CISM
Certified Information Security Manager
Study Guide

Mike Chapple, PhD, CISM

SYBEX
A Wiley Brand

Copyright © 2022 by John Wiley & Sons, Inc. All rights reserved.

Published by John Wiley & Sons, Inc., Hoboken, New Jersey.

Published simultaneously in Canada.

978-1-119-80193-1
978-1-119-80204-4 (ebk.)
978-1-119-80194-8 (ebk.)

No part of this publication may be reproduced, stored in a retrieval system, or transmitted in any form or by any means, electronic, mechanical, photocopying, recording, scanning, or otherwise, except as permitted under Section 107 or 108 of the 1976 United States Copyright Act, without either the prior written permission of the Publisher, or authorization through payment of the appropriate per-copy fee to the Copyright Clearance Center, Inc., 222 Rosewood Drive, Danvers, MA 01923, (978) 750-8400, fax (978) 750-4470, or on the web at www.copyright.com. Requests to the Publisher for permission should be addressed to the Permissions Department, John Wiley & Sons, Inc., 111 River Street, Hoboken, NJ 07030, (201) 748-6011, fax (201) 748-6008, or online at www.wiley.com/go/permission.

Limit of Liability/Disclaimer of Warranty: The publisher and the author make no representations or warranties with respect to the accuracy or completeness of the contents of this work and specifically disclaim all warranties, including without limitation warranties of fitness for a particular purpose. No warranty may be created or extended by sales or promotional materials. The advice and strategies contained herein may not be suitable for every situation. This work is sold with the understanding that the publisher is not engaged in rendering legal, accounting, or other professional services. If professional assistance is required, the services of a competent professional person should be sought. Neither the publisher nor the author shall be liable for damages arising herefrom. The fact that an organization or Website is referred to in this work as a citation and/or a potential source of further information does not mean that the author or the publisher endorses the information the organization or Website may provide or recommendations it may make. Further, readers should be aware the Internet Websites listed in this work may have changed or disappeared between when this work was written and when it is read.

For general information on our other products and services or for technical support, please contact our Customer Care Department within the United States at (800) 762-2974, outside the United States at (317) 572-3993 or fax (317) 572-4002.

Wiley also publishes its books in a variety of electronic formats. Some content that appears in print may not be available in electronic formats. For more information about Wiley products, visit our web site at www.wiley.com.

Library of Congress Control Number: 2021948030

Trademarks: WILEY, the Wiley logo, Sybex and the Sybex logo are trademarks or registered trademarks of John Wiley & Sons, Inc. and/or its affiliates, in the United States and other countries, and may not be used without written permission. CISM is a trademark or registered trademark of Information Systems Audit and Control Association, Inc. All other trademarks are the property of their respective owners. John Wiley & Sons, Inc. is not associated with any product or vendor mentioned in this book.

Cover image: ©Jeremy Woodhouse/Getty Images

Cover design: Wiley

SKY10074883_050924

To my wife, Renee. We are 22 years into this adventure together and every moment is better than the last. Here's to what's next!
—Mike

Acknowledgments

Books like this involve work from many people, and as an author, I truly appreciate the hard work and dedication that the team at Wiley shows. I would especially like to thank my acquisitions editor, Jim Minatel. I've worked with Jim for too many years to count and it's always an absolute pleasure working with a true industry pro.

I also greatly appreciated the editing and production team for the book, including David Clark, the project editor, who brought years of experience and great talent to the project; Ben Malisow, the technical editor, who provided insightful advice and gave wonderful feedback throughout the book; and Barath Kumar Rajasekaran, the production editor, who guided me through layouts, formatting, and final cleanup to produce a great book. I would also like to thank the many behind-the-scenes contributors, including the graphics, production, and technical teams who make the book and companion materials into a finished product.

Victoria Mastagh, my production assistant at CertMike.com, was instrumental in preparing the glossary, and Matthew Howard, my research assistant at Notre Dame, played a crucial role in pulling together the class slides that accompany the book for instructors.

My agent, Carole Jelen of Waterside Productions, continues to provide me with wonderful opportunities, advice, and assistance throughout my writing career.

Finally, I would like to thank my family, who supported me through the late evenings, busy weekends, and long hours that a book like this requires to write, edit, and get to press.

About the Author

Mike Chapple, Ph.D., CISM, is the author of over 30 books, including the best-selling *CISSP (ISC)² Certified Information Systems Security Professional Official Study Guide* (Sybex, 2021) and the *CISSP (ISC)² Official Practice Tests* (Sybex, 2021). He is an information security professional with two decades of experience in higher education, the private sector, and government.

Mike currently serves as Teaching Professor in the IT, Analytics, and Operations department at the University of Notre Dame's Mendoza College of Business, where he teaches undergraduate and graduate courses on cybersecurity, data management, and business analytics.

Mike previously served as executive vice president and chief information officer of the Brand Institute, a Miami-based marketing consultancy. Mike also spent four years in the information security research group at the National Security Agency and served as an active-duty intelligence officer in the U.S. Air Force.

Mike is a technical editor for *Information Security Magazine* and has written more than 25 books. He earned both his B.S. and Ph.D. degrees from Notre Dame in computer science and engineering. Mike also holds an M.S. in computer science from the University of Idaho and an MBA from Auburn University. Mike holds the Cybersecurity Analyst+ (CySA+), Security+, Certified Information Security Manager (CISM), Certified Cloud Security Professional (CCSP), and Certified Information Systems Security Professional (CISSP) certifications.

Learn more about Mike and his other security certification materials at his website, CertMike.com.

About the Technical Editor

Ben Malisow has worked in the fields of education/training, communication, information technology, security, and/or some combination of these industries, for over 25 years. Prior to his current position, Ben has provided information security consulting services and training to a diverse host of clients, including the Defense Advanced Research Projects Agency (DARPA), the Department of Homeland Security (at TSA), and the FBI. He has also served as an Air Force officer, after graduating from the Air Force Academy.

An experienced trainer, Ben has been an adjunct professor of English at the College of Southern Nevada, a computer teacher for troubled junior/senior high school students in Las Vegas, a senior instructor for the University of Texas - San Antonio, and he has taught computer security certification prep classes for Carnegie-Mellon University's CERT/SEI.

Ben has published widely in many fields. His latest books include *Exposed: How Revealing Your Data and Eliminating Privacy Increases Trust and Liberates Humanity* (Wiley, 2020), the *CCSP (ISC)² Official Study Guide* (Sybex, 2020), the *CCSP Official (ISC)² Practice Tests* (Sybex, 2018), and *How to Pass Your INFOSEC Exam* from Amazon Direct. Updates to his work and his podcast, "The Sensuous Sounds of INFOSEC," can be found at securityzed.com. His certification-preparation courses can be found on Udemy.com.

Contents at a Glance

Introduction   *xxi*

Assessment Test   *xxxii*

Chapter 1   Today's Information Security Manager   1

Chapter 2   Information Security Governance and Compliance   31

Chapter 3   Information Risk Management   63

Chapter 4   Cybersecurity Threats   91

Chapter 5   Information Security Program Development
and Management   115

Chapter 6   Security Assessment and Testing   145

Chapter 7   Cybersecurity Technology   181

Chapter 8   Incident Response   249

Chapter 9   Business Continuity and Disaster Recovery   297

Appendix   Answers to the Review Questions   357

Index   *377*

Contents

Introduction   *xxi*

Assessment Test   *xxxii*

Chapter   1   Today's Information Security Manager   1

Information Security Objectives   2
Role of the Information Security Manager   3
    Chief Information Security Officer   4
    Lines of Authority   4
    Organizing the Security Team   5
    Roles and Responsibilities   7
Information Security Risks   8
    The DAD Triad   8
    Incident Impact   9
Building an Information Security Strategy   12
    Threat Research   12
    SWOT Analysis   13
    Gap Analysis   13
    Creating SMART Goals   16
    Alignment with Business Strategy   16
    Leadership Support   17
    Internal and External Influences   17
    Cybersecurity Responsibilities   18
    Communication   19
    Action Plans   19
Implementing Security Controls   20
    Security Control Categories   21
    Security Control Types   21
Data Protection   23
Summary   25
Exam Essentials   25
Review Questions   27

Chapter   2   Information Security Governance and Compliance   31

Governance   33
    Corporate Governance   33
    Governance, Risk, and Compliance Programs   35
    Information Security Governance   35
    Developing Business Cases   36
    Third-Party Relationships   37

Understanding Policy Documents   38
  Policies   38
  Standards   40
  Procedures   42
  Guidelines   43
  Exceptions and Compensating Controls   44
  Developing Policies   45
Complying with Laws and Regulations   46
Adopting Standard Frameworks   47
  COBIT   47
  NIST Cybersecurity Framework   49
  NIST Risk Management Framework   52
  ISO Standards   53
  Benchmarks and Secure Configuration Guides   54
Security Control Verification and Quality Control   56
Summary   57
Exam Essentials   57
Review Questions   59

Chapter   3   **Information Risk Management**   **63**

Analyzing Risk   65
  Risk Identification   66
  Risk Calculation   67
  Risk Assessment   68
Risk Treatment and Response   72
  Risk Mitigation   73
  Risk Avoidance   74
  Risk Transference   74
  Risk Acceptance   75
Risk Analysis   75
Disaster Recovery Planning   78
  Disaster Types   78
  Business Impact Analysis   79
Privacy   79
  Sensitive Information Inventory   80
  Information Classification   80
  Data Roles and Responsibilities   82
  Information Lifecycle   83
  Privacy-Enhancing Technologies   83
  Privacy and Data Breach Notification   84
Summary   84
Exam Essentials   85
Review Questions   86

Chapter	4	**Cybersecurity Threats**	**91**
		Exploring Cybersecurity Threats	92
		Classifying Cybersecurity Threats	92
		Threat Actors	94
		Threat Vectors	99
		Threat Data and Intelligence	101
		Open Source Intelligence	101
		Proprietary and Closed Source Intelligence	104
		Assessing Threat Intelligence	105
		Threat Indicator Management and Exchange	107
		Public and Private Information Sharing Centers	108
		Conducting Your Own Research	108
		Summary	109
		Exam Essentials	109
		Review Questions	111
Chapter	5	**Information Security Program Development and Management**	**115**
		Information Security Programs	117
		Establishing a New Program	117
		Maintaining an Existing Program	121
		Security Awareness and Training	123
		User Training	123
		Role-Based Training	124
		Ongoing Awareness Efforts	124
		Managing the Information Security Team	125
		Hiring Team Members	126
		Developing the Security Team	126
		Managing the Security Budget	127
		Organizational Budgeting	127
		Fiscal Years	127
		Expense Types	128
		Budget Monitoring	129
		Integrating Security with Other Business Functions	130
		Procurement	130
		Accounting	133
		Human Resources	133
		Information Technology	135
		Audit	138
		Summary	139
		Exam Essentials	139
		Review Questions	141

Chapter   6   Security Assessment and Testing   145

Vulnerability Management   146
  Identifying Scan Targets   146
  Determining Scan Frequency   148
  Configuring Vulnerability Scans   149
  Scanner Maintenance   154
  Vulnerability Scanning Tools   155
  Reviewing and Interpreting Scan Reports   159
  Validating Scan Results   160
Security Vulnerabilities   161
  Patch Management   162
  Legacy Platforms   163
  Weak Configurations   164
  Error Messages   164
  Insecure Protocols   165
  Weak Encryption   166
Penetration Testing   167
  Adopting the Hacker Mindset   168
  Reasons for Penetration Testing   169
  Benefits of Penetration Testing   169
  Penetration Test Types   170
  Rules of Engagement   171
  Reconnaissance   173
  Running the Test   173
  Cleaning Up   174
Training and Exercises   174
Summary   175
Exam Essentials   176
Review Questions   177

Chapter   7   Cybersecurity Technology   181

Endpoint Security   182
  Malware Prevention   183
  Endpoint Detection and Response   183
  Data Loss Prevention   184
  Change and Configuration Management   185
  Patch Management   185
  System Hardening   185
Network Security   186
  Network Segmentation   186
  Network Device Security   188
  Network Security Tools   191
Cloud Computing Security   195

Benefits of the Cloud   196
Cloud Roles   198
Cloud Service Models   198
Cloud Deployment Models   202
Shared Responsibility Model   204
Cloud Standards and Guidelines   207
Cloud Security Issues   208
Cloud Security Controls   210
Cryptography   212
Goals of Cryptography   212
Symmetric Key Algorithms   214
Asymmetric Cryptography   215
Hash Functions   217
Digital Signatures   218
Digital Certificates   219
Certificate Generation and Destruction   220
Code Security   223
Software Development Life Cycle   223
Software Development Phases   224
Software Development Models   226
DevSecOps and DevOps   229
Code Review   230
Software Security Testing   232
Identity and Access Management   234
Identification, Authentication, and Authorization   234
Authentication Techniques   235
Authentication Errors   237
Single-Sign On and Federation   238
Provisioning and Deprovisioning   238
Account Monitoring   239
Summary   240
Exam Essentials   241
Review Questions   244

Chapter   8   Incident Response   249

Security Incidents   251
Phases of Incident Response   252
Preparation   253
Detection and Analysis   254
Containment, Eradication, and Recovery   255
Post-Incident Activity   267
Building the Incident Response Plan   269
Policy   269
Procedures and Playbooks   270

	Documenting the Incident Response Plan	270
	Creating an Incident Response Team	272
	Incident Response Providers	273
	CSIRT Scope of Control	273
	Coordination and Information Sharing	273
	Internal Communications	274
	External Communications	274
	Classifying Incidents	274
	Threat Classification	275
	Severity Classification	276
	Conducting Investigations	279
	Investigation Types	279
	Evidence	282
	Plan Training, Testing, and Evaluation	288
	Summary	289
	Exam Essentials	290
	Review Questions	292

Chapter 9	**Business Continuity and Disaster Recovery**	**297**
	Planning for Business Continuity	298
	Project Scope and Planning	299
	Organizational Review	300
	BCP Team Selection	301
	Resource Requirements	302
	Legal and Regulatory Requirements	303
	Business Impact Analysis	304
	Identifying Priorities	305
	Risk Identification	306
	Likelihood Assessment	308
	Impact Analysis	309
	Resource Prioritization	310
	Continuity Planning	310
	Strategy Development	311
	Provisions and Processes	311
	Plan Approval and Implementation	313
	Plan Approval	313
	Plan Implementation	314
	Training and Education	314
	BCP Documentation	314
	The Nature of Disaster	318
	Natural Disasters	319
	Human-Made Disasters	324
	System Resilience, High Availability, and Fault Tolerance	327
	Protecting Hard Drives	328

Protecting Servers 329
Protecting Power Sources 331
Recovery Strategy 331
Business Unit and Functional Priorities 332
Crisis Management 333
Emergency Communications 334
Workgroup Recovery 334
Alternate Processing Sites 334
Database Recovery 338
Recovery Plan Development 340
Emergency Response 341
Personnel and Communications 341
Assessment 342
Backups and Offsite Storage 342
Utilities 345
Logistics and Supplies 345
Training, Awareness, and Documentation 345
Testing and Maintenance 346
Read-Through Test 346
Structured Walk-Through 346
Simulation Test 347
Parallel Test 347
Full-Interruption Test 347
Lessons Learned 347
Maintenance 348
Summary 349
Exam Essentials 349
Review Questions 351

Appendix   **Answers to the Review Questions**   **357**

Chapter 1: Today's Information Security Manager 358
Chapter 2: Information Security Governance and Compliance 360
Chapter 3: Information Risk Management 362
Chapter 4: Cybersecurity Threats 363
Chapter 5: Information Security Program Development and
Management 365
Chapter 6: Security Assessment and Testing 368
Chapter 7: Cybersecurity Technology 370
Chapter 8: Incident Response 372
Chapter 9: Business Continuity and Disaster Recovery 374

Index 377

Introduction

If you're preparing to take the Certified Information Security Manager (CISM) exam, you'll undoubtedly want to find as much information as you can about information security and the art of leading and managing security teams. The more information you have at your disposal, the better off you'll be when taking the exam. This study guide was written with that in mind. The goal was to provide enough information to prepare you for the test, but not so much that you'll be overloaded with information that's outside the scope of the exam.

This book presents the material at an intermediate technical level. Experience with and knowledge of security concepts, operating systems, and application systems will help you get a full understanding of the challenges you'll face as a security manager.

I've included review questions at the end of each chapter to give you a taste of what it's like to take the exam. I recommend that you check out these questions first to gauge your level of expertise. You can then use the book mainly to fill in the gaps in your current knowledge. This study guide will help you round out your knowledge base before tackling the exam.

If you can answer 90 percent or more of the review questions correctly for a given chapter, you can feel safe moving on to the next chapter. If you're unable to answer that many correctly, reread the chapter and try the questions again. Your score should improve.

Don't just study the questions and answers! The questions on the actual exam will be different from the practice questions included in this book. The exam is designed to test your knowledge of a concept or objective, so use this book to learn the objectives behind the questions.

The CISM Exam

The CISM exam is designed to be a vendor-neutral certification for cybersecurity managers. ISACA recommends this certification for those who already have technical experience in the information security field and are either already serving in management roles or who want to shift from being an individual contributor into a management role.

The exam covers four major domains:

1. Information Security Governance
2. Information Security Risk Management
3. Information Security Program
4. Incident Management

These four areas include a range of topics, from enterprise risk management to responding to cybersecurity incidents. They focus heavily on scenario-based learning and the role of the information security manager in various scenarios. There's a lot of information that you'll need to learn, but you'll be well rewarded for possessing this credential. ISACA reports that the average salary of CISM credential holders is over $118,000.

The CISM exam includes only standard multiple-choice questions. Each question has four possible answer choices and only one of those answer choices is the correct answer. When you're taking the test, you'll likely find some questions where you think multiple answers might be correct. In those cases, remember that you're looking for the *best* possible answer to the question!

The exam costs $575 for ISACA members and $760 for nonmembers. More details about the CISM exam and how to take it can be found at:

`www.isaca.org/credentialing/cism`

You'll have four hours to take the exam and will be asked to answer 150 questions during that time period. Your exam will be scored on a scale ranging from 200 to 800, with a passing score of 450.

> ISACA frequently does what is called *item seeding*, which is the practice of including unscored questions on exams. It does so to gather psycho-metric data, which is then used when developing new versions of the exam. Before you take the exam, you will be told that your exam may include these unscored questions. So, if you come across a question that does not appear to map to any of the exam objectives—or for that matter, does not appear to belong in the exam—it is likely a seeded question. You never really know whether or not a question is seeded, however, so always make your best effort to answer every question.

Taking the Exam

Once you are fully prepared to take the exam, you can visit the ISACA website to register. Currently, ISACA offers two options for taking the exam: an in-person exam at a testing center and an at-home exam that you take on your own computer through a remote proctoring service.

In-Person Exams

ISACA partners with PSI Exams testing centers, so your next step will be to locate a testing center near you. In the United States, you can do this based on your address or your ZIP code, while non-U.S. test takers may find it easier to enter their city and country. You can search for a test center near you at the PSI Exams website:

`https://isacaavailability.psiexams.com`

Now that you know where you'd like to take the exam, simply set up a PSI testing account and schedule an exam on their site.

On the day of the test, bring a government-issued identification card or passport that contains your full name (exactly matching the name on your exam registration), your signature, and your photograph. Make sure to show up with plenty of time before the exam starts. Remember that you will not be able to take your notes, electronic devices (including smartphones and watches), or other materials in with you.

At-Home Exams

ISACA began offering online exam proctoring in 2020 in response to the coronavirus pandemic. When this book went to press, the at-home testing option was still available and appears likely to continue. Candidates using this approach will take the exam at their home or office and be proctored over a webcam by a remote proctor.

Due to the rapidly changing nature of the at-home testing experience, candidates wishing to pursue this option should check the ISACA website for the latest details. In fact, checking the ISACA website for exam policy changes is a good idea for all test takers.

After the CISM Exam

Once you have taken the exam, you will be notified of your score immediately, so you'll know if you passed the test right away. You should keep track of your score report with your exam registration records and the email address you used to register for the exam.

Meeting the Experience Requirement

The CISM program is designed to demonstrate that an individual is a qualified information security manager. That requires more than just passing a test—it also requires real hands-on work experience managing cybersecurity teams.

The CISM work experience requirement has two different components:

- You must have five years of information security work experience.
- You must have at least three years of information security management work experience. That work experience must come from at least three of the four CISM domains.

If you're a current information security manager, you may find it easy to meet these requirements. If you've been in the field for five years and have been a manager for at least three of those years, you're probably good to go because your time as an information security manager also counts toward your general information security experience requirement.

There are some waivers available that can knock one or two years off your experience requirement. All of these waivers apply only to the general information security work experience requirement, not the management requirement.

If you hold any of the following credentials, you qualify for a two-year reduction in the experience requirement:

- Certified Information Systems Security Professional (CISSP)
- Certified Information Systems Auditor (CISA)
- Master of Business Administration (MBA) degree
- Master's degree in information security or a related field

One year experience requirement waivers are available for holders of:

- Skill-based or general security certifications (such as the CompTIA Security+ credential)
- Bachelor's degree in information security or a related field
- One full year of general information systems management experience
- One full year of general security management experience

You must have earned all of the experience used toward your requirement within the 10 years preceding your application or within 5 years of the date you pass the exam.

Maintaining Your Certification

Information security is a constantly evolving field with new threats and controls arising regularly. All CISM holders must complete continuing professional education on an annual basis to keep their knowledge current and their skills sharp. The guidelines around continuing professional education are somewhat complicated, but they boil down to two main requirements:

- You must complete 120 hours of credit every three years to remain certified.
- You must have a minimum of 20 hours of credit every year during that cycle.

You must meet both of these requirements. For example, if you earn 120 credit hours during the first year of your certification cycle, you still must earn 20 additional credits in each of the next two years.

Continuing education requirements follow calendar years, and your clock will begin ticking on January 1 of the year after you earn your certification. You are allowed to begin earning credits immediately after you're certified. They'll just count for the next year.

There are many acceptable ways to earn CPE credits, many of which do not require travel or attending a training seminar. The important requirement is that you generally do not earn CPEs for work that you perform as part of your regular job. CPEs are intended to cover professional development opportunities outside of your day-to-day work. You can earn CPEs in several ways:

- Attending conferences
- Attending training programs
- Attending professional meetings and activities
- Taking self-study courses
- Participating in vendor marketing presentations
- Teaching, lecturing, or presenting
- Publishing articles, monographs, or books
- Participating in the exam development process
- Volunteering with ISACA
- Earning other professional credentials

- Contributing to the profession
- Mentoring

For more information on the activities that qualify for CPE credits, visit this site:

www.isaca.org/credentialing/how-to-earn-cpe

Study Guide Elements

This study guide uses several common elements to help you prepare. These include the following:

Summaries   The summary section of each chapter briefly explains the chapter, allowing you to easily understand what it covers.

Exam Essentials   The exam essentials focus on major exam topics and critical knowledge that you should take into the test. The exam essentials focus on the exam objectives provided by ISACA.

Chapter Review Questions   A set of questions at the end of each chapter will help you assess your knowledge and if you are ready to take the exam based on your knowledge of that chapter's topics.

Additional Study Tools

This book comes with some additional study tools to help you prepare for the exam. They include the following.

 Go to www.wiley.com/go/sybextestprep to register and gain access to this interactive online learning environment and test bank with study tools.

Sybex Test Preparation Software

Sybex's test preparation software lets you prepare with electronic test versions of the review questions from each chapter, the practice exam, and the bonus exam that are included in this book. You can build and take tests on specific domains, by chapter, or cover the entire set of CISM exam objectives using randomized tests.

Audio Reviews

The author of this book recorded files containing the exam essentials for each chapter in a convenient audio form. Use these audio reviews in the car, on the train, when you're out for a run, or whenever you have a few minutes to review what you've learned.

Electronic Flashcards

Our electronic flashcards are designed to help you prepare for the exam. Over 100 flashcards will ensure that you know critical terms and concepts.

Glossary of Terms

Sybex provides a full glossary of terms in PDF format, allowing quick searches and easy reference to materials in this book.

Bonus Practice Exams

In addition to the practice questions for each chapter, this book includes two full 150-question practice exams. We recommend that you use them both to test your preparedness for the certification exam.

Like all exams, the CISM certification from ISACA is updated periodically and may eventually be retired or replaced. At some point after ISACA is no longer offering this exam, the old editions of our books and online tools will be retired. If you have purchased this book after the exam was retired, or are attempting to register in the Sybex online learning environment after the exam was retired, please know that we make no guarantees that this exam's online Sybex tools will be available once the exam is no longer available.

CISM Exam Objectives

ISACA publishes relative weightings for each of the exam's objectives. The following table lists the four CISM domains and the extent to which they are represented on the exam.

Domain	% of Exam
1. Information Security Governance	17%
2. Information Security Risk Management	20%
3. Information Security Program	33%
4. Incident Management	30%

CISM Certification Exam Objective Map

The CISM exam covers two different types of objectives: topics and supporting tasks. I recommend that instead of focusing on these objectives in the order they appear in the exam objectives that you instead learn them in the order they are presented in this book. In my 25 years of experience teaching information security topics, I've found that approaching these topics in a more logical order will better prepare you for the exam.

If you're looking for where I've covered a specific objective in the book, use the following two tables to find the appropriate chapter.

Topic Mapping

Topic	Chapter(s)
Domain 1: Information Security Governance	
A. Enterprise Governance	**1,2**
1A1. Organizational Culture	1
1A2. Legal, Regulatory, and Contractual Requirements	2
1A3. Organizational Structures, Roles, and Responsibilities	1
B. Information Security Strategy	**1,2**
1B1. Information Security Strategy Development	1
1B2. Information Governance Frameworks and Standards	2
1B3. Strategic Planning (e.g., budgets, resources, business case)	2
Domain 2: Information Security Risk Management	
A. Information Security Risk Assessment	**3,4,6**
2A1. Emerging Risk and Threat Landscape	4
2A2. Vulnerability and Control Deficiency Analysis	6
2A3. Risk Assessment and Analysis	3
B. Information Security Risk Response	**3**
2B1. Risk Treatment/Risk Response Options	3
2B2. Risk and Control Ownership	3
2B3. Risk Monitoring and Reporting	3
Domain 3: Information Security Program	
A. Information Security Program Development	**2,3,5**
3A1. Information Security Program Resources (e.g., people, tools, technologies)	5
3A2. Information Asset Identification and Classification	3
3A3. Industry Standards and Frameworks for Information Security	2
3A4. Information Security Policies, Procedures, and Guidelines	2
3A5. Information Security Program Metrics	5

Topic	Chapter(s)
B. Information Security Program Management	**5,6,7**
3B1. Information Security Control Design and Selection	7
3B2. Information Security Control Implementation and Integrations	7
3B3. Information Security Control Testing and Evaluation	6
3B4. Information Security Awareness and Training	5
3B5. Management of External Services (e.g., providers, suppliers, third parties, fourth parties)	5
3B6. Information Security Program Communications and Reporting	5

Domain 4: Incident Management

A. Incident Management Readiness	**8,9**
4A1. Incident Response Plan	8
4A2. Business Impact Analysis (BIA)	9
4A3. Business Continuity Plan (BCP)	9
4A4. Disaster Recovery Plan (DRP)	9
4A5. Incident Classification/Categorization	8
4A6. Incident Management Training, Testing, and Evaluation	8
B. Incident Management Operations	**8**
4B1. Incident Management Tools and Techniques	8
4B2. Incident Investigation and Evaluation	8
4B3. Incident Containment Methods	8
4B4. Incident Response Communications (e.g., reporting, notification, escalation)	8
4B5. Incident Eradication and Recovery	8
4B6. Post-incident Review Practices	8

Supporting Task Mapping

Supporting Task	Chapter(s)
1. Identify internal and external influences to the organization that impact the information security strategy.	1, 4
2. Establish and/or maintain an information security strategy in alignment with organizational goals and objectives.	1
3. Establish and/or maintain an information security governance framework.	2
4. Integrate information security governance into corporate governance.	2
5. Establish and maintain information security policies to guide the development of standards, procedures, and guidelines.	2
6. Develop business cases to support investments in information security.	2
7. Gain ongoing commitment from senior leadership and other stakeholders to support the successful implementation of the information security strategy.	1
8. Define, communicate, and monitor information security responsibilities throughout the organization and lines of authority.	1
9. Compile and present reports to key stakeholders on the activities, trends, and overall effectiveness of the information security program.	5
10. Evaluate and report information security metrics to key stakeholders.	5
11. Establish and/or maintain the information security program in alignment with the information security strategy.	5
12. Align the information security program with the operational objectives of other business functions.	5
13. Establish and maintain information security processes and resources to execute the information security program.	5
14. Establish, communicate, and maintain organizational information security policies, standards, guidelines, procedures, and other documentation.	2
15. Establish, promote, and maintain a program for information security awareness and training.	5

Supporting Task	Chapter(s)
16. Integrate information security requirements into organizational processes to maintain the organization's security strategy.	5
17. Integrate information security requirements into contracts and activities of external parties.	5
18. Monitor external parties' adherence to established security requirements.	5
19. Define and monitor management and operational metrics for the information security program.	5
20. Establish and/or maintain a process for information asset identification and classification.	3
21. Identify legal, regulatory, organizational, and other applicable compliance requirements.	2
22. Participate in and/or oversee the risk identification, risk assessment, and risk treatment process.	3
23. Participate in and/or oversee the vulnerability assessment and threat analysis process.	4, 6
24. Identify, recommend, or implement appropriate risk treatment and response options to manage risk to acceptable levels based on organizational risk appetite.	3
25. Determine whether information security controls are appropriate and effectively manage risk to an acceptable level.	3, 7
26. Facilitate the integration of information risk management into business and IT processes.	3
27. Monitor for internal and external factors that may require reassessment of risk.	3
28. Report on information security risk, including noncompliance and changes in information risk, to key stakeholders to facilitate the risk management decision-making process.	3
29. Establish and maintain an incident response plan, in alignment with the business continuity plan and disaster recovery plan.	8
30. Establish and maintain an information security incident classification and categorization process.	8
31. Develop and implement processes to ensure the timely identification of information security incidents.	8

Supporting Task	Chapter(s)
32. Establish and maintain processes to investigate and document information security incidents in accordance with legal and regulatory requirements.	8
33. Establish and maintain incident handling process, including containment, notification, escalation, eradication, and recovery.	8
34. Organize, train, equip, and assign responsibilities to incident response teams.	8
35. Establish and maintain incident communication plans and processes for internal and external parties.	8
36. Evaluate incident management plans through testing and review, including table-top exercises, checklist review, and simulation testing at planned intervals.	8
37. Conduct post-incident reviews to facilitate continuous improvement, including root-cause analysis, lessons learned, corrective actions, and reassessment of risk.	8

Assessment Test

1. Seth's organization recently experienced a security incident where an attacker was able to place offensive content on the homepage of his organization's website. Seth would like to implement a series of security controls to prevent this type of attack from occurring in the future. What goal of information security is Seth most directly addressing?

   A. Integrity

   B. Availability

   C. Nonrepudiation

   D. Confidentiality

2. Kevin is conducting a SWOT analysis for his organization's cybersecurity program. He is especially proud of the talented and diverse team that exists within his organization. Where would he place this quality on the SWOT matrix?

   A. Upper-left quadrant

   B. Upper-right quadrant

   C. Lower-left quadrant

   D. Lower-right quadrant

3. Jen is building out a series of controls for her organization's information security program and is categorizing those controls by type. She is updating the organization's firewall to include next-generation capabilities. What type of control is she working on?

   A. Detective

   B. Preventive

   C. Compensating

   D. Deterrent

4. Belinda recently assumed the CISO role at a publicly traded company. She is sorting through the corporate governance model and identifying the roles that different people and groups play in the organization. Which one of the following roles has ultimate authority for the corporation?

   A. CEO

   B. CIO

   C. Board

   D. Board chair

5. Brandon leads the information security team for a large organization and is working with the software development team to provide them with application security testing services. He would like to document the roles and responsibilities of the two teams in a written agreement with the leader of the development team. What type of agreement would be most appropriate?

A. MOU

B. SLA

C. BPA

D. MSA

6. Monica is conducting a quantitative risk assessment of the risk that a fire poses to her organization's primary operating facility. She believes that a serious fire would destroy 50 percent of the facility, causing $10 million in damage. She expects that a fire of this nature would only occur once every 50 years, on average. What is the AV in this scenario?

A. $200,000

B. $5 million

C. $10 million

D. $20 million

7. After assessing the risk of fire, Monica decides to install new sprinkler systems throughout the facility to reduce the likelihood of a serious fire. What type of risk treatment action is she taking?

A. Risk avoidance

B. Risk acceptance

C. Risk transference

D. Risk mitigation

8. Victor is a security consultant who was recently hired to perform a penetration test of an organization. He is not an employee but an independent contractor. He is reporting his findings directly to the CIO, and the security team is not aware of the work he is doing. What term best describes Victor's work?

A. White hat

B. Gray hat

C. Black hat

D. Red hat

9. Peihua is working on the organizing documents for her organization's cybersecurity program. Her document will outline the parameters under which the organization will function. What type of document is she creating?

A. Charter

B. Scope statement

C. Business purpose statement

D. Statement of authority

10. Fred is helping his boss develop a set of metrics for the organization's security program. After consulting the ITIL framework used by his organization, he decides to track the number of major security incidents that occur each year. What type of metric is this?

   A. KGI

   B. KPI

   C. KSI

   D. KRI

11. Tim recently entered into an agreement with a service provider to perform weekly vulnerability scanning of his organization. The contract will last for three years. What type of expense best describes this purchase?

   A. Budgeted expense

   B. Nonbudgeted expense

   C. Capital expense

   D. Operational expense

12. Carl is conducting a review of his system's security. He is assuming that an attacker has already compromised the system and searching for signs of that compromise. What term best describes this work?

   A. Penetration testing

   B. Security assessment

   C. Threat hunting

   D. Black-box testing

13. Lisa's team is participating in a security exercise. They are testing the security of systems and attempting to break into systems controlled by others in the organization. What type of team is Lisa leading?

   A. Blue team

   B. White team

   C. Purple team

   D. Red team

14. Cindy is concerned that users in her organization might take sensitive data and email it to their personal email accounts for access after they leave the organization. Which one of the following security technologies would best protect against this risk?

   A. Firewall

   B. IPS

   C. DLP

   D. Configuration management

15. Andrea is placing a new server onto her organization's network. The server is a web server that will be accessible only by internal employees. What network zone would be the most appropriate location for this server?

A. Internet

B. Intranet

C. Extranet

D. DMZ

16. Matthew is responsible for managing the cloud infrastructure supporting his organization's website. As demand for the site increases, Matthew would like to scale the infrastructure's computing capability. Which one of the following is an example of horizontal scaling?

A. Adding memory and processing power to the server

B. Adding additional network bandwidth

C. Adding additional servers

D. Adding new load balancers

17. Danielle is revising her organization's cybersecurity incident response plan and would like a consistent scale for rating the severity of an incident. What organization produces a widely used severity rating scale?

A. NIST

B. FBI

C. NSA

D. CIA

18. Ricky is collecting evidence as part of an investigation that his organization believes will lead to a civil lawsuit against one of their suppliers. What is the standard of evidence that would normally be applied in this type of lawsuit?

A. Beyond a reasonable doubt

B. Beyond the shadow of doubt

C. Preponderance of the evidence

D. Absolute proof

19. Wally is assessing the controls used to protect his organization against the risk of data loss. Which one of the following controls would be the best defense against the accidental deletion of data by an authorized user?

A. RAID 1

B. RAID 5

C. Backups

D. Access controls

20. Melissa is preparing to test her organization's disaster recovery plan. During the test, she will activate the organization's backup processing facility and use it to process data as a test, but normal operations will continue in the primary facility. What type of test is she running?

A. Parallel test

B. Full interruption test

C. Simulation test

D. Structured walk-through

Answers to Assessment Test

1. **A.** The three main goals of information security are confidentiality, integrity, and availability, so we can eliminate nonrepudiation right away. There is also no indication that there was any disclosure of sensitive information, so we can also eliminate confidentiality. We could consider this an availability breach if the attacker made legitimate information unavailable, but integrity is a better answer here because the attacker definitely altered the content of the website without authorization. You'll find a thorough discussion of the goals of an information security program in Chapter 1.

2. **A.** This is an example of a strength. It is an internal force that is positive. Therefore, it would be placed in the upper-left quadrant. The upper-right quadrant is for internal negative forces or weaknesses. The lower-left quadrant is for external positive forces or opportunities. The lower-right quadrant is for external negative forces or threats. You'll find more information about SWOT analyses in Chapter 1.

3. **B.** Firewalls are best described as preventive controls because their purpose is to block an attack from succeeding. Detective controls seek to identify attacks that are taking place and, though a firewall can detect some attacks, this is not the primary purpose of the device. Firewalls may also serve as compensating controls in a regulatory environment, but there is no indication in this question that the firewall is being used as a compensating control. Firewalls are not normally visible to an attacker until after they have attempted an attack, so they cannot serve as deterrent controls. You'll find a discussion of control categories and types in Chapter 1.

4. **C.** The board of directors, acting as a group, has ultimate authority over the organization. They are elected by the shareholders who own the company and serve as the owner's representatives. They delegate much of their authority to the Chief Executive Officer (CEO) but retain ultimate control. You'll learn more about corporate governance models in Chapter 2.

5. **A.** In this case, Brandon needs an agreement with another internal organization. These types of agreements most commonly take the form of memoranda of understanding (MOU). More formal master service agreements (MSAs) and service level agreements (SLAs) are normally used with external service providers. Business partnership agreements (BPAs) are used when two organizations are entering into a joint effort. You'll learn more about different agreement types in Chapter 2.

6. **D.** The asset value (AV) is the total value of the asset being analyzed. In this case, we know that the data center would be 50 percent destroyed by a fire and that the damage caused by the fire would be valued at $10 million. We can then work backward to determine that if $10 million is 50 percent of the asset value, then the asset value is $20 million. You'll learn more about quantitative risk assessment in Chapter 3.

7. **D.** Monica is seeking to reduce the likelihood and/or impact of a risk. Therefore, she is engaging in risk mitigation activity. Risk avoidance involves changing business practices to make a risk irrelevant. Risk acceptance involves continuing business activities in the face of a risk. Risk transference involves shifting some of the impact of a risk to a third party, such as an insurance company. You'll learn more about risk treatment options in Chapter 3.

8. A. Victor is working as an authorized tester and, therefore, his work is definitely white-hat hacking. It is not relevant whether he is an employee or a contractor or what groups within the organization are aware of his testing. The only relevant factor is that he is performing authorized security testing on behalf of the organization. Gray-hat hackers perform similar work and report their results to the organization but do so without authorization. Black-hat hackers perform testing for malicious purposes. Red-hat hackers are not a common category of attacker. You'll learn more about different attacker types in Chapter 4.

9. A. Peihua is drafting the organization's security program charter. This is the organizing document for the program, and it outlines the parameters under which the program will function. This is a tricky question because the scope statement, business purpose statement, and statement of authority are all common elements of the charter. You'll learn more about the organizing documents for a security program in Chapter 5.

10. B. This metric is directly out of the ITIL framework's nine key performance indicators (KPIs) for a security program. KPIs are metrics that demonstrate the success of the program in achieving its objects and are a look at historical performance. Key goal indicators (KGIs) are similar but track progress toward a defined goal and there is no clear goal in this scenario. Key risk indicators (KRIs) look forward at risks that may jeopardize future security. You'll learn more about security metrics in Chapter 5.

11. D. There is no indication in the question of whether this expense is budgeted or nonbudgeted, so we can eliminate those two answer choices. Capital expenses are used to acquire and maintain large assets, whereas operational expenses cover day-to-day business costs. Tom is signing a services agreement and not purchasing an asset, so this agreement would best be classified as an operational expense. You'll learn more about security program budgeting in Chapter 5.

12. C. Carl is conducting a security assessment, but that is not the best answer here because there is a more specific correct answer. The presumption of compromise is the hallmark of threat hunting, a type of security assessment. You'll learn more about threat hunting and other security assessments in Chapter 6.

13. D. During a security exercise, teams like Lisa's who attempt to gain access to systems are classified as the red team. Blue team members are the defenders who secure systems from attack. White team members are observers and judges. Purple team events bring together members of the red and blue teams. You'll learn more about cybersecurity exercises in Chapter 6.

14. C. While it is possible that any security technology could play an indirect role in preventing the unauthorized exfiltration of information, data loss prevention (DLP) technology is specifically designed to protect against this threat, so that is the best possible answer to this question. You'll learn more about DLP and other security technologies in Chapter 7.

15. B. Servers intended for internal use should only be placed on the intranet, where they are accessible only to other internal systems. The DMZ would be an appropriate location for this server if it permitted public access. An extranet would be appropriate if the server was being accessed by business partners. The Internet is generally never a good location for a server. You'll learn more about firewalls and security zones in Chapter 7.

16. C. Any one of these solutions is an example of scaling the environment to meet increased demand. However, the question is specifically asking about computing capability. Adding computing capability requires modifying the servers, so we can eliminate the options about adding network bandwidth or load balancers. We're also asking specifically about horizontal scaling, which is adding additional servers, making that our correct answer. Adding additional memory or processing power to the existing server would be vertical scaling. You'll learn more about different scaling options in Chapter 7.

17. A. The National Institute for Standards and Technology (NIST) produces a widely used rating scale that categorizes security incidents based on the scope of their impact and the types of data involved. You'll learn more about this rating scale in Chapter 8.

18. C. Most civil cases do not follow the beyond-a-reasonable-doubt standard of proof. Instead, they use the weaker *preponderance of the evidence* standard. Meeting this standard simply requires that the evidence demonstrate that the outcome of the case is more likely than not. For this reason, evidence collection standards for civil investigations are not as rigorous as those used in criminal investigations. You'll learn more about security investigations and evidence standards in Chapter 8.

19. C. Backups allow the organization to recover data that was accidentally deleted. RAID technology is used to protect against the failure of a hard drive and would not protect against the loss of data by user action. Access controls would be effective to prevent an unauthorized user from deleting data but would not stop an authorized user from doing so. You'll learn more about data protection controls in Chapter 9.

20. A. This type of test, where the alternate processing facility is activated but the primary site retains operational control, is known as a parallel test. In a full interruption test, the primary site is shut down and operational control moves to the alternate site. Simulations and structured walk-throughs do not affect normal operations and do not activate the alternate site. You'll learn more about business continuity and disaster recovery programs and testing in Chapter 9.

Chapter

1

Today's Information Security Manager

THE CERTIFIED INFORMATION SECURITY MANAGER (CISM) DOMAINS AND SUBTOPICS COVERED IN THIS CHAPTER INCLUDE:

✓ **Domain 1: Information Security Governance**

- **A. Enterprise Governance**
    - **1A1. Organizational Culture**
    - **1A3. Organizational Structures, Roles and Responsibilities**
- **B. Information Security Strategy**
    - **1B1. Information Security Strategy Development**

THE CERTIFIED INFORMATION SECURITY MANAGER (CISM) SUPPORTING TASKS COVERED IN THIS CHAPTER INCLUDE:

✓ **1. Identify internal and external influences to the organization that impact the information security strategy.**

✓ **2. Establish and/or maintain an information security strategy in alignment with organizational goals and objectives.**

✓ **7. Gain ongoing commitment from senior leadership and other stakeholders to support the successful implementation of the information security strategy.**

✓ **8. Define, communicate, and monitor information security responsibilities throughout the organization and lines of authority.**

Information security managers are responsible for leading teams of cybersecurity professionals and helping them achieve the goals of the cybersecurity program while aligning those objectives with the needs of the business. This work is crucial to protecting their organizations in today's complex threat landscape. Managers must help their teams protect the confidentiality, integrity, and availability of information and information systems used by their organizations. Fulfilling this responsibility requires a strong understanding of the threat environment facing their organization and a commitment to designing and implementing a set of controls capable of rising to the occasion and answering those threats.

In the first section of this chapter, you will learn about the role that cybersecurity managers play in a modern organization. You will then learn the basic objectives of cybersecurity: confidentiality, integrity, and availability of your operations. In the sections that follow, you will learn about some of the controls that you can put in place to protect your most sensitive data from prying eyes. This chapter sets the stage for the remainder of the book, where you will dive more deeply into many different areas of cybersecurity management.

Information Security Objectives

When most people think of cybersecurity, they imagine hackers trying to break into an organization's system and steal sensitive information, ranging from Social Security numbers and credit cards to top-secret military information. Although protecting sensitive information from unauthorized disclosure is certainly one element of a cybersecurity program, it is important to understand that cybersecurity actually has three complementary objectives, as shown in Figure 1.1.

FIGURE 1.1 The three key objectives of cybersecurity programs are confidentiality, integrity, and availability.

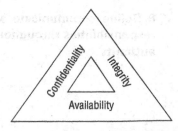

Confidentiality ensures that unauthorized individuals are not able to gain access to sensitive information. Cybersecurity professionals develop and implement security controls, including firewalls, access control lists, and encryption, to prevent unauthorized access to information. Attackers may seek to undermine confidentiality controls to achieve one of their goals: the unauthorized disclosure of sensitive information.

Integrity ensures that there are no unauthorized modifications to information or systems, either intentionally or unintentionally. Security professionals use integrity controls, such as hashing and integrity monitoring solutions, to enforce this requirement. Integrity threats may come from attackers actively seeking the alteration of information without authorization, or they may result from human error, mechanical failure, or environmental conditions, such as a power spike corrupting information.

Availability ensures that information and systems are ready to meet the needs of legitimate users at the time those users request them. Security professionals use availability controls, such as fault tolerance, clustering, and backups, to ensure that legitimate users gain access as needed. Similar to integrity threats, availability threats may come from attackers actively seeking the disruption of access, or they may come from human error, mechanical failure, or environmental conditions, such as a fire destroying a data center that contains valuable information or services.

Cybersecurity analysts often refer to these three goals, known as the *CIA Triad*, when performing their work. They often characterize risks, attacks, and security controls as meeting one or more of the three CIA Triad goals when describing them.

Role of the Information Security Manager

Information security managers are responsible for safeguarding the confidentiality, integrity, and availability of the information and systems used by their organization. But they must achieve these goals within the context of the organization's day-to-day activities and strategic objectives. The information security manager must wear the two hats shown in Figure 1.2: that of a cybersecurity subject matter expert and that of a business leader engaged with the organization's mission.

FIGURE 1.2 Information security managers must be both security experts and business leaders.

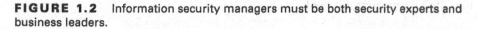
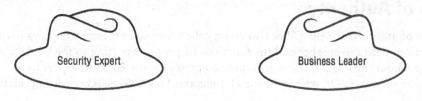

This "dual-hattedness" is perhaps the most significant defining characteristic of what makes an information security leader different from an information security professional. Information security professionals can narrow much of their focus to cybersecurity matters. Leaders, on the other hand, must maintain that organizational focus at the same time and use their expertise to help guide the organization in making decisions that are both sound from a business perspective and reasonable from a risk management perspective.

Depending on the size of an organization, information security management and leadership may be a role shared by several (or many!) different people, a consolidated role held by a single person, or even a partial role filled by someone who also bears other responsibilities within the organization. There is no one-size-fits-all answer to sizing the information security function for an organization—the selection is highly dependent on the nature of the organization's security requirements, the complexity of their operating environment, and the team they have in place.

Chief Information Security Officer

The most senior information security leader within an organization often bears the title of *chief information security officer (CISO)*. The CISO is a senior business executive who is responsible for overseeing all information security efforts within the organization. The CISO title is commonly accepted as the standard for an organization's information security leader, although some organizations may use different titles, including these:

- Vice president for information security (or assistant/associate vice president)
- Director of information security
- Information security manager

Many people believe that the use of these alternative titles indicates diminished status in the organization and a lack of prioritization for cybersecurity. In many cases, there is some truth behind this perception. In some cases, the use of the term *officer* may also imply that the individual bearing the title is an officer of the corporation or nonprofit organization. This has specific legal consequences that affect the CISO's responsibility and personal liability. However, it is important to note that just because someone has the title of CISO does not automatically make them an officer of the organization. Election or appointment as an officer is a formal process that requires the consent of the governing board.

The choice of a title also varies widely based on industry practices and organizational culture. For our purposes, we will continue to refer to the senior-most information security leader as the CISO throughout this book.

Lines of Authority

The lines of authority for the CISO also convey the role that cybersecurity plays in the organization, both the number and the functions of people reporting to the CISO, and the person to whom the CISO reports. It is quite common for the CISO to report to the chief information officer (CIO), who leads the IT function. This CISO/CIO reporting relationship clearly places responsibility for information security issues within the IT organization. In other cases, the CISO may report to other executives, such as:

- Chief executive officer (CEO)
- Chief risk officer (CRO)
- Chief security officer (CSO) (this role includes oversight of information security, physical security, and other security concerns)
- Chief operating officer (COO)
- Chief audit executive

The nature of this reporting relationship signals the importance that the organization places on the cybersecurity function as well as the perceived role of cybersecurity within the organization. For example, placing the information security function underneath a chief risk officer or chief security officer signals that the organization views information security risks within the context of a broader enterprise risk management or security program. As with titling, there is no "correct" placement of the CISO within the organizational structure, but organizations should be cognizant of the message they send to the security team and other employees based on their selection.

Although there are strong arguments for placing information security in several different parts of the organization, one general principle that should almost always be observed is that information security should not be buried underneath another function. This is particularly true when doing so may create a conflict of interest. For example, an organization might decide to place the information security function under a director of technology infrastructure who reports to the CIO. This approach is problematic for several reasons:

- It indicates that information security is not as important to the organization as other technology functions.
- It creates a potential conflict of interest when the information security team disagrees with an approach endorsed by the director to whom they report or when the security team is expected to report unflattering results of audits or tests performed on assets owned by that individual.
- It creates difficulties when the cybersecurity team has a conflict with another technology team that resides in a different part of the IT organization.

Organizing the Security Team

The CISO bears ultimate responsibility for protecting the confidentiality, integrity, and availability of the information and systems used by the organization. The specific controls and techniques used to achieve those goals will vary greatly, depending on the nature of the organization and its security requirements.

In almost every case, a team of information security professionals supports the CISO in their work, providing subject matter expertise and operational talents to achieve the organization's security objectives. In larger organizations, the CISO may leverage a management structure similar to the one shown in Figure 1.3, where a director who reports to the CISO leads each major cybersecurity function. The specific functions shown in Figure 1.3 are for illustrative purposes only and will vary from organization to organization.

FIGURE 1.3   Typical cybersecurity organizational structure

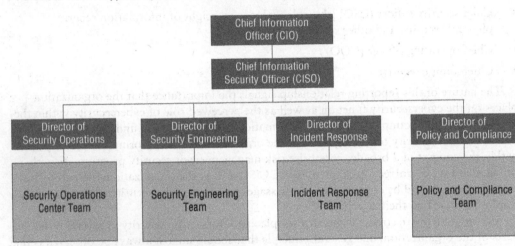

In larger organizations, these directors may each be supported by a series of managers, each of whom has individual contributors as direct reports. In midsized organizations, individual contributors may report to the directors. The need for additional layers of management is directly dependent on the number of people in the organization and should be optimized to reflect each manager's span of control. The *span of control* represents the number of individuals who directly report to a position. Different organizations have different philosophies on span of control, but it is commonly thought that managers with less than five direct reports likely have too small of a span of control and could take on additional responsibilities, whereas managers with more than 10 direct reports may have difficulty effectively managing a very large team.

Cybersecurity vs. Information Security

You may have noticed that we use the terms *cybersecurity* and *information security* almost interchangeably throughout this book. This is a deliberate choice, because the terms are commonly used this way in practice. However, we do want to point out that they do have two different meanings.

As you've already read, the goal of information security is to protect the confidentiality, integrity, and availability of an organization's information and information assets. The goal of cybersecurity is to protect the confidentiality, integrity, and availability of an organization's digital resources. These terms are closely related, but there are subtle differences.

Information security, properly defined, is responsible for the security of *all* information, whether in digital or analog form. An information security program would be responsible not only for electronic information systems but also for the protection of paper records and other nondigital assets. Cybersecurity, properly defined, is responsible for the security of all digital assets and may be thought of as a subset of the field of information security.

Although these definitional differences exist, the reality is that cybersecurity teams are almost always responsible for information security more broadly and most practitioners use these terms interchangeably. Therefore, for the sake of variety, we will do so as well in this book.

Roles and Responsibilities

Responsibility for different information security functions may be spread among a team and across the organization. For example, consider an organization's response to a cybersecurity incident. The organization may decide that the CISO has overall accountability for the incident response effort. However, the CISO does not do this on their own. They are supported by a variety of stakeholders who play different roles. The incident response team leader and members report to the CISO and carry out the actual response. Legal counsel provides valuable input on compliance issues and responsibilities. The CEO may need to be kept informed of incident progress. Tracking all of these stakeholders is crucial to ensuring that items don't slip through the cracks.

The RACI matrix is a common management tool used to specify how roles and responsibilities are shared throughout an organization. The matrix shows various security responsibilities and roles and then includes one of four letters indicating the level of involvement each role has in that responsibility. The options for filling in the RACI matrix are as follows:

- *Responsible (R)* roles are those who actually carry out the work involved. There must be at least one role assigned as responsible for each responsibility, although there may be more than one.

- *Accountable (A)* roles bear ultimate and final responsibility for achieving the objective. Consider this the "buck stops here" role for the responsibility. Each responsibility in the matrix must have one, and only one, accountable role.

- *Consulted (C)* roles are those who provide input that affects the responsibility because of their subject matter expertise.

- *Informed (I)* roles are those who are provided with regular updates on the status of the effort. They may need this information to complete their work, oversee the organization, or perform other tasks, but the key characteristic is that, unlike consulted roles, informed roles receive updates but do not provide input.

Figure 1.4 shows an abbreviated example of a RACI matrix for a few security roles in an organization.

FIGURE 1.4   RACI matrix for information security

	Incident Response	Privacy Compliance	Security Leadership
CEO	I		I
CIO	I	A	C
CISO	A	R	A
IR Leader	R	C	R
IR Team	R	C	
Compliance Leader	C	R	R
Compliance Team		R	
SOC Leader	C	I	R
SOC Team	C		
Legal Counsel	C	R	
Public Relations	C		

Information Security Risks

Security incidents occur when an organization experiences an adverse impact to the confidentiality, integrity, and/or availability of information or information systems. These incidents may occur as the result of malicious activity (such as an attacker targeting the organization and stealing sensitive information); accidental activity (such as an employee leaving an unencrypted laptop in the back of a rideshare); or natural activity (such as an earthquake destroying a data center).

Security professionals are responsible for understanding these risks and implementing controls designed to manage those risks to an acceptable level. To do so, they must first understand the effects that an incident might have on the organization and the impact it might have on an ongoing basis.

The DAD Triad

Earlier in this chapter, we introduced the CIA Triad, used to describe the three main goals of cybersecurity: confidentiality, integrity, and availability. Figure 1.5 shows a related model: the *DAD Triad*. This model explains the three important threats to cybersecurity efforts: *disclosure*, *alteration*, and *denial*. Each of these three threats maps directly to one of the main goals of cybersecurity:

- *Disclosure* is the exposure of sensitive information to unauthorized individuals, otherwise known as *data loss*. Disclosure is a violation of the principle of confidentiality. Attackers who gain access to sensitive information and remove it from the organization are said to be performing *data exfiltration*. Disclosure may also occur accidentally, such as when an administrator misconfigures access controls or an employee loses a device.

- *Alteration* is the unauthorized modification of information and is a violation of the principle of integrity. Attackers may seek to modify records contained in a system for financial gain, such as adding fraudulent transactions to a financial account. Alteration may occur as the result of natural activity, such as a power surge causing a "bit flip" that modifies stored data. Accidental alteration is also a possibility, if users unintentionally modify information stored in a critical system as the result of a typo or other unintended activity.

- *Denial* is the disruption of an authorized user's legitimate access to information. Denial events violate the principle of availability. This availability loss may be intentional, such as when an attacker launches a distributed denial-of-service (DDoS) attack against a website. Denial may also occur as the result of accidental activity, such as the failure of a critical server, or as the result of natural activity, such as a natural disaster impacting a communications circuit.

FIGURE 1.5   The three key threats to cybersecurity programs are disclosure, alteration, and denial.

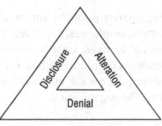

The CIA and DAD triads are very useful tools for cybersecurity planning and risk analysis. Whenever you find yourself tasked with a broad goal of assessing the security controls used to protect an asset or the threats to an organization, you can turn to the CIA and DAD triads. For example, if you're asked to assess the threats to your organization's website, you may apply the DAD Triad in your analysis:

- Does the website contain sensitive information that would damage the organization if disclosed to unauthorized individuals?

- If an attacker were able to modify information contained on the website, would this unauthorized alteration cause financial, reputational, or operational damage to the organization?

- Does the website perform mission-critical activities that could damage the business significantly if an attacker were able to disrupt the site?

That's just one example of using the DAD Triad to inform a risk assessment. You can use the CIA and DAD models in almost any situation to serve as a helpful starting point for a more detailed risk analysis.

Incident Impact

The impacts of a security incident may be wide-ranging, depending on the nature of the incident and the type of organization affected. We can categorize the potential impact of a security incident using the same categories that businesses generally use to describe any type of risk: financial, reputational, strategic, operational, and compliance.

Let's explore each of these risk categories a little further.

Financial Risk

Financial risk is, as the name implies, the risk of monetary damage to the organization as the result of a data breach, service disruption, or other security incident. This may be very direct financial damage, such as the costs of rebuilding a data center after it is physically destroyed or the costs of contracting experts for incident response and forensic analysis services.

Financial risk may also be indirect and come as a second-order consequence of the breach. For example, if an employee loses a laptop containing plans for a new product, the organization suffers direct financial damages of a few thousand dollars from the loss of the physical laptop. However, the indirect financial damage may be more severe—competitors may get ahold of those product plans and beat the organization to market, resulting in potentially significant revenue loss.

Reputational Risk

Reputational risk occurs when the negative publicity surrounding a security breach causes the loss of goodwill among customers, employees, suppliers, and other stakeholders. It is often difficult to quantify reputational damage, since these stakeholders may not directly say that they will reduce or eliminate their volume of business with the organization as a result of the security breach. However, the breach may still have an impact on their future decisions about doing business with the organization.

Identity Theft

When a security breach strikes an organization, the effects of that breach often extend beyond the walls of the breached organization, affecting customers, employees, and other individual stakeholders. The most common impact on these groups is the risk of identity theft posed by the exposure of personally identifiable information (PII) to unscrupulous individuals.

Organizations should take special care to identify, inventory, and protect PII elements, especially those that are prone to use in identity theft crimes. These include Social Security numbers, bank account and credit card information, driver's license numbers, passport data, and similar sensitive identifiers.

Strategic Risk

Strategic risk is the risk that an organization will become less effective in meeting its major goals and objectives as a result of the breach. Consider again the example of an employee losing a laptop that contains new product development plans. In addition to the financial impact discussed earlier, this incident may pose strategic risk to the organization in two different ways. First, if the organization does not have another copy of those plans, they may be unable to bring the new product to market or may suffer significant product development delays. Second, if competitors gain hold of those plans, they may be able to bring competing products to market more quickly or even beat the organization to market, gaining first-mover advantage. Both of these effects demonstrate strategic risk to the organization's ability to carry out its business plans.

Operational Risk

Operational risk is risk to the organization's ability to carry out its day-to-day functions. Operational risks may slow down business processes, delay delivery of customer orders, or require the implementation of time-consuming manual workarounds to normally automated practices.

Operational risk and strategic risk are closely related, so it might be difficult to distinguish between them. Think about the difference in terms of the nature and degree of the impact on the organization. If a risk threatens the very existence of an organization or the ability of the organization to execute its business plans, that is a strategic risk that seriously jeopardizes the organization's ongoing viability. On the other hand, if the risk only causes inefficiency and delay within the organization, it fits better into the operational risk category.

Compliance Risk

Compliance risk occurs when a security breach causes an organization to run afoul of legal or regulatory requirements. For example, the Health Insurance Portability and Accountability Act (HIPAA) requires that health-care providers and other covered entities protect the confidentiality, integrity, and availability of protected health information (PHI). If an organization loses patient medical records, they run afoul of HIPAA requirements and are subject to sanctions and fines from the U.S. Department of Health and Human Services. That's an example of compliance risk.

Organizations face many different types of compliance risk in today's regulatory landscape. The nature of those risks depends on the jurisdictions where the organization operates, the industry that the organization functions within, and the types of data that the organization handles. We discuss these compliance risks in more detail in Chapter 2, "Information Security Governance and Compliance."

Risks Often Cross Categories

Don't feel like you need to shoehorn every risk into one and only one of these categories. In most cases, a risk will cross multiple risk categories. For example, if an organization suffers a data breach that exposes customer PII to unknown individuals, the organization will likely suffer reputational damage due to negative media coverage. However, the organization may also suffer financial damage. Some of this financial damage may come in the form of lost business due to the reputational damage. Other financial damage may come

(continues)

(continued)

as a consequence of compliance risk if regulators impose fines on the organization. Still more financial damage may occur as a direct result of the breach, such as the costs associated with providing customers with identity protection services and notifying them about the breach.

Building an Information Security Strategy

Perhaps the most important responsibility of an information security leader is the creation, implementation, and maintenance of an *information security strategy* for the organization. This strategy begins with an assessment of the current state of the organization and a comparison to the desired state of security based on the organization's control objectives. It then outlines a plan for working from that current state to achieve the desired state through clearly articulated goals.

Before developing an information security strategy, information security leaders should gather information about the current and desired states of the organization. They do this through a series of analyses, including threat research, SWOT analysis, and gap analyses.

Threat Research

Developing a cybersecurity strategy requires a strong understanding of the threat environment facing cybersecurity professionals. A strategy is only effective if it combats the threats that pose the greatest risk to the organization. These threats may be described using two important factors:

- *Threat actors* are the individuals or groups seeking to undermine the security of an organization.

- *Threat vectors* are the tactics, tools, and techniques used by threat actors to achieve their objectives.

Cybersecurity threat actors differ significantly in their skills, capabilities, resources, and motivation. Protecting your organization's information and systems requires a solid understanding of the nature of these different threats so that you may develop a set of security controls that comprehensively protect your organization against them.

We dedicate an entire chapter of this book to understanding the cybersecurity threat landscape and conducting threat research. You will learn more about these topics in Chapter 4, "Cybersecurity Threat."

SWOT Analysis

SWOT analysis is a technique commonly used by organizations to assess their current state and develop their forward-looking strategy. SWOT is an acronym describing the four major elements of the analysis:

- *Strengths* are internal characteristics of the organization that provide it with an advantage toward achieving its goals/mission. For example, a cybersecurity team might consider its cybersecurity awareness program as a strength if it is particularly effective.

- *Weaknesses* are internal characteristics of the organization that place it at a disadvantage toward achieving its goals/mission. For example, a cybersecurity team might identify the lack of application security skills as a weakness.

- *Opportunities* are external factors that the organization might exploit to better achieve its goals/mission. For example, a cybersecurity team might consider the use of managed service providers as an opportunity to relieve the burden on the team and focus their work on value-added activities.

- *Threats* are external factors that might jeopardize the organization's ability to achieve its goals/mission. For example, a new privacy law passed by a jurisdiction within which the company operates might pose a threat to the organization.

The SWOT analysis may be conducted at any level of the organization. Senior leaders may conduct a SWOT analysis that analyzes the business overall. The CISO may conduct a SWOT analysis for the broad information security function, whereas the director of the incident response team may conduct a SWOT analysis for that specific function.

Organizations typically develop a SWOT analysis through a collaborative process that seeks inputs from all levels of the team, from individual contributors to senior management. The exercise of creating a SWOT analysis helps the organization think critically about its current position and how it will be affected by both internal and external forces moving forward.

A SWOT analysis may be quite detailed, but teams usually document the result of their work in a generalized chart similar to the one shown in Figure 1.6. This matrix organizes positive factors (strengths and opportunities) on the left side and negative factors (weaknesses and threats) on the right side. Similarly, internal factors (strengths and weaknesses) appear on the top, and external factors (opportunities and threats) appear on the bottom.

Gap Analysis

After identifying the risks that they face, organizations define their security requirements by writing a series of *control objectives* that describe how they plan to manage those risks. These control objectives are described from a strategic perspective in a general manner and provide a basis for the evaluation of the organization's current information security program against its desired state.

FIGURE 1.6   Cybersecurity SWOT analysis example

	Positive	Negative
Internal	**Strengths** 1. Experienced team 2. Strong technology infrastructure 3. Ability to innovate	**Weaknesses** 1. Incident response skills 2. Disorganized vendor management process 3. Lack of consolidated logging
External	**Opportunities** 1. Managed service provider offerings 2. Vendor-provided training	**Threats** 1. New state-level compliance requirements 2. Security failures at service providers

Control Objectives

In many cases, organizations draw these control objectives from industry standard frameworks, such as the Control Objectives for Information Technology (COBIT). Developed by ISACA, COBIT provides broad objective statements that apply to any IT organization. For example, the COBIT control objective for managed security states:

> Keep the impact and occurrence of information security incidents within the enterprise's risk appetite levels.

You'll learn more about the COBIT framework and other approaches to developing control objectives in Chapter 2.

With those control objectives in hand, cybersecurity managers can conduct an assessment of the current state of their controls and determine the degree to which they are achieving their control objectives. This process, known as a *gap analysis*, identifies areas of deficiency and opportunities for improvement that, if prioritized for remediation, may become the basis for goals in the organization's information security strategy.

Maturity Models

In addition to performing an objectives-based gap analysis, organizations may use *maturity models* to assess the state of their IT organization against industry best practices. ISACA offers the *Capability Maturity Model Integration (CMMI)* as a method to assess maturity of an organization. The use of these models is particularly common in software development efforts and in U.S. government contracting work, but the model may also be applied to security and other processes.

FIGURE 1.7   CMMI levels

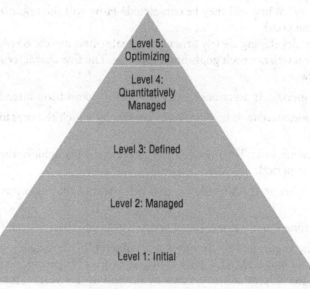

Under CMMI, an organization assesses each process as being at one of the five levels shown in Figure 1.7:

- At *Level 1: Initial,* the organization has unpredictable processes that are poorly controlled. This level is characterized by reactive management and a "firefighting" approach.

- When an organization achieves *Level 2: Managed,* it begins to implement organized processes on a per-project basis but is still operating in reactive mode.

- Moving on to *Level 3: Defined,* the organization has standard processes that are used organization wide and are adapted for use within each project. This level marks a shift from reactive to proactive management.

- *Level 4: Quantitatively Managed* organizations build measurement and controls on top of their processes to allow them to quickly identify and remediate deficiencies and address control gaps before issues arise.

- At the top tier of the CMMI, *Level 5: Optimizing* organizations use a continuous process improvement approach to adjust and fine-tune the way that they work to achieve peak efficiency and effectiveness.

Creating SMART Goals

Drafting the goals for an information security strategy can be a daunting task. Information security managers need to create goals that motivate the organization to succeed, move the organization toward the desired security state, and are reasonable to achieve. Strategies should not be vague but rather clearly articulated. For example, a goal of "Improve our vulnerability management program" is difficult to specifically envision. What types of improvement are necessary? When will they be completed? How will the organization know whether it has achieved the goal?

Organizations developing clearly articulated goals often use the SMART framework to describe the characteristics each goal should possess. The five characteristics of a SMART goal are as follows:

▪ The goal is *specific*. It describes clearly what the organization intends to achieve.

▪ The goal is *measurable*. It includes clear criteria by which the organization can measure success.

▪ The goal is *achievable*. The organization can realistically achieve the goal within the specified time period.

▪ The goal is *relevant*. If achieved, the goal will advance the organization's strategic objectives.

▪ The goal is *time-bound*. It includes a specific deadline for achievement.

Let's revisit the vague goal of "Improve our vulnerability management program." We can transform this goal into a SMART goal by recasting it as "Implement daily network vulnerability scanning for all production systems by the end of this year." This goal is much more specific—we are going to conduct network vulnerability scans on a daily basis. It is also measurable. We will know that we have achieved the goal once we are scanning 100 percent of production systems on a daily basis. Whether the goal is achievable within the next year or relevant to the organization's strategy is a judgment that must be made by management.

 Don't confuse "achievable" with "easy." Leaders should push their teams to achieve difficult goals by assigning stretch goals that force teams out of their comfort zone to achieve higher levels of productivity. At the same time, teams should not be set up for failure. Balancing the appropriate level of stress to place on the organization is an important job of the information security manager.

Alignment with Business Strategy

Information security functions exist for only one purpose: to serve the business. Certainly, security teams are focused on protecting the confidentiality, integrity, and availability of that business's information and systems, but information security managers must remain constantly aware that they do so in service of the organization achieving its business goals and objectives.

This is often one of the most important challenges facing leaders of cybersecurity teams. It's easy for technical subject matter experts to get lost in the weeds of their work and come to think of cybersecurity as an end in and of itself, but cybersecurity is only effective when it facilitates the achievement of organizational goals and objectives. Information security efforts must align with the business's goals, objectives, functions, processes, and practices.

Leadership Support

As a supporting function, information security initiatives do not generate revenue. Security functions are a cost center from a financial perspective. Every dollar spent on cybersecurity issues is a dollar that cannot be invested elsewhere in the business or returned to shareholders as profit. Therefore, senior business leaders and other stakeholders are often wary of investments in cybersecurity, and achieving their support is crucial to the success of the program.

One of the most important responsibilities of the information security manager is to gain ongoing commitment from senior leadership and other important stakeholders for investments of time and money in the security program. This requires helping leaders understand how information security efforts support the organization's goals and objectives. It also requires developing business cases for cybersecurity initiatives that demonstrate the impact of those initiatives on the business and include clear criteria for determining their successful implementation.

You'll learn more about building business cases for cybersecurity in Chapter 2.

Internal and External Influences

As you develop a security strategy for your organization, your core task is to achieve your security objectives in a manner that aligns with your organization's business strategy. That said, it would be naïve to believe that this happens in a bubble. Your organization's approach to security is influenced by a number of internal and external factors:

- The broader *business environment* within which your organization operates. The demands of customers and pressures placed on the organization by competitors will influence the level of commitment to and investment in cybersecurity, both positively and negatively.

- Your organization's *risk tolerance*. This is the degree of risk that you are willing to undertake as you seek to achieve your business objectives. You will learn more about risk tolerance and risk management in Chapter 3, "Information Risk Management."

- The *regulatory environment* within which your organization operates. This may include federal and state laws and industry codes of practice. You will learn more about regulatory requirements that may apply to your organization in Chapter 2.

- Changes in the *threat landscape*. As adversaries adapt their tactics and techniques, your cybersecurity strategy must evolve to combat those changes. You will learn more about the cybersecurity threat landscape in Chapter 4.

- *Emerging technologies* in use in your field. If competitive pressures or innovation strategies guide your organization toward the use of emerging technologies, those technologies will challenge the status quo in your security program.

- *Social media* spreads news at faster rates than ever before. Even if your organization does not directly discuss cybersecurity issues on social media, rest assured that your customers and other stakeholders will.

- *Third-party considerations* also play a role. Although the media, industry groups, vendors, and other third parties may not have regulatory authority, they may also bring pressure to bear on your organization, forcing changes in cybersecurity strategies.

Cybersecurity Responsibilities

You've heard the old adage: security is everybody's responsibility. There's wisdom in that old saying—cybersecurity professionals aren't the only ones who must protect the organization's information and information systems. As you build out your information security strategy, be sure to clearly document the roles of major contributors. These include three critical roles in data governance: data owners, data stewards, and data custodians.

Data owners are the senior-level officials who bear overall responsibility for particular datasets. The data owner sets policies and guidelines for data use and data security and has the authority to make final decisions regarding a dataset. Data owners are usually the business leaders who have responsibility for the mission area most closely related to the dataset. For example, an organization's vice president for human resources might be the data owner for employment information.

Practically speaking, most individuals who are senior enough to hold the position of data owner do not have the time available to get involved in the daily decisions of data governance. They usually delegate that responsibility to a *data steward*. The data steward handles the implementation of the high-level policies set by the data owner. For example, a data steward might make day-to-day decisions about who may access a dataset. In the case of the employee dataset, if the data owner is the vice president for human resources, that vice president might delegate data stewardship responsibility to a director for HR information services. In most cases, there is a reporting relationship between the data owner and the data steward.

Data custodians are the individuals who actually store and process the information in question. IT staff often find themselves in the position of data custodians because of their roles as system owners and administrators. Technologists are rarely data owners or data stewards, but they are usually data custodians for almost all of the data in the organization due to the nature of their jobs. Data stewards ensure that appropriate data protections are in place, including encryption, backups, access controls, and other mechanisms that meet the requirements set forth by data owners and stewards.

Data processors are third-party organizations that handle data on behalf of a data owner. For example, if the IT team at an organization stores data in a cloud service, that cloud service provider is a data processor.

Consider an example that helps tie these terms together. If your bank collects financial information from you to process loan applications and an IT administrator at the bank uses a cloud service to store those records, we have several roles at play. You are the data subject, because the records are about you. The bank, as an organization, is responsible for that data and likely designates a senior officer, such as the vice president of loans, as the data owner. The IT administrator who handles the records is a data custodian, and the cloud service they use is a data processor.

Individual users also bear responsibility for protecting the security of information and systems that they use and access. Cybersecurity responsibility training should be provided to all end users but should also have a particular focus on two categories of user:

- *High-risk users* who are the likely targets of cyberattacks. This may be because they are high-profile individuals likely to attract attention or because they engage in activities that place them at higher risk, such as frequently traveling to high-risk destinations.

- *Privileged users* who would pose a higher-than-average risk if their accounts were compromised. This includes technologists with administrative access to systems, finance professionals with the ability to initiate funds transfers, executives with access to sensitive information, and other similar highly privileged groups.

Strong cybersecurity programs clearly define the responsibilities of each of these groups, communicate to them regularly, and monitor their progress toward achieving security objectives.

Communication

Cybersecurity strategies are only effective if they are clearly communicated to stakeholders throughout the organization. You will need to use messaging and methods for this communication that fit within your organization's normal business processes. You will want to consider the normal culture within your organization and traditional channels of communication and take advantage of those as much as possible. For example, if employees are used to receiving important messages at their weekly team meetings, try to inject security messaging into those meetings. If they prefer brief informal communication by Slack, communicate that way. Bring the cybersecurity message to users where they already are and they'll be much more receptive to that messaging.

At the same time, cybersecurity messages must be concise. Highlight the essential aspects of information security in a way that translates to actionable advice for the audience. They don't need to hear all of the details behind cybersecurity strategies. They just need to understand that their assistance is important and what, exactly, is being asked of them.

Action Plans

As you put a cybersecurity strategy in place, you'll want to develop an action plan that outlines both the short-term and long-term steps that you will take to move your organization from its current state to its desired state. As with communication efforts, you'll be more successful if you align those plans with the normal project planning methods used by your organization.

Figure 1.8 shows an example of a one-page plan that covers the four-year rollout of an organization's information security strategy.

FIGURE 1.8   Communicating the security strategy

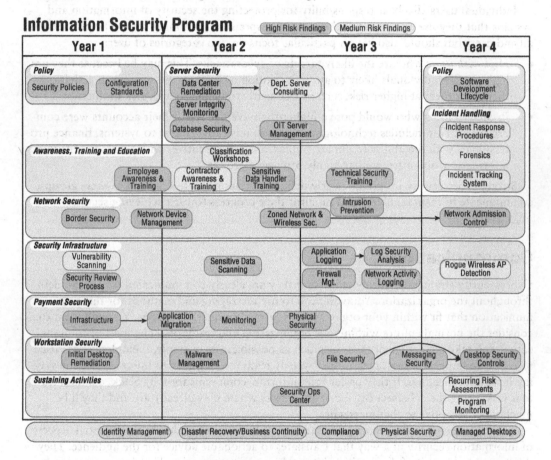

Implementing Security Controls

As an organization analyzes its risk environment, technical and business leaders determine the level of protection required to preserve the confidentiality, integrity, and availability of their information and systems. They express these requirements by writing the *control objectives* that the organization wishes to achieve. These control objectives are statements of a desired security state, but they do not, by themselves, actually carry out security activities. *Security controls* are specific measures that fulfill the security objectives of an organization.

Security Control Categories

Security controls are categorized based on their mechanism of action: the way that they achieve their objectives. There are three different categories of security control:

- *Technical controls* enforce confidentiality, integrity, and availability in the digital space. Examples of technical security controls include firewall rules, access control lists, intrusion prevention systems, and encryption.

- *Operational controls* include the processes that we put in place to manage technology in a secure manner. These include user access reviews, log monitoring, and vulnerability management.

- *Managerial controls* are procedural mechanisms that focus on the mechanics of the risk management process. Examples of administrative controls include periodic risk assessments, security planning exercises, and the incorporation of security into the organization's change management, service acquisition, and project management practices.

 If you're not familiar with some of the controls provided as examples in this chapter, don't worry about it! We'll discuss them all in detail later in the book.

Organizations should select a set of security controls that meets their control objectives based on the criteria and parameters that they either select for their environment or have imposed on them by outside regulators. For example, an organization that handles sensitive information might decide that confidentiality concerns surrounding that information require the highest level of control. At the same time, they might conclude that the availability of their website is not of critical importance. Given these considerations, they would dedicate significant resources to the confidentiality of sensitive information while perhaps investing little, if any, time and money protecting their website against a denial-of-service attack.

Many control objectives require a combination of technical, operational, and management controls. For example, an organization might have the control objective of preventing unauthorized access to a data center. They might achieve this goal by implementing biometric access control (technical control), performing regular reviews of authorized access (operational control), and conducting routine risk assessments (managerial control).

Security Control Types

We can also divide security controls into types, based on their desired effect. The types of security control include the following:

- *Preventive controls* intend to stop a security issue before it occurs. Firewalls and encryption are examples of preventive controls.

- *Detective controls* identify security events that have already occurred. Intrusion detection systems are detective controls.

- *Corrective controls* remediate security issues that have already occurred. Restoring backups after a ransomware attack is an example of a corrective control.

- *Deterrent controls* seek to discourage an attacker from attempting to violate security policies. Vicious guard dogs and barbed wire fences are examples of deterrent controls.

- *Physical controls* are security controls that impact the physical world. Examples of physical security controls include fences, perimeter lighting, locks, fire suppression systems, and burglar alarms.

- *Compensating controls* are controls designed to mitigate the risk associated with exceptions made to a security policy.

Exploring Compensating Controls

The Payment Card Industry Data Security Standard (PCI DSS) includes one of the most formal compensating control processes in use today. It sets out three criteria that must be met for a compensating control to be satisfactory:

- The control must meet the intent and rigor of the original requirement.

- The control must provide a similar level of defense as the original requirement, such that the compensating control sufficiently offsets the risk that the original PCI DSS requirement was designed to defend against.

- The control must be "above and beyond" other PCI DSS requirements.

For example, an organization might find that it needs to run an outdated version of an operating system on a specific machine because software necessary to run the business will only function on that operating system version. Most security policies would prohibit using the outdated operating system because it might be susceptible to security vulnerabilities. The organization could choose to run this system on an isolated network with either very little or no access to other systems as a compensating control.

The general idea is that a compensating control finds alternative means to achieve an objective when the organization cannot meet the original control requirement. Although PCI DSS offers a very formal process for compensating controls, the use of compensating controls is a common strategy in many different organizations, even those not subject to PCI DSS. Compensating controls balance the fact that it simply isn't possible to implement every required security control in every circumstance with the desire to manage risk to the greatest feasible degree.

In many cases, organizations adopt compensating controls to address a temporary exception to a security requirement. In those cases, the organization should also develop remediation plans designed to bring the organization back into compliance with the letter and intent of the original control.

Data Protection

Security professionals spend significant amounts of their time focusing on the protection of sensitive data. We serve as stewards and guardians, protecting the confidentiality, integrity, and availability of the sensitive data created by our organizations and entrusted to us by our customers and other stakeholders.

As we think through data protection techniques, it's helpful to consider the three states in which data might exist:

- *Data at rest* is stored data that resides on hard drives, tapes, in the cloud, or on other storage media. This data is prone to pilfering by insiders or external attackers who gain access to systems and are able to browse through their contents.

- *Data in motion* is data that is in transit over a network. When data travels on an untrusted network, it is open to eavesdropping attacks by anyone with access to those networks.

- *Data in processing* is data that is actively in use by a computer system. This includes the data stored in memory while processing takes place. An attacker with control of the system may be able to read the contents of memory and steal sensitive information.

We can use different security controls to safeguard data in all of these states, building a robust set of defenses that protects our organization's vital interests.

Data Encryption

Encryption technology uses mathematical algorithms to protect information from prying eyes, both while it is in transit over a network and while it resides on systems. Encrypted data is unintelligible to anyone who does not have access to the appropriate decryption key, making it safe to store and transmit encrypted data over otherwise insecure means.

We'll dive deeply into encryption tools and techniques in Chapter 7, "Cybersecurity Technology."

Data Loss Prevention

Data loss prevention (DLP) systems help organizations enforce information handling policies and procedures to prevent data loss and theft. They search systems for stores of sensitive information that might be unsecured and monitor network traffic for potential attempts to remove sensitive information from the organization. They can act quickly to block the transmission before damage is done and alert administrators to the attempted breach.

DLP systems work in two different environments:

- Host-based DLP
- Network DLP

Host-based DLP uses software agents installed on systems that search those systems for the presence of sensitive information. These searches often turn up Social Security numbers, credit card numbers, and other sensitive information in the most unlikely places!

Detecting the presence of stored sensitive information allows security professionals to take prompt action to either remove it or secure it with encryption. Taking the time to secure or remove information now may pay handsome rewards down the road if the device is lost, stolen, or compromised.

Host-based DLP can also monitor system configuration and user actions, blocking undesirable actions. For example, some organizations use host-based DLP to block users from accessing USB-based removable media devices that they might use to carry information out of the organization's secure environment.

Network-based DLP systems are dedicated devices that sit on the network and monitor outbound network traffic, watching for any transmissions that contain unencrypted sensitive information. They can then block those transmissions, preventing the unsecured loss of sensitive information.

DLP systems may simply block traffic that violates the organization's policy, or in some cases, they may automatically apply encryption to the content. This automatic encryption is commonly used with DLP systems that focus on email.

DLP systems also have two mechanisms of action:

- *Pattern matching*, where they watch for the telltale signs of sensitive information. For example, if they see a number that is formatted like a credit card or Social Security number, they can automatically trigger on that. Similarly, they may contain a database of sensitive terms, such as "credit card" or "blood pressure," and trigger when they see those terms in a transmission.

- *Watermarking*, where systems or administrators apply electronic tags to sensitive documents and then the DLP system can monitor systems and networks for unencrypted content containing those tags.

Watermarking technology is also commonly used in *digital rights management* (DRM) solutions that enforce copyright and data ownership restrictions.

Data Minimization

Data minimization techniques reduce risk by reducing the amount of sensitive information that we maintain on a regular basis. The best way to achieve data minimization is to simply destroy data when it is no longer necessary to meet our original business purpose.

If we can't completely remove data from a dataset, we can often transform it into a format where the original sensitive information is de-identified. The *de-identification* (or "anonymization") process removes the ability to link data back to an individual, reducing its sensitivity.

An alternative to de-identifying data is transforming it into a format where the original information can't be retrieved. This is a process called *data obfuscation*, and we have several tools at our disposal to assist with it:

- *Hashing* uses a hash function to transform a value in our dataset to a corresponding hash value. If we apply a strong hash function to a data element, we may replace the value in our file with the hashed value. Hashing uses a one-way function, meaning that it is not possible to retrieve the original value if you only have access to the hashed value.

- *Tokenization* replaces sensitive values with a unique identifier using a lookup table. For example, we might replace a widely known value, such as a student ID, with a randomly generated 10-digit number. We'd then maintain a lookup table that allows us to convert those back to student IDs if we need to determine someone's identity. Of course, if you use this approach, you must keep the lookup table secure!

- *Masking* partially redacts sensitive information by replacing some or all sensitive fields with blank characters. For example, we might replace all but the last four digits of a credit card number with X's or *'s to render the card number unreadable.

Although it isn't possible to retrieve the original value directly from the hashed value, there is one major flaw to this approach. If someone has a list of possible values for a field, they can conduct something called a *rainbow table attack*. In this attack, the attacker computes the hashes of those candidate values and then checks to see if those hashes exist in our data file.

For example, imagine that we have a file listing all the students at our college who have failed courses but we hash their student IDs. If an attacker has a list of all students, they can compute the hash values of all student IDs and then check to see which hash values are on the list. For this reason, hashing should only be used with caution.

Summary

Cybersecurity managers are responsible for ensuring the confidentiality, integrity, and availability of information and systems maintained by their organizations. Confidentiality ensures that unauthorized individuals are not able to gain access to sensitive information. Integrity ensures that there are no unauthorized modifications to information or systems, either intentionally or unintentionally. Availability ensures that information and systems are ready to meet the needs of legitimate users at the time those users request them. Together, these three goals are known as the CIA Triad.

As cybersecurity analysts seek to protect their organizations, they must evaluate risks to the CIA Triad. This includes the design and implementation of an appropriate mixture of security controls drawn from the managerial, operational, and technical control categories. These controls should also be varied in type, including a mixture of preventive, detective, corrective, deterrent, physical, and compensating controls.

Exam Essentials

Know the three objectives of cybersecurity. *Confidentiality* ensures that unauthorized individuals are not able to gain access to sensitive information. *Integrity* ensures that there are no unauthorized modifications to information or systems, either intentionally or unintentionally. *Availability* ensures that information and systems are ready to meet the needs of legitimate users at the time those users request them.

Describe how information security strategies should be aligned with organizational goals and objectives. As information security managers develop their plans, they should use reliable techniques to assess the current state of the program, such as threat research, SWOT analysis, and gap analysis. They may then identify the initiatives that will move the organization from the current state to its desired state.

Explain how security strategies are influenced by internal and external factors.   Security strategies must be aligned with the business, but they must also incorporate other influences. Information security managers must remain abreast of emerging technologies, social media, the business environment, the organization's risk tolerance, regulatory requirements, third-party considerations, and the threat landscape as they develop, monitor, and revise cybersecurity strategies.

Know why stakeholder commitment and communication are essential to success.   As information security leaders roll out new strategies, they must ensure that they have the support of senior leaders and other stakeholders. They may do this by clearly outlining how information security supports the organization's broader goals and objectives, identifying the business impact of security initiatives, and identifying clear success criteria.

Explain how security controls may be categorized based on their mechanism of action and their intent.   Controls are grouped into the categories of managerial, operational, and technical based on the way that they achieve their objectives. They are divided into the types of preventive, detective, corrective, deterrent, compensating, and physical based on their intended purpose.

Describe the diverse impacts of data breaches on organizations.   When an organization suffers a data breach, the resulting data loss often results in both direct and indirect damages. The organization suffers immediate financial repercussions due to the costs associated with the incident response, as well as long-term financial consequences due to reputational damage. This reputational damage may be difficult to quantify, but it may also have a lasting impact. In some cases, organizations may suffer operational damage if they experience availability damages, preventing them from accessing their own information.

Explain why data must be protected in transit, at rest, and in use.   Attackers may attempt to eavesdrop on network transmissions containing sensitive information. This information is highly vulnerable when in transit unless protected by encryption technology. Attackers also might attempt to breach data stores, stealing data at rest. Encryption serves to protect stored data as well as data in transit. Data is also vulnerable while in use on a system and should be protected during data processing activities.

Know how data loss prevention (DLP) systems block data exfiltration attempts.   DLP technology enforces information handling policies to prevent data loss and theft. DLP systems may function at the host level, using software agents to search systems for the presence of sensitive information. They may also work at the network level, watching for transmissions of unencrypted sensitive information. DLP systems detect sensitive information using pattern-matching technology and/or digital watermarking.

Explain how data minimization reduces risk by reducing the amount of sensitive information that we maintain.   In cases where we cannot simply discard unnecessary information, we can protect information through de-identification and data obfuscation. The tools used to achieve these goals include hashing, tokenization, and masking of sensitive fields.

Review Questions

1. Matt is updating the organization's threat assessment process. What category of control is Matt implementing?

   A. Operational

   B. Technical

   C. Corrective

   D. Managerial

2. Jade's organization recently suffered a security breach that affected stored credit card data. Jade's primary concern is the fact that the organization is subject to sanctions for violating the provisions of the Payment Card Industry Data Security Standard. What category of risk is concerning Jade?

   A. Strategic

   B. Compliance

   C. Operational

   D. Financial

3. Chris is responding to a security incident that compromised one of his organization's web servers. He believes that the attackers defaced one or more pages on the website. What cybersecurity objective did this attack violate?

   A. Confidentiality

   B. Nonrepudiation

   C. Integrity

   D. Availability

4. Which one of the following elements is *most* important to gaining the support of senior leaders for cybersecurity initiatives?

   A. Using plain, understandable language

   B. Communicating often and in the format desired by the leaders

   C. Demonstrating the alignment between business objectives and security needs

   D. Adopting emerging technologies

5. Tonya is concerned about the risk that an attacker will attempt to gain access to her organization's database server. She is searching for a control that would discourage the attacker from attempting to gain access. What type of security control is she seeking to implement?

   A. Preventive

   B. Detective

   C. Corrective

   D. Deterrent

6. Which one of the following individuals bears ultimate responsibility for protecting an organization's data?

   A. Data steward

   B. End users

   C. Data custodian

   D. Data owner

7. Brooke is conducting a SWOT analysis for her organization's cybersecurity program. She recently learned about a cybersecurity insurance offering that may allow the organization to transfer some financial risk and is considering purchasing a policy. Where would this offering fit in the SWOT analysis?

   A. Strength

   B. Weakness

   C. Opportunity

   D. Threat

8. Tina is tuning her organization's intrusion prevention system to prevent false positive alerts. What type of control is Tina implementing?

   A. Technical control

   B. Physical control

   C. Managerial control

   D. Operational control

9. Dan is the CISO of an organization and he is spearheading the development of a new security operations center (SOC). He bears responsibility for the success of this initiative. In the RACI matrix entry for this initiative, how would Dan *best* be labeled?

   A. R

   B. A

   C. C

   D. I

10. Tony is reviewing the status of his organization's defenses against a breach of their file server. He believes that a compromise of the file server could reveal information that would prevent the company from continuing to do business. What term *best* describes the risk that Tony is considering?

    A. Strategic

    B. Reputational

    C. Financial

    D. Operational

11. Which one of the following data elements is not commonly associated with identity theft?

   A. Social Security number

   B. Driver's license number

   C. Frequent flyer number

   D. Passport number

12. What term best describes an organization's desired security state?

   A. Control objectives

   B. Security priorities

   C. Strategic goals

   D. Best practices

13. Jerry is developing a cybersecurity awareness program for members of his team who have administrative access to sensitive systems. What category *best* describes the users he is targeting?

   A. Privileged users

   B. High-risk users

   C. End users

   D. Data owners

14. Which one of the following individuals is the *least* appropriate direct manager of a chief information security officer?

   A. Chief information officer

   B. Chief risk officer

   C. Chief executive officer

   D. Senior director for identity and access management

15. Greg recently conducted an assessment of his organization's security controls and discovered a potential gap: the organization does not use full-disk encryption on laptops. What type of control gap exists in this case?

   A. Detective

   B. Corrective

   C. Deterrent

   D. Preventive

16. Toni is developing a new goal for her information security program. She has currently written it as "We will acquire and implement a new intrusion prevention system that will reduce successful network intrusions by 50%." What element of the SMART framework is lacking from this goal?

   A. Specific

   B. Measurable

C. Achievable

D. Relevant

E. Time-bound

17. Nolan is writing an after-action report on a security breach that took place in his organization. The attackers stole thousands of customer records from the organization's database. What cybersecurity principle was most impacted in this breach?

A. Availability

B. Nonrepudiation

C. Confidentiality

D. Integrity

18. Which one of the following objectives is not one of the three main objectives that information security professionals must achieve to protect their organizations against cybersecurity threats?

A. Integrity

B. Nonrepudiation

C. Availability

D. Confidentiality

19. What is the *most* appropriate span of control for a cybersecurity leader?

A. 2

B. 4

C. 7

D. 12

20. Brian is conducting a maturity assessment of his organization's cybersecurity team using Capability Maturity Model Integration (CMMI). He notes that the team does use defined processes but that they develop them in a reactive manner for each project they undertake. What level of maturity would *best* describe this team?

A. Defined

B. Repeatable

C. Initial

D. Quantitatively managed

E. Managed

Chapter

2

Information Security Governance and Compliance

THE CERTIFIED INFORMATION SECURITY MANAGER (CISM) DOMAINS AND SUBTOPICS COVERED IN THIS CHAPTER INCLUDE:

✓ **Domain 1: Information Security Governance**

- **A. Enterprise Governance**

    - **1A2. Legal, Regulatory, and Contractual Requirements**

- **B. Information Security Strategy**

    - **1B2. Information Governance Frameworks and Standards**

    - **1B3. Strategic Planning (e.g. budgets, resources, business case)**

✓ **Domain 3: Information Security Program**

- **A. Information Security Program Development**

    - **3A3. Industry Standards and Frameworks for Information Security**

    - **3A4. Information Security Policies, Procedures, and Guidelines**

THE CERTIFIED INFORMATION SECURITY MANAGER (CISM) SUPPORTING TASKS COVERED IN THIS CHAPTER INCLUDE:

✓ **3. Establish and/or maintain an information security governance framework.**

✓ **4. Integrate information security governance into corporate governance.**

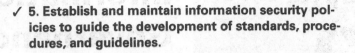

✓ 5. Establish and maintain information security policies to guide the development of standards, procedures, and guidelines.

✓ 6. Develop business cases to support investments in information security.

✓ 14. Establish, communicate, and maintain organizational information security policies, standards, guidelines, procedures, and other documentation.

✓ 21. Identify legal, regulatory, organizational, and other applicable compliance requirements

Policy serves as the foundation for any cybersecurity program, setting out the principles and rules that guide the execution of security efforts throughout the enterprise. Often, organizations base these policies on best practice frameworks developed by industry groups such as the National Institute of Standards and Technology (NIST) or the International Organization for Standardization (ISO). In many cases, organizational policies are also influenced and directed by external compliance obligations that regulators impose on the organization. In this chapter, you will learn about the important elements of the cybersecurity policy framework as well as the compliance obligations imposed on organizations by governments and other regulators.

Governance

Governance programs are the sets of procedures and controls put in place to allow an organization to effectively direct its work. Without governance, running a large organization would be virtually impossible. Imagine if thousands of employees throughout the organization each had to make their own determinations about which work was most important, who should carry out each function, and how the organization would conduct its work. The organization would quickly find itself in a state of unmanageable chaos. Governance efforts function at all layers of an organization to coordinate the development and execution of strategic plans. This ensures that every aspect of an organization's work aligns with the organization's strategy and goals.

Corporate Governance

At the highest levels of the organization, corporate governance programs ensure that the organization sets an appropriate strategic direction, develops a plan to implement that strategy, and then executes on its strategic plan. This is done through a hierarchical model, such as the one shown in Figure 2.1, which is the common governance model for publicly traded corporations.

This approach is designed for use in an environment where the owners are so numerous or unengaged that they are unable to carry out day-to-day oversight of the company. This is the situation where a publicly traded company typically finds itself. The owners of that company's stock own the corporation, but they may number in the thousands or millions and their membership may change on a daily basis. It would quickly cripple a public corporation if all of its shareholders were required to vote on every action taken by the company. To alleviate this burden, the shareholders of the company conduct regular meetings where they elect a group of individuals to direct the actions of the corporation on their behalf. This group, known as the *board of directors*, has ultimate authority over the organization as the owners' representatives.

FIGURE 2.1 Typical corporate governance model

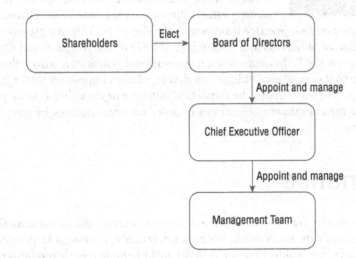

These directors are typically drawn from the major shareholders and have expertise in corporate governance, perhaps having served as senior corporate executives themselves. Although some members of the board may also be employed as senior leaders within the organization, it is considered a best practice in corporate governance for a majority of the members of the board to be *independent directors*, meaning that they have no significant relationship with the company other than their board membership. In fact, the major stock exchanges each have requirements about the number of independent directors that a corporation must have to qualify for listing on the exchange.

Boards typically meet on a fairly infrequent basis, perhaps monthly or quarterly, so it is not practical for a board to dictate the day-to-day operations of the company. Instead, they hire a *chief executive officer (CEO)* who manages the company's operations. The CEO is hired by the board, may be dismissed by the board, and has their performance reviews and compensation determined by the board.

Of course, the CEO also can't control every single function of the organization, so they must hire a team of executives, managers, and individual contributors to perform this work. Once again, the flow of governance cascades downward. The shareholder owners of the company delegate authority to run the organization to their elected board of directors. The board then hires and manages the CEO, who then hires and manages other senior executives, who hire and manage middle managers, who hire and manage teams of individual contributors. The size of the management hierarchy depends on the size of the organization and is intended to preserve a reasonable span of control for each manager, as discussed in Chapter 1, "Today's Information Security Manager."

 The governance model described here is the one used for publicly traded companies. Nonprofit organizations follow a similar model, with the major difference being that the board members are either elected by the membership of the organization or elected in a "self-perpetuating" model, where current board members vote to elect new board members. Privately owned organizations may follow many different governance models. For example, the sole owner of a corporation may also serve as the CEO or carry out the functions of a board on their own. Alternatively, multiple owners of a corporation may each appoint a number of board members proportional to their ownership stake. There are many possible variations on this model, but the key point is that the owners control the organization either directly or through a board that they control.

Governance, Risk, and Compliance Programs

Organizations carry out the work of governance through the creation and implementation of a *governance, risk, and compliance (GRC) program*. GRC programs integrate three related tasks:

- *Governance* of the organization, as discussed in this chapter
- *Risk management*, as discussed in Chapter 3, "Information Risk Management"
- *Compliance*, as discussed later in this chapter

Information Security Governance

Information security governance is a natural extension of corporate governance. The board delegates operational authority to the CEO, who then delegates specific areas of authority to subordinate executives. For example, the CEO might delegate financial authority to the chief financial officer (CFO) and operational authority to the chief operations officer (COO). Similarly, the CEO delegates information security responsibility to the chief information security officer (CISO) or other responsible executive, following one of the options discussed in Chapter 1.

This hierarchical approach to governance helps ensure that information security governance efforts are integrated into corporate governance efforts, ensuring that the organization's information security program supports broader organizational goals and objectives. The CISO and CEO must work together to ensure the proper alignment of the information security program with corporate governance.

The CISO then works with other peers on the senior management team to design and implement an information security governance framework that guides the activity of the information security function and ensures alignment with the organization's information security strategy. This governance framework may take many different forms. It normally involves the establishment of a management structure for the cybersecurity team that aligns with management approaches used elsewhere in the organization.

The information security governance framework should also include the mechanisms that the security team will use to enforce security requirements across the organization. This is particularly important because the CISO does not exercise operational control over the entire organization but needs management leverage to ensure the organization meets its cybersecurity requirements. This is normally done through the creation of policies that apply to the entire organization, as discussed later in this chapter.

The lines of authority for the cybersecurity function flow through the defined corporate governance mechanisms of the organization. The CISO and other security leaders should utilize existing reporting and communications channels when available and establish new channels when necessary. They should also include escalation procedures in the event that the cybersecurity team requires management assistance getting traction in other areas of the organization.

Developing Business Cases

The implementation and management of information security personnel, projects, and tools requires investments of financial and human resources by the organization. Those resources are, of course, finite, and there is normally stiff competition within the organization over their allocation. Other business leaders may want the same resources assigned to initiatives they find to be a higher priority, whereas shareholders may prefer that the resources be returned to them as profit in the form of dividends.

Therefore, cybersecurity managers must be able to make coherent business cases that justify their proposed investments. These business cases outline the rationale for the investment and justify it as the best possible use of the requested resources. Cybersecurity managers should investigate the business case process used by the rest of their organization and adopt it as closely as possible. These formats may vary, but they typically include several core components:

- A *scope statement* that concisely describes the proposed initiative
- The *strategic context* that demonstrates the need for the initiative and how the investment aligns with the organization's broader strategic goals
- A *cost analysis* that outlines the financial and human resource costs of the initiative, on both a one-time and a recurring basis
- An *evaluation of alternatives* that describes other possible approaches for achieving the strategic goals addressed by this project and explains why the current proposal is the best available option

- A *project plan* that describes the detailed implementation plan for the initiative
- A *management plan* that describes how the organization will oversee the processes created by this initiative on an ongoing basis in a manner that integrates with the information security and corporate governance frameworks

Third-Party Relationships

Many risks facing an organization come from external partners with whom the organization does business. These risks may be the result of a vendor relationship that arises somewhere along the organization's supply chain, or they may be the result of other business partnerships. The nature of these risks requires oversight, and therefore, it is important to integrate third-party relationships into an organization's information security governance program. Organizations may deploy some standard agreements and practices to manage these risks. Commonly used agreements include the following:

- *Master service agreements (MSAs)* provide an umbrella contract for the work that a vendor does with an organization over an extended period of time. The MSA typically includes detailed security and privacy requirements. Each time the organization enters into a new project with the vendor, they may then create a *statement of work (SOW)* that contains project-specific details and references the MSA.
- *Service-level agreements (SLAs)* are written contracts that specify the conditions of service that will be provided by the vendor and the remedies available to the customer if the vendor fails to meet the SLA. SLAs commonly cover issues such as system availability, data durability, and response time.
- A *memorandum of understanding (MOU)* is a letter written to document aspects of the relationship. MOUs are an informal mechanism that allows the parties to document their relationship to avoid future misunderstandings. MOUs are commonly used in cases where an internal service provider is offering a service to a customer that is in a different business unit of the same company.
- *Business partnership agreements (BPAs)* exist when two organizations agree to do business with each other in a partnership. For example, if two companies jointly develop and market a product, the BPA might specify each partner's responsibilities and the division of profits.
- *Nondisclosure agreements (NDAs)* protect the confidentiality of information used in the relationship. NDAs may be mutual, protecting the confidentiality of information belonging to both parties in the relationship, or one-way, protecting the confidential information belonging to only the customer or the supplier.

Organizations will need to select the agreement type(s) most appropriate for their specific circumstances.

All things come to an end, and third-party relationships are no exception. Organizations should take steps to ensure that they have an orderly transition when a vendor relationship ends, or the vendor is discontinuing a product or service on which the organization depends.

This should include specific steps that both parties will follow to have an orderly transition when the vendor announces a product's *end of life (EOL)* or a service's *end of service life (EOSL)*. These same steps may be followed if the organization chooses to stop using the product or service on its own.

Understanding Policy Documents

An organization's *information security policy framework* contains a series of documents designed to describe the organization's cybersecurity program. The scope and complexity of these documents vary widely, depending on the nature of the organization and its information resources. These frameworks generally include four different types of document:

- Policies
- Standards
- Procedures
- Guidelines

In the remainder of this section, you'll learn the differences between each of these document types. However, keep in mind that the definitions of these categories vary significantly from organization to organization and it is very common to find the lines between them blurred. Though at first glance that may seem incorrect, it's a natural occurrence as security theory meets the real world. As long as the documents are achieving their desired purpose, there's no harm in using whatever naming system is preferred in your organization.

Policies

Policies are broad statements of management intent. Compliance with policies is mandatory. An information security policy will generally contain generalized statements about cybersecurity objectives, including the following:

- A statement of the importance of cybersecurity to the organization
- Requirements that all staff and contracts take measures to protect the confidentiality, integrity, and availability of information and information systems
- Statement on the ownership of information created and/or possessed by the organization
- Designation of the CISO or other individual as the executive responsible for cybersecurity issues
- Delegation of authority granting the CISO the ability to create standards, procedures, and guidelines that implement the policy

In many organizations, the process to create a policy is laborious and requires senior management approval, often from the CEO. Keeping policy statements broadly worded provides the CISO with the flexibility to adapt and change specific security requirements with changes in the business and technology environments. For example, the five-page information security policy at the University of Notre Dame simply states:

> The Information Governance Committee will create handling standards for each Highly Sensitive data element. Data stewards may create standards for other data elements under their stewardship. These information handling standards will specify controls to manage risks to University information and related assets based on their classification. All individuals at the University are responsible for complying with these controls.

This type of policy allows an organization to maintain a high-level document and use it to guide the development of standards, procedures, and guidelines that remain in alignment with enterprise goals and objectives.

By way of contrast, the federal government's Centers for Medicare and Medicaid Services (CMS) has a 95-page information security policy. This mammoth document contains incredibly detailed requirements, such as:

> A record of all requests for monitoring must be maintained by the CMS CIO along with any other summary results or documentation produced during the period of monitoring. The record must also reflect the scope of the monitoring by documenting search terms and techniques. All information collected from monitoring must be controlled and protected with distribution limited to the individuals identified in the request for monitoring and other individuals specifically designated by the CMS Administrator or CMS CIO as having a specific need to know such information.

The CMS document even goes so far as to include a complex chart describing the many cybersecurity roles held by individuals throughout the agency. An excerpt from that chart appears in Figure 2.2.

This approach may meet the needs of CMS, but it is hard to imagine the long-term maintenance of that document. Lengthy security policies often quickly become outdated as necessary changes to individual requirements accumulate and become neglected because staff are weary of continually publishing new versions of the policy.

FIGURE 2.2   Excerpt from CMS roles and responsibilities chart

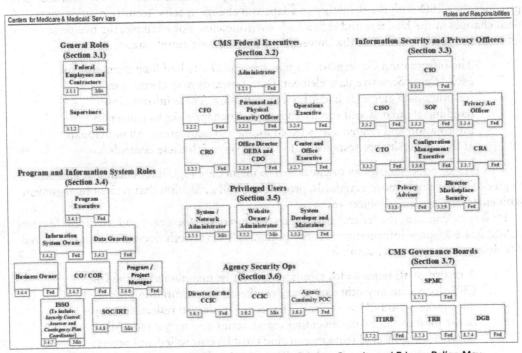

Source: Centers for Medicare and Medicaid Services Information Systems Security and Privacy Policy, May 21, 2019. (www.cms.gov/Research-Statistics-Data-and-Systems/CMS-Information-Technology/ InformationSecurity/Downloads/CMS-IS2P2.pdf)

Standards

Standards provide mandatory requirements describing how an organization will carry out its information security policies. These may include the specific configuration settings used for a common operating system, the controls that must be put in place for highly sensitive information, or any other security objective. Standards are typically approved at a lower organizational level than policies and, therefore, may change more regularly. Organizations may choose to develop their own standards, adopt standards created by external groups, or use a hybrid approach where they modify existing standards to meet their needs.

For example, the University of California (UC) at Berkeley maintains a detailed document titled the *Minimum Security Standards for Electronic Information*, available at https://security.berkeley.edu/minimum-security-standards-electronic-information. This document divides information into four different data protection levels (DPLs) and then describes what controls are required, optional, and not required for data at different levels, using a detailed matrix. An excerpt from this matrix appears in Figure 2.3.

FIGURE 2.3 Excerpt from UC Berkeley Minimum Security Standards for Electronic Information

MSSEI Controls	DPL 0 (TBD)	DPL 1 Individual	DPL 1 Privileged	DPL 1 Institutional	DPL 2 Individual	DPL 2 Privileged	DPL 2 Institutional	DPL 3 (TBD)	Guidelines
1.1 Removal of non-required covered data		o	√	√	√	√	√		see secure deletion guideline and UCOP disposition schedules database
1.2 Covered system inventory			√	√		√	√		1.2 guideline
1.3 Covered system registration			+	√		√	√		1.3 guideline
1.4 Annual registration renewal			√	√		√	√		1.4 guideline
2.1 Managed software inventory			+	√	o	√	√		2.1 guideline
3.1 Secure configurations	o		+	√	√	√	√		3.1 guideline
4.1 Continuous vulnerability assessment & remediation			+	√		√	√		4.1 guideline

Source: University of California at Berkeley Minimum Security Standards for Electronic Information

The standard then provides detailed descriptions for each of these requirements with definitions of the terms used in the requirements. For example, requirement 3.1 in Figure 2.3 simply reads "Secure configurations." Later in the document, UC Berkeley expands this to read "Resource Custodians must utilize well-managed security configurations for hardware, software, and operating systems based on industry standards." It goes on to define "well-managed" as including the following:

- Devices must have secure configurations in place prior to deployment.

- Any deviations from defined security configurations must be approved through a change management process and documented. A process must exist to annually review deviations from the defined security configurations for continued relevance.

- A process must exist to regularly check configurations of devices and alert the Resource Custodian of any changes.

This approach provides a document hierarchy that is easy to navigate for the reader and provides access to increasing levels of detail as needed. Notice also that many of the requirement lines in Figure 2.3 offer links to guidelines. Clicking those links leads to advice to organizations subject to this policy that begins with this text:

> UC Berkeley security policy mandates compliance with Minimum Security Standard for Electronic Information for devices handling covered data. The recommendations below are provided as optional guidance.

This is a perfect example of three elements of the information security policy framework working together. Policy sets out the broad objectives of the security program and requires compliance with standards, which includes details of required security controls. Guidelines, discussed later in this chapter, provide advice to organizations seeking to comply with the policy and standards.

In some cases, organizations may encounter industry-specific standards. These best practices, developed by industry groups, are custom-tailored to the needs of the industry. In some heavily regulated industries, compliance with these standards may be required by law or contractual agreement. In other fields, the standards are just helpful resources. Failure to follow industry best practices may be seen as negligence and can cause legal liability for the organization. Many of these industry standards are expressed in the "Adopting Standard Frameworks" section, later in this chapter.

Procedures

Procedures are detailed, step-by-step processes that individuals and organizations must follow in specific circumstances. Similar to checklists, procedures ensure a consistent process for achieving a security objective. Organizations may create procedures for building new systems, releasing code to production environments, responding to security incidents, and many other tasks. Compliance with procedures is mandatory.

For example, Visa publishes a document titled *What to Do if Compromised* (`https://usa.visa.com/dam/VCOM/download/merchants/cisp-what-to-do-if-compromised.pdf`) that lays out a mandatory process that merchants suspecting a credit card compromise must follow. Although the document doesn't contain the word *procedure* in the title, the introduction clearly states that the document "establishes procedures and timelines for reporting and responding to a suspected or confirmed Compromise Event." The document provides requirements covering the following areas of incident response:

- Notify Visa of the incident within three days.
- Provide Visa with an initial investigation report.
- Provide notice to other relevant parties.
- Provide exposed payment account data to Visa.
- Conduct PCI forensic investigation.
- Conduct independent investigation.
- Preserve evidence.

Each of these sections provides detailed information on how Visa expects merchants to handle incident response activities. For example, the forensic investigation section describes the use of Payment Card Industry Forensic Investigators (PFI) and reads as follows:

> Upon discovery of an account data compromise, or receipt of an independent forensic investigation notification, an entity must:

- Engage a PFI (or sign a contract) within five (5) business days.
- Provide Visa with the initial forensic (i.e. preliminary) report within ten (10) business days from when the PFI is engaged (or the contract is signed).
- Provide Visa with a final forensic report within ten (10) business days of the completion of the review.

There's not much room for interpretation in this type of language. Visa is laying out a clear and mandatory procedure describing what actions the merchant must take, the type of investigator they should hire, and the timeline for completing different milestones.

Organizations commonly include the following procedures in their policy frameworks:

- *Monitoring procedures* that describe how the organization will perform security monitoring activities, including the possible use of continuous monitoring technology
- *Evidence production procedures* that describe how the organization will respond to subpoenas, court orders, and other legitimate requests to produce digital evidence
- *Patching procedures* that describe the frequency and process of applying patches to applications and systems under the organization's care

Of course, cybersecurity teams may decide to include many other types of procedures in their frameworks, as dictated by the organization's operational needs.

Guidelines

Guidelines provide best practices and recommendations related to a given concept, technology, or task. Compliance with guidelines is not mandatory, and guidelines are offered in the spirit of providing helpful advice. That said, the "optionality" of guidelines may vary significantly depending on the organization's culture.

In April 2016, the chief information officer (CIO) of the state of Washington published a 25-page document providing guidelines on the use of electronic signatures by state agencies. The document is not designed to be obligatory but, rather, offers advice to agencies seeking to adopt electronic signature technology. The document begins with a purpose section that outlines three goals for guidelines:

1. Help agencies determine if, and to what extent, their agency will implement and rely on electronic records and electronic signatures.

2. Provide agencies with information they can use to establish policy or rule governing their use and acceptance of digital signatures.

3. Provide direction to agencies for sharing of their policies with the Office of the Chief Information Officer (OCIO) pursuant to state law.

The first two stated objectives line up completely with the function of guidelines. Phrases like "help agencies determine" and "provide agencies with information" are common in guideline documents. There is nothing mandatory about them, and in fact, the guidelines explicitly state that Washington state law "does not mandate that any state agency accept or require electronic signatures or records."

The third objective might seem a little strange to include in guidelines. Phrases like "provide direction" are more commonly found in policies and procedures. Browsing through the document, the text relating to this objective is only a single paragraph within a 25-page document:

> The Office of the Chief Information Officer maintains a page on the OCIO. wa.gov website listing links to individual agency electronic signature and record submission policies. As agencies publish their policies, the link and agency contact information should be emailed to the OCIO Policy Mailbox. The information will be added to the page within 5 working days. Agencies are responsible for notifying the OCIO if the information changes.

Reading this paragraph, the text does appear to clearly outline a mandatory procedure and would not be appropriate in a guideline document that fits within the strict definition of the term. However, it is likely that the committee drafting this document thought it would be much more convenient to the reader to include this explanatory text in the related guideline rather than drafting a separate procedure document for a fairly mundane and simple task.

 The full Washington state document, *Electronic Signature Guidelines*, is available for download from the Washington State CIO's website at https://ocio.wa.gov/sites/default/files/ Electronic_Signature_Guidelines_FINAL.pdf.

Exceptions and Compensating Controls

When adopting new security policies, standards, and procedures, organizations should also provide a mechanism for exceptions to those rules. Inevitably, unforeseen circumstances will arise that require a deviation from the requirements. The policy framework should lay out the specific requirements for receiving an exception and the individual or committee with the authority to approve exceptions.

The state of Washington uses an exception process that requires the requestor document the following information:

- Standard/requirement that requires an exception
- Reason for noncompliance with the requirement
- Business and/or technical justification for the exception
- Scope and duration of the exception
- Risks associated with the exception
- Description of any supplemental controls that mitigate the risks associated with the exception

- Plan for achieving compliance
- Identification of any unmitigated risks

Many exception processes require the use of *compensating controls* to mitigate the risk associated with exceptions to security standards. The Payment Card Industry Data Security Standard (PCI DSS) includes one of the most formal compensating control processes in use today. It sets out three criteria that must be met for a compensating control to be satisfactory:

1. The control must meet the intent and rigor of the original requirement.
2. The control must provide a similar level of defense as the original requirement such that the compensating control sufficiently offsets the risk that the original PCI DSS requirement was designed to defend against.
3. The control must be "above and beyond" other PCI DSS requirements.

For example, an organization might find that it needs to run an outdated version of an operating system on a specific machine because software necessary to run the business will only function on that operating system version. Most security policies would prohibit using the outdated operating system because it might be susceptible to security vulnerabilities. The organization could choose to run this system on an isolated network with either very little or no access to other systems as a compensating control.

The general idea is that a compensating control finds alternative means to achieve an objective when the organization cannot meet the original control requirement. Although PCI DSS offers a very formal process for compensating controls, the use of compensating controls is a common strategy in many different organizations, even those not subject to PCI DSS. Compensating controls balance the fact that it simply isn't possible to implement every required security control in every circumstance with the desire to manage risk to the greatest feasible degree.

In many cases, organizations adopt compensating controls to address a temporary exception to a security requirement. In those cases, the organization should also develop remediation plans designed to bring the organization back into compliance with the letter and intent of the original control.

Developing Policies

When developing new policies, cybersecurity managers should align their work with any other policy development mechanisms that may exist within their organization. The more that a leader is able to align cybersecurity policy efforts with existing processes, the easier it will be to gain traction for those initiatives. In any event, cybersecurity managers should follow a few key principles when working on policy development initiatives:

Obtain input from all relevant stakeholders. Think carefully about all of the leaders and teams that might be affected by the policy and work to understand their perspective while crafting the policy. This doesn't mean that everyone in the organization must agree with a proposed policy but that everyone should feel that their input was solicited and heard during the process.

Follow the chain of command.   Knowledge of the organizational structure is essential to the success of a policy initiative. Cybersecurity managers must be aware of both the formal governance lines of authority as well as the informal mechanisms of the organization for getting things done.

Accommodate the organizational culture.   There's a good reason that there isn't a one-size-fits-all security policy that every organization can adopt. That's because every organization is different. Make sure that the policies you create fit into the organizational culture and match the "tone at the top" from other leaders.

Meet internal and external requirements.   Cybersecurity programs are heavily regulated, both by internal governance processes and external laws and regulations. In many cases, these requirements may dictate some of the contents of security policies. At the very least, security policies should not contradict these requirements.

After a policy is drafted, it should move through the policy approval mechanisms used by the organization. After receiving final sign-off, the cybersecurity manager may then communicate the policy to affected individuals and teams and begin the process of implementing the new policy. Depending on the nature of the change, this may involve using a phased approach that allows the organization to gradually adapt to the new requirements. After approving policies, organizations should place those policies into a maintenance mode where they are reviewed on an annual basis to ensure that they continue to meet the organization's security objectives.

Complying with Laws and Regulations

Legislators and regulators around the world take an interest in cybersecurity due to the potential adverse impact incidents can have on individuals, government, and society. Whereas the European Union (EU) has a broad-ranging data protection regulation, cybersecurity analysts in the United States are forced to deal with a patchwork of security regulations covering different industries and information categories.

Here are some of the major information security regulations that organizations are facing:

- The *Health Insurance Portability and Accountability Act (HIPAA)* includes security and privacy rules that affect health-care providers, health insurers, and health information clearinghouses in the United States.

- The *Payment Card Industry Data Security Standard (PCI DSS)* provides detailed rules about the storage, processing, and transmission of credit and debit card information. PCI DSS is not a law but rather a contractual obligation that applies to credit card merchants and service providers worldwide.

- The *Gramm–Leach–Bliley Act (GLBA)* covers the handling of personally identifiable information by U.S. financial institutions, broadly defined to include many groups that you wouldn't normally think of as financial institutions, such as colleges and universities that administer student loans, real estate appraisers, and debt collectors. GLBA requires that those institutions have a formal security program and designate an individual as having overall responsibility for that program.

- The *Sarbanes–Oxley (SOX) Act* applies to the financial records of U.S. publicly traded companies and requires that those companies have a strong degree of assurance for the IT systems that store and process those records.
- The *General Data Protection Regulation (GDPR)* implements security and privacy requirements for the personal information of European Union residents worldwide.
- The *Family Educational Rights and Privacy Act (FERPA)* requires that U.S. educational institutions implement security and privacy controls for student educational records.
- Various *data breach notification laws* describe the requirements that individual states place on organizations that suffer data breaches regarding notification of individuals affected by the breach.

Remember that this is only a brief listing of security regulations. Many other laws and obligations exist that apply to specific jurisdictions, industries, and data types. You should always consult your organization's legal counsel and subject matter experts when designing a compliance strategy for your organization. You'll need to understand the various national, territory, and state laws that apply to your operations, and the advice of a well-versed attorney is crucial when interpreting and applying cybersecurity regulations to your specific business and technical environment.

Many regulatory requirements include mandates that organizations periodically provide reports and/or assessments of their compliance. Cybersecurity managers should work with other business leaders and compliance professionals to develop processes that ensure these obligations are fulfilled in a timely manner.

Adopting Standard Frameworks

Developing a new cybersecurity program is a formidable undertaking. Organizations will have a wide variety of control objectives and tools at their disposal to meet those objectives. Teams facing the task of developing a new security program or evaluating an existing program may find it challenging to cover a large amount of ground without a roadmap. Fortunately, several standard security frameworks are available to assist with this task and provide a standardized approach to developing cybersecurity programs.

COBIT

ISACA promotes the Control Objectives for Information Technology (COBIT) as an IT management and governance framework. In the most recent version of COBIT from 2019, ISACA includes two sets of foundational principles. These consist of six principles for a governance system within an organization and three for a governance framework covering many organizations. The six principles for a governance system are as follows:

- "Each enterprise needs a governance system to satisfy stakeholder needs and to generate value from the use of information and technology.

- A governance system for enterprise information and technology is built from a number of components that can be of different types and work together in a holistic way.

- A governance system should be dynamic.

- A governance system should clearly distinguish between governance and management activities and structures.

- A governance system should be tailored to the enterprise's needs.

- A governance system should cover the enterprise end-to-end, focusing not only on the IT function but on all technology and information processing the enterprise puts in place to achieve its goals."

These six concepts define crucial characteristics of IT governance. From these, ISACA defines three principles for IT governance frameworks that describe how frameworks should be designed:

- "A governance framework should be based upon a conceptual model, identifying the key components and relationships among components, to maximize consistency and allow automation.

- A governance framework should be open and flexible. It should allow the addition of new content and the ability to address new issue in the most flexible way, while maintaining integrity and consistency.

- A governance framework should align to relevant major related standards, frameworks, and regulations."

ISACA designed COBIT to follow these principles and focuses on the ability of an organization to achieve objectives that fall within five domains:

- *Evaluate, Direct, and Monitor (EDM)* objectives provide for effective IT governance and the selection and monitoring of strategic goals.

- *Align, Plan, and Organize (APO)* objectives describe how the IT function should be organized and how it should structure its work.

- *Build, Acquire, and Implement (BAI)* objectives describe how the IT organization should create and acquire new information systems and integrate them into the business.

- *Deliver, Service, and Support (DSS)* objectives describe how the organization should manage the operational tasks of information technology.

- *Monitor, Evaluate, and Assess (MEA)* objectives describe how the organization should measure its effectiveness against performance targets, control objectives, and any external requirements it faces.

Each of these domains is broken into very specific objectives that are described in the COBIT 2019 Core Model. The organization meets these objectives by creating a governance system that consists of seven major components:

- Processes
- Services, infrastructure, and applications

- People, skills, and competencies
- Culture, ethics, and behavior
- Information
- Principles, policies, and procedures
- Organizational structures

NIST Cybersecurity Framework

The National Institute for Standards and Technology (NIST) is responsible for developing cybersecurity standards across the U.S. federal government. The guidance and standard documents they produce in this process often have wide applicability across the private sector and are commonly referred to by nongovernmental security analysts due to the fact that they are available in the public domain and are typically of very high quality.

In 2018, NIST released version 1.1 of its Cybersecurity Framework (CSF) designed to assist organizations attempting to meet one or more of the following five objectives:

- Describe their current cybersecurity posture.
- Describe their target state for cybersecurity.
- Identify and prioritize opportunities for improvement within the context of a continuous and repeatable process.
- Assess progress toward the target state.
- Communicate among internal and external stakeholders about cybersecurity risk.

The NIST framework includes three components:

- The Framework Core, shown in Figure 2.4, is a set of five security functions that apply across all industries and sectors: identify, protect, detect, respond, and recover. The framework then divides these functions into categories, subcategories, and informative references. Figure 2.5 shows a small excerpt of this matrix in completed form, looking specifically at the Identify (ID) function and the Asset Management category. If you would like to view a fully completed matrix, see the NIST document *Framework for Improving Critical Infrastructure Cybersecurity*.

- The Framework Implementation assesses how an organization is positioned to meet cybersecurity objectives. Table 2.1 shows the framework implementation tiers and their criteria. This approach is an example of a *maturity model* that describes the current and desired positioning of an organization along a continuum of progress. In the case of the NIST maturity model, organizations are assigned to one of four maturity model tiers.

- Framework profiles describe how a specific organization might approach the security functions covered by the Framework Core. An organization might use a framework profile to describe its current state and then a separate profile to describe its desired future state.

FIGURE 2.4   NIST Cybersecurity Framework Core Structure

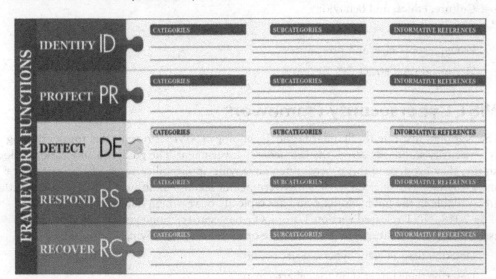

Source: Framework for Improving Critical Infrastructure Cybersecurity, National Institute of Standards and Technology (https://nvlpubs.nist.gov/nistpubs/CSWP/NIST.CSWP.04162018.pdf)

FIGURE 2.5   Asset Management Cybersecurity Framework

Function	Category	Subcategory	Informative References
IDENTIFY (ID)	Asset Management (ID.AM): The data, personnel, devices, systems, and facilities that enable the organization to achieve business purposes are identified and managed consistent with their relative importance to business objectives and the organization's risk strategy.	ID.AM-1: Physical devices and systems within the organization are inventoried	• CCS CSC 1 • COBIT 5 BAI09.01, BAI09.02 • ISA 62443-2-1:2009 4.2.3.4 • ISA 62443-3-3:2013 SR 7.8 • ISO/IEC 27001:2013 A.8.1.1, A.8.1.2 • NIST SP 800-53 Rev. 4 CM-8
		ID.AM-2: Software platforms and applications within the organization are inventoried	• CCS CSC 2 • COBIT 5 BAI09.01, BAI09.02, BAI09.05 • ISA 62443-2-1:2009 4.2.3.4 • ISA 62443-3-3:2013 SR 7.8 • ISO/IEC 27001:2013 A.8.1.1, A.8.1.2 • NIST SP 800-53 Rev. 4 CM-8
		ID.AM-3: Organizational communication and data flows are mapped	• CCS CSC 1 • COBIT 5 DSS05.02 • ISA 62443-2-1:2009 4.2.3.4 • ISO/IEC 27001:2013 A.13.2.1 • NIST SP 800-53 Rev. 4 AC-4, CA-3, CA-9, PL-8
		ID.AM-4: External information systems are catalogued	• COBIT 5 APO02.02 • ISO/IEC 27001:2013 A.11.2.6 • NIST SP 800-53 Rev. 4 AC-20, SA-9
		ID.AM-5: Resources (e.g., hardware, devices, data, time, and software) are prioritized based on their classification, criticality, and business value	• COBIT 5 APO03.03, APO03.04, BAI09.02 • ISA 62443-2-1:2009 4.2.3.6 • ISO/IEC 27001:2013 A.8.2.1 • NIST SP 800-53 Rev. 4 CP-2, RA-2, SA-14
		ID.AM-6: Cybersecurity roles and responsibilities for the entire workforce and third-party stakeholders (e.g., suppliers, customers, partners) are established	• COBIT 5 APO01.02, DSS06.03 • ISA 62443-2-1:2009 4.3.2.3.3 • ISO/IEC 27001:2013 A.6.1.1

Source: Framework for Improving Critical Infrastructure Cybersecurity, National Institute of Standards and Technology (https://nvlpubs.nist.gov/nistpubs/CSWP/NIST.CSWP.04162018.pdf)

TABLE 2.1 NIST Cybersecurity Framework implementation tiers

Tier	Risk management process	Integrated risk management program	External participation
Tier 1: Partial	Organizational cybersecurity risk management practices are not formalized, and risk is managed in an ad hoc and sometimes reactive manner.	There is limited awareness of cybersecurity risk at the organizational level. The organization implements cybersecurity risk management on an irregular, case-by-case basis due to varied experience or information gained from outside sources.	The organization does not understand its role in the larger ecosystem with respect to either its dependencies or its dependents.
Tier 2: Risk Informed	Risk management practices are approved by management but may not be established as organizationwide policy.	There is an awareness of cybersecurity risk at the organizational level, but an organizationwide approach to managing cybersecurity risk has not been established.	Generally, the organization understands its role in the larger ecosystem with respect to either its own dependencies or its dependents, but not both.
Tier 3: Repeatable	The organization's risk management practices are formally approved and expressed as policy.	There is an organizationwide approach to manage cybersecurity risk.	The organization understands its role, dependencies and its dependents in the larger ecosystem and may contribute to the community's broader understanding of risks.
Tier 4: Adaptive	The organization adapts its cybersecurity practices based on previous and current cybersecurity activities, including lessons learned and predictive indicators.	There is an organizationwide approach to managing cybersecurity risk that uses risk-informed policies, processes, and procedures to address potential cybersecurity events.	The organization understands its role, dependencies, and dependents in the larger ecosystem and contributes to the community's broader understanding of risks.

Source: Framework for Improving Critical Infrastructure Cybersecurity, National Institute of Standards and Technology

The NIST Cybersecurity Framework provides organizations with a sound approach to developing and evaluating the state of their cybersecurity programs.

NIST Risk Management Framework

In addition to the CSF, NIST publishes a Risk Management Framework (RMF). The RMF is a mandatory standard for federal agencies that provides a formalized process that federal agencies must follow to select, implement, and assess risk-based security and privacy controls. Figure 2.6 provides an overview of the NIST RMF process. More details may be found in NIST SP 800-37, Risk Management Framework for Information Systems and Organizations (https://nvlpubs.nist.gov/nistpubs/SpecialPublications/NIST.SP.800-37r2.pdf).

FIGURE 2.6   NIST Risk Management Framework

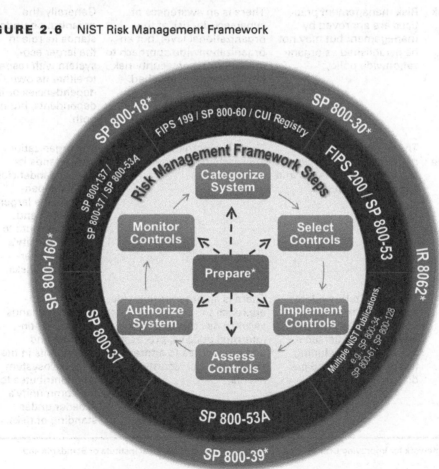

Source: FISMA Implementation Project Risk Management Framework (RMF) Overview, National Institute of Standards and Technology (https://csrc.nist.gov/projects/risk-management/rmf-overview)

Exam Note

NIST publishes both the CSF and RMF, and it can be a little confusing to keep them straight. The RMF is a formal process for implementing security controls and authorizing system use, whereas the CSF provides a broad structure for cybersecurity controls.

ISO Standards

The *International Organization for Standardization (ISO)* publishes a series of standards that offer best practices for cybersecurity and privacy. As you prepare for the CISM exam, you should be familiar with five specific ISO standards: ISO 27001, ISO 27002, ISO 27004, ISO 27701, and ISO 31000.

ISO 27001

ISO 27001 is a standard titled "Information technology—Security techniques—Information security management systems—Requirements." This standard includes control objectives covering 14 categories:

- Information security policies
- Organization of information security
- Human resource security
- Asset management
- Access control
- Cryptography
- Physical and environmental security
- Operations security
- Communications security
- System acquisition, development, and maintenance
- Supplier relationships
- Information security incident management
- Information security aspects of business continuity management
- Compliance with internal requirements, such as policies, and with external requirements, such as laws

The ISO 27001 standard was once the most commonly used information security standard, but it is declining in popularity outside of highly regulated industries that require ISO compliance. Organizations in those industries may choose to formally adopt ISO 27001 and pursue *certification* programs, where an external assessor validates their compliance with the standard and certifies them as operating in accordance with ISO 27001.

ISO 27002

ISO 27002 goes beyond control objectives and describes the actual controls that an organization may implement to meet cybersecurity objectives. ISO designed this supplementary document for organizations that wish to:

- Select information security controls
- Implement information security controls
- Develop information security management guidelines

Due to its advisory nature, ISO 27002 may be considered more of a guideline than a standard.

ISO 27004

ISO 27004 helps organizations implement a consistent process for the monitoring, measurement, analysis, and evaluation of its information security management function.

ISO 27701

Whereas ISO 27001 and ISO 27002 focus on cybersecurity controls, *ISO 27701* contains standard guidance for managing privacy controls. ISO views this document as an extension to their ISO 27001 and ISO 27002 security standards.

Exam Note

Be careful with the numbering of the ISO standards, particularly ISO 27001 and ISO 27701. They look nearly identical, but it is important to remember that ISO 27001 covers cybersecurity and ISO 27701 covers privacy.

ISO 31000

ISO 31000 provides guidelines for risk management programs. This document is not specific to cybersecurity or privacy but covers risk management in a general way so that it may be applied to any type of risk.

Benchmarks and Secure Configuration Guides

The NIST and ISO frameworks are high-level descriptions of cybersecurity and risk management best practices. They don't offer practical guidance on actually implementing security controls. However, government agencies, vendors, and industry groups publish a variety of benchmarks and secure configuration guides that help organizations understand how they can securely operate commonly used platforms, including operating systems, web servers, application servers, and network infrastructure devices. These often serve as the baselines for an organization's own security standards. They also play an important role in risk assessments, serving as the standard by which an organization may be measured.

These benchmarks and configuration guides examine the nitty-gritty details of securely operating commonly used systems. Figure 2.7 shows an excerpt from a security configuration benchmark for Windows Server 2019.

FIGURE 2.7   Windows Server 2019 security benchmark excerpt

> *2.3.10.10 (L1) Ensure 'Network access: Restrict anonymous access to Named Pipes and Shares' is set to 'Enabled' (Scored)*
>
> **Profile Applicability:**
>
> - Level 1 - Domain Controller
> - Level 1 - Member Server
>
> **Description:**
>
> When enabled, this policy setting restricts anonymous access to only those shares and pipes that are named in the `Network access: Named pipes that can be accessed anonymously` and `Network access: Shares that can be accessed anonymously` settings. This policy setting controls null session access to shares on your computers by adding `RestrictNullSessAccess` with the value `1` in the
>
> `HKEY_LOCAL_MACHINE\SYSTEM\CurrentControlSet\Services\LanManServer\Parameters`
>
> registry key. This registry value toggles null session shares on or off to control whether the server service restricts unauthenticated clients' access to named resources.
>
> The recommended state for this setting is: `Enabled`.
>
> **Rationale:**
>
> Null sessions are a weakness that can be exploited through shares (including the default shares) on computers in your environment.
>
> **Audit:**
>
> Navigate to the UI Path articulated in the Remediation section and confirm it is set as prescribed. This group policy setting is backed by the following registry location:
>
> ```
> HKEY_LOCAL_MACHINE\SYSTEM\CurrentControlSet\Services\LanManServer\Parameters:
> RestrictNullSessAccess
> ```
>
> **Remediation:**
>
> To establish the recommended configuration via GP, set the following UI path to `Enabled`:
>
> ```
> Computer Configuration\Policies\Windows Settings\Security Settings\Local
> Policies\Security Options\Network access: Restrict anonymous access to Named
> Pipes and Shares
> ```

Source: Center for Internet Security (CIS) (`cisecurity.org/cis-benchmarks`)

The excerpt shown in Figure 2.7 comes from the *Center for Internet Security (CIS),* an industry organization that publishes hundreds of benchmarks for commonly used platforms.

To give you a sense of the level of detail involved, Figure 2.7 shows a portion of one page from a document that contains 993 pages detailing appropriate security settings for Windows Server 2019.

Security Control Verification and Quality Control

Quality control procedures verify that an organization has sufficient security controls in place and that those security controls are functioning properly. Every security program should include procedures for conducting regular internal tests of security controls and supplement those informal tests with formal evaluations of the organization's security program. Those evaluations may come in two different forms: audits and assessments.

Audits are formal reviews of an organization's security program or specific compliance issues conducted on behalf of a third party. Audits require rigorous, formal testing of controls and result in a formal statement from the auditor regarding the entity's compliance. Audits may be conducted by internal audit groups at the request of management or by external audit firms, typically at the request of an organization's governing body or a regulator.

Organizations providing services to other organizations often hire an independent assessor to perform a *service organization controls (SOC)* audit under the American Institute for Certified Public Accountants (AICPA) Statement on Standards for Attestation Engagements 18 (SSAE 18). There are three different categories of SOC assessment:

- *SOC 1 engagements* assess the organization's controls that might impact the accuracy of financial reporting.

- *SOC 2 engagements* assess the organization's controls that affect the security (confidentiality, integrity, and availability) and privacy of information stored in a system. SOC 2 audit results are confidential and are normally only shared outside the organization under an NDA.

- *SOC 3 engagements* also assess the organization's controls that affect the security (confidentiality, integrity, and availability) and privacy of information stored in a system. However, SOC 3 audit results are intended for public disclosure.

In addition to the three categories of SOC assessment, there are two different types of SOC report. Both reports begin by providing a description by management of the controls put in place. They differ in the scope of the opinion provided by the auditor:

- *Type 1 reports* provide the auditor's opinion on the description provided by management and the suitability of the design of the controls as of a specific date.

- *Type 2 reports* go further and also provide the auditor's opinion on the operating effectiveness of the controls—that is, the auditor actually confirms that the controls are functioning properly over a period of time.

Exam Note

The differences between SOC categories and types are confusing, and you should review them before taking the CISM exam.

Assessments are less formal reviews of security controls that are typically requested by the security organization itself in an effort to engage in process improvement. During an assessment, the assessor typically gathers information by interviewing employees and taking them at their word, rather than performing the rigorous independent testing associated with an audit.

Summary

Information security governance programs ensure that the function achieves its objectives in an efficient and effective manner. Information security governance efforts must align with corporate governance efforts to ensure that the information security program remains aligned with corporate strategy.

Policies form the basis of every strong information security program. A solid policy framework consists of policies, standards, procedures, and guidelines that work together to describe the security control environment of an organization. In addition to complying with internally developed policies, organizations must often comply with externally imposed compliance obligations. Security frameworks, such as COBIT, the NIST Cybersecurity Framework, and ISO 27001, provide a common structure for security programs based on accepted industry best practices. Organizations should implement and test security controls to achieve security control objectives that are developed based on the business and technical environment of the organization.

Exam Essentials

Governance programs guide and direct security efforts. Information security governance efforts should integrate with other corporate governance programs to support both the business's goals and its security strategy. Organizations should draw on existing governance frameworks, such as COBIT and the ISO standards, to avoid redundant effort and to align with industry best practices.

Policy frameworks consist of policies, standards, procedures, and guidelines. Policies are high-level statements of management intent for the information security program. Standards describe the detailed implementation requirements for policies. Procedures offer step-by-step instructions for carrying out security activities. Compliance with policies, standards, and procedures is mandatory. Guidelines offer optional advice that complements other elements of the policy framework.

Organizations often adopt a set of security policies covering different areas of their security programs.   Common policies used in security programs include an information security policy, an acceptable use policy, a data ownership policy, a data retention policy, an account management policy, and a password policy. The specific policies adopted by any organization will depend on that organization's culture and business needs.

Policy documents should include exception processes.   Exception processes should outline the information required to receive an exception to security policy and the approval authority for each exception. The process should also describe the requirements for compensating controls that mitigate risks associated with approved security policy exceptions.

Organizations face a variety of security compliance requirements.   Merchants and credit card service providers must comply with the Payment Card Industry Data Security Standard (PCI DSS). Organizations handling the personal information of European Union residents must comply with the EU General Data Protection Regulation (GDPR). All organizations should be familiar with the national, territory, and state laws that affect their operations.

Standards frameworks provide an outline for structuring and evaluating cybersecurity programs.   Organizations may choose to base their security programs on a framework, such as the NIST Cybersecurity Framework (CSF) or International Organization for Standardization (ISO) standards. U.S. federal government agencies and contractors should also be familiar with the NIST Risk Management Framework (RMF). These frameworks sometimes include maturity models that allow an organization to assess its progress. Some frameworks also offer certification programs that provide independent assessments of an organization's progress toward adopting a framework.

Audits and assessments monitor compliance with requirements.   Audits are externally commissioned, formal reviews of the capability of an organization to achieve its control objectives. Assessments are less rigorous reviews of security issues, often performed or commissioned by IT staff. Organizations providing services to other entities may wish to conduct a service organization controls (SOC) audit under SSAE 18.

Review Questions

1. Joe is authoring a document that explains to system administrators one way in which they might comply with the organization's requirement to encrypt all laptops. What type of document is Joe writing?

   A. Policy

   B. Guideline

   C. Procedure

   D. Standard

2. Victor is designing an information security governance program for his organization. Which one of the following statements about governance programs is not correct?

   A. Governance programs should clearly distinguish between governance and management activities.

   B. Governance programs should be created once and developed in a manner that does not require future changes.

   C. Security governance programs should be aligned with corporate governance programs.

   D. Governance programs should cover the enterprise end-to-end.

3. What law creates privacy obligations for those who handle the personal information of European Union residents?

   A. HIPAA

   B. FERPA

   C. GDPR

   D. PCI DSS

4. Which one of the following is *not* one of the five core security functions defined by the NIST Cybersecurity Framework?

   A. Identify

   B. Contain

   C. Respond

   D. Recover

5. What ISO standard provides guidance on privacy controls?

   A. 27002

   B. 27001

   C. 27701

   D. 31000

6. Which one of the following documents must normally be approved by the CEO or a similarly high-level executive?

   A. Standard

   B. Procedure

   C. Guideline

   D. Policy

7. Greg would like to create an umbrella agreement that provides the security terms and conditions for all future work that his organization does with a vendor. What type of agreement should Greg use?

   A. BPA

   B. MOU

   C. MSA

   D. SLA

8. What organization is known for creating independent security benchmarks covering hardware and software platforms from many different vendors?

   A. Microsoft

   B. Center for Internet Security

   C. Cloud Security Alliance

   D. Cisco

9. In a publicly traded corporation, who is directly responsible for hiring and firing the chief executive officer?

   A. Senior executive team

   B. Shareholders

   C. Board of directors

   D. Chief financial officer

10. Which one of the following would *not* normally be found in an organization's information security policy?

    A. Statement of the importance of cybersecurity

    B. Requirement to use AES-256 encryption

    C. Delegation of authority

    D. Designation of responsible executive

11. Darren is working with an independent auditor to produce an audit report that he will share with his customers under NDA to demonstrate that he has appropriate security controls in place. The auditor will not be assessing the effectiveness of those controls. What type of audit report should Darren expect?

    A. SOC 2 Type 1

    B. SOC 2 Type 2

C. SOC 3 Type 1

D. SOC 3 Type 2

12. Danielle is developing a business case to support a proposed investment in her organization's vulnerability management program. Which of the following components would she *not* normally include in the business case?

A. Cost analysis

B. Implementation plan

C. Rollback plan

D. Strategic context

13. What compliance obligation applies to merchants and service providers who work with credit card information?

A. FERPA

B. SOX

C. HIPAA

D. PCI DSS

14. Gwen is developing a new security policy for her organization. Which one of the following statements does not reflect best practices for policy development?

A. All stakeholders should agree with the proposed policy.

B. The policy should follow normal corporate policy approval processes.

C. Policies should match the "tone at the top" from senior business leaders.

D. Cybersecurity managers are typically responsible for communicating and implementing approved security policies.

15. Kevin is developing the business case for a new information security incident response program. Which one of the following statements is true about the costs associated with this initiative?

A. The business case does not need to address costs, since this is done within the budgeting process.

B. The business case should only include the one-time costs that are associated with implementing the new initiative.

C. The business case should only include the new recurring costs that are created by the initiative.

D. The business case should include both one-time and recurring costs associated with the initiative.

16. Which individual in an organization bears ultimate accountability to the board of directors for achieving the organization's strategic plan?

A. CISO

B. CIO

    C. CFO

    D. CEO

17. The board of directors of Kate's company recently hired an independent firm to review the state of the organization's security controls and certify those results to the board. What term best describes this engagement?

    A. Assessment

    B. Control review

    C. Gap analysis

    D. Audit

18. Which one of the following is not an objective domain in the COBIT framework?

    A. Secure, Protect, and Defend (SPD)

    B. Evaluate, Direct, and Monitor (EDM)

    C. Align, Plan, and Organize (APO)

    D. Deliver, Service, and Support (DSS)

19. Which one of the following is not a common use of the NIST Cybersecurity Framework?

    A. Describe the current cybersecurity posture of an organization.

    B. Describe the target future cybersecurity posture of an organization.

    C. Communicate with stakeholders about cybersecurity risk.

    D. Create specific technology requirements for an organization.

20. Which one of the following items is *not* normally included in a request for an exception to security policy?

    A. Description of a compensating control

    B. Description of the risks associated with the exception

    C. Proposed revision to the security policy

    D. Business justification for the exception

Chapter

3

Information Risk Management

THE CERTIFIED INFORMATION SECURITY MANAGER (CISM) DOMAINS AND SUBTOPICS COVERED IN THIS CHAPTER INCLUDE:

✓ **Domain 2: Information Risk Management**

- **A. Information Security Risk Assessment**
  - **2A3. Risk Assessment and Analysis**
- **B. Information Security Risk Response**
  - **2B1. Risk Treatment/Risk Response Options**
  - **2B2. Risk and Control Ownership**
  - **2B3. Risk Monitoring and Reporting**

✓ **Domain 3: Information Security Program**

- **A. Information Security Program Development**
  - **3A2. Information Asset Identification and Classification**

THE CERTIFIED INFORMATION SECURITY MANAGER (CISM) SUPPORTING TASKS COVERED IN THIS CHAPTER INCLUDE:

✓ **20. Establish and/or maintain a process for information asset identification and classification.**

✓ **22. Participate in and/or oversee the risk identification, risk assessment, and risk treatment process.**

✓ **24. Identify, recommend, or implement appropriate risk treatment and response options to manage risk to acceptable levels based on organizational risk appetite.**

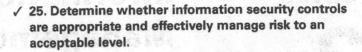

✓ **25. Determine whether information security controls are appropriate and effectively manage risk to an acceptable level.**

✓ **26. Facilitate the integration of information risk management into business and IT processes.**

✓ **27. Monitor for internal and external factors that may require reassessment of risk.**

✓ **28. Report on information security risk, including noncompliance and other changes in information risk, to key stakeholders to facilitate the risk management decision-making process.**

Organizations face an almost dizzying array of cybersecurity risks, ranging from the reputational and financial damage associated with a breach of personal information to the operational issues caused by a natural disaster. The discipline of risk management seeks to bring order to the process of identifying and addressing these risks. In this chapter, we examine the risk management process and discuss a category of risk that is closely related to cybersecurity: the privacy and protection of personal information.

Analyzing Risk

We operate in a world full of risks. If you left your home and drove to your office this morning, you encountered a large number of risks. You could have been involved in an automobile accident, encountered a train delay, or been struck by a bicycle on the sidewalk. We're aware of these risks at the back of our minds, but we don't let them paralyze us. Instead, we take simple precautions to help manage the risks that we think have the greatest potential to disrupt our lives.

In an *enterprise risk management (ERM)* program, organizations take a formal approach to risk analysis that begins with identifying risks, continues with determining the severity of each risk, and then results in adopting one or more *risk management* strategies to address each risk.

Before we move too deeply into the risk assessment process, let's define a few important terms that we'll use during our discussion:

- *Threats* are any possible events that might have an adverse impact on the confidentiality, integrity, and/or availability of our information or information systems.

- *Vulnerabilities* are weaknesses in our systems or controls that could be exploited by a threat.

- *Risks* occur at the intersection of a vulnerability and a threat that might exploit that vulnerability. A threat without a corresponding vulnerability does not pose a risk, nor does a vulnerability without a corresponding threat.

Figure 3.1 illustrates this relationship between threats, vulnerabilities, and risks.

FIGURE 3.1   Risk exists at the intersection of a threat and a corresponding vulnerability.

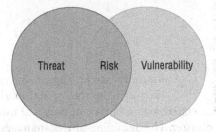

Consider the example from earlier of walking down the sidewalk on your way to work. The fact that you are on the sidewalk without any protection is a vulnerability. A bicycle speeding down that sidewalk is a threat. The result of this combination of factors is that you are at risk of being hit by the bicycle on the sidewalk. If you remove the vulnerability by parking in a garage beneath your building, you are no longer at risk for that particular threat. Similarly, if the city erects barriers that prevent bicycles from entering the sidewalk, you are also no longer at risk. Of course, your new situation may introduce *new* threats, such as the parking garage collapsing!

Let's consider another example drawn from the cybersecurity domain. Organizations regularly conduct vulnerability scans designed to identify potential vulnerabilities in their environment. One of these scans might identify a server that exposes TCP port 22 to the world, allowing brute-force SSH attempts by an attacker. Exposing port 22 presents a vulnerability to a brute-force attack. An attacker with a brute-force scanning tool presents a threat. The combination of the port exposure and the existence of attackers presents a risk.

In this case, you don't have any way to eliminate attackers, so you can't really address the threat, but you do have control over the services running on your systems. If you shut down the SSH service and close port 22, you eliminate the vulnerability and, therefore, also eliminate the risk.

Of course, we can't always completely eliminate a risk because it isn't always feasible to shut down services. We might decide instead to take actions that reduce the risk. We'll talk more about those options when we get to risk management strategies later in this chapter.

Risk Identification

The *risk identification process* requires identifying the threats and vulnerabilities that exist in your operating environment. These risks may come from a wide variety of sources ranging from malicious hackers to hurricanes. Consider some of the different categories of risk facing organizations:

- *External risks* are those risks that originate from a source outside the organization. This is an extremely broad category of risk, including cybersecurity adversaries, malicious code, and natural disasters, among many other types of risk.

- *Internal risks* are those risks that originate from within the organization. They include malicious insiders, mistakes made by authorized users, equipment failures, and similar risks.

- *Multiparty risks* are those that impact more than one organization. For example, a power outage to a city block is a multiparty risk because it affects all of the buildings on that block. Similarly, the compromise of an SaaS provider's database is a multiparty risk because it compromises the information of many different customers of the SaaS provider.

- *Legacy systems* pose a unique type of risk to organizations. These outdated systems often do not receive security updates, and cybersecurity professionals must take extraordinary measures to protect them against unpatchable vulnerabilities.

- *Intellectual property (IP) theft* risks occur when a company possesses trade secrets or other proprietary information that, if disclosed, could compromise the organization's business advantage.

- *Software compliance/licensing risks* occur when an organization licenses software from a vendor and intentionally or accidentally runs afoul of usage limitations that expose the customer to financial and legal risk.

This is not an exhaustive list of all the possible types of risk facing your organization. It's intended to help illustrate the different types of risk that exist as a starting point for your own risk analysis based on the specific situations facing your organization.

Risk Calculation

Not all risks are equal. Returning to the example of a pedestrian on the street, the risk of being hit by a bicycle is far more worrisome than the risk of being struck down by a meteor. That makes intuitive sense, but let's explore the underlying thought process that leads to that conclusion. It's a process called *risk calculation*.

When we evaluate any risk, we do so by using two different factors:

- The *likelihood of occurrence*, or probability, that the risk will occur. We might express this as the percentage of chance that a threat will exploit a vulnerability over a specified period of time, such as within the next year.

- The magnitude of the *impact* that the risk will have on the organization if it does occur. We might express this as the financial cost that we will incur as the result of a risk, although there are other possible measures.

Using these two factors, we can assign each risk a conceptual score by combining the probability and the magnitude. This leads many risk analysts to express the severity of a risk using this formula:

Risk Severity = Likelihood × Impact

It's important to point out that this equation does not always have to be interpreted literally. Although you may wind up multiplying these values together in some risk assessment processes, it's best to think of this conceptually as combining the likelihood and impact to determine the severity of a risk.

When we assess the risks of being struck by a bicycle or a meteor on the street, we can use these factors to evaluate the risk severity. There might be a high probability that we will be struck by a bicycle. That type of accident might have a moderate magnitude, leaving us willing to consider taking steps to reduce our risk. Being struck by a meteor would clearly have a catastrophic magnitude of impact, but the probability of such an incident is incredibly unlikely, leading us to acknowledge the risk and move on without changing our behavior.

The laws and regulations facing an industry may play a significant role in determining the impact of a risk. For example, an organization subject to the European Union's General Data Protection Regulation (GDPR) faces significant fines if they have a data breach affecting the personal information of EU residents. The size of these fines would factor significantly into the impact assessment of the risk of a privacy breach. Organizations must, therefore, remain aware of the current regulations that affect their risk posture.

Risk Assessment

Risk assessments are a formalized approach to risk prioritization that allows organizations to conduct their reviews in a structured manner. Risk assessments follow two different analysis methodologies:

- *Quantitative risk assessments* use numeric data in the analysis, resulting in assessments that allow the very straightforward prioritization of risks.

- *Qualitative risk assessments* substitute subjective judgments and categories for strict numerical analysis, allowing the assessment of risks that are difficult to quantify.

As organizations seek to provide clear communication of risk factors to stakeholders, they often combine elements of quantitative and qualitative risk assessments. Let's review each of these approaches.

Quantitative Risk Assessment

Most quantitative risk assessment processes follow a similar methodology that includes the following steps:

1. *Determine the asset value (AV) of the asset affected by the risk.* This *asset value (AV)* is expressed in dollars, or other currency, and may be determined by using the cost to acquire the asset, the cost to replace the asset, or the depreciated cost of the asset, depending on the organization's preferences.

2. *Determine the likelihood that the risk will occur.* Risk analysts consult subject matter experts and determine the likelihood that a risk will occur in a given year. This is expressed as the number of times the risk is expected to happen each year and is described as the *annualized rate of occurrence (ARO)*. A risk that is expected to occur twice a year has an ARO of 2.0, whereas a risk that is expected once every one hundred years has an ARO of 0.01.

3. *Determine the amount of damage that will occur to the asset if the risk materializes.* This is known as the *exposure factor (EF)* and is expressed as the percentage of the asset expected to be damaged. The exposure factor of a risk that would completely destroy an asset is 100 percent, whereas a risk that would damage half of an asset has an EF of 50 percent.

4. *Calculate the single loss expectancy.* The *single loss expectancy (SLE)* is the amount of financial damage expected each time this specific risk materializes. It is calculated by multiplying the AV by the EF.

5. *Calculate the annualized loss expectancy.* The *annualized loss expectancy (ALE)* is the amount of damage expected from a risk each year. It is calculated by multiplying the SLE and the ARO.

It's important to note that these steps assess the quantitative scale of a single risk; that is one combination of a threat and a vulnerability. Organizations conducting quantitative risk assessments would repeat this process for every possible threat/vulnerability combination.

Let's walk through an example of a quantitative risk assessment. Imagine that you are concerned about the risk associated with a denial-of-service (DoS) attack against your email server. Your organization uses that server to send email messages to customers offering products for sale. It generates $1,000 in sales for each hour that it is in operation. After consulting threat intelligence sources, you believe that a DoS attack is likely to occur three times a year and last for three hours before you are able to control it.

The asset in this case is not the server itself, because the server will not be physically damaged. The asset is the ability to send email and you have already determined that it is worth $1,000 per hour. The asset value for three hours of server operation is, therefore, $3,000.

Your threat intelligence estimates that the risk will occur three times per year, making your annualized rate of occurrence 3.0.

After consulting your email team, you believe that the server would operate at 10 percent capacity during a DoS attack, as some legitimate messages would get out. Therefore, your exposure factor is 90 percent, because 90 percent of the capacity would be consumed by the attack.

Your single loss expectancy is calculated by multiplying the asset value ($3,000) by the exposure factor (90 percent) to get the expected loss during each attack. This gives you an SLE of $2,700.

Your annualized loss expectancy is the product of the SLE ($2,700) and the ARO (3.0), or $8,100.

Exam Note

Be prepared to explain the terminology of quantitative risk assessment and perform these calculations when you take the CISM exam. When you encounter these questions, watch out for scenarios that provide you with more information than you may need to answer the question. Question writers sometimes provide extra facts to lead you astray!

Organizations can use the ALEs that result from a quantitative risk assessment to prioritize their remediation activities and determine the appropriate level of investment in controls that mitigate risks. This implements a cost/benefit approach to risk management. For example, it would not normally make sense (at least in a strictly financial sense) to spend more than the ALE on an annual basis to protect against a risk. In the previous example, if a DoS prevention service would block all of those attacks, it would make financial sense to purchase it if the cost is less than $8,100 per year.

Qualitative Risk Assessment

Quantitative techniques work very well for evaluating financial risks and other risks that can be clearly expressed in numeric terms. Many risks, however, do not easily lend themselves to quantitative analysis. For example, how would you describe reputational damage, public health and safety, or employee morale in quantitative terms? You might be able to draw some inferences that tie these issues back to financial data, but the bottom line is that quantitative techniques simply aren't well suited to evaluating these risks.

Qualitative risk assessment techniques seek to overcome the limitations of quantitative techniques by substituting subjective judgment for objective data. Qualitative techniques still use the same probability and magnitude factors to evaluate the severity of a risk but do so using subjective categories. For example, Figure 3.2 shows a simple qualitative risk assessment that evaluates the probability and magnitude of several risks on a subjective Low/Medium/High scale. Risks are placed on this chart based on the judgments made by subject matter experts.

FIGURE 3.2 Qualitative risk assessments use subjective rating scales to evaluate probability and magnitude.

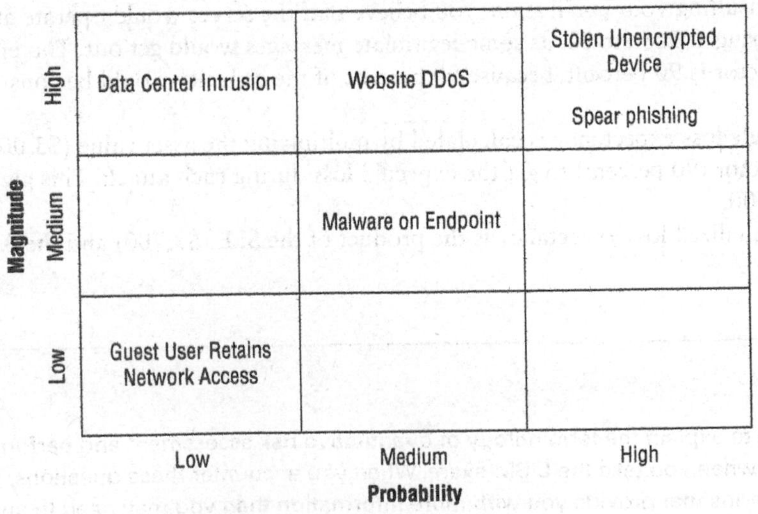

Although it's not possible to directly calculate the financial impact of risks that are assessed using qualitative techniques, this risk assessment scale makes it possible to prioritize risks. For example, reviewing the risk assessment in Figure 3.2, we can determine that the greatest risks facing this organization are stolen unencrypted devices and spear phishing attacks. Both of these risks share a high probability and high magnitude of impact. If we're considering using funds to add better physical security to the data center, this risk assessment informs us that our time and money would likely be better spent on full-disk encryption for mobile devices and a secure email gateway.

Exam Note

Many organizations combine quantitative and qualitative techniques to get a comprehensive perspective of both the tangible and intangible risks that they face.

Supply Chain Assessment

When evaluating the risks to your organization, don't forget about the risks that occur based on third-party relationships. You rely on many different vendors to protect the confidentiality, integrity, and availability of your data. Performing vendor due diligence is a crucial security responsibility.

For example, how many cloud service providers handle your organization's sensitive information? Those vendors become a crucial part of your supply chain from both operational and security perspectives. If they don't have adequate security controls in place, your data is at risk.

Similarly, the hardware that you use in your organization comes through a supply chain as well. How certain are you that it wasn't tampered with on the way to your organization? Documents leaked by former NSA contractor Edward Snowden revealed that the U.S. government intercepted hardware shipments to foreign countries and implanted malicious code deep within their hardware. Performing hardware source authenticity assessments validates that the hardware you received was not tampered with after leaving the vendor.

Reassessing Risk

Risk assessment is not a one-time project—it is an ongoing process. A variety of internal and external factors change over time, modifying existing risk scenarios and creating entirely new potential risks. For example, if a new type of attacker begins targeting organizations in your industry, that is a new risk factor that should prompt a reassessment of risk. Similarly, if you enter a new line of business, that also creates new potential risks.

Risk managers should monitor the internal and external environment for changes in circumstances that require risk reassessment. These might include changes in the threat landscape, evolving regulatory requirements, or even geopolitical changes. Organizations should maintain a set of *key risk indicators (KRIs)* that facilitate risk monitoring. These KRIs are quantitative measures of risk that may be easily monitored for situations where they exceed a defined threshold value or worrisome trends.

Reassessments of risk should take place whenever KRIs or other factors suggest that the environment is undergoing a significant change. Risk managers should also conduct periodic reassessments even in the absence of obvious changes to help the organization identify previously undetected issues. The results of these reassessments may prompt changes in elements of the organization's information security program.

Risk Treatment and Response

With a completed risk assessment in hand, organizations can then turn their attention to addressing those risks. *Risk treatment* is the process of systematically responding to the risks facing an organization. The risk assessment serves two important roles in the risk management process:

- The risk assessment provides guidance in prioritizing risks so that the risks with the highest probability and magnitude are addressed first.
- Quantitative risk assessments help determine whether the potential impact of a risk justifies the costs incurred by adopting a specific risk management approach.

Risk managers should work their way through the risk assessment and identify an appropriate management strategy for each risk included in the assessment. Managers have four strategies to choose from: risk mitigation, risk avoidance, risk transference, and risk acceptance. In the next several sections, we discuss each of these strategies using two examples.

First, we discuss the financial risk associated with the theft of a laptop from an employee. In this example, we are assuming that the laptop does not contain any unencrypted sensitive information. The risk that we are managing is the financial impact of losing the actual hardware.

Second, we discuss the business risk associated with a distributed denial-of-service (DDoS) attack against an organization's website.

We use these two scenarios to help you understand the different options available when selecting a risk management strategy and the trade-offs involved in that selection process.

Risk Mitigation

Risk mitigation is the process of applying security controls to reduce the probability and/or magnitude of a risk. Risk mitigation is the most common risk management strategy, and the vast majority of the work of security professionals revolves around mitigating risks through the design, implementation, and management of security controls. Many of these controls involve engineering tradeoffs between functionality, performance, and security.

When you choose to mitigate a risk, you may apply one security control or a series of security controls. Each of those controls should reduce the probability that the risk will materialize, the magnitude of the risk should it materialize, or both the probability and magnitude.

In our first scenario, we are concerned about the theft of laptops from our organization. If we want to mitigate that risk, we could choose from a variety of security controls. For example, purchasing cable locks for laptops might reduce the probability that a theft will occur.

FIGURE 3.3   (a) STOP tag attached to a device. (b) Residue remaining on device after attempted removal of a STOP tag.

(a)   (b)

We could also choose to purchase a device registration service that provides tamperproof registration tags for devices, such as the STOP tags shown in Figure 3.3. These tags provide a prominent warning to potential thieves when attached to a device, as shown in Figure 3.3(a). This serves as a deterrent to theft, reducing the probability that the laptop will be stolen in the first place. If a thief does steal the device and removes the tag, it leaves the permanent residue, shown in Figure 3.3(b). Anyone finding the device is instructed to contact the registration vendor for instructions, reducing the potential impact of the theft if the device is returned.

In our second scenario, a DDoS attack against an organization's website, we could choose among several mitigating controls. For example, we could simply purchase more bandwidth and server capacity, allowing us to absorb the bombardment of a DDoS attack and thus reducing the impact of an attack. We could also choose to purchase a third-party DDoS mitigation service that prevents the traffic from reaching our network in the first place, thus reducing the probability of an attack.

Risk Avoidance

Risk avoidance is a risk management strategy by which we change our business practices to completely eliminate the potential that a risk will materialize. Risk avoidance may initially seem like a highly desirable approach. After all, who wouldn't want to eliminate the risks facing their organization? There is, however, a major drawback. Risk avoidance strategies typically have a serious detrimental impact on the business.

For example, consider the laptop theft risk discussed earlier in this chapter. We could adopt a risk avoidance strategy and completely eliminate the risk by not allowing employees to purchase or use laptops. This approach is unwieldy and would likely be met with strong opposition from employees and managers due to the negative impact on employee productivity.

Similarly, we could avoid the risk of a DDoS attack against the organization's website by simply shutting down the website. If there is no website to attack, there's no risk that a DDoS attack can affect the site. But it's highly improbable that business leaders will accept shutting down the website as a viable approach. In fact, you might consider being driven to shut down your website to avoid DDoS attacks as the *ultimate* denial-of-service attack!

Risk Transference

Risk transference shifts some of the impact of a risk from the organization experiencing the risk to another entity. The most common example of risk transference is purchasing an insurance policy that covers a risk. When purchasing insurance, the customer pays a premium to the insurance carrier. In exchange, the insurance carrier agrees to cover losses from risks specified in the policy.

In the example of laptop theft, property insurance policies may cover the risk. If an employee's laptop is stolen, the insurance policy would provide funds to cover either the value of the stolen device or the cost to replace the device, depending on the type of coverage.

It's unlikely that a property insurance policy would cover a DDoS attack. In fact, many general business policies exclude all cybersecurity risks. An organization seeking insurance coverage against this type of attack should purchase *cybersecurity insurance*, either as a separate policy or as a rider on an existing business insurance policy. This coverage would repay some or all of the cost of recovering operations and may also cover lost revenue during an attack.

Risk Acceptance

Risk acceptance is the final risk management strategy, and it boils down to deliberately choosing to take no other risk management strategy and to simply continue operations as normal in the face of the risk. A risk acceptance approach may be warranted if the cost of mitigating a risk is greater than the impact of the risk itself.

> **WARNING**
>
> Risk acceptance is a deliberate decision that comes as the result of a thoughtful analysis. It should not be undertaken as a default strategy. Simply stating that "we accept this risk" without analysis is not an example of an accepted risk; it is an example of an unmanaged risk!

In our laptop theft example, we might decide that none of the other risk management strategies are appropriate. For example, we might feel that the use of cable locks is an unnecessary burden and that theft recovery tags are unlikely to work, leaving us without a viable risk mitigation strategy. Business leaders might require that employees have laptop devices, eliminating risk avoidance as a viable option. And the cost of a laptop insurance policy might be too high to justify. In that case, we might decide that we will simply accept the risk and cover the cost of stolen devices when thefts occur. That's risk acceptance.

In the case of the DDoS risk, we might go through a similar analysis and decide that risk mitigation and transference strategies are too costly. In the event we continue to operate the site, we might do so, accepting the risk that a DDoS attack could take the site down.

Exam Note

Understand the four risk treatment/response options (risk mitigation, risk avoidance, risk acceptance, and risk transference) when you take the CISM exam. Be prepared to provide examples of these strategies and to identify which strategy is being used in a given scenario.

Risk Analysis

As you work to manage risks, you will implement controls designed to mitigate those risks. As you prepare for the exam, here are a few key terms that you can use to describe different states of risk:

- The *inherent risk* facing an organization is the original level of risk that exists before implementing any controls. Inherent risk takes its name from the fact that it is the level of risk inherent in the organization's business.

- The *residual risk* is the risk that remains after an organization implements controls designed to mitigate, avoid, and/or transfer the inherent risk.
- An organization's *risk appetite* is the level of risk that the organization is willing to accept as a cost of doing business.

These three concepts are connected by the way in which an organization manages risk. An organization begins with its inherent risk and then implements risk management strategies to reduce that level of risk. It continues doing so until the residual risk is at or below the organization's risk appetite.

Control Risk

The world of public accounting brings us the concept of control risk. Control risk is the risk that arises from the potential that a lack of internal controls within the organization will cause a material misstatement in the organization's financial reports. Information technology risks can contribute to control risks if they jeopardize the integrity or availability of financial information. For this reason, financial audits often include tests of the controls protecting financial systems.

Organizations can implement practices that address these concepts only if they have a high degree of risk awareness. Organizations must understand the risks they face and the controls they can implement to manage those risks. They must also conduct regular risk control assessments and self-assessments to determine whether those controls continue to operate effectively.

Risk Reporting

As risk managers work to track and manage risks, they must communicate their results to other risk professionals and business leaders. The risk register is the primary tool that risk management professionals use to track risks facing the organization. Figure 3.4 shows an excerpt from a risk register used to track IT risks in higher education.

The risk register is a lengthy document that often provides far too much detail for business leaders. When communicating risk management concepts to senior leaders, risk professionals often use a *risk matrix*, or heat map, such as the one shown in Figure 3.5. This approach quickly summarizes risks and allows senior leaders to quickly focus on the most significant risks facing the organization and how those risks might impact organizational goals and objectives.

Circumstances will also arise where leaders and managers within the organization will need to understand changes in the organization's risk profile. These may be urgent situations based on an active emergency or slower-moving discussions based on the evolving risk landscape. Information security managers should establish a regular reporting rhythm, with periodic risk reports delivered at a regular frequency, as well as a mechanism for rapidly providing urgent updates. In all cases, risk managers should write their reports with a strong understanding of their audience, tailoring the content to the knowledge, needs, and specific concerns of each target group.

FIGURE 3.4   Risk register excerpt

ID	Risk Statement	Risk Causes	Risk Impacts	Likelihood	Impact	Score
20	No coordinated vetting and review process for third-party or cloud-computing services used to store, process, or transmit institutional data	Lack of senior management support; lack of communication of central vetting process to staff/employees; failure to understand the need to protect institutional data	Multiple redundant services in place (inefficient and costly for the institution); institution unaware who its business partners are; institution unaware if institutional data are held by third parties; institution unable to ensure that third parties are following compliance requirements	1	2	2
21	Failure to create and maintain sufficient and current policies and standards to protect the confidentiality, integrity, and availability of institutional data and IT resources (e.g., hardware, devices, data, and software)	Lack of senior management support; failure to understand information security concepts; lack of funding to support policy development activities; lack of funding for training; lack of user training	Improper use of university IT systems and institutional data; failure of users to protect critical institutional data when using IT resources (leading to data breach); institution subject to regulatory violations and fines; institutional reputation loss; poor perception/reputation of IT	2	3	6
22	Data breach or leak of sensitive information (e.g., academic, business, or research data)	Lack of senior management support; complex regulatory environments impacting higher education IT systems and data (e.g., FERPA, HIPAA, GLBA, PCI, accessibility, export controls, etc.); complexity of IT systems, infrastructure, and services; lack of funding for data handling training; lack of user training; intentional user malfeasance; unintentional user error; hacking or infiltration by third parties	Institution subject to regulatory violations and fines; costs of breach notification; costs of redress for individuals; loss of alumni donations; loss of research data; costs to mitigate underlying breach event; institutional reputation loss; poor perception/reputation of IT	3	3	9

Source: EDUCAUSE IT Risk Register (library.educause.edu/resources/2015/10/it-risk-register)

FIGURE 3.5   Risk matrix

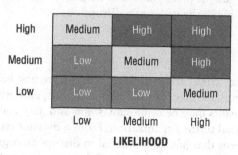

Enterprise Risk Management

As organizations seek to adopt a systematic approach to enterprise risk management, they should work to integrate risk management practices into normal business and information technology processes. Mature organizations don't treat risk management efforts as siloed projects but rather as integral components of their day-to-day work.

Here are some examples of business areas that should incorporate risk management:

- *Software and systems development* efforts create and modify software and systems on a regular basis. New and modified systems are a potential source of risk to the organization, and integrating risk assessment and response practices into these development efforts helps ensure that the organization integrates security from the start and does not need to "bolt on" security controls after the fact in a costly and error-prone approach.

- *Procurement* processes bring new vendors and systems into the organization, another source of potential risk. Any new or renewing relationship with a vendor should include a formal risk assessment that identifies potential risks associated with the relationship and implements appropriate risk treatments before moving forward.

- *Project management* procedures govern much of the work performed in the modern organization and, like software and systems development, often result in change to business practices and technology. Project management procedures should incorporate risk assessments that identify new or changed risks that arise during the course of a project and address them appropriately.

The goal of integrating risk management into everyday business activity is to enable a consistent and comprehensive risk management program across the business.

Disaster Recovery Planning

No matter how many controls we put in place, the reality is that disasters will sometimes strike our organization and cause disruptions. *Disaster recovery planning (DRP)* is the discipline of developing plans to recover operations as quickly as possible in the face of a disaster. The disaster recovery planning process creates a formal, broad disaster recovery plan for the organization and, when required, develops specific functional recovery plans for critical business functions. The goal of these plans is to help the organization recover normal operations as quickly as possible in the wake of a disruption.

Disaster Types

Disasters of any type may strike an organization. When we first hear the word *disaster*, we often immediately conjure up images of hurricanes, floods, and other natural environmental disasters. However, disasters may be of human origin and may come as a result of forces external as well as internal to the organization. From a disaster recovery planning perspective, a disaster is any event that has the potential to disrupt an organization's business. The occurrence of a disaster triggers the activation of the organization's disaster recovery plan.

As part of the DRP process, organizations should conduct site risk assessments for each of their facilities. These risk assessments identify and prioritize the risks posed to the facility, including both internal and external risks from environmental disasters and those caused by humans.

Business Impact Analysis

The *business impact analysis (BIA)* is a formal process designed to identify the mission-essential functions within an organization and facilitate the identification of the critical systems that support those functions.

Four core metrics are used in the BIA process that you should understand when preparing for the exam:

- The *mean time between failures (MTBF)* is a measure of the reliability of a system. It is the expected amount of time that will elapse between system failures. For example, if the MTBF is six months, you can expect that the system will fail once every six months, on average.

- The *mean time to repair (MTTR)* is the average amount of time to restore a system to its normal operating state after a failure.

- The *recovery time objective (RTO)* is the amount of time that the organization can tolerate a system being down before it is repaired. The service team is meeting expectations when the time to repair is less than the RTO.

- The *recovery point objective (RPO)* is the amount of data that the organization can tolerate losing during an outage.

Each of these metrics allows the organization to evaluate the impact of different risks on its operations and the acceptability of the state of its disaster recovery controls.

As organizations evaluate the state of their environment, they should pay particular attention to *single points of failure*. These are systems, devices, or other components that, if they fail, would cause an outage. For example, if a server only has one power supply, the failure of that power supply would bring down the server, making it a single point of failure. Adding a redundant power supply to the server resolves that single point of failure. Similarly, if that server is the only server providing the organization's web page, the server then becomes a single point of failure. Adding a second server to a cluster resolves that single point of failure.

Privacy

Cybersecurity professionals are responsible for protecting the confidentiality, integrity, and availability of all information under their care. This includes personally identifiable information (PII) that, if improperly disclosed, would jeopardize the privacy of one or more individuals.

When privacy breaches occur, they clearly have a negative impact on the individuals whose information was lost in the breach. Those individuals may find themselves exposed to identity theft and other personal risks. Privacy breaches also have organizational consequences for the business that loses control of personal information. These consequences may include reputational damage, fines, and the loss of important intellectual property that may now fall into the hands of a competitor.

Organizations seeking to codify their privacy practices may adopt a *privacy notice* that outlines their privacy commitments. In some cases, laws or regulations may require that organizations adopt a privacy notice. In addition, organizations may include privacy statements in their terms of agreement with customers and other stakeholders.

Sensitive Information Inventory

Organizations often deal with many different types of sensitive and personal information. The first step in managing this sensitive data is developing an inventory of the types of data maintained by the organization and the places where it is stored, processed, and transmitted.

Organizations should include the following types of information in their inventory:

- *Personally identifiable information (PII)* includes any information that uniquely identifies an individual person, including customers, employees, and third parties.

- *Protected health information (PHI)* includes medical records maintained by health-care providers and other organizations that are subject to the Health Insurance Portability and Accountability Act (HIPAA).

- *Financial information* includes any personal financial records maintained by the organization.

- *Government information* maintained by the organization may be subject to other rules, including the data classification requirements discussed in the next section.

Once the organization has an inventory of this sensitive information, it can begin to take steps to ensure that it is appropriately protected from loss or theft.

Information Classification

Information classification programs organize data into categories based on the sensitivity of the information and the impact on the organization should the information be inadvertently disclosed. For example, the U.S. government uses the following four major classification categories:

- *Top Secret* information requires the highest degree of protection. The unauthorized disclosure of Top Secret information could reasonably be expected to cause exceptionally grave damage to national security.

- *Secret* information requires a substantial degree of protection. The unauthorized disclosure of Secret information could reasonably be expected to cause serious damage to national security.

- *Confidential* information requires some protection. The unauthorized disclosure of Confidential information could reasonably be expected to cause identifiable damage to national security.

- *Unclassified* information is information that does not meet the standards for classification under the other categories. Information in this category is still not publicly releasable without authorization.

Businesses generally don't use the same terminology for their levels of classified information. Instead, they might use friendlier terms, such as Highly Sensitive, Sensitive, Internal, and Public.

Data classification allows organizations to clearly specify the security controls required to protect information with different levels of sensitivity. For example, the U.S. government requires the use of brightly colored cover sheets, such as those shown in Figure 3.6 (although the figure is black and white), to identify classified information in printed form.

FIGURE 3.6 Cover sheets used to identify classified U.S. government information

Information classification decisions may then drive *asset classification* as well. When performing asset classification, managers identify the highest-level classification of information that is stored, processed, or transmitted by the device in question. The device is then assigned a classification level that may then be used to determine the appropriate security controls to apply to that device. This approach allows organizations to apply costly and time-consuming controls only when necessary, ensuring that measures taken to protect assets are proportional to their business value.

Data Roles and Responsibilities

One of the most important things that we can do to protect our data is to create clear *data ownership* policies and procedures. Using this approach, the organization designates specific senior executives as the data owners for different data types. For example, the vice president of Human Resources might be the data owner for employment and payroll data, whereas the vice president for Sales might be the data owner for customer information.

Every organization should have a clear process in place for assigning ownership of information assets using consistent criteria. Clear lines of data ownership place responsibility for data in the hands of executives who best understand the impact of decisions about that data on the business. They don't make all of these decisions in isolation, however. Data owners delegate some of their responsibilities to others in the organization and also rely on advice from subject matter experts, such as cybersecurity analysts and data protection specialists.

As you prepare for the exam, you should be familiar with other important data privacy roles:

- *Data controllers* are the entities who determine the reasons for processing personal information and direct the methods of processing that data. This term is used primarily in European law, and it serves as a substitute for the term *data owner* to avoid a presumption that anyone who collects data has an ownership interest in that data.

- *Data stewards* are individuals who carry out the intent of the data controller and are delegated both authority and responsibility from the controller.

- *Data custodians* are individuals or teams who do not have controller or stewardship responsibility but who are responsible for the secure safekeeping of information. For example, a data controller or data steward might delegate responsibility for securing PII to an information security team. In that case, the information security team serves as a data custodian.

- *Data processors* are service providers that process personal information on behalf of a data controller. For example, a credit card processing service might be a data processor for a retailer. The retailer retains responsibility as the data controller. The credit card processing service that the retailer uses is a data processor.

- *Data subjects* are the individuals about whom data is collected, stored, and processed. The data subject for a record containing personally identifiable information is the person whom the record is about.

Data Protection Officers

Organizations should identify a specific individual who bears overall responsibility for carrying out the organization's data privacy efforts. This person, often given the title of chief privacy officer, bears the ultimate responsibility for data privacy and must coordinate across functional teams to achieve the organization's privacy objectives.

The European Union's General Data Protection Regulation (GDPR) formalizes this role, requiring that every data controller designate a data protection officer (DPO) and grant that individual the autonomy to carry out their responsibilities free from undue internal influence.

Information Lifecycle

Data protection should continue at all stages of the information lifecycle, from the time the data is originally collected until the time it is eventually disposed of.

At the early stages of the data lifecycle, organizations should practice *data minimization*, where they collect the smallest possible amount of information necessary to meet their business requirements. Information that is not necessary should either be immediately discarded or, better yet, not collected in the first place.

Although information remains within the care of the organization, the organization should practice *purpose limitation*. This means that information should be used only for the purpose that it was originally collected and that was consented to by the data subjects.

At the end of the lifecycle, the organization should implement *data retention* standards that guide the end of the data lifecycle. Data should be kept for only as long as it remains necessary to fulfill the purpose for which it was originally collected. At the conclusion of its lifecycle, data should be securely destroyed.

Exam Note

Reducing the amount of data that you retain is a great way to minimize your security risk. Remember this as you answer exam questions that ask you to identify the best or most effective strategy for reducing risk.

Privacy-Enhancing Technologies

If we can't completely remove data from a dataset, we can often transform it into a format where the original sensitive information is anonymized. Although true anonymization may be quite difficult to achieve, we can often use pseudo-anonymization techniques, such as de-identification. The *de-identification* process removes the ability to link data back to an individual, reducing its sensitivity.

An alternative to de-identifying data is transforming it into a format where the original information can't be retrieved. This is a process called *data obfuscation*, and we have several tools at our disposal to assist with it:

- *Hashing* uses a hash function to transform a value in our dataset to a corresponding hash value. If we apply a strong hash function to a data element, we may replace the value in our file with the hashed value.

- *Tokenization* replaces sensitive values with a unique identifier using a lookup table. For example, we might replace a widely known value, such as a student ID, with a randomly generated 10-digit number. We'd then maintain a lookup table that allows us to convert those back to the student ID if we need to determine someone's identity. Of course, if you use this approach, you need to keep the lookup table secure!

- *Data masking* partially redacts sensitive information by replacing some or all sensitive fields with blank characters. For example, we might replace all but the last four digits of a credit card number with Xs or asterisks to render the card number unreadable.

Although it isn't possible to retrieve the original value directly from the hashed value, this approach has one major flaw: if someone has a list of possible values for a field, they can conduct something called a *rainbow table attack*. In this attack, the attacker computes the hashes of those candidate values and then checks to see if those hashes exist in your data file.

For example, imagine that we have a file listing all the students at our college who have failed courses but we hash their student IDs. If an attacker has a list of all students, they can compute the hash values of all student IDs and then check to see which hash values are on the list. For this reason, hashing should only be used with caution.

Privacy and Data Breach Notification

In the unfortunate event of a data breach, the organization should immediately activate its cybersecurity incident response plan. The details of this incident response plan are discussed thoroughly in Chapter 8, "Incident Response," and should include procedures for the notification of key personnel and escalation of serious incidents.

Organizations may also have a responsibility under national and regional laws to make public notifications and disclosures in the wake of a data breach. This responsibility may be limited to notifying the individuals involved or, in some cases, may require notification of government regulators and/or the news media.

In the United States, every state has a data breach notification law, with different requirements for triggering notifications. The European Union's GDPR also includes a breach notification requirement. The United States lacks a federal law requiring broad notification for all security breaches but does have industry-specific laws and requirements that require notification in some circumstances.

The bottom line is that breach notification requirements vary by industry and jurisdiction, and an organization experiencing a breach may be required to untangle many overlapping requirements. For this reason, organizations experiencing a data breach should consult with an attorney who is well versed in this field.

Summary

Cybersecurity efforts are all about risk management. In this chapter, you learned about the techniques that cybersecurity analysts use to identify, assess, and manage a wide variety of risks. You learned about the differences between risk mitigation, risk avoidance, risk transference, and risk acceptance and when it is appropriate to use each. You also learned how the disaster recovery planning process can help prevent disruptions to a business and the role of security professionals in protecting the privacy of personally identifiable information.

Exam Essentials

Know how risk identification and assessment helps organizations prioritize cybersecurity efforts.   Cybersecurity analysts try to identify all of the risks facing their organization and then conduct a business impact analysis to assess the potential degree of risk based on the probability that it will occur and the magnitude of the potential effect on the organization. This work allows security professionals to prioritize risks and communicate risk factors to others in the organization.

Know that vendors are a source of external risk.   Organizations should conduct their own systems assessments as part of their risk assessment practices, but they should conduct supply chain assessments as well. Performing vendor due diligence reduces the likelihood that a previously unidentified risk at a vendor will negatively impact the organization. Hardware source authenticity techniques verify that hardware was not tampered with after leaving the vendor's premises.

Be familiar with the risk management strategies that organizations may adopt.   Risk avoidance strategies change business practices to eliminate a risk. Risk mitigation techniques reduce the probability or magnitude of a risk. Risk transference approaches move some of the risk to a third party. Risk acceptance acknowledges the risk and continues normal business operations despite the presence of the risk.

Understand how disaster recovery planning builds resiliency.   Disaster recovery plans activate when an organization experiences a natural or human-made disaster that disrupts normal operations. The disaster recovery plan helps the organization quickly recover its information and systems and resume normal operations.

Be familiar with the privacy controls that protect personal information.   Organizations handling sensitive personal information should develop privacy programs that protect that information from misuse and unauthorized disclosure. The plan should cover personally identifiable information (PII), protected health information (PHI), financial information, and other records maintained by the organization that might impact personal privacy.

Review Questions

1. Jen identified a missing patch on a Windows server that might allow an attacker to gain remote control of the system. After consulting with her manager, she applied the patch. From a risk management perspective, what has she done?

   A. Removed the threat

   B. Reduced the threat

   C. Removed the vulnerability

   D. Reduced the vulnerability

2. You notice a high number of SQL injection attacks against a web application run by your organization, so you install a web application firewall to block many of these attacks before they reach the server. How have you altered the severity of this risk?

   A. Reduced the magnitude

   B. Eliminated the vulnerability

   C. Reduced the probability

   D. Eliminated the threat

   Questions 3–7 refer to the following scenario:

   Aziz is responsible for the administration of an e-commerce website that generates $100,000 per day in revenue for his firm. The website uses a database that contains sensitive information about the firm's customers.

   Aziz is assessing the risk of a denial-of-service attack against the database where the attacker would destroy the data contained within the database. He expects that it would cost approximately $500,000 to reconstruct the database from existing records. After consulting threat intelligence, he believes that there is a 5 percent chance of a successful attack in any given year.

3. What is the asset value (AV)?

   A. $5,000

   B. $100,000

   C. $500,000

   D. $600,000

4. What is the exposure factor (EF)?

   A. 5%

   B. 20%

   C. 50%

   D. 100%

5. What is the single loss expectancy (SLE)?

   A. $5,000

   B. $100,000

    C. $500,000

    D. $600,000

6. What is the annualized rate of occurrence (ARO)?

    A. 0.05

    B. 0.20

    C. 2.00

    D. 5.00

7. What is the annualized loss expectancy (ALE)?

    A. $5,000

    B. $25,000

    C. $100,000

    D. $500,000

Questions 8–11 refer to the following scenario:

Grace recently completed a risk assessment of her organization's exposure to data breaches and determined that there is a high level of risk related to the loss of sensitive personal information. She is considering a variety of approaches to managing this risk.

8. Grace's first idea is to add a web application firewall to protect her organization against SQL injection attacks. What risk management strategy does this approach adopt?

    A. Risk acceptance

    B. Risk avoidance

    C. Risk mitigation

    D. Risk transference

9. Grace is considering dropping the customer activities that collect and store sensitive personal information. What risk management strategy would Grace's approach use?

    A. Risk acceptance

    B. Risk avoidance

    C. Risk mitigation

    D. Risk transference

10. Grace's company decided to install the web application firewall and continue doing business. They are still worried about other risks to the information that were not addressed by the firewall and are considering purchasing an insurance policy to cover those risks. What strategy does this use?

    A. Risk acceptance

    B. Risk avoidance

    C. Risk mitigation

    D. Risk transference

11. In the end, Grace found that the insurance policy was too expensive and opted not to purchase it. She is taking no additional action. What risk management strategy is Grace using in this situation?

   A. Risk acceptance

   B. Risk avoidance

   C. Risk mitigation

   D. Risk transference

12. Under the European Union's GDPR, what term is assigned to the individual who leads an organization's privacy efforts?

   A. Data protection officer

   B. Data controller

   C. Data steward

   D. Data processor

13. Helen's organization maintains medical records on behalf of its customers, who are individual physicians. What term best describes the role of Helen's organization?

   A. Data processor

   B. Data controller

   C. Data owner

   D. Data steward

14. Gene recently conducted an assessment and determined that his organization can be without its main transaction database for a maximum of two hours before unacceptable damage occurs to the business. What metric has Gene identified?

   A. MTBF

   B. MTTR

   C. RTO

   D. RPO

15. Tina works for a hospital system and manages the system's patient records. What category of personal information best describes the information that is likely to be found in those records?

   A. PCI

   B. PHI

   C. PFI

   D. PII

16. Asa believes that her organization is taking data collected from customers for technical support and using it for marketing without their permission. What principle is most likely being violated?

   A. Data minimization

   B. Data retention

   C. Purpose limitation

   D. Data sovereignty

17. Which one of the following U.S. government classification levels requires the highest degree of security control?

   A. Secret

   B. Confidential

   C. Top Secret

   D. Unclassified

18. Which of the following data protection techniques is reversible when conducted properly?

   A. Tokenization

   B. Masking

   C. Hashing

   D. Shredding

19. What term is given to an individual or organization who determines the reasons for processing personal information?

   A. Data steward

   B. Data controller

   C. Data processor

   D. Data custodian

20. Brian recently conducted a risk mitigation exercise and has determined the level of risk that remains after implementing a series of controls. What term best describes this risk?

   A. Inherent risk

   B. Control risk

   C. Risk appetite

   D. Residual risk

Cybersecurity Threats

THE CERTIFIED INFORMATION SECURITY MANAGER (CISM) DOMAINS AND SUBTOPICS COVERED IN THIS CHAPTER INCLUDE:

✓ **Domain 2: Information Risk Management**

- ▪ **A. Information Security Risk Assessment**

  - ▪ **2A1. Emerging Risk and Threat Landscape**

THE CERTIFIED INFORMATION SECURITY MANAGER (CISM) SUPPORTING TASKS COVERED IN THIS CHAPTER INCLUDE:

✓ **1. Identify internal and external influences to the organization that impact the information security strategy.**

✓ **23. Participate in and/or oversee the vulnerability assessment and threat analysis process.**

Cybersecurity threats have become increasingly sophisticated and diverse over the past three decades. An environment that was once populated by lone hobbyists is now shared by skilled technologists, organized criminal syndicates, and even government-sponsored attackers, all seeking to exploit the digital domain to achieve their own objectives. Cybersecurity professionals seeking to safeguard the confidentiality, integrity, and availability of their organization's assets must have a strong understanding of the threat environment to develop appropriate defensive mechanisms.

In the first part of this chapter, you will learn about the modern cybersecurity threat environment, including the major types of threat and the characteristics that differentiate them. In the sections that follow, you will learn how to build your own organization's threat intelligence capability to stay current as the threat environment evolves.

Exploring Cybersecurity Threats

Cybersecurity threat actors differ significantly in their skills, capabilities, resources, and motivation. Protecting your organization's information and systems requires a solid understanding of the nature of these different threats so that you can develop a set of security controls that comprehensively protect your organization against their occurrence.

Classifying Cybersecurity Threats

Before we explore specific types of threat actors, let's examine the characteristics that differentiate the types of cybersecurity threat actors. Understanding our adversary is crucial to defending against them.

Internal vs. External   We most often think about the threat actors who exist outside our organizations: competitors, criminals, and the curious. However, some of the most dangerous threats come from within our own environments. We'll discuss the insider threat later in this chapter.

Level of Sophistication/Capability   Threat actors vary greatly in their level of cybersecurity sophistication and capability. As we explore different types of threat actors in this chapter, we'll discuss how they range from the unsophisticated script kiddie simply running code borrowed from others to the advanced persistent threat (APT) actor exploiting vulnerabilities discovered in their own research labs and unknown to the security community.

Resources/Funding   Just as threat actors vary in their sophistication, they also vary in the resources available to them. Highly organized attackers sponsored by criminal syndicates or national governments often have virtually limitless resources, whereas less organized attackers may simply be hobbyists working in their spare time.

Intent/Motivation   Attackers also vary in their motivation and intent. The script kiddie may simply be out for the thrill of the attack, whereas competitors may be engaged in highly targeted corporate espionage. Nation-states seek to achieve political objectives; criminal syndicates often focus on direct financial gain.

As we work through this chapter, we'll explore different types of threat actors. As we do so, take some time to reflect back on these characteristics. In addition, you may wish to reference them when you hear news of current cybersecurity attacks in the media and other sources. Dissect those stories and analyze the threat actors involved. If the attack came from an unknown source, think about the characteristics that are most likely associated with the attacker. These can be important clues during a cybersecurity investigation. For example, a ransomware attack seeking payment from the victim is more likely associated with a criminal syndicate seeking financial gain than a competitor engaged in corporate espionage.

The Hats Hackers Wear

The cybersecurity community uses a shorthand lingo to refer to the motivations of attackers, describing them as having different-colored hats. The origins of this approach date back to old Western films where the "good guys" wore white hats and the "bad guys" wore black hats to help distinguish them in the film.

Cybersecurity professionals have adopted this approach to describe different types of cybersecurity adversaries:

- *White-hat hackers*, also known as authorized attackers, are those who act with authorization and seek to discover security vulnerabilities with the intent of correcting them. White-hat attackers may either be employees of the organization or contractors hired to engage in penetration testing.

- *Black-hat hackers*, also known as unauthorized attackers, are those with malicious intent. They seek to defeat security controls and compromise the confidentiality, integrity, or availability of information and systems for their own, unauthorized, purposes.

- *Gray-hat hackers*, also known as semi-authorized attackers, are those who fall somewhere between white- and black-hat hackers. They act without proper authorization, but they do so with the intent of informing their targets of any security vulnerabilities.

It's important to understand that simply having good intent does not make gray-hat hacking legal or ethical. The techniques used by gray-hat attackers can still be punished as criminal offenses.

Threat Actors

Now that we have a set of attributes that we can use to discuss the different types of threat actors, let's explore the most common types that security professionals encounter in their work.

Script Kiddies

The term *script kiddie* is a derogatory term for people who use hacking techniques but have limited skills. Often such attackers rely almost entirely on automated tools they download from the Internet. These attackers often have little knowledge of how their attacks actually work, and they are simply seeking convenient targets of opportunity.

You might think that with their relatively low skill level, script kiddies are not a real security threat. However, that isn't the case for two important reasons. First, simplistic hacking tools are freely available on the Internet. If you're vulnerable to them, anyone can easily find tools to automate denial-of-service (DoS) attacks, create viruses, make a Trojan horse, or even distribute ransomware as a service. Personal technical skills are no longer a barrier to attacking a network.

Second, script kiddies are plentiful and unfocused in their work. Although the nature of your business might not find you in the crosshairs of a sophisticated military-sponsored attack, script kiddies are much less discriminating in their target selection. They often just search for and discover vulnerable victims without even knowing the identity of their target. They might root around in files and systems and only discover who they've penetrated after their attack succeeds.

In general, the motivations of script kiddies revolve around trying to prove their skill. In other words, they may attack your network simply because it is there. Secondary school and university networks are common targets of script kiddies' attacks because many of these attackers are school-aged individuals.

Fortunately, the number of script kiddies is often offset by their lack of skill and lack of resources. These individuals tend to be rather young, they work alone, and they have very few resources. And by resources, we mean time as well as money. A script kiddie normally can't attack your network 24 hours a day. They usually have to work a job, go to school, and attend to other life functions.

Hacktivists

Hacktivists use hacking techniques to accomplish some activist goal. They might deface the website of a company whose policies they disagree with. Or they might attack a network due to a political issue. The defining characteristic of hacktivists is that they believe they are motivated by the greater good even if their activity violates the law.

Their activist motivation means that measures that might deter other attackers will be less likely to deter a hacktivist. Because they believe that they are engaged in a just crusade, they will, at least in some instances, risk getting caught to accomplish their goals. They may even view being caught as a badge of honor and a sacrifice for their cause.

The skill levels of hacktivists vary widely. Some are only script kiddies, whereas others are quite skilled, having honed their craft over the years. In fact, some cybersecurity researchers believe that some hacktivists are actually employed as cybersecurity professionals as their "day job" and perform hacktivist attacks in their spare time. Highly skilled hacktivists pose a significant danger to their targets.

The resources of hacktivists also vary somewhat. Many are working alone and have very limited resources. However, some are part of organized efforts. The hacking group Anonymous, who uses the logo seen in Figure 4.1, is the most well-known hacktivist group. They collectively decide their agenda and their targets. Over the years, Anonymous has waged cyberattacks against targets as diverse as the Church of Scientology, PayPal, Visa and Mastercard, Westboro Baptist Church, and even government agencies.

FIGURE 4.1   Logo of the hacktivist group Anonymous

Source: en.wikipedia.org/wiki/File:Anonymous_emblem.svg

This type of anonymous collective of attackers can prove quite powerful. Large groups will always have more time and other resources than a lone attacker. Due to their distributed and anonymous nature, it is difficult to identify, investigate, and prosecute participants in their hacking activities. The group lacks a hierarchical structure, and the capture of one member is unlikely to compromise the identities of other members.

Hacktivists tend to be external attackers, but in some cases, internal employees who disagree strongly with their company's policies engage in hacktivism. In those instances, it is more likely that the hacktivist will attack the company by releasing confidential information. Government employees and self-styled whistleblowers fit this pattern of activity, seeking to bring what they consider unethical government actions to the attention of the public.

For example, many people consider Edward Snowden a hacktivist. In 2013, Snowden, a former contractor with the U.S. National Security Agency, shared a large cache of sensitive government documents with journalists. Snowden's actions provided unprecedented insight into the digital intelligence gathering capabilities of the United States and its allies.

Criminal Syndicates

Organized crime appears in any case where there is money to be made, and cybercrime is no exception. The ranks of cybercriminals include links to traditional organized crime families in the United States, outlaw gangs, the Russian Mafia, and even criminal groups organized specifically for the purpose of engaging in cybercrime.

The common thread among these groups is motive and intent. The motive is simply illegal financial gain. Organized criminal syndicates do not normally embrace political issues or causes, and they are not trying to demonstrate their skills. In fact, they would often prefer to remain in the shadows, drawing as little attention to themselves as possible. They simply want to generate as much illegal profit as they possibly can.

In their 2019 Internet Organised Crime Threat Assessment (IOCTA), Europol found that organized crime groups were active in a variety of cybercrime categories, including the following:

- *Cyber-dependent crime*, including ransomware, data compromise, distributed denial-of-service (DDoS) attacks, website defacement, and attacks against critical infrastructure

- *Child sexual exploitation*, including child pornography, abuse, and solicitation

- *Payment fraud*, including credit card fraud and business email compromises

- *Dark web* activity, including the sale of illegal goods and services

- *Terrorism* support, including facilitating the actions of terrorist groups online

- *Cross-cutting crime factors*, including social engineering, money mules, and the criminal abuse of cryptocurrencies

Organized crime tends to have attackers who range from moderately skilled to highly skilled. It is rare for script kiddies to be involved in these crimes, and if they are, they tend to be caught rather quickly. The other defining factor is that organized crime groups tend to have more resources, both in terms of time and money, than do hacktivists or script kiddies. They often embrace the idea that "it takes money to make money" and are willing to invest in their criminal enterprises in the hopes of yielding a significant return on their investments.

Advanced Persistent Threats

In recent years, a great deal of attention has been given to state actors hacking into either foreign governments or corporations. The security company Mandiant created the term *advanced persistent threats (APTs)* to describe a series of attacks that they first traced to sources connected to the Chinese military. In subsequent years, the security community discovered similar organizations linked to the government of virtually every technologically advanced country.

The term *APT* tells you a great deal about the attacks themselves. First, they use advanced techniques, not simply tools downloaded from the Internet. Second, the attacks are persistent, occurring over a significant period of time. In some cases, the attacks continue for years as attackers patiently stalked their targets, awaiting the right opportunity to strike.

The APT attacks that Mandiant reported are emblematic of *nation-state attacks*. They tend to be characterized by highly skilled attackers with significant resources. A nation has the labor force, time, and money to finance ongoing, sophisticated attacks.

The motive can be political or economic. In some cases, the attack is done for traditional espionage goals: to gather information about the target's defense capabilities. In other cases, the attack might be targeting intellectual property or other economic assets.

Zero-Day Attacks

APT attackers often conduct their own security vulnerability research in an attempt to discover vulnerabilities that are not known to other attackers or cybersecurity teams. After they uncover a vulnerability, they do not disclose it but rather store it in a vulnerability repository for later use.

Attacks that exploit these vulnerabilities are known as *zero-day attacks*. Zero-day attacks are particularly dangerous because they are unknown to product vendors, and therefore, no patches are available to correct them. APT actors who exploit zero-day vulnerabilities are often able to easily compromise their targets.

Stuxnet is one of the most well-known examples of an APT attack. The Stuxnet attack, traced to the U.S. and Israeli governments, exploited zero-day vulnerabilities to compromise the control networks at an Iranian uranium enrichment facility.

Insiders

Insider attacks occur when an employee, contractor, vendor, or other individual with authorized access to information and systems uses that access to wage an attack against the organization. These attacks are often aimed at disclosing confidential information, but insiders may also seek to alter information or disrupt business processes.

An insider might be of any skill level. They could be a script kiddie or very technically skilled. Insiders may also have differing motivations behind their attacks. Some are motivated by certain activist goals, whereas others are motivated by financial gain. Still others may simply be upset that they were passed over for a promotion or slighted in some other manner.

An insider will usually be working alone and have limited financial resources and time. However, the fact that they are insiders gives them an automatic advantage. They already have some access to your network and some level of knowledge. Depending on the insider's job role, they might have significant access and knowledge.

Behavioral assessments are a tool used to identify possible insider threats. Cybersecurity teams should work with human resources partners to identify insiders exhibiting unusual behavior and intervene before the situation escalates.

The Threat of Shadow IT

Dedicated employees often seek to achieve their goals and objectives through whatever means allows them to do so. Sometimes, this involves purchasing technology services that aren't approved by the organization. For example, when file sharing and synchronization services first came on the market, many employees turned to personal Dropbox accounts to sync work content between their business and personal devices. They did not do this with any malicious intent. On the contrary, they were trying to benefit the business by being more productive.

This situation, where individuals and groups seek out their own technology solutions, is a phenomenon known as *shadow IT*. Shadow IT poses a risk to the organization because it puts sensitive information in the hands of vendors outside of the organization's control. Cybersecurity teams should remain vigilant for shadow IT adoption and remember that the presence of shadow IT in an organization means that business needs are not being met by the enterprise IT team. Consulting with shadow IT users often identifies acceptable alternatives that both meet business needs and satisfy security requirements.

Competitors

Competitors may engage in corporate espionage designed to steal sensitive information from your organization and use it to their own business advantage. This may include theft of customer information, stealing proprietary software, identifying confidential product development plans, or gaining access to any other information that would benefit the competitor.

In some cases, competitors will use a disgruntled insider to get information from your company. They may also seek insider information available for purchase on the *dark web*, a shadowy anonymous network often used for engaging in illicit activity. Figure 4.2 shows an actual dark web market with corporate information for sale.

These markets don't care how they get the information; their only concern is selling it. In some cases, hackers break into a network, steal sensitive data they find, and then sell the information to a dark web market. In other cases, insiders sell confidential information on the dark web. In fact, some dark web markets are advertising that they wish to buy

FIGURE 4.2   Dark web market

confidential data from corporate insiders. This provides a ready resource for competitors to purchase your company's information on the dark web.

Your organization may want to consider other specific threat actors based on your threat models and profile, so you should not consider this a complete list. You should conduct periodic organizational threat assessments to determine what types of threat actors are most likely to target your organization, and why.

Threat Vectors

Threat actors targeting an organization need some means to gain access to that organization's information or systems. *Threat vectors* are the means that threat actors use to obtain that access.

Email and Social Media

Email is one of the most commonly exploited threat vectors. Phishing messages, spam messages, and other email-borne attacks are a simple way to gain access to an organization's network. These attacks are easy to execute and can be launched against many users simultaneously. The benefit for the attacker is that they generally need to succeed only one time to launch a broader attack. Even if 99.9 percent of users ignore a phishing message, the attacker needs the login credentials of only a single user to begin their attack.

Social media may be used as a threat vector in similar ways. Attackers might directly target users on social media, or they might use social media in an effort to harvest information about users that may be used in another type of attack.

Direct Access

Bold attackers may seek to gain direct access to an organization's network by physically entering the organization's facilities. One of the most common ways they do this is by entering public areas of a facility, such as a lobby, customer store, or other easily accessible location, and sitting and working on their laptops, which are surreptitiously connected to unsecured network jacks on the wall.

Alternatively, attackers who gain physical access to a facility may be able to find an unsecured computer terminal, network device, or other system. Security professionals must assume that an attacker who is able to physically touch a component will be able to compromise that device and use it for malicious purposes.

Wireless Networks

Wireless networks offer an even easier path to an organization's network. Attackers don't need to gain physical access to the network or your facilities if they are able to sit in the parking lot and access your organization's wireless network. Unsecured or poorly secured wireless networks pose a significant security risk.

Removable Media

Attackers also commonly use removable media, such as USB drives, to spread malware and launch their attacks. An attacker might distribute inexpensive USB sticks in parking lots, airports, or other public areas, hoping that someone will find the device and plug it into their computer, curious to see what it contains. As soon as that happens, the device triggers a malware infection that silently compromises the finder's computer and places it under the control of the attacker.

Cloud

Cloud services can also be used as an attack vector. Attackers routinely scan popular cloud services for files with improper access controls, systems that have security flaws, or accidentally published API keys and passwords. Organizations must include the cloud services that they use as an important component of their security program.

The vulnerabilities facing organizations operating in cloud environments bear similarities to those found in on-premises environments, but the controls often differ.

Third-Party Risks

Sophisticated attackers may attempt to interfere with an organization's IT supply chain, gaining access to devices at the manufacturer or while the devices are in transit from the manufacturer to the end user. Tampering with a device before the end user receives it allows attackers to insert backdoors that grant them control of the device once the customer installs it on their network. This type of third-party risk is difficult to anticipate and address.

Other issues may also arise in the supply chain, particularly if a vendor fails to continue to support a system that the organization depends on, provide required system integrations, or provide adequate security for outsourced code development or data storage. Strong vendor management practices can identify these issues quickly as they arise and allow the organization to address the risks appropriately.

Threat Data and Intelligence

Threat intelligence is the set of activities and resources available to cybersecurity professionals seeking to learn about changes in the threat environment. Building a threat intelligence program is a crucial part of any organization's approach to cybersecurity. If you're not familiar with current threats, you won't be able to build appropriate defenses to protect your organization against those threats. Threat intelligence information can also be used for *predictive analysis* to identify likely risks to the organization.

There are many sources of threat intelligence, ranging from open source intelligence (OSINT) that you can gather from publicly available sources, to commercial services that provide proprietary or closed source intelligence information. An increasing number of products and services have the ability to consume threat feed data, allowing you to leverage it throughout your infrastructure and systems.

Regardless of their source, threat feeds are intended to provide up-to-date detail about threats in a way that your organization can leverage. Threat feeds often include technical details about threats, such as IP addresses, hostnames and domains, email addresses, URLs, file hashes, file paths, CVE numbers, and other details about a threat. Additional information is often included to help make the information relevant and understandable, including details of what may make your organization a target or vulnerable to the threat, descriptions of threat actors, and even details of their motivations and methodologies.

Vulnerability databases are also an essential part of an organization's threat intelligence program. Reports of vulnerabilities certainly help direct an organization's defensive efforts, but they also provide valuable insight into the types of exploits being discovered by researchers.

Threat intelligence sources may also provide *indicators of compromise (IoCs)*. These are the telltale signs that an attack has taken place and may include file signatures, log patterns, and other evidence left behind by attackers. IoCs may also be found in *file* and *code repositories* that offer threat intelligence information.

Open Source Intelligence

Open source threat intelligence is threat intelligence that is acquired from publicly available sources. Many organizations have recognized how useful open sharing of threat information can be, and open source threat intelligence has become broadly available. In fact, now the challenge is often about deciding what threat intelligence sources to use, ensuring that they are reliable and up-to-date, and leveraging them well.

A number of sites maintain extensive lists of open source threat information sources:

- Senki.org provides a list: `www.senki.org/operators-security-toolkit/open-source-threat-intelligence-feeds`
- The Open Threat Exchange operated by AT&T is part of a global community of security professionals and threat researchers: `https://cybersecurity.att.com/open-threat-exchange`

- The MISP Threat Sharing project, `www.misp-project.org/feeds`, provides standardized threat feeds from many sources, with community-driven collections.

- Threatfeeds.io hosts a list of open source threat intelligence feeds, with details of when they were added and modified, who maintains them, and other useful information: `https://threatfeeds.io`.

In addition to open source and community threat data sources, there are many government and public sources of threat intelligence data. For example, Figure 4.3 shows a recent alert listing from the Cybersecurity and Infrastructure Security Agency (CISA) website.

FIGURE 4.3   Recent alert listing from the CISA website

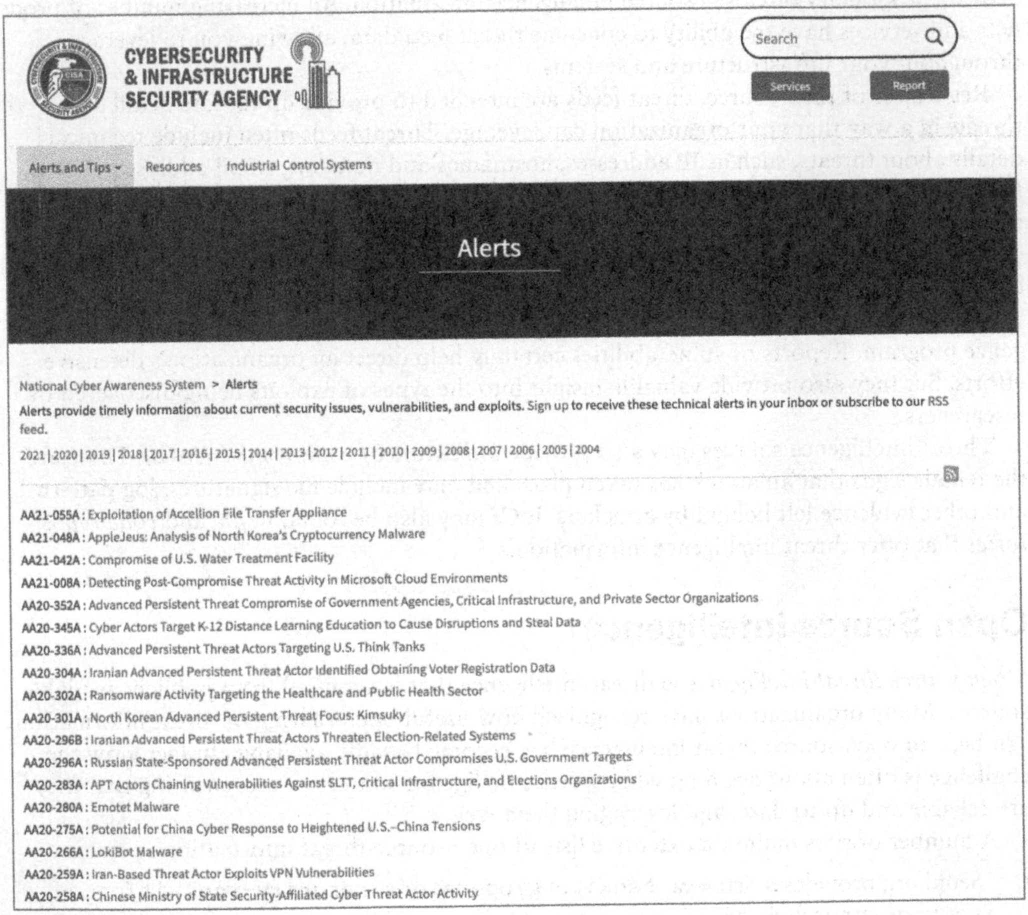

CYBERSECURITY & INFRASTRUCTURE SECURITY AGENCY

Search

Services   Report

Alerts and Tips ▾   Resources   Industrial Control Systems

Alerts

National Cyber Awareness System > Alerts

Alerts provide timely information about current security issues, vulnerabilities, and exploits. Sign up to receive these technical alerts in your inbox or subscribe to our RSS feed.

2021 | 2020 | 2019 | 2018 | 2017 | 2016 | 2015 | 2014 | 2013 | 2012 | 2011 | 2010 | 2009 | 2008 | 2007 | 2006 | 2005 | 2004

AA21-055A : Exploitation of Accellion File Transfer Appliance
AA21-048A : AppleJeus: Analysis of North Korea's Cryptocurrency Malware
AA21-042A : Compromise of U.S. Water Treatment Facility
AA21-008A : Detecting Post-Compromise Threat Activity in Microsoft Cloud Environments
AA20-352A : Advanced Persistent Threat Compromise of Government Agencies, Critical Infrastructure, and Private Sector Organizations
AA20-345A : Cyber Actors Target K-12 Distance Learning Education to Cause Disruptions and Steal Data
AA20-336A : Advanced Persistent Threat Actors Targeting U.S. Think Tanks
AA20-304A : Iranian Advanced Persistent Threat Actor Identified Obtaining Voter Registration Data
AA20-302A : Ransomware Activity Targeting the Healthcare and Public Health Sector
AA20-301A : North Korean Advanced Persistent Threat Focus: Kimsuky
AA20-296B : Iranian Advanced Persistent Threat Actors Threaten Election-Related Systems
AA20-296A : Russian State-Sponsored Advanced Persistent Threat Actor Compromises U.S. Government Targets
AA20-283A : APT Actors Chaining Vulnerabilities Against SLTT, Critical Infrastructure, and Elections Organizations
AA20-280A : Emotet Malware
AA20-275A : Potential for China Cyber Response to Heightened U.S.–China Tensions
AA20-266A : LokiBot Malware
AA20-259A : Iran-Based Threat Actor Exploits VPN Vulnerabilities
AA20-258A : Chinese Ministry of State Security-Affiliated Cyber Threat Actor Activity

Here are some other popular government sites that provide threat intelligence information:

- CISA's Computer Emergency Readiness Team (CERT) site: us-cert.cisa.gov
- The U.S. Department of Defense Cyber Crime Center site: www.dc3.mil
- CISA's Automated Indicator Sharing (AIS) program, www.dhs.gov/cisa/automated-indicator-sharing-ais, and their Information Sharing and Analysis Organizations program, www.dhs.gov/cisa/information-sharing-and-analysis-organizations-isaos

Many countries provide their own cybersecurity sites, like the Australian Signals Directorate's Cyber Security Centre: www.cyber.gov.au. You should become familiar with major intelligence providers, worldwide and for each country you operate in or work with.

These are some major vendor websites:

- Microsoft's threat intelligence blog: www.microsoft.com/security/blog/tag/threat-intelligence
- Cisco's threat security site (https://tools.cisco.com/security/center/home.x), which includes an experts' blog with threat research information as well as the Cisco Talos reputation lookup tool (talosintelligence.com)

Here are several helpful public sources:

- The SANS Internet Storm Center (isc.sans.edu) provides timely reporting on current Internet threat conditions.
- VirusShare (virusshare.com) contains details about malware uploaded to VirusTotal.
- Spamhaus (www.spamhaus.org) focuses on block lists, including spam via the Spamhaus Block List (SBL), hijacked and compromised computers on the Exploits Block List (XBL), the Policy Block List (PBL), the Don't Route or Peer lists (DROP) listing netblocks that you may not want to allow traffic from, and a variety of other information.

These are just a small portion of the open source intelligence resources available to security practitioners, but they give you a good idea of what is available.

Exploring the Dark Web

The *dark web* is a network run over standard Internet connections but using multiple layers of encryption to provide anonymous communication. Hackers often use sites on the dark web to share information and sell credentials and other data stolen during their attacks.

Threat intelligence teams should familiarize themselves with the dark web and include searches of dark web marketplaces for credentials belonging to their organization or its

(continues)

(continued)

clients. The sudden appearance of credentials on dark web marketplaces likely indicates that a successful attack took place and requires further investigation.

You can access the dark web using the Tor browser. You'll find more information on the Tor browser at the Tor Project website: www.`torproject.org`.

Proprietary and Closed Source Intelligence

Commercial security vendors, government organizations, and other security-centric organizations also create and make use of proprietary, or *closed source intelligence*. They do their own information gathering and research, and they may use custom tools, analysis models, or other proprietary methods to gather, curate, and maintain their threat feeds.

There are a number of reasons that proprietary threat intelligence may be used. The organization may want to keep their threat data secret, they may want to sell or license it and their methods and sources are their trade secrets, or they may not want to take the chance that threat actors will learn about the data they are gathering.

Commercial closed source intelligence is often part of a service offering, which can be a compelling resource for security professionals. The sheer amount of data available via open source threat intelligence feeds can be overwhelming for many organizations. Combing through threat feeds to identify relevant threats, and then ensuring that they are both well defined and applied appropriately for your organization, can require massive amounts of effort. Validating threat data can be difficult in many cases, and once you are done making sure you have quality threat data, you still have to do something with it!

When a Threat Feed Fails

The authors of this book learned a lesson about up-to-date threat feeds a number of years ago after working with an IDS and IPS vendor. The vendor promised up-to-date feeds and signatures for current issues, but they tended to run behind other vendors in the marketplace. In one case, a critical Microsoft vulnerability was announced, and exploit code was available from Microsoft and in active use in the industry within less than 48 hours. Despite repeated queries, the vendor did not provide detection rules for over two weeks. Unfortunately, manual creation of rules on this vendor's platform did not work well, resulting in exposure of systems that should have been protected.

It is critical that you have reliable, up-do-date feeds to avoid situations like this. You may want to have multiple feeds that you can check against each other—often one feed may be faster or release information sooner, so multiple good-quality, reliable feeds can be a big help!

Threat maps provide a geographic view of threat intelligence. Many security vendors offer high-level maps that provide real-time insight into the cybersecurity threat landscape. For example, FireEye offers the public threat map shown in Figure 4.4 at

`www.fireeye.com/cyber-map/threat-map.html`

FIGURE 4.4   FireEye Cybersecurity Threat Map

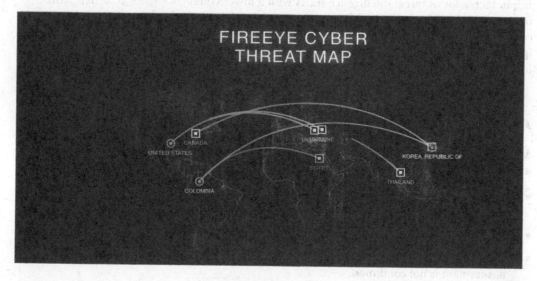

Organizations may also use threat-mapping information to gain insight into the sources of attacks aimed directly at their networks. However, threat map information should always be taken with a grain of salt because geographic attribution is notoriously unreliable. Attackers often relay their attacks through cloud services and other compromised networks, hiding their true geographic location from threat analysis tools.

Assessing Threat Intelligence

Regardless of the source of your threat intelligence information, you need to assess it. A number of common factors come into play when you assess a threat intelligence source or a specific threat intelligence notification:

- Is it timely? A feed that is operating on delay can cause you to miss a threat or to react after the threat is no longer relevant.

- Is the information accurate? Can you rely on what it says, and how likely is it that the assessment is valid? Does it rely on a single source or multiple sources? How often are those sources correct?

■   Is the information relevant? If it describes the wrong platform, software, or reason for the organization to be targeted, the data may be very timely, very accurate, and completely irrelevant to your organization.

One way to summarize the threat intelligence assessment data is via a *confidence score*. Confidence scores allow organizations to filter and use threat intelligence based on how much trust they can give it. That doesn't mean that lower confidence information isn't useful; in fact, a lot of threat intelligence starts with a lower confidence score, and that score increases as the information solidifies and as additional sources of information confirm it or are able to do a full analysis. Low-confidence threat information shouldn't be completely ignored, but it also shouldn't be relied on to make important decisions without taking the low-confidence score into account.

Assessing the Confidence Level of Your Intelligence

Many threat feeds will include a confidence rating, along with a descriptive scale. For example, ThreatConnect uses six levels of confidence:

- Confirmed (90–100) uses independent sources or direct analysis to prove that the threat is real.

- Probable (70–89) relies on logical inference but does not directly confirm the threat.

- Possible (50–69) is used when some information agrees with the analysis but the assessment is not confirmed.

- Doubtful (30–49) is assigned when the assessment is possible but not the most likely option, or the assessment cannot be proven or disproven by the information that is available.

- Improbable (2–29) means that the assessment is possible but is not the most logical option, or it is refuted by other information that is available.

- Discredited (1) is used when the assessment has been confirmed to be inaccurate or incorrect.

You can read through all of ThreatConnect's rating system at threatconnect.com/blog/best-practices-indicator-rating-and-confidence.

Your organization may use a different scale—1–5, 1–10, and High/Medium/Low scales are all commonly used to allow threat intelligence users to quickly assess the quality of the assessment and its underlying data.

Threat Indicator Management and Exchange

Managing threat information at any scale requires standardization and tooling to allow the threat information to be processed and used in automated ways. Indicator management can be much easier with a defined set of terms. That's where structured markup languages like STIX and OpenIOC come in.

Structured Threat Information Expression (STIX) is an XML language originally sponsored by the U.S. Department of Homeland Security. In its current version, STIX 2.0 defines 12 STIX domain objects, including things like attack patterns, identities, malware, threat actors, and tools. These objects are then related to each other by one of two STIX relationship object models: either as a relationship or a sighting. A STIX 2.0 JSON description of a threat actor might read as follows:

```
{
 "type": "threat-actor",
 "created": "2019-10-20T19:17:05.000Z",
 "modified": "2019-10-21T12:22:20.000Z",
 "labels": [ "crime-syndicate"],
 "name": "Evil Maid, Inc",
 "description": "Threat actors with access to hotel rooms",
 "aliases": ["Local USB threats"],
 "goals": ["Gain physical access to devices", "Acquire data"],
 "sophistication": "intermediate",
 "resource_level": "government",
 "primary_motivation": "organizational-gain"
}
```

Fields like sophistication and resource level use defined vocabulary options to allow STIX 2.0 users to consistently use the data as part of automated and manual systems.

TIP Using a single threat feed can leave you in the dark! Many organizations leverage multiple threat feeds to get the most up-to-date information. Thread feed combination can also be challenging since threat feeds may not use the same format, classification model, or other elements. You can work around this issue by finding sources that already combine multiple feeds or by finding feeds that use the same description frameworks, like STIX.

Since its creation, STIX has been handed off to the Organization for the Advancement of Structured Information Standards (OASIS), an international nonprofit consortium that maintains many other projects related to information formatting, including XML and HTML.

A companion to STIX is the *Trusted Automated Exchange of Intelligence Information (TAXII)* protocol. TAXII is intended to allow cyberthreat information to be communicated at the application layer via HTTPS. TAXII is specifically designed to support STIX data exchange. You can read more about both STIX and TAXII in detail at the OASIS GitHub documentation site: oasis-open.github.io/cti-documentation.

Another option is the *Open Indicators of Compromise (OpenIOC)* format. Like STIX, OpenIOC is an XML-based framework. The OpenIOC schema was developed by Mandiant, and it uses Mandiant's indicators for its base framework. A typical IOC includes metadata such as the author, the name of the IOC, and a description of the indicator. The full definition of the IOC may also include details of the actual compromise(s) that led to the indicator's discovery.

Public and Private Information Sharing Centers

In addition to threat intelligence vendors and resources, threat intelligence communities have been created to share threat information. In the United States, organizations known as Information Sharing and Analysis Centers (ISACs) help infrastructure owners and operators share threat information and provide tools and assistance to their members. The National Council of ISACs lists the sector-based ISACs at www.nationalisacs.org/member-isacs-3.

The ISAC concept was introduced in 1998, as part of Presidential Decision Directive-63 (PDD-63), which asked critical infrastructure sectors to establish organizations to share information about threats and vulnerabilities. ISACs operate on a trust model, allowing in-depth sharing of threat information for both physical threats and cyberthreats. Most ISACs operate 24/7, providing ISAC members in their sector with incident response and threat analysis.

In addition to ISACs, there are specific U.S. agencies or department partners for each critical infrastructure area. A list breaking them down by sector can be found at www.dhs.gov/cisa/critical-infrastructure-sectors.

Outside the United States, government bodies and agencies with similar responsibilities exist in many countries. The UK Centre for the Protection of National Infrastructure (www.cpni.gov.uk) is tasked with providing threat information, resources, and guidance to industry and academia as well as to other parts of the government and law enforcement.

Conducting Your Own Research

As a security professional, you should continue to conduct your own research into emerging cybersecurity threats. Here are sources you might consult as you build your threat research toolkit:

- Vendor security information websites.
- Vulnerability and threat feeds from vendors, government agencies, and private organizations.
- Academic journals and technical publications, such as Internet Request for Comments (RFC) documents. RFC documents are particularly informative because they contain the detailed technical specifications for Internet protocols.
- Professional conferences and local industry group meetings.
- Social media accounts of prominent security professionals.

As you reference these sources, keep an eye out for information on adversary *tactics, techniques, and procedures (TTPs)*. Learning more about the ways that attackers function allows you to improve your own threat intelligence program.

Summary

Cybersecurity professionals must have a strong working understanding of the threat landscape in order to assess the risks facing their organizations and the controls required to mitigate those risks. Cybersecurity threats may be classified based on their internal or external status, their level of sophistication and capability, their resources and funding, and their intent and motivation.

Threat actors take many forms, ranging from relatively unsophisticated script kiddies who are simply seeking the thrill of a successful hack to advanced nation-state actors who use cyberattacks as a military weapon to achieve political advantage. Hacktivists, criminal syndicates, competitors, and other threat actors may all target the same organizations for different reasons.

Cyberattacks come through a variety of threat vectors. The most common vectors include email and social media; other attacks may come through direct physical access, supply chain exploits, network-based attacks, and other vectors. Organizations should build robust threat intelligence programs to help them stay abreast of emerging threats and adapt their controls to function in a changing environment.

Exam Essentials

Be able to describe several key attributes in which threat actors differ. We can classify threat actors using four major criteria. First, threat actors may be internal to the organization, or they may come from external sources. Second, threat actors differ in their level of sophistication and capability. Third, they differ in their available resources and funding. Finally, different threat actors have different motivations and levels of intent.

Know the many different sources of threat actors. Threat actors may be very simplistic in their techniques, such as script kiddies using exploit code written by others, or quite sophisticated, such as the advanced persistent threat posed by nation-state actors and criminal syndicates. Hacktivists may seek to carry out political agendas, whereas competitors may seek financial gain. We can group hackers into white-hat, gray-hat, and black-hat categories based on their motivation and authorization.

Be able to explain how attackers exploit different vectors to gain initial access to an organization. Attackers may attempt to gain initial access to an organization remotely over the Internet, through a wireless connection, or by attempting direct physical access. They may also approach employees over email or social media. Attackers may seek to use removable media to trick employees into unintentionally compromising their networks, or they may seek to spread exploits through cloud services. Sophisticated attackers may attempt to interfere with an organization's supply chain.

Know how threat intelligence provides organizations with valuable insight into the threat landscape.   Security teams may leverage threat intelligence from public and private sources to learn about current threats and vulnerabilities. They may seek out detailed indicators of compromise and perform predictive analytics on their own data. Threat intelligence teams often supplement open source and closed source intelligence that they obtain externally with their own research.

Be able to explain why security teams must monitor supply chain risks.   Modern enterprises depend on hardware, software, and cloud service vendors to deliver IT services to their internal and external customers. Vendor management techniques protect the supply chain against attackers seeking to compromise these external links into an organization's network. Security professionals should pay particular attention to risks posed by outsourced code development, cloud data storage, and integration between external and internal systems.

Review Questions

1. Which of the following measures is not commonly used to assess threat intelligence?

   A. Timeliness

   B. Detail

   C. Accuracy

   D. Relevance

2. What language is STIX based on?

   A. PHP

   B. HTML

   C. XML

   D. Python

3. Kolin is a penetration tester who works for a cybersecurity company. His firm was hired to conduct a penetration test against a health-care system, and Kolin is working to gain access to the systems belonging to a hospital in that system. What term best describes Kolin's work?

   A. White hat

   B. Gray hat

   C. Green hat

   D. Black hat

4. Which one of the following attackers is most likely to be associated with an APT?

   A. Nation-state actor

   B. Hacktivist

   C. Script kiddie

   D. Insider

5. What organizations did the U.S. government help create to share knowledge between organizations in specific verticals?

   A. DHS

   B. SANS

   C. CERTS

   D. ISACs

6. Which of the following threat actors typically has the greatest access to resources?

   A. Nation-state actors

   B. Organized crime

   C. Hacktivists

   D. Insider threats

7. Of the threat vectors shown here, which one is most commonly exploited by attackers who are at a distant location?

   A. Email

   B. Direct access

   C. Wireless

   D. Removable media

8. Which one of the following is the best example of a hacktivist group?

   A. Chinese military

   B. U.S. government

   C. Russian mafia

   D. Anonymous

9. What type of assessment is particularly useful for identifying insider threats?

   A. Behavioral

   B. Instinctual

   C. Habitual

   D. IOCs

10. Cindy wants to send threat information via a standardized protocol specifically designed to exchange cyberthreat information. What should she choose?

    A. STIX 1.0

    B. OpenIOC

    C. STIX 2.0

    D. TAXII

11. Greg believes that an attacker may have installed malicious firmware in a network device before it was provided to his organization by the supplier. What type of threat vector best describes this attack?

    A. Supply chain

    B. Removable media

    C. Cloud

    D. Direct access

12. Ken is conducting threat research on Transport Layer Security (TLS) and would like to consult the authoritative reference for the protocol's technical specification. What resource would best meet his needs?

    A. Academic journal

    B. Internet RFCs

    C. Subject matter experts

    D. Textbooks

13. Wendy is scanning cloud-based repositories for sensitive information. Which one of the following should concern her most if discovered in a public repository?

    A. Product manuals

    B. Source code

    C. API keys

    D. Open source data

14. Which one of the following threat research tools is used to visually display information about the location of threat actors?

    A. Threat map

    B. Predictive analysis

    C. Vulnerability feed

    D. STIX

15. Vince recently received the hash values of malicious software that several other firms in his industry found installed on their systems after a compromise. What term best describes this information?

    A. Vulnerability feed

    B. IoC

    C. TTP

    D. RFC

16. Ursula recently discovered that a group of developers are sharing information over a messaging tool provided by a cloud vendor but not sanctioned by her organization. What term best describes this use of technology?

    A. Shadow IT

    B. System integration

    C. Vendor management

    D. Data exfiltration

17. Tom's organization recently learned that his vendor is discontinuing support for their customer relationship management (CRM) system. What should concern Tom the most from a security perspective?

    A. Unavailability of future patches

    B. Lack of technical support

    C. Theft of customer information

    D. Increased costs

18. Which one of the following information sources would not be considered an OSINT source?

    A. DNS lookup

    B. Search engine research

    C. Port scans

    D. WHOIS queries

19. Edward Snowden was a government contractor who disclosed sensitive government documents to journalists to uncover what he believed were unethical activities. Which two of the following terms best describe Snowden's activities? (Choose two.)

   A. Insider

   B. State actor

   C. Hacktivist

   D. APT

   E. Organized crime

20. Renee is a cybersecurity hobbyist. She receives an email about a new web-based grading system being used by her son's school and she visits the site. She notices that the URL for the site looks like this:

`https://www.myschool.edu/grades.php&studentID=1023425`

She realizes that 1023425 is her son's student ID number and then attempts to access the following similar URLs:

`https://www.myschool.edu/grades.php&studentID=1023423`

`https://www.myschool.edu/grades.php&studentID=1023424`

`https://www.myschool.edu/grades.php&studentID=1023426`

`https://www.myschool.edu/grades.php&studentID=1023427`

When she does so, she accesses the records of other students. She closes the records and immediately informs the school principal of the vulnerability. What term best describes Renee's work?

   A. White-hat hacking

   B. Green-hat hacking

   C. Gray-hat hacking

   D. Black-hat hacking

Chapter
5

Information Security Program Development and Management

THE CERTIFIED INFORMATION SECURITY MANAGER (CISM) DOMAINS AND SUBTOPICS COVERED IN THIS CHAPTER INCLUDE:

✓ **Domain 3: Information Security Program**

- **A. Information Security Program Development**

    - **3A1. Information Security Program Resources (e.g. people, tools, technologies)**

    - **3A5. Information Security Program Metrics**

- **B. Information Security Program Management**

    - **3B4. Information Security Awareness and Training**

    - **3B5. Management of External Services (e.g., providers, suppliers, third parties, fourth parties)**

    - **3B6. Information Security Program Communications and Reporting**

THE CERTIFIED INFORMATION SECURITY MANAGER (CISM) SUPPORTING TASKS COVERED IN THIS CHAPTER INCLUDE:

✓ **9. Compile and present reports to key stakeholders on the activities, trends, and overall effectiveness of the information security program.**

✓ **10. Evaluate and report information security metrics to key stakeholders.**

✓ **11. Establish and/or maintain the information security program in alignment with the information security strategy.**

✓ **12. Align the information security program with the operational objectives of other business functions.**

✓ **13. Establish and maintain information security processes and resources to execute the information security program.**

✓ **15. Establish, promote, and maintain a program for information security awareness and training.**

✓ **16. Integrate information security requirements into organizational processes to maintain the organization's security strategy.**

✓ **17. Integrate information security requirements into contracts and activities of external parties.**

✓ **18. Monitor external parties' adherence to established security requirements.**

✓ **19. Define and monitor management and operational metrics for the information security program.**

The main responsibility of the information security manager is to develop, implement, and maintain an information security program that enumerates and satisfies the organization's security objectives. The work involved in this effort will vary based on the organization's degree of cybersecurity maturity and may include efforts to both enhance and maintain the current state of affairs.

In this chapter, you will learn about the process used to establish a new information security program and maintain an existing program. You will learn how security awareness and training efforts provide individuals at all levels of the organization with the knowledge they need to support security objectives. You will discover how to manage a cybersecurity budget and how to effectively integrate an information security program with other critical business functions.

Information Security Programs

The main responsibility of the chief information security officer (CISO) or other senior-most information security leader in an organization is to develop, implement, and maintain the organization's *information security program*. This program is the collection of policies, standards, processes, activities, and projects that work together to achieve the goals set forth in the organization's information security strategy.

In Chapter 1, "Today's Information Security Manager," you learned about the process that the organization follows to develop an information security strategy. You can think of the information security program as where that strategy is realized. Security leaders and managers work with their teams and other stakeholders to advance efforts that seek to realize the vision described in that strategy. Depending on the current state of the organization, this effort may involve significant initiatives to design and implementation of new controls, projects aimed at enhancing existing controls, and the routine operational work that ensures controls continue to function efficiently and effectively. The information security program is the work performed by the information security team.

Establishing a New Program

New cybersecurity managers in an organization without a mature security function may find themselves developing a program from the ground up. This effort should begin with the development of an information security strategy that identifies appropriate standards, conducts a gap analysis, and understands the threat environment, as discussed in Chapter 1.

With that strategy in hand, managers may begin to outline the set of initiatives required to bring the organization from its current state to the desired state of information security.

As they establish the program, they should ensure that its work remains aligned with the information security strategy that guides their effort.

Defining Program Scope

The first step in developing a new information security program is creating a clear statement of the program's *scope*. This is the definition of the activities that are (and are not) included in the program's work. There are two important elements to the program's scope:

- The type of security objectives that are included in the program. Does the program cover all aspects of information security or are there exceptions? For example, physical security and the security of paper documents might be excluded from the information security program if they are covered by other work.

- The portion of the organization covered by the information security program. A security program might cover the entire organization, or its work might be limited to a business unit or other portion of the organizational structure.

In most cases, the scope statement may be concise, communicating the nature of the program clearly to all employees. For example, a broadly defined security program might use this scope statement:

> The information security program is responsible for securing the confidentiality, integrity, and availability of all information stored, processed, or transmitted by the organization in any form: physical or digital.

If some security objectives are omitted from the scope of the program, this may be mentioned explicitly. For example, if the security program does not include paper records or physical security, the program's scope might be defined as follows:

> The information security program is responsible for securing the confidentiality, integrity, and availability of all information stored, processed, or transmitted by the organization in digital form.

If the program applies only to a specific area of the organization or excludes a specific area of the organization, this would also be included in the scope statement. For example, many universities have associated health systems and those health systems often have separate information security functions. In that situation, the university's main information security program might have a scope statement that describes this scope limitation:

> The information security program is responsible for securing the confidentiality, integrity, and availability of all information stored, processed, or transmitted by the organization in any form: physical or digital. The program does not apply to elements of the University Health System governed by the UHS Cybersecurity Program.

Developing a Program Charter

With a scope statement in hand, information security managers may then begin creating the information security program *charter*. The charter is the organizing document for the cybersecurity program. Building on the scope, the charter outlines the parameters under which the program will function. Common components of an information security program charter include the following:

- A *scope statement* identifying the scope of the information security program. This is simply reiterating the scope statement created for the program in a location where all interested stakeholders may reference it.

- A *business purpose* clearly linking the information security program objectives to business objectives. For example, the University of Pennsylvania uses this business purpose statement in their Information Security and Privacy Program Charter (`www.isc.upenn.edu/information-security-and-privacy-program-charter`):

  > Penn is committed to preeminence in research, teaching, and service. As a result, Penn owns significant assets in the form of information. Penn's informational assets include, but are not limited to, student education records, employment records, financial information, research data, protected health information, alumni and donor information, Penn operational data, Penn intellectual property, and other data relating to Penn's infrastructure, technology resources, and information security. The improper use of such information, the unauthorized or inadvertent disclosure, alteration or destruction of information assets, or a significant interruption in their availability, can disrupt Penn's ability to fulfill its mission. Such actions can also result in regulatory, legal, financial and/or reputational risk to Penn and to the individuals whose data Penn maintains.

- A *statement of authority* for the program, normally delegating institutional authority to a specific individual. For example, the charter for the Wayne State University Information Security Program (`https://tech.wayne.edu/docs/wsu-security-program-charter.pdf`) does this as follows:

  > The Sr. Director of Information Security under the division of Computing & Information Technology is designated as the Chief Information Security Officer ("Program Officer") responsible for coordinating and overseeing the Information Security Program. The Program Officer may designate other representatives of the University to oversee and coordinate portions of the program.

- *Roles and responsibilities* for other stakeholders who have the responsibility to help carry out the activities of the information security program. These may include:
  - Senior leaders
  - Information security team members
  - Other technologists
  - Internal and external auditors
  - Data owners, stewards, and custodians
  - Other employees and stakeholders

- *Governance structure and processes* that will continue to ensure that the organization's information security program remains in alignment with the organization's business goals.

- *Program documentation procedures* that formalize how the organization will establish, communicate, and maintain information security standards, guidelines, procedures, and other documentation.

- *Enforcement mechanisms* that establish how the organization will guide and enforce compliance with information security policies and provide consequences for individuals and units that fail to comply with information security program requirements.

- A *review process* that will be conducted on a periodic basis to ensure that the information security program continues to achieve the information security objectives, that those information security objectives continue to align with business objectives, and that the information security program is functioning properly.

- An *approval statement* that clearly describes the authority under which the program is enacted. This is normally done through the signature of the CEO or other senior leader. This approval statement gives force to the delegation of authority and other details outlined in the charter.

The specific contents of any organization's information security program charter will depend on the organization's business and security objectives, operational culture, and other factors. Rather than being overly concerned about the specific section headings included in a charter, information security managers should ensure that the charter provides the framework under which they may effectively implement the program.

Maintaining Business Alignment

The role of cybersecurity programs is to enable organizations to meet their business objectives while protecting the confidentiality, integrity, and availability of information and systems. To achieve this purpose, cybersecurity managers must have an intimate understanding of the business and work diligently to align security efforts with business needs.

For example, let's consider a case where security and business objectives might be misaligned. Imagine the security program for an eBook publisher. A CISO might look at this publisher, analyze industry best practices, and decide to advocate for a security policy that mandates that all access to corporate resources requires multifactor authentication. That's a common enough security practice, and many organizations do enforce this type of policy today.

However, this type of policy might not be compatible with the normal business activity of a book publisher. They sell digital books to readers who want to access them on computers, tablets, and smartphones. If the organization's multifactor authentication policy applies to *all* access to the company's information, that would include their books and require that all of their customers use multifactor authentication to read their books. That's not a very appealing concept for a customer and might cause them to simply take their business elsewhere. In this case, we have a misalignment between the business objective of providing customers with simple, easy access to their books, and the security objective of multifactor authentication.

The publisher might correct this misalignment by clarifying the security objective to apply only to sensitive corporate information and to specifically exclude customer access to books. This newly aligned objective better balances security requirements and business goals.

Steering committees are a great way to facilitate alignment between security and business objectives. The security manager can convene a group that represents business units and get their input in the development of security plans. This group's feedback can help avoid security missteps like the one made by our eBook publisher.

In addition to using steering committees, security teams should closely monitor the business's operational activity to watch for signs of misalignment. As issues crop up, they should be entered into the organization's issue tracking tool and monitored closely until they are satisfactorily resolved.

The alignment of security and business objectives is not a one-time task. It's an ongoing activity that must be a priority of security teams to ensure that these objectives remain aligned as business needs and the security landscape evolve.

Maintaining an Existing Program

Once an organization has an existing information security program, information security managers must operate and maintain that program. This involves monitoring the program to ensure that it remains in alignment with business objectives and the information security strategy as well as providing regular reporting to stakeholders.

Metrics and Monitoring

Organizations evaluate their security programs through the use of *metrics* that assess the efficiency and effectiveness of critical security controls. Metrics are measurements that provide insight into the health of a security program both at a single point in time and on a long-term basis.

It's critical that organizations define the metrics and performance measurements they will use in advance of reporting the data. This ensures the integrity of the process and prevents cherry-picking of favorable results for reporting purposes.

Security programs use three primary types of metrics to demonstrate their effectiveness and the state of the organization's security controls. These key indicators offer program management and operational metrics that evaluate the effectiveness and efficiency of the information security program:

- *Key performance indicators (KPIs)* are metrics that demonstrate the success of the security program in achieving its objectives. KPIs are mutually agreed-upon measures that evaluate whether a security program is meeting its defined goals. Generally speaking, KPIs are a look back at historical performance, providing a measuring stick to evaluate the past success of the program.

- *Key goal indicators (KGIs)* are similar to KPIs but measure progress toward defined goals. For example, if an organization has a goal to eliminate all stored Social Security numbers (SSNs), a KGI might track the percentage of SSNs that have been removed.

- *Key risk indicators (KRIs)* are measures that seek to quantify the security risk facing an organization. KRIs, unlike KPIs and KGIs, are a look forward instead of back. They attempt to show how much risk exists that may jeopardize the future security of the organization.

Key Performance Indicators (KPIs)

Every organization will have to define its own KPIs, but the Information Technology Infrastructure Library (ITIL) framework provides a good starting point. They offer nine KPIs that security programs may choose to leverage:

- Percentage of the decrease in security breaches reported to the service desk
- Percentage of the decrease in the impact of security breaches
- Percentage of the increase in SLAs with appropriate security clauses
- Number of preventive security measures the organization implemented in response to security threats
- Amount of elapsed time between the identification of a security threat and the implementation of an appropriate control
- Number of major security incidents
- Number of security incidents that created service outages or impairments
- Number of security test, training, and awareness events that took place
- Number of shortcomings identified during security tests

Key Risk Indicators (KRIs)

KRIs must also be customized to the needs of the organization. ISACA recommends selecting KRIs based on four criteria:

- The potential *impact* of the KRI, or the likelihood that the indicator will identify potential risks that are significant to the business
- The *effort* required to implement, measure, and support the indicator on an ongoing basis
- The *reliability* of the indicator as a good predictor of risk
- The *sensitivity* of the indicator, meaning that it is able to accurately capture variances in the risk

Selecting and monitoring a strong set of KPIs and KRIs provides business and technology leaders with a solid assessment of the state of their security programs.

Reporting

Information security managers are responsible not only for developing and monitoring the key metrics of their security programs, but also for ensuring that key stakeholders remain aware of the program's status.

One common mistake made by information security managers is to develop a dashboard or web page with updated metrics and then simply inform stakeholders that they may view those metrics whenever they like. This approach may seem open and transparent, but it suffers from two major drawbacks:

- Stakeholders who are not involved in security on a day-to-day basis are unlikely to revisit the site unless prompted to do so periodically.

- Providing metrics is only one piece of the picture. Security managers should also provide context around those metrics to explain changes and update stakeholders on the progress of the program.

Managers should compile and present reports to key stakeholders on the activities, trends, and overall effectiveness of the information security program and underlying business processes. They may do this using formal written reports, in-person or recorded briefings, and/or informal email updates. In most cases, managers will use a mixture of these methods in a manner that is appropriate for the needs and culture of their organization.

Security Awareness and Training

The success of a security program depends on the behavior (both actions and inaction) of many different people. Security training and awareness programs help ensure that employees and other stakeholders are aware of their information security responsibilities and that those responsibilities remain top-of-mind. Information security managers are responsible for establishing, promoting, and maintaining an information security training and awareness program to foster an effective security culture in their organizations.

User Training

Users within your organization should receive regular *security training* to ensure that they understand the risks associated with your computing environment and their role in minimizing those risks. Strong training programs take advantage of a diversity of training techniques, including the use of *computer-based training (CBT)*.

Not every user requires the same level of training. Organizations should use *role-based training* to make sure that individuals receive the appropriate level of training based on their job responsibilities. For example, a systems administrator should receive detailed and highly technical training, whereas a customer service representative requires less technical training with a greater focus on social engineering and pretexting attacks that they may encounter in their work.

Phishing attacks often target users at all levels of the organization, and every security awareness program should include specific antiphishing campaigns designed to help users recognize suspicious requests and respond appropriately. These campaigns often involve the use of *phishing simulations*, which send users fake phishing messages to test their skills. Users who click on the simulated phishing message are sent to a training program designed to help them better recognize fraudulent messages.

Security awareness training also commonly incorporates elements of *gamification*, designed to make training more enjoyable and help users retain the message of the campaign. *Capture the flag (CTF)* exercises are a great example of this. CTF programs pit technologists against one another in an attempt to attack a system and achieve a specific goal, such as stealing a sensitive file. Participants in the CTF exercise gain an appreciation for attacker techniques and learn how to better defend their own systems against similar attacks.

You'll also want to think about the frequency of your training efforts. You'll need to balance the time required to conduct training with the benefit from reminding users of their responsibilities. One approach used by many organizations is to conduct initial training whenever an employee joins the organization or assumes new job responsibilities and then use annual refresher training to cover the same material and update users on new threats and controls.

The team responsible for providing security training should review materials on a regular basis to ensure that the content remains relevant. Changes in the security landscape and the organization's business may require updating the material to remain fresh and relevant.

Role-Based Training

All users should receive some degree of security education, but organizations should also customize training to meet specific role-based requirements. For example, employees handling credit card information should receive training on PCI DSS requirements. Human resources team members should be trained on handling personally identifiable information. IT staffers need specialized skills to implement security controls. Training should be custom-tailored to an individual's role in the organization.

Ongoing Awareness Efforts

In addition to formal training programs, an information security program should include *security awareness* efforts. These are less formal efforts that are designed to remind employees about the security lessons they've already learned. Unlike security training, awareness efforts don't require a commitment of time to sit down and learn new material. Instead, they use posters, videos, email messages, and similar techniques to keep security top-of-mind for those who've already learned the core lessons.

Figure 5.1 shows an example of a security awareness poster developed by the U.S. Department of Energy.

FIGURE 5.1   Security awareness poster

Source: U.S. Department of Energy

Managing the Information Security Team

Building and managing teams is one of the most often-overlooked aspects of an information security manager's responsibilities. When other leaders think about the security function, their minds often quickly turn to technology controls. They think about firewalls, ransomware, access controls, authentication systems, and the many technical trappings of a security program.

It's easy to lose sight of the fact that information security managers are also team managers. They're responsible for recruiting, retaining, motivating, and training the staff members who deliver on the objectives of the information security program. Without a trained and motivated team, the organization simply can't meet its security objectives.

Hiring Team Members

Hiring decisions are some of the most important decisions that security managers make and, in many cases, they're made in haste. Think about this purely from a financial perspective. It's easy for a senior security hire to command a salary of $150,000. With benefits, that number can easily creep up to $200,000. If the person you hire stays with the company for five years, that makes the hire a million-dollar decision.

Putting aside the financial aspects of hiring decisions, the people you hire are the ones who will implement your security program. If you make bad hiring decisions, you jeopardize your ability to meet your program's objectives and put the organization's security at risk. Therefore, managers should spend significant time on hiring decisions to ensure they're confident that they are hiring the right person for each opening, rather than simply trying to fill openings. If you settle for a mediocre candidate, you'll regret that decision later.

Developing the Security Team

Once you have staff on board, it's your responsibility as a manager to motivate, train, and retain that personnel to run your security program effectively. As you do this, you should seek to manage the skills of your security team to both challenge your staff and ensure that you have a cross-trained team ready to pick up new responsibilities if someone leaves the organization.

There are two important components to your skill set development program:

- *Training programs* help employees keep their skills current and develop skills in new areas of cybersecurity. You should allocate a portion of your budget to provide each employee with the training they need to keep their skills sharp and advance in their profession.

- *Certifications* help employees validate their skills and are an important recruiting and retention tool. You recognize that or you wouldn't be reading a cybersecurity certification book right now! As you develop the skills of your employees, provide them with opportunities to pursue certifications that both interest them and advance the organization's security objectives.

Time spent developing your team is time well spent. The best cybersecurity managers dedicate a significant portion of their time to attracting and retaining talented teams.

Managing the Security Budget

Security managers also have financial responsibility for their organization's security program. This means that they must participate in developing, implementing, and monitoring a budget.

Many security managers came up through the technical ranks and find themselves in their first management role, unfamiliar with many of the nontechnical skills required for the job. If that's your situation, you might find yourself unfamiliar with the skills and tools that can assist you with this task.

Organizational Budgeting

A *budget* is just a financial plan for the team. It outlines how much money is available to you over the course of the year and how you plan to spend that money.

Most organizations go through an annual budget planning cycle where the organization's leadership decides the following year's budget a few months before the year begins. This means that you'll have to work backward and will often find yourself preparing a budget at least six months in advance of it going into effect. Or, looking at it another way, depending on where you are in the budget cycle, it could be up to 18 months until the next time that you receive a budget adjustment. That's why planning in advance is so important.

As you go through the budget planning process, you'll need to follow the guidelines set by your organization. There are two major approaches to budgeting:

- *Incremental budgeting* approaches start with the prior year's budget and then make adjustments by either raising or lowering the budget. If your organization uses this approach, you'll frequently hear phrases like "We have a 3% budget increase this year" or "We're cutting the budget by 5%." It's up to the manager to advocate for additional budget and to make the new numbers work.

- *Zero-based budgeting* approaches begin from zero each year, and managers are asked to justify their entire budget, rather than start with the assumption that they will have the same amount of funding as they did the previous year.

Fiscal Years

There's one more important concept in budget planning that you should know. Budgets work on the concept of a *fiscal year*. Every organization selects their own fiscal year that is 12 months long, and it may or may not coincide with the calendar year. When the organization sets budgets and provides financial reporting, it does so based on the fiscal year rather than the calendar year.

For example, an organization might have a fiscal year that begins on July 1. Figure 5.2 illustrates how that would work in calendar years 2021 and 2022.

FIGURE 5.2   Relationship between calendar years and fiscal years

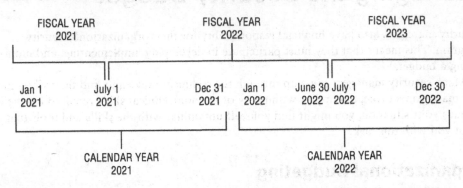

If the new fiscal year begins on July 1, the organization moves into fiscal year 2021 (abbreviated FY21) on July 1, 2020, and that fiscal year runs through June 30, 2021. The next day, July 1, 2021, marks the beginning of FY22.

In this approach, the first half of calendar year 2021 (abbreviated CY21) is actually the second half of FY20, which began in July 2019. So, in this approach, each calendar year is divided across two fiscal years. Budgets begin anew every July.

> **WARNING**   The example provided in this chapter of a July 1 fiscal year start date is just one possibility. Organizations may choose any start date they wish for their fiscal year and often do so to better align the fiscal year with the operating realities of their business.

You definitely need to understand the fiscal year used by your organization so that you can appropriately plan your budget. You don't want to run out of money early or leave money that you needed for a project on the table when a fiscal year rolls over.

Expense Types

There are two different types of expenses in the world of business budgeting: capital expenses and operational expenses. If you've ever heard anyone using the phrase "different flavors of money," this is what they're talking about. Money that falls into the capital expense budget typically can't be used for operational expenses, and vice versa. Therefore, it's important to understand each type of money and how it may be used.

Capital expenses (CapEx) are costs that an organization incurs as part of building out and maintaining its large assets. For example, if you buy or renovate a building, that's a fixed asset, and the costs associated with it are capital expenses.

Other examples of capital expenses are:

▪ Purchasing expensive computing equipment

▪ Buying vehicles

▪ Buying new multifunction printers

Operational expenses (OpEx) are those costs of running the business day to day that don't involve purchasing or maintaining an asset. The most common example of operational expenses are payroll costs. You're paying your employees to run your business, but you're not purchasing the employee, so your employees are not a financial asset. This makes payroll an operational expense.

Other examples of operational expenses are:

- Electricity costs
- Hardware maintenance agreements
- Office supplies

The line between capital and operational expenses can be a little fuzzy and will depend on your organization's financial practices. Some organizations use a dollar threshold to help differentiate between the two, whereas others have more complex guidelines. You should check with your financial accounting team for help sorting this out.

Both capital and operating expenses may be one-time or recurring. For example, your security team's payroll is a recurring operational expense, whereas the cost of hiring a security consultant to review your firewall rules is likely treated as a one-time operational expense. Similarly, the building of a new data center is a one-time capital expense whereas the replacement of your servers is a recurring capital expense.

Capital expenses and operating expenses are treated very differently by tax laws and financial reporting regulations. That's the reason that accountants are so concerned with differentiating between the two and why it's difficult to move money between capital and operating budgets in some organizations.

Budget Monitoring

Budget planning is typically an annual chore that follows a very well-defined lifecycle. However, a security manager's budget responsibility doesn't end once the planning cycle concludes. In fact, the work has only just begun. During the course of the year, security managers must monitor their budget and track expenses to ensure that they finish the year within expectations.

Clearly, it's a bad idea to exceed your budget. You might be spending money that doesn't exist, and at the very least, you're going to wind up in hot water with your boss. Security managers should keep close tabs on their budgets and make sure that they don't finish the year in the red with a budget shortfall.

The longer you are in business, the more likely it is that you will experience unexpected expenses. You might not be able to predict what unexpected expenses will come up, but it is a fairly safe bet that something you didn't expect will surface. Managers can compensate for this by setting aside a contingency budget designed to cover unexpected expenses.

Although it's definitely a bad idea to exceed your budget, that also doesn't mean that it's a good idea to leave a lot of money on the table. Unless there were very unusual circumstances, a large surplus at the end of the year probably means that you didn't plan very well. You don't run the risk of spending money that isn't there, but you are preventing your company from using those funds elsewhere. In financial terms, you're creating an opportunity cost by holding funds that the organization could use to take advantage of some other opportunity.

You'll need to develop your own patterns for budget monitoring and reporting. For example, you might begin by reviewing your budget and spending on a weekly basis. Over time, as you get comfortable with financial planning, you might back off to a biweekly or monthly schedule.

Integrating Security with Other Business Functions

Information security teams function within an organization that contains many other line-of-business and support functions. Just as security managers expect others in the organization to assist with the implementation of the security program, security teams must also work within the parameters set by other areas for their scope of control.

As a business leader, the CISO must understand how to align information security program requirements with those of other business functions. Aligning security objectives with the operational objectives of other business functions helps ensure that the information security program adds value to the business and protects its interests.

Procurement

The *procurement* function in an organization is responsible for acquiring the products and services that the organization needs to carry out its business. It normally consists of a team of contracting and vendor management specialists who assist other departments with purchases, providing subject matter expertise on contracting and negotiation, and ensuring that the purchase complies with the organization's requirements.

The acquisition of products and services always has the potential to create and influence information security risks. Therefore, it is crucial that information security managers work effectively with procurement teams to integrate information security requirements into their activities. This occurs at three significant steps in the vendor management lifecycle: vendor evaluation, contracting, and ongoing vendor management.

Vendor Evaluation

Vendors play an important role in the information technology operations of every organization. Whether it's the simple purchasing of hardware or software from an external company or the provision of cloud computing services from a strategic partner, vendors are integral in providing the IT services that we offer our customers. Security professionals must pay careful attention to managing these business partnerships in a way that protects the confidentiality, integrity, and availability of their organization's information and IT systems. This process, known as conducting *vendor due diligence*, protects us against many of the risks associated with acquiring hardware, software, and services.

Perhaps the most important rule of thumb is that you should always ensure that vendors follow security policies and procedures that are at least as effective as those you would apply in your own environment. Vendors extend your organization's technology environment and, if they handle data on your behalf, you should expect that they execute the same degree of care that you would in your own operations and meet your minimum security requirements. Otherwise, vendors may become the weak link in the supply chain and jeopardize your security objectives.

Security professionals charged with managing vendor relationships should follow consistent policies and procedures to efficiently and effectively evaluate vendors. It's not unusual for a large organization to add on dozens or even hundreds of new vendors in a single year, and organizations often change vendors due to pricing, functionality, or other concerns.

Depending on your organization's procurement environment, the evaluation of a new vendor may include anything from a formal *request for proposals (RFP)* to an informal evaluation and selection process. In either case, security should play an important role, contributing to the requirements sent to vendors and playing a role in the evaluation process.

During this evaluation, you should also assess the quality and effectiveness of the provider's own information security and risk management programs. What controls, methodologies, and policies do they have in place to control risks that might affect your organization?

Contracting

As organizations begin to increasingly use vendors for services that include the storage, processing, and transmission of sensitive information, they must pay careful attention to the vendor's information management practices. Data ownership issues often arise in supplier relationships, particularly when the vendor is creating information on behalf of the customer. Agreements put in place prior to beginning a new vendor relationship should contain clear language about data ownership.

In most cases, a customer will want to ensure that they retain uninhibited ownership of the information. They will also want contract terms that specify that the vendor's right to use the information is limited to activities performed on behalf of, and with the knowledge and consent of, the customer. In addition, customers should ensure that the contract includes language that requires the vendor to securely delete all customer information within an acceptable period of time after the relationship ends. Customers should also consider including contract language that provides them with the right to audit vendor compliance with the contract terms.

Customers should also include language in vendor agreements that prohibits the vendor from sharing customer information with third parties without explicit consent from the customer.

In cases where vendor personnel will come into contact with sensitive information and resources, the contract should ensure that those employees are subject to a rigorous personnel security program.

Finally, the customer should include data protection requirements in the contract. This is particularly important if the vendor will be the sole custodian of critical information belonging to the customer. The contract should specify that the vendor is responsible for

preserving the information and implementing appropriate fault tolerance and backup procedures to prevent data loss. In cases where the information is especially critical, the agreement
may even include provisions that specify the exact controls the vendor must put in place to
protect information.

These provisions should certainly be used when negotiating contracts with outsourced
service providers, but they are also suitable for use in formal relationships with joint ven-
tures, other business partners, and even customers.

Vendor and Supplier Management

Procurement teams are also responsible for managing relationships with existing vendors,
suppliers, and providers. These include organizations that range from the suppliers of your
IT hardware to the provider of your Internet connectivity.

 Remember that your vendors and suppliers also have vendors and
suppliers that help them provide services to you. If your business is
dependent upon the security of a third-party supplier, you also must
investigate the security of the fourth-party organizations that support
your supplier's operations.

Vendor Onboarding

The vendor onboarding process should include conversations between the vendor and the
customer that verify the details of the contract and ensure that everything gets off on the
right foot.

Onboarding often involves setting up the technical arrangements for data transfer, and
organizations should ensure that they are satisfied with the encryption technology and other
controls in place to protect information while in transit and maintain its security while at
rest in vendor systems.

The onboarding process should also include establishing procedures for security incident
notification. If the vendor experiences a security incident, the vendor should promptly notify
affected customers, and the channels for those communications should be clearly established.

Vendor Maintenance and Monitoring

After the vendor is set up and running, the security team's job is not over. The vendor should
then enter a maintenance phase where the customer continues to monitor security practices. This may include site visits and recurring conversations and the review of independent
audit and assessment reports.

The maintenance phase will likely also involve the handling of security incidents that
occur at the vendor's site. If the vendor never reports a security incident, this may be a red
flag, since almost every organization occasionally experiences a security breach of some kind.

Vendor Offboarding

All good things must eventually come to an end, and the reality is that even the most productive business relationships will terminate at some point. The offboarding process is the
final step in the vendor lifecycle. It includes ensuring that the vendor destroys all confidential
information in its possession and that the relationship is unwound in an orderly fashion.

Depending on business requirements, the lifecycle may then begin anew with the selection of a new vendor. Of course, it is always preferable to begin the vendor selection process for a new provider before terminating the relationship with an existing provider!

 If you'd like to explore this topic in more detail, you may wish to review ISO Standard 27036 (www.iso.org/standard/59689.html), which covers information security for supplier relationships. In particular, part 4 of the standard contains guidance on the security of cloud service providers.

Accounting

Information security managers also serve as financial managers, responsible for the management of a budget, as discussed earlier in this chapter. Therefore, security managers should have a strong understanding of their organization's accounting practices and the tools available to them to help manage their budgets.

In addition, accounting teams can often serve as a backstop to catch purchases of technology with security implications that did not go through the organization's formal procurement process. It is far more desirable to catch purchases before they occur and integrate security into the selection and implementation process, but accounting teams can help security managers detect purchases that might otherwise slip through the cracks.

Human Resources

The Human Resources (HR) team is responsible for coordinating all of the employee actions that take place in an organization, including hiring new employees, transferring employees to new roles, and terminating departing employees. These activities have direct security implications, and therefore, it is crucial that information security teams work closely with their HR counterparts.

Hiring Employees

From a security perspective, hiring a new employee is one of the most important decisions that an organization makes. An organization's employees have privileged access to all kinds of sensitive information and systems. Of course, it's impossible to filter out all of the bad apples, but organizations have a responsibility to ensure that security plays a prominent role in the hiring process. Spending a little extra time on security issues before hiring an employee can avoid costly mistakes.

PRE-EMPLOYMENT SCREENING

Every organization should perform pre-employment screening to verify the background of potential hires. The timing and contents of this screening will vary based on the type of organization and legal constraints in the specific state or country where the employee is hired.

Some common components of pre-employment screening are as follows:

- Checking for a criminal background in all states where the employee has lived or worked.

- Verifying that an employee is not listed on the sex offender registry. This is often a mandatory part of pre-employment screening for positions where the employee will work with children, such as in a school or childcare facility.

- Checking references provided by the employee as well as using personal contacts at past employers to learn more about a candidate.

- Verifying that the educational and employment experience on a résumé is accurate by contacting schools and employers.

 WARNING   In some cases, organizations may perform credit checks to further investigate an employee's background, although obtaining and using this information requires written consent and is heavily regulated, so many organizations skip this portion of checks.

EMPLOYMENT AGREEMENTS

Organizations should use written employment agreements that spell out the employee's responsibilities in many different areas. For the purposes of the CISM exam, you should know that this may include security-related responsibilities. Here are two specific areas that should be included in all employment agreements:

- *Nondisclosure agreements (NDAs)*, where the employee agrees not to disclose any confidential information learned during the course of employment, even after the employee leaves the organization

- *Asset return agreements*, where the employee agrees to return all of the organization's property at the end of employment, including both information and physical assets

EMPLOYEE ORIENTATION

Employers should use the hiring and orientation process as an opportunity to familiarize employees with the organization's security policies through training and, perhaps, a written acknowledgment from each new hire that they have read and agree to the organization's security policies. In cases where the organization is subject to compliance requirements, the orientation should include specific training on those requirements.

Transferring Employees

Internal employee transfers may create security concerns as well. When an employee moves into a new role, make sure that they've received the appropriate onboarding for their new role and that their old permissions have been properly revoked.

Failing to properly handle internal employee transfers often leads to a situation known as *privilege creep*. This occurs when an employee accepts a new position within the company and is then granted the new access permissions necessary to carry out that new work but never has the privileges associated with their old job revoked. The employee then has unnecessary permissions, which violates the security principle of least privilege.

Terminating Employees

Every employee eventually leaves an organization for one reason or another. In the happiest case, they're retiring after years of successful employment. In other cases, they're voluntarily leaving because they found a more attractive position. Sometimes the termination is on less positive grounds and the employee is being forced out of the organization through layoffs or firing. No matter the reason, it's very important that security teams play a role in the employee termination process.

Exit Interviews

Organizations should do everything they can to make an employee's separation as pleasant as possible, within the constraints of the employee's specific circumstances. One way to do this is through an exit interview, usually conducted by a senior manager or a member of the HR department. *Exit interviews* are used to gather information about the employee's experience at the company and wish them well in their future endeavors.

Exit interviews are also a useful time to gently remind the employee about their responsibilities under their nondisclosure agreement and that they must continue to protect confidential information. It's tricky to do this well because you don't want to offend the employee, but you do want to offer a reminder. One good way to do this is by saying something like "And, as you know, your nondisclosure agreement will remain in place even after you leave us. If you ever have any questions about the types of information covered by that agreement, please feel free to give us a call. We'd be happy to help you sort it out."

Revoking Access

Organizations should also carefully think through when they revoke access to information and systems. In the case of a voluntary separation, this is usually easy, and the employee's access is revoked at the end of their last day of employment. In the case of an involuntary separation, things get a little trickier. If the employee is being terminated immediately, the likelihood of a revenge attack becomes higher. In those cases, organizations should cut off access at the same time the employee is being notified of their termination. If you cut off access too early, you run the risk of alerting the employee to the firing. If you do it too late, the employee may gain access to systems after the termination meeting.

Retrieving Company Property

Finally, don't forget to retrieve all of the organization's property in the employee's possession. This includes keys, access badges, laptops, mobile devices, paper and electronic files, and any other company property issued to the employee. If you don't retrieve assets on the last day of employment, your likelihood of ever retrieving them is low.

Information Technology

Information security managers and their teams may reside in different parts of the organization, as we discussed in Chapter 1. In some organizations, information security may be a unit within the information technology team, whereas other organizations may enforce separation between security and IT teams. In either case, the information security and information technology functions are closely linked and interdependent. Therefore, security managers must maintain good relationships with their IT counterparts.

The duties of these teams overlap in many different ways, but there are two particular areas of focus: access management and change management.

Access Management

One of the fundamental responsibilities of information technology and/or information security professionals is performing account and access management tasks. This includes designing strong processes that implement the principles of least privilege and separation of duties, implementing job rotation schemes, and managing the account lifecycle.

Least Privilege

The principle of *least privilege* states that an individual should only have the minimum set of privileges necessary to complete their assigned job duties. Least privilege is important for two reasons.

First, least privilege minimizes the potential damage from an insider attack. If an employee turns malicious, the damage they can cause will be limited by the privileges assigned to them by job role. It's unlikely, for example, that an accountant would be able to deface the company website because an accountant's job responsibilities have nothing to do with updating web content.

Second, least privilege limits the ability of an external attacker to quickly gain privileged access when compromising an employee's account. Unless they happen to compromise a system administrator's account, they will find themselves limited by the privileges of the account that they steal.

Separation of Duties

The *separation of duties* principle states that sensitive business functions should require the involvement of at least two people. This reduces the likelihood of fraud by requiring collusion between two employees to commit fraud.

A common example of separation of duties is found in accounting departments. One way that employees might steal funds from the organization is to set up fake vendors in the system and then issue checks to those vendors for services that were never rendered. To prevent this, organizations typically separate the ability to set up a new vendor and issue a check to a vendor and say that no employee should ever have both of those privileges.

Job Rotation

Many organizations also implement job rotation schemes designed to move people around from job to job on a periodic basis. This approach has obvious personnel benefits by providing teams with a diverse set of experiences and allowing them to experience many different aspects of the organization's operations. It also has the security benefit of reducing the likelihood of fraud. If you know that someone else will be looking at your work during a job rotation, you are less likely to conduct illegitimate activity that might be detected during a rotation.

Mandatory Vacations

Mandatory vacation policies attempt to achieve the same goal by requiring that staff in key positions take a minimum number of consecutive vacation days each year and not have access to corporate systems during that time period. This enforced absence provides an opportunity for fraudulent activity to come to light when the employee does not have the access necessary to cover it up.

Account Maintenance

Security professionals are also responsible for managing the account and credential lifecycle. This requires a series of account maintenance activities:

- Granting new users access to systems and ensuring that they have the correct access privileges for their job role
- Modifying access privileges when a user changes jobs or a user's job requires new access
- Reviewing access on a regular basis and removing any unnecessary access
- Removing the access of terminated users, completing the account management lifecycle

Account Monitoring

Security administrators must pay careful attention to the permissions and use of end-user accounts to protect against and detect security incidents. They should pay particular attention to two account security issues.

The first is inaccurate permissions assigned to accounts that either prevent a user from doing their work or violate the principle of least privilege. These permissions are often the result of privilege creep, a condition that occurs when users switch jobs and gain new permissions but never have their old permissions revoked.

To protect against inaccurate permissions, administrators should perform regular user account audits in cooperation with managers from around the organization. During each of these manual reviews, the administrators should pull a listing of all of the permissions assigned to each account and then review that listing with managers to ensure that it is appropriate for the user's role, making any necessary adjustments. Reviewers should pay careful attention to users who switched jobs since the last account review.

Some organizations may use a formal attestation process where auditors review documentation to ensure that managers have formally approved each user's account and access permissions.

The second issue is the unauthorized use of permissions either by someone other than the legitimate user accessing the account or by the user performing some illegitimate action. Protecting against the unauthorized use of permissions is tricky because it can be hard to detect. This requires the use of *continuous account monitoring* systems that watch for suspicious activity and alert administrators to strange actions.

A continuous account monitoring system may flag violations of access policies, such as logons from strange geographic locations. For example, the system might flag:

- Users connecting from two distant locations at the same time, such as a user connecting from both the home office and a remote location in Eastern Europe at the same time— cases like this are known as *impossible travel time logins* and should be treated as suspicious events.

- Logins from unusual network locations, such as a user who always logs in from the HR network suddenly appearing on a guest network, and logons at unusual times of day, such as a mail clerk logging into the system in the middle of the night.
- Deviations from normal behavior, such as users accessing files that they do not normally access.
- High volumes of activity that may represent bulk downloading of sensitive information.

The specific circumstances that merit attention will vary from organization to organization, but performing this type of behavior-based continuous account monitoring is an important security control.

Change Management

Change management processes ensure that organizations follow a standardized process for requesting, reviewing, approving, and implementing changes to information systems. They have the goal of minimizing the probability and impact of disruptions to normal IT services because of change. This includes an assessment of the security impact of a proposed change.

The standard tool used for change management is the *request for change (RFC)*. In an organization practicing strong change control, any individual who wants to change a system writes the change in an RFC that includes some standard elements:

- Description of the change
- Explanation of the expected impact
- Assessment of the risk involved
- Plan for rolling back the change if it fails
- Identity of the individuals or groups involved in the change
- Proposed schedule for the change
- Systems and services affected by the change

Once someone submits an RFC for review, it must be approved by a relevant authority. For minor changes, this may simply be the person's manager. In the case of major changes, the organization's *change advisory board (CAB)* may review and approve the change.

Some routine changes have preapproved status and may be made as soon as the RFC is submitted. For example, if storage engineers replace backup tapes each month, they might have a preapproved change in the change management system for that activity. They still submit an RFC, but the RFC is immediately approved due to the fact that it is for a preapproved change, and work may then begin on schedule with no other action required.

Audit

Information security and information technology teams are often subject to both internal and external audits. The purpose of these audits is to confirm that the organization complies with its own policies, industry best practices, and legal and regulatory requirements.

Information security managers should maintain productive relationships with those who coordinate these audits and, in particular, with the internal auditing function in their organization. This relationship must be carefully navigated because auditors require independence from the functions they are auditing and will not be willing to engage in a relationship that puts their independence into question. However, the objectives of auditors and information security functions are often aligned, and the two groups may leverage that relationship productively, as long as they are careful to ensure that auditors retain their independence.

We discussed audits in more detail in Chapter 2, "Information Security Governance and Compliance."

Summary

The information security program serves as the umbrella organizational unit for all of an organization's efforts to protect the confidentiality, integrity, and availability of information and systems. The chief information security officer (CISO), or other senior-most information security leader, bears overall responsibility for ensuring that the information security program is properly designed, implemented, and operated.

The CISO must ensure that the information security program remains aligned with the objectives of the business overall as well as the operational objectives of other business functions, including procurement, accounting, human resources, information technology, and audit functions. In addition, the CISO should put monitoring procedures in place to evaluate the effectiveness of the program over time and detect opportunities for improvement.

Exam Essentials

Be able to describe the purpose of the charter.   The core of the charter is the scope statement, which defines the security objectives included in the program and the portion of the organization covered by the program. The charter should also address the business purpose of the program, a statement of authority, roles and responsibilities, governance structures, documentation, enforcement mechanisms, and processes for periodic program reviews.

Know how metrics are used to assess the efficiency and effectiveness of the information security program.   Key performance indicators (KPIs) are metrics that demonstrate the success of the security program in achieving its objectives. KPIs look at historical performance. Key goal indicators (KGIs) measure progress toward defined goals. Key risk indicators (KRIs) try to quantify the security risk facing an organization. KRIs look forward at future potential risks.

Be able to explain how security training and awareness ensures that individuals understand their responsibilities.   Security training programs impart new knowledge to employees and other stakeholders. They should be tailored to meet the specific requirements of an individual's role in the organization. Security awareness programs seek to remind users of the information they have already learned, keeping their security responsibilities top-of-mind.

Know that security managers are people managers.   Security managers lead a team of professionals and are responsible for the motivation, development, and management of those team members. This includes providing training that helps employees keep their skills current and certifications that help employees validate their skills.

Know that security managers are financial managers.   Security managers bear responsibility for managing a budget allocated to the information security program. They must understand how the fiscal year used by their organization affects funds availability and how to work within the budgeting and accounting processes used by their organization.

Be able to explain how information security must work closely with other business functions.   Security managers should cultivate relationships with other business leaders to ensure that security is well integrated with other business functions. This includes integrating with the human resources function for employee hiring, transfers, and termination. It also includes aligning with procurement and accounting functions for product and service acquisitions. Security leaders should also work carefully with other information technology leaders and the organization's auditors.

Review Questions

1. Which one of the following elements is *least* likely to be found in an information security program charter?

    A. Scope statement

    B. Project schedule

    C. Roles and responsibilities

    D. Governance structure

2. Victoria's organization has a disconnect between the human resources function and the information security function. As a result, employee transfers are not being properly handled. What is the greatest security risk resulting from this situation?

    A. Privilege escalation

    B. Separation of duties

    C. Privilege creep

    D. Two-person control

3. Leo is responsible for managing his organization's information security budget. Which one of the following circumstances is the most preferred situation?

    A. Expenses greatly exceed budget.

    B. Expenses slightly exceed budget.

    C. Expenses are slightly under budget.

    D. Expenses are greatly under budget.

4. Andrew is concerned that his security program is not well aligned with business goals and would like to convene a group to help guide his work. What type of group would best meet his needs?

    A. Change advisory board (CAB)

    B. Senior leadership

    C. Board

    D. Steering committee

5. Norma is developing a new information security standard for her organization and would like to ensure that the policy has appropriate authority and goes through an appropriate approval process. Where should she look to verify this is the case?

    A. Scope statement

    B. RFC

    C. NDA

    D. Charter

6. Dan would like to add a new element to his organization's information security awareness program. Which one of the following tools would be most appropriate?

    A. End user training

    B. Certification

    C. Capture the flag

    D. Posters

7. Alexis is working to develop standard language for use with vendors that will ensure that her organization retains ownership of data handled by the vendor. Where would be the best location to include this language?

    A. Contract

    B. NDA

    C. MOU

    D. SOW

8. Bob is developing a set of measures designed to evaluate how well the information security program in his organization is functioning. He will provide monthly reporting on these metrics, looking back at the program's functioning over the past month. What term best describes these metrics?

    A. KMIs

    B. KGIs

    C. KRIs

    D. KPIs

9. Tanya is hiring a new incident analyst to help supplement the capabilities of her team. She is identifying the line item in her budget that will cover the salary and benefits for this new employee. What term best describes this expense?

    A. One-time

    B. Capital

    C. Unbudgeted

    D. Operational

10. Gary's organization uses a fiscal year budgeting system, with the fiscal year beginning on January 1. He is planning for an expense that will occur in June 2024. During what fiscal and calendar year will this expense occur?

    A. CY24 and FY24

    B. CY24 and FY25

    C. CY24 and FY23

    D. CY25 and FY24

11. The Acme Widgets Company is putting new controls in place for its accounting department. Management is concerned that a rogue accountant may be able to create a new false vendor and then issue checks to that vendor as payment for services that were never rendered. What security control can best help prevent this situation?

    A. Mandatory vacation

    B. Separation of duties

    C. Defense in depth

    D. Job rotation

12. An accounting employee at Doolittle Industries was recently arrested for participation in an embezzlement scheme. The employee transferred money to a personal account and then shifted funds around between other accounts every day to disguise the fraud for months. Which one of the following controls might have best allowed the earlier detection of this fraud?

    A. Separation of duties

    B. Least privilege

    C. Defense in depth

    D. Mandatory vacation

13. After completing the first year of his security awareness program, Charles reviews the data about how many personnel completed training compared to how many were assigned the training to determine whether he hit the 95 percent completion rate he was aiming for. What is this type of measure called?

    A. A KPI

    B. A metric

    C. An awareness control

    D. A return on investment rate

14. Which one of the following efforts allows security professionals to validate their knowledge to current and potential employers?

    A. Training

    B. Certification

    C. Awareness

    D. Accreditation

15. Which one of the following statements about change management programs is correct?

    A. All changes must be approved by the change advisory board (CAB).

    B. Minor changes do not require an RFC.

    C. Some RFCs may be immediately approved on an automated basis.

    D. The primary purpose of change management is to create a paper trail to support audits.

16. Wendy is designing a pre-employment screening program for her organization. Which one of the following screening techniques is commonly omitted due to legal and privacy concerns?

    A. Credit checks

    B. Criminal background checks

    C. Reference checks

    D. Education verification

17. Elliott is evaluating a new content management system that an outside service provider will host for his organization. What is the most appropriate minimum security standard for him to require of possible vendors?

    A. Handling information in the same manner the organization would

    B. Compliance with the vendor's own policies

    C. Compliance with all laws and regulations

    D. Elimination of all identified security risks

18. Abe works for an organization that has several subsidiaries that operate independently. Those subsidiaries report to different leaders and have their own independent security programs. If the governance model does not change, what would be the appropriate way for Abe's security program to address this situation?

    A. Limit the objectives of his program.

    B. Limit the scope of his program.

    C. Include the subsidiaries in his program.

    D. Replace the subsidiary programs with his own.

19. Sally is developing a set of metrics that will help her organization assess changes in the threat environment and adjust their security program accordingly. What type of metrics is she developing?

    A. KMIs

    B. KGIs

    C. KRIs

    D. KPIs

20. Tia recently created a set of high-level security metrics for senior leaders who need to understand the effectiveness of the security program. What would be the best way for her to communicate these metrics?

    A. Continue to post them on a dashboard that is available to stakeholders to peruse at their convenience.

    B. Provide stakeholders with access to a web page that contains detailed security metrics.

    C. Email a copy of the dashboard to stakeholders periodically.

    D. Provide reporting to stakeholders that contextualizes these metrics.

Chapter

6

Security Assessment and Testing

THE CERTIFIED INFORMATION SECURITY MANAGER (CISM) DOMAINS AND SUBTOPICS COVERED IN THIS CHAPTER INCLUDE:

✓ **Domain 2: Information Security Risk Management**

   ■ **A. Information Security Risk Assessment**

      ■ **2A2. Vulnerability and Control Deficiency Analysis**

✓ **Domain 3: Information Security Program**

   ■ **B. Information Security Program Management**

      ■ **3B3. Information Security Control Testing and Evaluation**

THE CERTIFIED INFORMATION SECURITY MANAGER (CISM) SUPPORTING TASKS COVERED IN THIS CHAPTER INCLUDE:

✓ **23. Participate in and/or oversee the vulnerability assessment and threat analysis process.**

Many security threats exist in today's cybersecurity landscape. In previous chapters, you've read about the threats posed by hackers with varying motivations, malicious code, and social engineering. Cybersecurity professionals are responsible for building, operating, and maintaining security controls that protect against these threats. An important component of this maintenance is performing regular security assessment and testing to ensure that controls are operating properly and that the environment contains no exploitable vulnerabilities.

This chapter begins with a discussion of vulnerability management, including the design, scheduling, and interpretation of vulnerability scans. It then moves on to discuss penetration testing, an assessment tool that puts cybersecurity professionals in the role of attackers to test security controls. The chapter concludes with a discussion of cybersecurity exercises that may be used as part of an ongoing training and assessment program.

Vulnerability Management

Our technical environments are complex. We operate servers, endpoint systems, network devices, and many other components that each run millions of lines of code and process complex configurations. No matter how much we work to secure these systems, it is inevitable that they will contain security weaknesses and that new weaknesses will arise on a regular basis. We call these weaknesses *vulnerabilities*.

Vulnerability management programs play a crucial role in identifying, prioritizing, and remediating vulnerabilities in our environments. They use *vulnerability scanning* to detect new vulnerabilities as they arise and then implement a remediation workflow that addresses the highest-priority vulnerabilities. Every organization should incorporate vulnerability management into their cybersecurity program.

Identifying Scan Targets

Once an organization decides that it wishes to conduct vulnerability scanning and determines which, if any, regulatory requirements apply to their scans, they move on to the more detailed phases of the planning process. The next step is to identify the systems that will be covered by the vulnerability scans. Some organizations choose to cover all systems in their scanning process, whereas others scan systems differently (or not at all), depending on the answers to many different questions, including the following:

- What is the data classification of the information stored, processed, or transmitted by the system?

- Is the system exposed to the Internet or other public or semipublic networks?
- What services are offered by the system?
- Is the system in a production, test, or development environment?

Organizations also use automated techniques to identify the systems that may be covered by a scan. Cybersecurity professionals use scanning tools to search the network for connected systems, whether they were previously known or unknown, and to build an *asset inventory*. Figure 6.1 shows an example of an asset map developed using the Qualys vulnerability scanner's asset inventory functionality.

FIGURE 6.1   Qualys asset map

Administrators may then supplement this inventory with additional information about the type of system and the information it handles. This information then helps make determinations about which systems are critical and which are noncritical. Asset inventory and *asset criticality* information help guide decisions about the types of scans that are performed, the frequency of those scans, and the priority administrators should place on remediating vulnerabilities detected by the scan.

Determining Scan Frequency

Cybersecurity professionals depend on automation to help them perform their duties in an efficient, effective manner. Vulnerability scanning tools allow the automated scheduling of scans to take the burden off administrators. Figure 6.2 shows an example of how these scans might be configured in Tenable's Nessus product. Nessus was one of the first vulnerability scanners on the market and remains widely used today. Administrators may designate a schedule that meets their security, compliance, and business requirements.

FIGURE 6.2   Configuring a Nessus scan

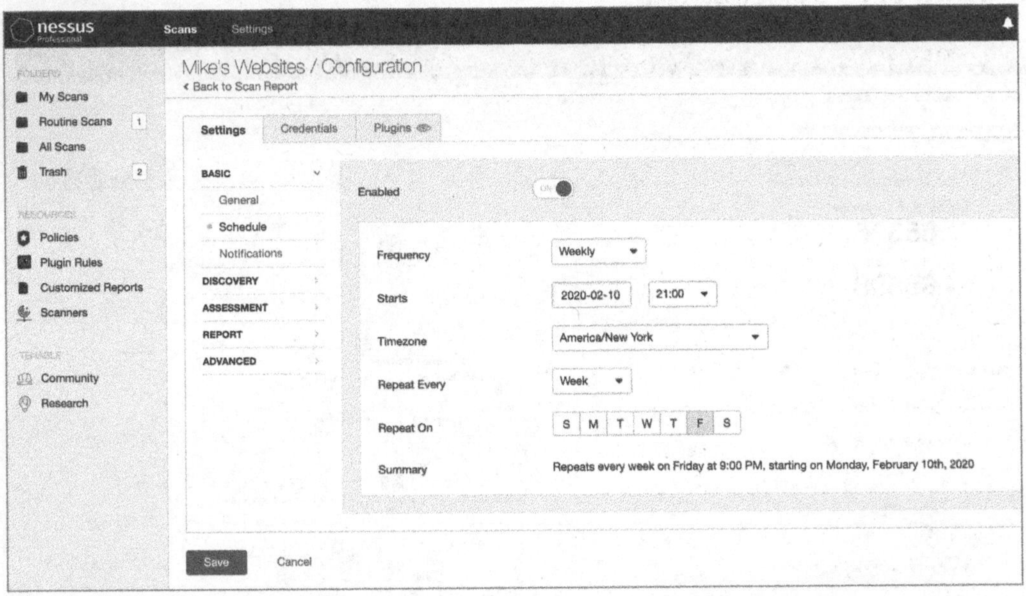

Administrators should configure these scans to provide automated alerting when they detect new vulnerabilities. Many security teams configure their scans to produce automated email reports of scan results, such as the report shown in Figure 6.3.

Many different factors influence how often an organization decides to conduct vulnerability scans against its systems:

- The organization's *risk appetite* is its willingness to tolerate risk within the environment. If an organization is extremely risk averse, it may choose to conduct scans more frequently to minimize the amount of time between when a vulnerability comes into existence and when it is detected by a scan.

- *Regulatory requirements,* such as those imposed by the Payment Card Industry Data Security Standard (PCI DSS) or the Federal Information Security Management Act (FISMA), may dictate a minimum frequency for vulnerability scans. These requirements may also come from corporate policies.

- *Technical constraints* may limit the frequency of scanning. For example, the scanning tool may only be capable of performing a certain number of scans per day, and organizations may need to adjust scan frequency to ensure that all scans complete successfully.

- *Business constraints* may limit the organization from conducting resource-intensive vulnerability scans during periods of high business activity to avoid disruption of critical processes.

- *Licensing limitations* may curtail the bandwidth consumed by the scanner or the number of scans that may be conducted simultaneously.

FIGURE 6.3   Sample Nessus scan report

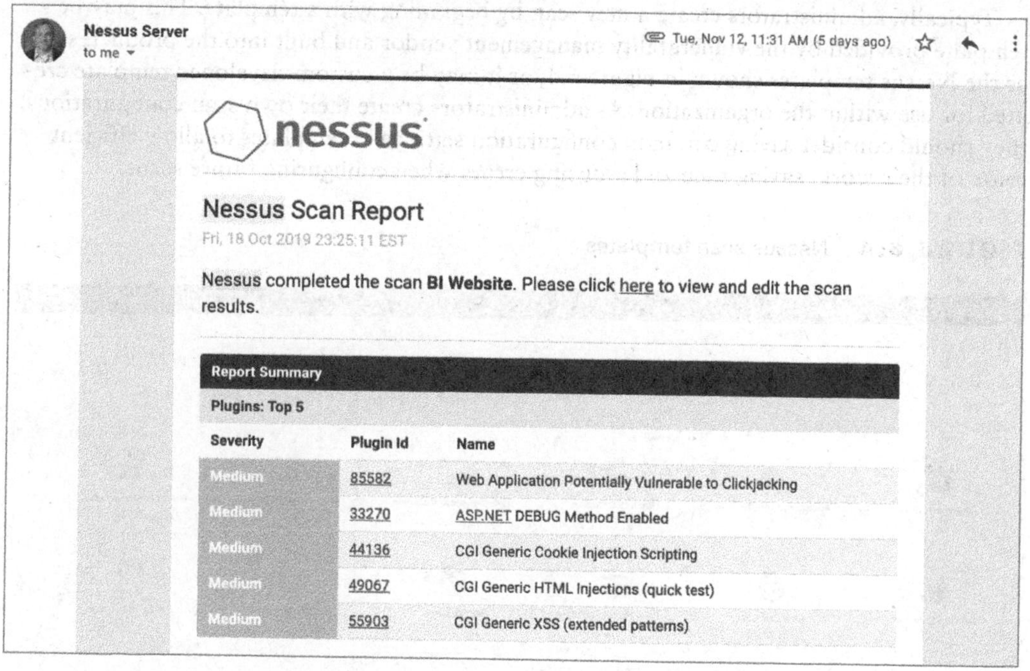

Cybersecurity professionals must balance each of these considerations when planning a vulnerability scanning program. It is usually wise to begin small and slowly expand the scope and frequency of vulnerability scans over time to avoid overwhelming the scanning infrastructure or enterprise systems.

Configuring Vulnerability Scans

Vulnerability management solutions provide administrators with the ability to configure many different parameters related to scans. In addition to scheduling automated scans and producing reports, administrators may customize the types of checks performed by the scanner, provide credentials to access target servers, install scanning agents on target servers, and conduct scans from a variety of network perspectives. It is important to conduct regular *configuration reviews* of vulnerability scanners to ensure that scan settings match current requirements.

Scan Sensitivity Levels

Cybersecurity professionals configuring vulnerability scans should pay careful attention to the configuration settings related to the scan sensitivity level. These settings determine the types of checks that the scanner will perform and should be customized to ensure that the scan meets its objectives while minimizing the possibility of disrupting the target environment.

Typically, administrators create a new scan by beginning with a template. This may be a template provided by the vulnerability management vendor and built into the product, such as the Nessus templates shown in Figure 6.4, or it may be a custom-developed template created for use within the organization. As administrators create their own scan configurations, they should consider saving common configuration settings in templates to allow efficient reuse of their work, saving time and reducing errors when configuring future scans.

FIGURE 6.4 Nessus scan templates

Administrators may also improve the efficiency of their scans by configuring the specific plug-ins that will run during each scan. Each plug-in performs a check for a specific vulnerability, and these plug-ins are often grouped into families based on the operating system, application, or device that they involve. Disabling unnecessary plug-ins improves the speed of the scan by bypassing unnecessary checks and also may reduce the number of false positive results detected by the scanner.

For example, an organization that does not use the Amazon Linux operating system may choose to disable all checks related to Amazon Linux in their scanning template. Figure 6.5 shows an example of disabling these plug-ins in Nessus.

FIGURE 6.5   Disabling unused plug-ins

Status	Plugin Family ▼	Total	Status
ENABLED	AIX Local Security Checks	11287	DISABLED
DISABLED	Amazon Linux Local Security Checks	760	DISABLED
ENABLED	Backdoors	108	DISABLED
ENABLED	CentOS Local Security Checks	2231	DISABLED
ENABLED	CGI abuses	3514	DISABLED
ENABLED	CGI abuses : XSS	630	DISABLED
ENABLED	CISCO	756	DISABLED

Nessus — Scans 2 — Policies

My Scan Policy

Policies > Settings   Credentials   Compliance   **Plugins**

Save   Cancel

Some plug-ins perform tests that may actually disrupt activity on a production system or, in the worst case, damage content on those systems. These *intrusive plug-ins* are a tricky situation. Administrators want to run these scans because they may identify problems that could be exploited by a malicious source. At the same time, cybersecurity professionals clearly don't want to *cause* problems on the organization's network and, as a result, may limit their scans to *nonintrusive plug-ins*.

One way around this problem is to maintain a test environment containing copies of the same systems running on the production network and running scans against those test systems first. If the scans detect problems in the test environment, administrators may correct the underlying causes on both test and production networks before running scans on the production network.

Supplementing Network Scans

Basic vulnerability scans run over a network, probing a system from a distance. The scan provides a realistic view of the system's security by simulating what an attacker might see from another network vantage point. However, the firewalls, intrusion prevention systems, and other security controls that exist on the path between the scanner and the target server may affect the scan results, providing an inaccurate view of the server's security independent of those controls.

Additionally, many security vulnerabilities are difficult to confirm using only a remote scan. Vulnerability scans that run over the network may detect the possibility that a vulnerability exists but be unable to confirm it with confidence, causing a false positive result that requires time-consuming administrator investigation.

Modern vulnerability management solutions can supplement these remote scans with trusted information about server configurations. This information may be gathered in two ways. First, administrators can provide the scanner with credentials that allow the scanner to connect to the target server and retrieve configuration information. This information can then be used to determine whether a vulnerability exists, improving the scan's accuracy over noncredentialed alternatives. For example, if a vulnerability scan detects a potential issue that can be corrected by an operating system update, the credentialed scan can check whether the update is installed on the system before reporting a vulnerability.

Figure 6.6 shows an example of the *credentialed scanning* options available within Qualys. Credentialed scans may access operating systems, databases, and applications, among other sources.

> **TIP**
>
> Credentialed scans typically only retrieve information from target servers and do not make changes to the server itself. Therefore, administrators should enforce the principle of least privilege by providing the scanner with a read-only account on the server. Doing so reduces the likelihood of a security incident related to the scanner's credentialed access.

FIGURE 6.6   Configuring credentialed scanning

Authentication

Authentication enables the scanner to log into hosts at scan time to extend detection capabilities. See the online help to learn how to configure this option.

- ☑ Windows
- ☑ Unix/Cisco IOS
- ☑ Oracle
- ☐ Oracle Listener
- ☐ SNMP
- ☐ VMware
- ☐ DB2
- ☐ HTTP
- ☐ MySQL

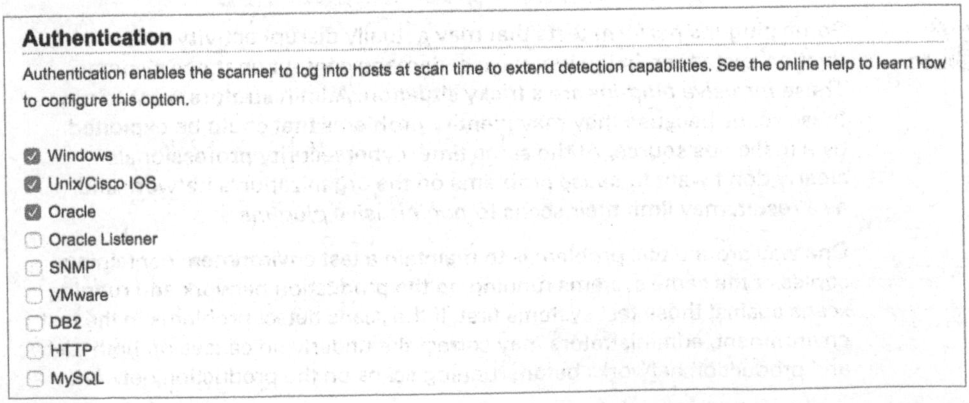

In addition to credentialed scanning, some scanners supplement the traditional *server-based scanning* approach to vulnerability scanning with a complementary *agent-based scanning* approach. In this approach, administrators install small software agents on each target server. These agents conduct scans of the server configuration, providing an "inside-out" vulnerability scan, and then report information back to the vulnerability management platform for analysis and reporting.

> System administrators are typically wary of installing agents on the servers that they manage for fear that the agent will cause performance or stability issues. If you choose to use an agent-based approach to scanning, you should approach this concept conservatively, beginning with a small pilot deployment that builds confidence in the agent before proceeding with a more widespread deployment.

Scan Perspective

Comprehensive vulnerability management programs provide the ability to conduct scans from a variety of *scan perspectives*. Each scan perspective conducts the scan from a different location on the network, providing a different view into vulnerabilities. For example, an external scan is run from the Internet, giving administrators a view of what an attacker located outside the organization would see as potential vulnerabilities. Internal scans might run from a scanner on the general corporate network, providing the view that a malicious insider might encounter. Finally, scanners located inside the data center and agents located on the servers offer the most accurate view of the real state of the server by showing vulnerabilities that might be blocked by other security controls on the network. Controls that might affect scan results include the following:

- Firewall settings
- Network segmentation
- Intrusion detection systems (IDSs)
- Intrusion prevention systems (IPSs)

> The internal and external scans required by PCI DSS are a good example of scans performed from different perspectives. The organization may conduct its own internal scans but must supplement them with external scans conducted by an approved scanning vendor.

Vulnerability management platforms have the ability to manage different scanners and provide a consolidated view of scan results, compiling data from different sources. Figure 6.7 shows an example of how the administrator may select the scanner for a newly configured scan using Qualys.

FIGURE 6.7   Choosing a scan appliance

Launch Vulnerability Scan	Turn help tips: On I **Off** Launch Help

General Information

Give your scan a name, select a scan profile (a default is selected for you with recommended settings), and choose a scanner from the Scanner Appliance menu for internal scans, if visible.

Title: [   ] ▣

Option Profile: *   [Initial Options (default)   ] ⁺ᴿ Select

Scanner Appliance: [✓ External ▾] ⬇ View

        Default
        ✓ External
        All Scanners in Asset Group
        All Scanners in TagSet
        Build my list
        AWS_Internal

Choose Target Ho

Tell us which hosts (IP addresses) you want to scan.

◉ Assets   ○ Tags

Asset Groups   [Select items...   ] ↻ ▾   ⁺ᴿ Select

IPs/Ranges   [   ]   ⁺ᴿ Select

    Example: 192.168.0.87-192.168.0.92, 192.168.0.200

Exclude IPs/Ranges [   ]   ⁺ᴿ Select

    Example: 192.168.0.87-192.168.0.92, 192.168.0.200

Notification

☐ Send notification when this scan is finished

Scanner Maintenance

As with any technology product, vulnerability management solutions require care and feeding. Administrators should conduct regular maintenance of their vulnerability scanner to ensure that the scanning software and *vulnerability feeds* remain up-to-date.

> Scanning systems do provide automatic updating capabilities that keep the scanner and its vulnerability feeds up-to-date. Organizations should take advantage of these features, but it is always a good idea to check in once in a while and manually verify that the scanner is updating properly.

Scanner Software

Scanning systems themselves aren't immune from vulnerabilities. As shown in Figure 6.8, even vulnerability scanners can have security issues! Regular patching of scanner software protects an organization against scanner-specific vulnerabilities and also provides important bug fixes and feature enhancements to improve scan quality.

Vulnerability Plug-in Feeds

Security researchers discover new vulnerabilities every week, and vulnerability scanners can only be effective against these vulnerabilities if they receive frequent updates to their plug-ins. Administrators should configure their scanners to retrieve new plug-ins on a regular basis, preferably daily. Fortunately, as shown in Figure 6.9, this process is easily automated.

FIGURE 6.8 Nessus vulnerability in the NIST National Vulnerability Database

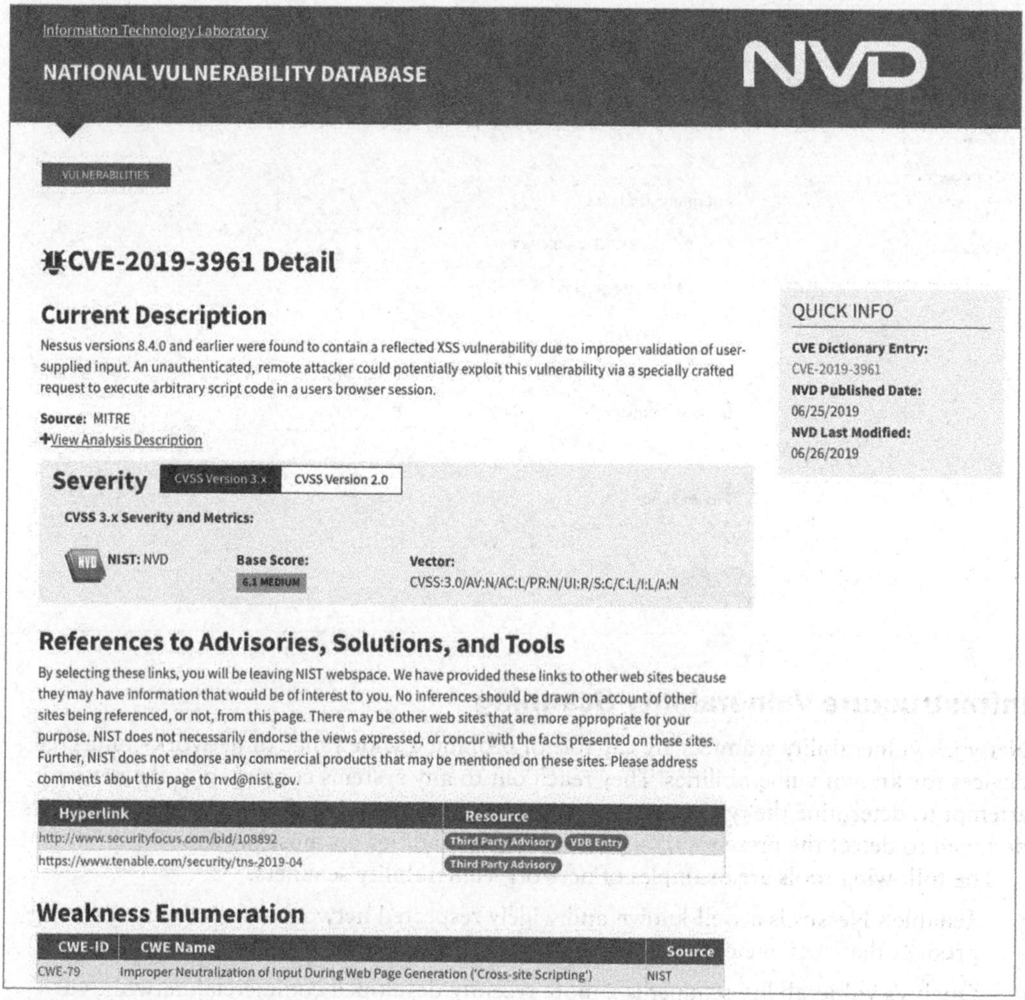

Source: NIST

Vulnerability Scanning Tools

As you fill out your cybersecurity toolkit, you will want to have a network vulnerability scanner, an application scanner, and a web application scanner available for use. Vulnerability scanners are often leveraged for preventive scanning and testing and are also found in penetration testers toolkits where they help identify systems that testers can exploit. This fact also means they're a favorite tool of attackers!

FIGURE 6.9 Nessus Automatic Updates

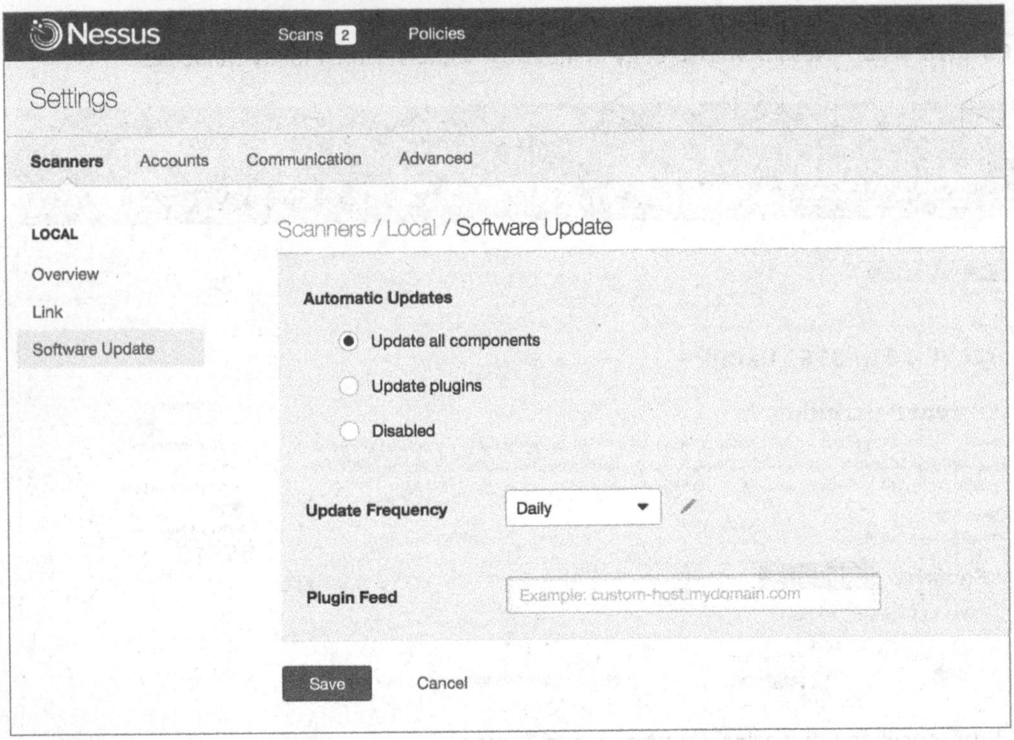

Infrastructure Vulnerability Scanning

Network vulnerability scanners are capable of probing a wide range of network-connected devices for known vulnerabilities. They reach out to any systems connected to the network, attempt to determine the type of device and its configuration, and then launch targeted tests designed to detect the presence of any known vulnerabilities on those devices.

The following tools are examples of network vulnerability scanners:

- Tenable's Nessus is a well-known and widely respected network vulnerability scanning product that was one of the earliest products in this field.

- Qualys's vulnerability scanner is a more recently developed commercial network vulnerability scanner that offers a unique deployment model using a software-as-a-service (SaaS) management console to run scans using appliances located in both on-premises data centers and the cloud.

- Rapid7's Nexpose is another commercial vulnerability management system that offers capabilities similar to those of Nessus and Qualys.

- The open source OpenVAS offers a free alternative to commercial vulnerability scanners.

These are four of the most commonly used network vulnerability scanners. Many other products are on the market today, and every mature organization should have at least one scanner in their toolkit. Many organizations choose to deploy two different vulnerability scanning products in the same environment as a defense-in-depth control.

Application Scanning

Application scanning tools are commonly used as part of the software development process. These tools analyze custom-developed software to identify common security vulnerabilities. Application testing occurs using three techniques:

- *Static testing* analyzes code without executing it. This approach points developers directly at vulnerabilities and often provides specific remediation suggestions.

- *Dynamic testing* executes code as part of the test, running all the interfaces that the code exposes to the user with a variety of inputs, searching for vulnerabilities.

- *Interactive testing* combines static and dynamic testing, analyzing the source code while testers interact with the application through exposed interfaces.

Application testing should be an integral part of the software development process. Many organizations introduce testing requirements into the software release process, requiring that any code released into production have a test that shows no significant vulnerabilities in the test results.

Web Application Scanning

Web application scanners are specialized tools used to examine the security of web applications. These tools test for web-specific vulnerabilities, such as SQL injection, cross-site scripting (XSS), and cross-site request forgery (CSRF) vulnerabilities. They work by combining traditional network scans of web servers with detailed probing of web applications, using such techniques as sending known malicious input sequences and fuzzing in attempts to break the application.

Nikto is a popular web application scanning tool. It is an open source tool that is freely available for anyone to use. As shown in Figure 6.10, it uses a command-line interface and is somewhat difficult to use.

Another open source tool available for web application scanning is Arachni. This tool, shown in Figure 6.11, is a packaged scanner available for Windows, macOS, and Linux operating systems.

Most organizations do use web application scanners, but they choose to use commercial products that offer advanced capabilities and user-friendly interfaces. Although there are dedicated web application scanners, such as Acunetix, on the market, many firms use the web application scanning capabilities of traditional network vulnerability scanners, such as Nessus, Qualys, and Nexpose.

FIGURE 6.10 Nikto web application scanner

```
 Scripting (XSS). http://www.cert.org/advisories/CA-2000-02.html.
+ /servlet/org.apache.catalina.ContainerServlet/<script>alert('Vulnerable')</script>: Apache-Tomcat is vulnerab
le to Cross Site Scripting (XSS) by invoking java classes. http://www.cert.org/advisories/CA-2000-02.html.
+ /servlet/org.apache.catalina.Context/<script>alert('Vulnerable')</script>: Apache-Tomcat is vulnerable to Cro
ss Site Scripting (XSS) by invoking java classes. http://www.cert.org/advisories/CA-2000-02.html.
+ /servlet/org.apache.catalina.Globals/<script>alert('Vulnerable')</script>: Apache-Tomcat is vulnerable to Cro
ss Site Scripting (XSS) by invoking java classes. http://www.cert.org/advisories/CA-2000-02.html.
+ /servlet/org.apache.catalina.servlets.WebdavStatus/<script>alert('Vulnerable')</script>: Apache-Tomcat is vul
nerable to Cross Site Scripting (XSS) by invoking java classes. http://www.cert.org/advisories/CA-2000-02.html.
+ /nosuchurl/><script>alert('Vulnerable')</script>: JEUS is vulnerable to Cross Site Scripting (XSS) when reque
sting non-existing JSP pages. http://securitytracker.com/alerts/2003/Jun/1007004.html
+ /~/<script>alert('Vulnerable')</script>?aspxerrorpath=null: Cross site scripting (XSS) is allowed with .
aspx file requests (may be Microsoft .net). http://www.cert.org/advisories/CA-2000-02.html
+ /~/<script>alert('Vulnerable')</script>.aspx: Cross site scripting (XSS) is allowed with .aspx file requests
(may be Microsoft .net). http://www.cert.org/advisories/CA-2000-02.html
+ /~/<script>alert('Vulnerable')</script>.asp: Cross site scripting (XSS) is allowed with .asp file requests (m
ay be Microsoft .net). http://www.cert.org/advisories/CA-2000-02.html
+ /node/view/666\"><script>alert(document.domain)</script>: Drupal 4.2.0 RC is vulnerable to Cross Site Scripti
ng (XSS). http://www.cert.org/advisories/CA-2000-02.html.
+ /mailman/listinfo/<script>alert('Vulnerable')</script>: Mailman is vulnerable to Cross Site Scripting (XSS).
Upgrade to version 2.0.8 to fix. http://www.cert.org/advisories/CA-2000-02.html.
+ OSVDB-27095: /bb000001.pl<script>alert('Vulnerable')</script>: Actinic E-Commerce services is vulnerable to C
ross Site Scripting (XSS). http://www.cert.org/advisories/CA-2000-02.html.
+ OSVDB-54589: /a.jsp/<script>alert('Vulnerable')</script>: JServ is vulnerable to Cross Site Scripting (XSS) w
hen a non-existent JSP file is requested. Upgrade to the latest version of JServ. http://www.cert.org/advisorie
s/CA-2000-02.html.
+ /<script>alert('Vulnerable')</script>.thtml: Server is vulnerable to Cross Site Scripting (XSS). http://www.c
ert.org/advisories/CA-2000-02.html.
+ /<script>alert('Vulnerable')</script>.shtml: Server is vulnerable to Cross Site Scripting (XSS). http://www.c
ert.org/advisories/CA-2000-02.html.
+ /<script>alert('Vulnerable')</script>.jsp: Server is vulnerable to Cross Site Scripting (XSS). http://www.cer
t.org/advisories/CA-2000-02.html.
+ /<script>alert('Vulnerable')</script>.aspx: Cross site scripting (XSS) is allowed with .aspx file requests (m
ay be Microsoft .net). http://www.cert.org/advisories/CA-2000-02.html.
```

FIGURE 6.11 Arachni web application scanner

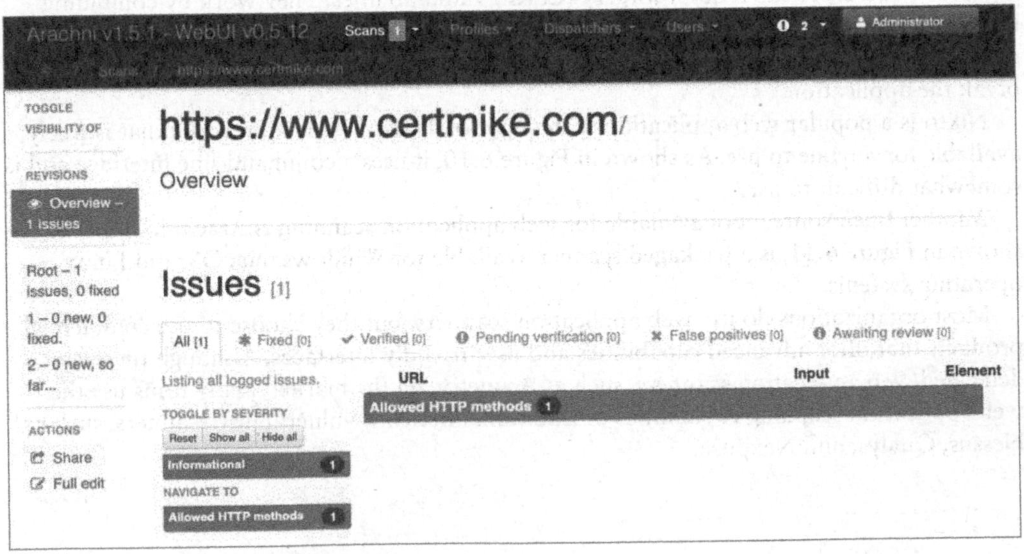

Reviewing and Interpreting Scan Reports

Vulnerability scan reports provide analysts with a significant amount of information that assists with the interpretation of the report. These reports provide detailed information about each vulnerability that they identify. Figure 6.12 shows an example of a single vulnerability reported by the Nessus vulnerability scanner.

Let's take a look at this report, section by section, beginning in the top left and proceeding in a counterclockwise fashion.

At the very top of the report, we see two critical details: the *name of the vulnerability*, which offers a descriptive title, and the *overall severity* of the vulnerability, expressed as a general category, such as low, medium, high, or critical. In this example report, the scanner is reporting that a server is running an outdated and insecure version of the SSL protocol. It is assigned to the high severity category.

Next, the report provides a *detailed description* of the vulnerability. In this case, the report provides a detailed description of the flaws in the SSL protocol and explaining that SSL is no longer considered acceptable for use.

The next section of the report provides a *solution* to the vulnerability. When possible, the scanner offers detailed information about how system administrators, security professionals, network engineers, and/or application developers may correct the vulnerability. In this case, the reader is instructed to disable SSL 2.0 and 3.0 and replace their use with a secure version of the TLS protocol.

In the section of the report titled "See Also," the scanner provides *references* where administrators can find more details on the vulnerability described in the report. In this case, the scanner refers the reader to several blog posts, Nessus documentation pages, and Internet Engineering Task Force (IETF) documents that provide more details on the vulnerability.

The *output* section of the report shows the detailed information returned by the remote system when probed for the vulnerability. This information can be extremely valuable to an analyst because it often provides the verbatim output returned by a command. Analysts can use this to better understand why the scanner is reporting a vulnerability, identify the location of a vulnerability, and potentially identify false positive reports. In this case, the output section shows the specific insecure ciphers being used.

The *port/hosts* section provides details on the server(s) that contain the vulnerability as well as the specific services on that server that have the vulnerability. In this case, the server's IP address is obscured for privacy reasons, but we can see that the server is running insecure versions of SSL on both ports 443 and 4433.

The *vulnerability information* section provides some miscellaneous information about the vulnerability. In this case, we see that the SSL vulnerability has appeared in news reports.

The *risk information* section includes useful information for assessing the severity of the vulnerability. In this case, the scanner reports that the vulnerability has an overall risk factor of High (consistent with the tag next to the vulnerability title).

The final section of the vulnerability report provides details on the vulnerability scanner plug-in that detected the issue. This vulnerability was reported by Nessus plug-in ID 20007, which was published in October 2005 and updated in March 2019.

FIGURE 6.12   Nessus vulnerability scan report

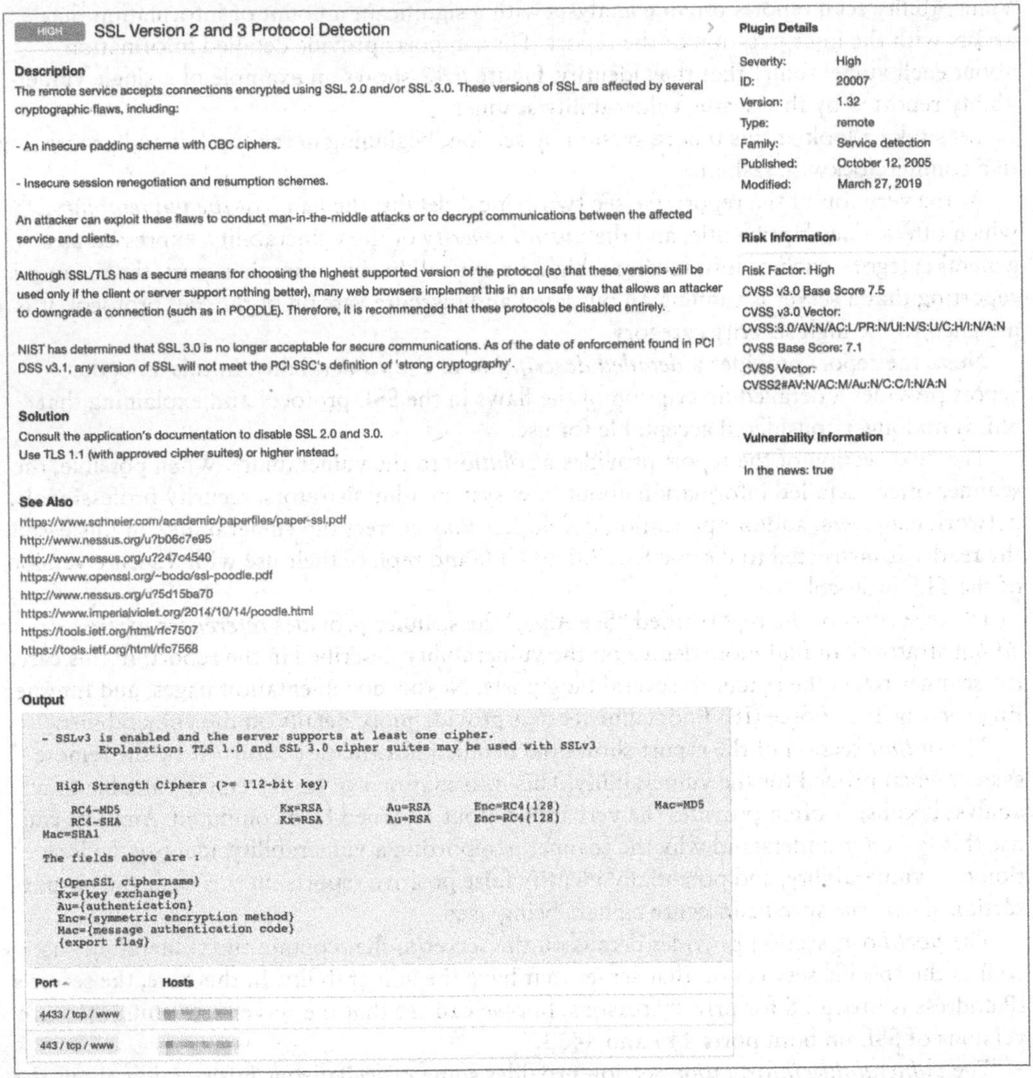

Validating Scan Results

Cybersecurity analysts interpreting reports often perform their own investigations to confirm the presence and severity of vulnerabilities. These investigations may include the use of external data sources that supply additional information valuable to the analysis.

False Positives

Vulnerability scanners are useful tools, but they aren't foolproof. Scanners do sometimes make mistakes for a variety of reasons. The scanner might not have sufficient access to the target system to confirm a vulnerability, or it might simply have an error in a plug-in that generates an erroneous vulnerability report. When a scanner reports a vulnerability that does not exist, this is known as a *false positive error*.

When a vulnerability scanner reports a vulnerability, this is known as a *positive report*. This report may either be accurate (a *true positive* report) or inaccurate (a *false positive* report). Similarly, when a scanner reports that a vulnerability is not present, this is a *negative report*. The negative report may either be accurate (a *true negative* report) or inaccurate (a *false negative* report).

Cybersecurity analysts should confirm each vulnerability reported by a scanner. In some cases, this may be as simple as verifying that a patch is missing or an operating system is outdated. In other cases, verifying a vulnerability requires a complex manual process that simulates an exploit. For example, verifying a SQL injection vulnerability may require actually attempting an attack against a web application and verifying the result in the back-end database.

When verifying a vulnerability, analysts should draw on their own expertise as well as that of others throughout the organization. Database administrators, system engineers, network technicians, software developers, and other experts have domain knowledge that is essential to the evaluation of a potential false positive report.

Reconciling Scan Results with Other Data Sources

Vulnerability scans should never take place in a vacuum. Cybersecurity analysts interpreting these reports should also turn to other sources of security information as they perform their analysis. Valuable information sources for this process include the following:

- *Log reviews* from servers, applications, network devices, and other sources that might contain information about possible attempts to exploit detected vulnerabilities

- *Security information and event management (SIEM)* systems that correlate log entries from multiple sources and provide actionable intelligence

- *Configuration management systems* that provide information on the operating system and applications installed on a system

Each of these information sources can prove invaluable when an analyst attempts to reconcile a scan report with the reality of the organization's computing environment.

Security Vulnerabilities

Each vulnerability scanning system contains plug-ins able to detect thousands of possible vulnerabilities, ranging from major SQL injection flaws in web applications to more mundane information disclosure issues with network devices. Though it's impossible to discuss each of these vulnerabilities in a book of any length, cybersecurity analysts should be familiar with the most commonly detected vulnerabilities and some of the general categories that cover many different vulnerability variants.

Patch Management

Applying security patches to systems should be one of the core practices of any information security program, but this routine task is often neglected due to a lack of resources for preventive maintenance. One of the most common alerts from a vulnerability scan is that one or more systems on the network are running an outdated version of an operating system or application and require security patches.

Figure 6.13 shows an example of one of these scan results. The server located at 10.64.142.211 has a remote code execution vulnerability. Though the scan result is fairly brief, it does contain quite a bit of helpful information.

FIGURE 6.13   Missing patch vulnerability

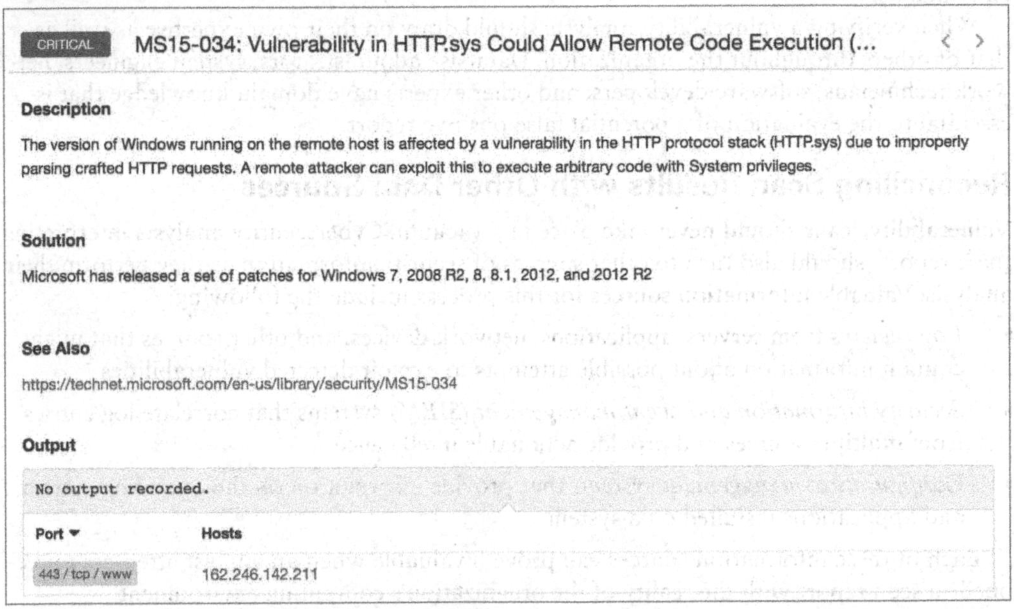

CRITICAL   MS15-034: Vulnerability in HTTP.sys Could Allow Remote Code Execution (...   ⟨ ⟩

Description

The version of Windows running on the remote host is affected by a vulnerability in the HTTP protocol stack (HTTP.sys) due to improperly parsing crafted HTTP requests. A remote attacker can exploit this to execute arbitrary code with System privileges.

Solution

Microsoft has released a set of patches for Windows 7, 2008 R2, 8, 8.1, 2012, and 2012 R2

See Also

https://technet.microsoft.com/en-us/library/security/MS15-034

Output

No output recorded.

Port ▼	Hosts
443 / tcp / www	162.246.142.211

Fortunately, there is an easy way to fix this problem. The Solution section tells us that Microsoft released patches for the affected operating systems, and the See Also section provides a direct link to the Microsoft security bulletin (MS15-034) that describes the issue and solution in greater detail.

The vulnerability shown in Figure 6.13 highlights the importance of operating a *patch management* program that routinely patches security issues. The issue shown in Figure 6.13 exposes improper or weak patch management at the operating system level, but these weaknesses can also exist in applications and firmware.

Legacy Platforms

Software vendors eventually discontinue support for every product they make. This is true for operating systems as well as applications. Once they announce the final end of support for a product, organizations that continue running the outdated software put themselves at a significant risk of attack. The vendor simply will not investigate or correct security flaws that arise in the product after that date. Organizations continuing to run the unsupported product are on their own from a security perspective, and unless you happen to maintain a team of operating system developers, that's not a good situation to find yourself in.

Perhaps the most famous end of support for a major operating system occurred in July 2015 when Microsoft discontinued support for the more-than-a-decade-old Windows Server 2003. Figure 6.14 shows an example of the report generated by Nessus when it identifies a server running this outdated operating system.

FIGURE 6.14 Unsupported operating system vulnerability

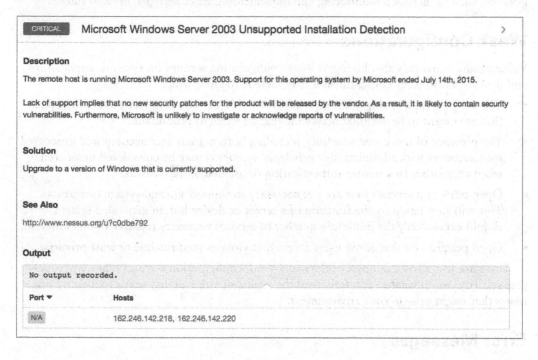

| CRITICAL | Microsoft Windows Server 2003 Unsupported Installation Detection | > |

Description

The remote host is running Microsoft Windows Server 2003. Support for this operating system by Microsoft ended July 14th, 2015.

Lack of support implies that no new security patches for the product will be released by the vendor. As a result, it is likely to contain security vulnerabilities. Furthermore, Microsoft is unlikely to investigate or acknowledge reports of vulnerabilities.

Solution

Upgrade to a version of Windows that is currently supported.

See Also

http://www.nessus.org/u?c0dbe792

Output

No output recorded.

Port ▼	Hosts
N/A	162.246.142.218, 162.246.142.220

We can see from this report that the scan detected two servers on the network running Windows Server 2003. The description of the vulnerability provides a stark assessment of what lies in store for organizations continuing to run any unsupported operating system:

> Lack of support implies that no new security patches for the product will be released by the vendor. As a result, it is likely to contain security vulnerabilities. Furthermore, Microsoft is unlikely to investigate or acknowledge reports of vulnerabilities.

The solution for organizations running unsupported operating systems is simple in its phrasing but complex in implementation. "Upgrade to a version of Windows that is currently supported" is a pretty straightforward instruction, but it may pose a significant challenge for organizations running applications that simply can't be upgraded to newer versions of Windows. In cases where the organization must continue using an unsupported operating system, best practice dictates isolating the system as much as possible, preferably not connecting it to any network, and applying as many compensating security controls as possible, such as increased monitoring and implementing strict network firewall rules.

Weak Configurations

Vulnerability scans may also highlight weak configuration settings on systems, applications, and devices. These weak configurations may include the following:

- The use of default settings that pose a security risk, such as administrative setup pages that are meant to be disabled before moving a system to production.

- The presence of unsecured accounts, including both normal user account and unsecured root accounts with administrative privileges. Accounts may be considered unsecured when they either lack strong authentication or use default passwords.

- Open ports and services that are not necessary to support normal system operations. This will vary based on the function of a server or device but, in general, a system should expose only the minimum number of services necessary to carry out its function.

- Open permissions that allow users access that violates the principle of least privilege.

These are just a few examples of the many weak configuration settings that may jeopardize security. You'll want to carefully read the results of vulnerability scans to identify other issues that might arise in your environment.

Error Messages

Many application development platforms support *debug modes* that give developers crucial error information needed to troubleshoot applications in the development process. Debug mode typically provides detailed information on the inner workings of an application and server, as well as supporting databases. Although this information can be useful to developers, it can inadvertently assist an attacker seeking to gain information about the structure of a database, authentication mechanisms used by an application, or other details. For this reason, vulnerability scans do alert on the presence of debug mode on scanned servers. Figure 6.15 shows an example of this type of scan result.

FIGURE 6.15 Debug mode vulnerability

MEDIUM **ASP.NET DEBUG Method Enabled**

Description

It is possible to send debug statements to the remote ASP scripts. An attacker might use this to alter the runtime of the remote scripts.

Solution

Make sure that DEBUG statements are disabled or only usable by authenticated users.

See Also

http://support.microsoft.com/default.aspx?scid=kb;en-us;815157

Output

```
The request
DEBUG /memberservices/showError.aspx HTTP/1.1
Host: 162.246.142.204
Accept-Charset: iso-8859-1,utf-8;q=0.9,*;q=0.1
Accept-Language: en
Command: stop-debug
Connection: Keep-Alive
User-Agent: Mozilla/4.0 (compatible; MSIE 8.0; Windows NT 5.1; Trident/4.0)
Pragma: no-cache
Accept: image/gif, image/x-xbitmap, image/jpeg, image/pjpeg, image/png, */*

Produces the following output :
HTTP/1.1 200 OK
Cache-Control: private
Content-Length: 2
Content-Type: text/html; charset=utf-8
Server: Microsoft-IIS/8.5
X-AspNet-Version: 4.0.30319
X-Powered-By: ASP.NET
```

In this example, the target system appears to be a Windows server supporting the ASP.NET development environment. The Output section of the report demonstrates that the server responds when sent a DEBUG request by a client.

Solving this issue requires the cooperation of developers and disabling debug modes on systems with public exposure. In mature organizations, software development should always take place in a dedicated development environment that is only accessible from private networks. Developers should be encouraged (or ordered!) to conduct their testing only on systems dedicated to that purpose, and it would be entirely appropriate to enable debug mode on those servers. There should be no need for supporting this capability on public-facing systems.

Insecure Protocols

Many of the older protocols used on networks in the early days of the Internet were designed without security in mind. These protocols typically do not have encryption to protect usernames, passwords, and the content sent over an open network, exposing users to eavesdropping attacks. Telnet is one example of an insecure protocol used to gain command-line access to a remote server. The File Transfer Protocol (FTP) provides the ability to transfer files between systems but does not incorporate security features. Figure 6.16 shows an example of a scan report that detected a system that supports the insecure FTP protocol.

FIGURE 6.16   FTP cleartext authentication vulnerability

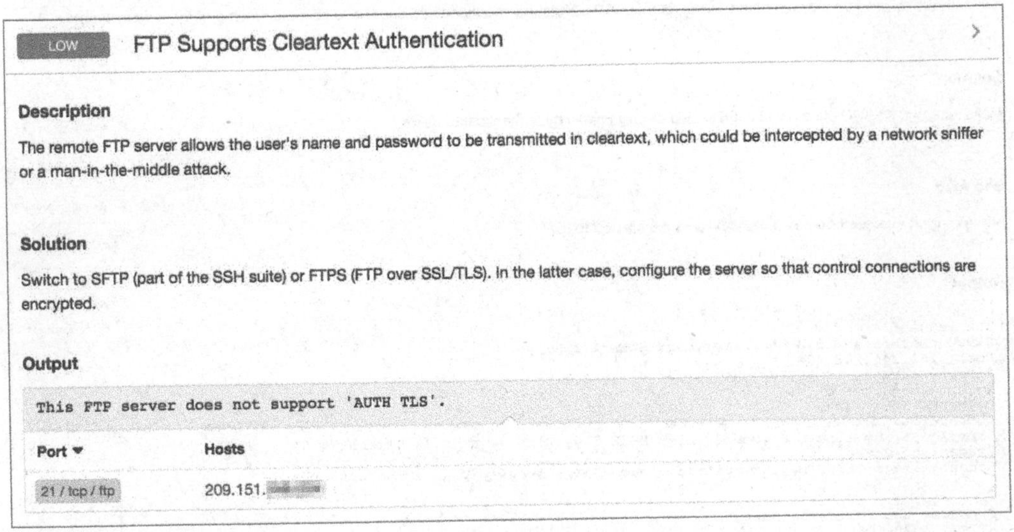

The solution for this issue is to simply switch to a more secure protocol. Fortunately, encrypted alternatives exist for both Telnet and FTP. System administrators can use Secure Shell (SSH) as a secure replacement for Telnet when seeking to gain command-line access to a remote system. Similarly, the Secure File Transfer Protocol (SFTP) and FTP-Secure (FTPS) both provide a secure method to transfer files between systems.

Weak Encryption

Encryption is a crucial security control used in every cybersecurity program to protect stored data and data in transit over networks. As with any control, however, encryption must be configured securely to provide adequate protection. You'll learn more about securely implementing encryption in Chapter 7, "Cybersecurity Technology."

When you implement encryption, you have two important choices to make:

- The algorithm to use in order to perform encryption and decryption
- The encryption key to use with that algorithm

The choices that you make for both of these characteristics may have a profound impact on the security of your environment. If you use a weak encryption algorithm, it may be easily defeated by an attacker. If you choose an encryption key that is easily guessable because of its length or composition, an attacker may find it using a cryptographic attack. For example, Figure 6.17 shows a scan report from a system that supports the insecure RC4 cipher.

FIGURE 6.17   Insecure SSL cipher vulnerability

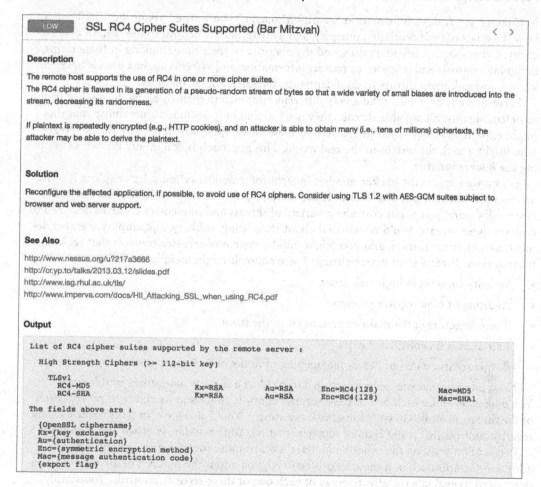

Penetration Testing

Penetration testing seeks to bridge the gap between the rote use of technical tools to test an organization's security and the power of those tools when placed in the hands of a skilled and determined attacker. Penetration tests are authorized, legal attempts to defeat an organization's security controls and perform unauthorized activities. These tests are time-consuming and require staff who are equally skilled and determined as the real-world attackers that will attempt to compromise the organization. However, they're also the most effective way for an organization to gain a complete picture of their security posture.

Adopting the Hacker Mindset

In Chapter 1, "Today's Information Security Manager," you learned about the CIA Triad and how the goals of confidentiality, integrity, and availability are central to the field of cybersecurity. Cybersecurity defenders do spend the majority of their time thinking in these terms, designing controls and defenses to protect information and systems against a wide array of known and unknown threats to confidentiality, integrity, and availability.

Penetration testers must take a very different approach in their thinking. Instead of trying to defend against all possible threats, they need to find only a single vulnerability that they might exploit to achieve their goals. To find these flaws, they must think like the adversary who might attack the system in the real world. This approach is commonly known as adopting the *hacker mindset*.

Before we explore the hacker mindset in terms of technical systems, let's explore it using an example from the physical world. If you were responsible for the physical security of an electronics store, you might consider a variety of threats and implement controls designed to counter those threats. You'd be worried about shoplifting, robbery, and employee embezzlement, among other threats, and you might build a system of security controls that seeks to prevent those threats from materializing. These controls might include the following:

- Security cameras in high-risk areas
- Auditing of cash register receipts
- Theft detectors at the main entrance/exit to the store
- Exit alarms on emergency exits
- Burglar alarm wired to detect the opening of doors outside business hours

Now, imagine that you've been engaged to conduct a security assessment of this store. You'd likely examine each one of these security controls and assess its ability to prevent each of the threats identified in your initial risk assessment. You'd also look for gaps in the existing security controls that might require supplementation. Your mandate is broad and high-level.

Penetration tests, on the other hand, have a much more focused mandate. Instead of adopting the approach of a security professional, you adopt the mindset of an attacker. You don't need to evaluate the effectiveness of each one of these security controls. You simply need to find either one flaw in the existing controls or one scenario that was overlooked in planning those controls.

In this example, a penetration tester might enter the store during business hours and conduct reconnaissance, gathering information about the security controls that are in place and the locations of critical merchandise. The tester might notice that, though the burglar alarm is tied to the doors, it does not include any sensors on the windows. The tester might then return in the middle of the night, smash a window, and grab valuable merchandise. Recognizing that the store has security cameras in place, the attacker might wear a mask and park a vehicle outside of the range of the cameras. That's the hacker mindset. Testers need to think like criminals.

There's a corollary to the hacker mindset that is important for both attackers and defenders to keep in mind. When conducting a penetration test (or a real-world attack), the attacker needs to win only once. They might attempt hundreds or thousands of potential attacks against a target. The fact that an organization's security defenses block 99.99 percent of those attacks is irrelevant if one of the attacks succeeds. Cybersecurity professionals need to win *every* time; attackers need to win only once.

Reasons for Penetration Testing

The modern organization dedicates extensive time, energy, and funding to a wide variety of security controls and activities. We install firewalls, intrusion prevention systems, security information and event management devices, vulnerability scanners, and many other tools. We equip and staff 24-hour security operations centers (SOCs) to monitor those technologies and watch our systems, networks, and applications for signs of compromise. There's more than enough work to completely fill our days twice over. Why on Earth would we want to take on the additional burden of performing penetration tests? After all, they are time-consuming to perform internally and expensive to outsource.

The answer to this question is that penetration testing provides us with visibility into our organization's security posture that simply isn't available by other means. Penetration testing is not intended to replace all the other cybersecurity activities of an organization. Instead, it complements and builds on those efforts. Penetration testers bring their unique skills and perspective to the table and can take the output of security tools and place them within the attacker's mindset, asking the question, "If I were an attacker, how could I use this information to my advantage?"

Benefits of Penetration Testing

We've already discussed *how* a penetration tester carries out their work at a high level. Let's now take a moment to consider *why* we conduct penetration testing. What benefits does it bring to the organization?

First and foremost, penetration testing provides us with knowledge that we can't obtain elsewhere. By conducting thorough penetration tests, we learn whether an attacker with the same knowledge, skills, and information as our testers would likely be able to penetrate our defenses. If they can't gain a foothold, we can then be reasonably confident that our networks are secure against attack by an equivalently talented attacker under the present circumstances.

Second, in the event that testers are successfully breaching security controls, penetration testing provides us with an important blueprint for remediation. Cybersecurity professionals can trace the actions of the testers as they progressed through the different stages of the attack and close the series of open doors that the testers passed through. This provides us with a more robust defense against future attacks.

Finally, penetration tests can provide us with essential, focused information on specific targets. We might conduct a penetration test prior to the deployment of a new system that is specifically focused on exercising the security features of that new environment. Unlike the broad nature of an open-ended penetration test, these focused tests can drill into the defenses around a specific target and provide actionable insight that can prevent a vulnerability from initial exposure.

> **Threat Hunting**
>
> The discipline of threat hunting is closely related to penetration testing but has a separate and distinct purpose. As with penetration testing, cybersecurity professionals engaged in threat hunting seek to adopt the attacker's mindset and imagine how hackers might seek to defeat an organization's security controls. The two disciplines diverge in what they accomplish with this information.
>
> Although penetration testers seek to evaluate the organization's security controls by testing them in the same manner as an attacker might, threat hunters use the attacker mindset to search the organization's technology infrastructure for the artifacts of a successful attack. They ask themselves what a hacker might do and what type of evidence they might leave behind and then go in search of that evidence.
>
> Threat hunting builds on a cybersecurity philosophy known as the "presumption of compromise." This approach assumes that attackers have already successfully breached an organization and searches out the evidence of successful attacks. When threat hunters discover a potential compromise, they then go into incident handling mode, seeking to contain, eradicate, and recover from the compromise. They also conduct a postmortem analysis of the factors that contributed to the compromise in an effort to remediate deficiencies. This post-event remediation is another similarity between penetration testing and threat hunting: Organizations leverage the output of both processes in similar ways.
>
> Threat hunters work with a variety of intelligence sources, using the concept of intelligence fusion to combine information from threat feeds, security advisories and bulletins, and other sources. They then seek to trace the path that an attacker followed as they maneuver through a target network.

Penetration Test Types

Once the type of assessment is known, one of the first things to decide about a penetration test is how much knowledge testers will have about the environment. Three typical classifications are used to describe this:

- *White-box* tests, also referred to as *known environment tests*, are tests performed with full knowledge of the underlying technology, configurations, and settings that make up the target. Testers will typically have such information as network diagrams, lists of systems and IP network ranges, and even credentials to the systems they are testing. White-box tests allow for effective testing of systems without requiring testers to spend time identifying targets and determining which may be a way in. This means that a white-box test is often more complete, since testers can get to every system, service, or other target that is in scope, and they will have credentials and other materials that will allow them to be tested. Of course, since testers can see everything inside an environment, they may not provide an accurate view of what an external attacker would see, and controls that would have been effective against most attackers may be bypassed.

- *Black-box* tests, also referred to as *unknown environment tests*, are intended to replicate what an attacker would encounter. Testers are not provided with access to or information about an environment, and instead, they must gather information, discover vulnerabilities, and make their way through an infrastructure or systems as an attacker would. This approach can be time-consuming, but it can help provide a reasonably accurate assessment of how secure the target is against an attacker of similar or lesser skill. It is important to note that the quality and skillset of your penetration tester or team is very important when conducting a black-box penetration test—if the threat actor you expect to target your organization is more capable, a black-box tester can't provide you with a realistic view of what they could do.

- *Gray-box* tests, also referred to as *partially known environment tests*, are a blend of black-box and white-box testing. A gray-box test may provide some information about the environment to the penetration testers without giving full access, credentials, or configuration details. A gray-box test can help focus penetration testers time and effort while also providing a more accurate view of what an attacker would actually encounter.

Bug Bounty Programs

Bug bounty programs provide organizations with an opportunity to benefit from the wisdom and talent of cybersecurity professionals outside their own teams. These programs allow outsiders to conduct security testing of an organization's public services and normally incentivize that research by offering financial rewards (or "bounties") to testers who successfully discover vulnerabilities.

Supporters of bug bounty programs often point out that outsiders will probe your security whether you like it or not. Running a formal bug bounty program provides them with the incentive to let you know when they discover security issues.

Rules of Engagement

Once you have determined the type of assessment and the level of knowledge testers will have about the target, the rest of the *rules of engagement* (RoE) can be written. Essential elements include the following:

- The timeline for the engagement and when testing can be conducted. Some assessments will intentionally be scheduled for noncritical timeframes to minimize the impact of potential service outages, whereas others may be scheduled during normal business hours to help test the organization's reaction to attacks.

- What locations, systems, applications, or other potential targets are included or excluded. This also often includes discussions about third-party service providers that may be impacted by the test, such as Internet services providers, software-as-a-service or other cloud service providers, or outsourced security monitoring services. Any special technical constraints should also be discussed in the RoE.

- Data handling requirements for information gathered during the penetration test. This is particularly important when engagements cover sensitive organizational data or systems. Requirements for handling often include confidentiality requirements for the findings, such as encrypting data during and after the test, and contractual requirements for disposing of the penetration test data and results after the engagement is over.

- What behaviors to expect from the target. Defensive behaviors like shunning, blacklisting, or other active defenses may limit the value of a penetration test. If the test is meant to evaluate defenses, this may be useful. If the test is meant to test a complete infrastructure, shunning or blocking the penetration testing team's efforts can waste time and resources.

- What resources are committed to the test. In white- and gray-box testing scenarios, time commitments from the administrators, developers, and other experts on the targets of the test are not only useful but also necessary for an effective test.

- Legal concerns should also be addressed, including a review of the laws that cover the target organization, any remote locations, and any service providers who will be in scope.

- When and how communications will occur. Should the engagement include daily or weekly updates regardless of progress, or will the penetration testers simply report when they are done with their work? How should the testers respond if they discover evidence of a current compromise?

Permission

The tools and techniques we cover in this book are the bread and butter of a penetration tester's job, but they can also be illegal to use without permission. Before you plan (and especially before you execute) a penetration test, you should have appropriate permission. In most cases, you should be sure to have appropriate documentation for that permission in the form of a signed agreement, a memo from senior management, or a similar "get out of jail free" card from a person or people in the target organization with the rights to give you permission.

Why is it called a "get out of jail free" card? It's the document that you would produce if something went wrong. Permission from the appropriate party can help you stay out of trouble if something goes wrong!

Scoping agreements and the rules of engagement must define more than just what will be tested. In fact, documenting the limitations of the test can be just as important as what will be included. The testing agreement or scope documentation should contain disclaimers explaining that the test is valid only at the point in time that it is conducted, and that the scope and methodology chosen can impact the comprehensiveness of the test. After all, a white-box penetration test is far more likely to find issues buried layers deep in a design than a black-box test of well-secured systems!

Problem handling and resolution is another key element of the rules of engagement. Although penetration testers and clients always hope that the tests will run smoothly and won't cause any disruption, testing systems and services, particularly in production environments using actual attack and exploit tools, can cause outages and other problems. In those cases, having a clearly defined communication, notification, and escalation path on both sides of the engagement can help minimize downtime and other issues for the target organization. Penetration testers should carefully document their responsibilities and limitations of liability and ensure that clients know what could go wrong and that both sides agree on how it should be handled. That way, both the known and unknown impacts of the test can be addressed appropriately.

Reconnaissance

Penetration tests begin with a reconnaissance phase, where the testers seek to gather as much information as possible about the target organization. In a white-box test, the testers enter the exercise with significant knowledge, but they still seek to supplement this knowledge with additional techniques.

Passive reconnaissance techniques seek to gather information without directly engaging with the target. Chapter 4, "Cybersecurity Threats," covered a variety of open source intelligence (OSINT) techniques that fit into the category of passive reconnaissance.

Active reconnaissance techniques directly engage the target in intelligence gathering. These techniques include the use of port scanning to identify open ports on systems, *footprinting* to identify the operating systems and applications in use, and vulnerability scanning to identify exploitable vulnerabilities.

One common goal of penetration testers is to identify wireless networks that may present a means of gaining access to an internal network of the target without gaining physical access to the facility. Testers use a technique called *war driving*, where they drive by facilities in a car equipped with high-end antennas and attempt to eavesdrop on or connect to wireless networks. Recently, testers have expanded this approach to the use of drones and uncrewed aerial vehicles (UAVs) in a technique known as *war flying*.

Running the Test

During the penetration test, the testers follow the same process used by attackers. You'll learn more about this process in the discussion of the Cyber Kill Chain in Chapter 8, "Incident Response." However, you should be familiar with some fundamental phases of the test as you prepare for the exam:

- *Initial access* occurs when the attacker exploits a vulnerability to gain access to the organization's network.

- *Privilege escalation* uses hacking techniques to shift from the initial access gained by the attacker to more advanced privileges, such as root access on the same system.

- *Pivoting,* or *lateral movement,* occurs as the attacker uses the initial system compromise to gain access to other systems on the target network.

- Attackers establish *persistence* on compromised networks by installing backdoors and using other mechanisms that will allow them to regain access to the network, even if the initial vulnerability is patched.

Penetration testers make use of many of the same tools used by real attackers as they perform their work. *Exploitation frameworks,* such as Metasploit, simplify the use of vulnerabilities by providing a modular approach to configuring and deploying vulnerability exploits.

Cleaning Up

At the conclusion of a penetration test, the testers conduct close-out activities that include presenting their results to management and cleaning up the traces of their work. Testers should remove any tools that they installed on systems as well as any persistence mechanisms that they put in place. The close-out report should provide the target with details on the vulnerabilities discovered during the test and advice on improving the organization's cybersecurity posture.

Training and Exercises

Organizations conduct a wide variety of training programs designed to help employees understand their cybersecurity role. Cybersecurity analysts often participate in training programs that are set up as exercises using a competition-style format, pitting a team of attackers against a team of defenders.

Running exercises helps to identify vulnerabilities in the organization's systems, networks, and applications, similar to the results achieved from penetration testing. Exercises also provide employees with hands-on experience both attacking and defending systems. This helps boost cybersecurity skills and awareness among the technical staff.

When conducting an exercise, participants are often divided into three teams:

- *Red team* members are the attackers who attempt to gain access to systems.

- *Blue team* members are the defenders who must secure systems and networks from attacks. The blue team also monitors the environment during the exercise, conducting active defense techniques. The blue team commonly gets a head start with some time to secure systems before the attack phase of the exercise begins.

- *White team* members are the observers and judges. They serve as referees to settle disputes over the rules and watch the exercise to document lessons learned from the test. The white team is able to observe the activities of both the red and blue teams and is also responsible for ensuring that the exercise does not cause production issues.

Purple Teaming

At the end of an exercise, it's common to bring the red and the blue teams together to share information about tactics and lessons learned. Each team walks the other through their role in the exercise, helping everyone learn from the process. This combination of knowledge from the red and blue teams is often referred to as *purple teaming*, because combining red and blue makes purple.

Capture the flag (CTF) exercises are a fun way to achieve training objectives. In a CTF exercise, the red team begins with set objectives, such as disrupting a website, stealing a file from a secured system, or causing other security failures. The exercise is scored based on how many objectives the red team was able to achieve compared to how many the blue team prevented them from executing.

Exercises don't need to take place using production systems. In many cases, an organization might set up special environment solely for the purpose of the exercise. This provides a safe playground for the test and minimizes the probability that an attack will damage production systems. Other exercises may not even use real systems at all. *Tabletop exercises* simply gather participants in the same room to walk through their response to a fictitious exercise scenario.

Summary

Security assessment and testing plays a crucial role in the ongoing management of a cybersecurity program. The techniques discussed in this chapter help cybersecurity professionals maintain effective security controls and stay abreast of changes in their environment that might alter their security posture.

Vulnerability scanning identifies potential security issues in systems, applications, and devices, providing teams with the ability to remediate those issues before they are exploited by attackers. The vulnerabilities that may be detected during these scans include improper patch management, weak configurations, default accounts, and the use of insecure protocols and ciphers.

Penetration testing puts security professionals in the role of attackers and asks them to conduct offensive operations against their targets in an effort to discover security issues. The results of penetration tests provide a roadmap for improving security controls.

Exam Essentials

Be able to list the vulnerabilities that exist in modern computing environments. Cybersecurity professionals should remain aware of the risks posed by vulnerabilities both on-premises and in the cloud. Improper or weak patch management can be the source of many of these vulnerabilities, providing attackers with a path to exploit operating systems, applications, and firmware. Weak configuration settings that create vulnerabilities include open permissions, unsecured root accounts, errors, weak encryption settings, insecure protocol use, default settings, and open ports and services. When a scan detects a vulnerability that does not exist, the report is known as a false positive. When a scan does not detect a vulnerability that actually exists, the report is known as a false negative.

Know the purpose of threat hunting. Threat hunting activities presume that an organization is already compromised and search for indicators of those compromises. Threat hunting efforts include the use of advisories, bulletins, and threat intelligence feeds in an intelligence fusion program. They search for signs that attackers gained initial access to a network and then conducted maneuver activities on that network.

Know the purpose of vulnerability scans. Vulnerability scans leverage application, network, and web application testing to check for known issues. These scans may be conducted in a credentialed or noncredentialed fashion and may be intrusive or nonintrusive, depending on the organization's needs. Analysts reviewing scans should also review logs and configurations for additional context.

Describe how penetration testing places security professionals in the role of attackers. Penetration tests may be conducted in a manner that provides the testers with full access to information before the test (white box), no information at all (black box), or somewhere in between those two extremes (gray box). Testers conduct tests within the rules of engagement and normally begin with reconnaissance efforts, including war driving, war flying, footprinting, and open source intelligence (OSINT). They use this information to gain initial access to a system. From there, they seek to conduct privilege escalation to increase their level of access and lateral movement/pivoting to expand their access to other systems. They seek to achieve persistence to allow continued access after the vulnerability they initially exploited is patched. At the conclusion of the test, they conduct cleanup activities to restore systems to normal working order and remove traces of their activity.

Describe how bug bounty programs incentivize vulnerability reporting. Bug bounty programs allow external security professionals to probe the security of an organization's public-facing systems. Testers who discover vulnerabilities are provided with financial rewards for their participation. This approach is a good way to motivate hackers to work for good, rather than using discovered vulnerabilities against a target.

Know how to use cybersecurity exercises to ensure that teams are prepared for security incidents. Exercises are designed to test the skills of security professionals. Blue teams are responsible for managing the organization's defenses. Offensive hacking is used by red teams as they attempt to gain access to systems on the target network. White teams serve as the neutral moderators of the exercise. Purple teaming is conducted after an exercise to bring together the red and blue teams for knowledge sharing.

Review Questions

1. Which one of the following security assessment techniques assumes that an organization has already been compromised and searches for evidence of that compromise?

    A. Vulnerability scanning

    B. Penetration testing

    C. Threat hunting

    D. War driving

2. Renee is configuring her vulnerability management solution to perform credentialed scans of servers on her network. What type of account should she provide to the scanner?

    A. Domain administrator

    B. Local administrator

    C. Root

    D. Read-only

3. Ryan is planning to conduct a vulnerability scan of a business-critical system using dangerous plug-ins. What would be the best approach for the initial scan?

    A. Run the scan against production systems to achieve the most realistic results possible.

    B. Run the scan during business hours.

    C. Run the scan in a test environment.

    D. Do not run the scan to avoid disrupting the business.

4. Tina is searching for potential gaps in her organization's incident response plan and gathers the team together for an exercise. They do not use any actual IT systems (production or test) in their work but simply discuss how they would respond to a scenario. What term best describes this test?

    A. Red team exercise

    B. Blue team exercise

    C. Tabletop exercise

    D. Purple team exercise

5. Tara recently analyzed the results of a vulnerability scan report and found that a vulnerability reported by the scanner did not exist because the system was actually patched as specified. What type of error occurred?

    A. False positive

    B. False negative

    C. True positive

    D. True negative

6. Brian ran a penetration test against a school's grading system and discovered a flaw that would allow students to alter their grades by exploiting a SQL injection vulnerability. What type of control should he recommend to the school's cybersecurity team to prevent students from engaging in this type of activity?

    A. Confidentiality

    B. Integrity

    C. Alteration

    D. Availability

7. Which one of the following is least likely to affect the type and frequency of vulnerability scans run by an organization?

    A. Technical constraints

    B. License limitations

    C. Regulatory Requirements

    D. Holidays

8. During a vulnerability scan, Brian discovered that a system on his network contained this vulnerability:

    > **THREAT:**
    > Microsoft Server Message Block (SMB) Protocol is a Microsoft network file sharing protocol used in Microsoft Windows.
    > The Microsoft SMB Server is vulnerable to multiple remote code execution vulnerabilities due to the way that the Microsoft Server Message Block 1.0 (SMBv1) server handles certain requests.
    > This security update is rated Critical for all supported editions of Windows Vista, Windows Server 2008, Windows 7, Windows Server 2008 R2, Windows Server 2012 and 2012 R2, Windows 8.1 and RT 8.1, Windows 10 and Windows Server 2016.
    >
    > **IMPACT:**
    > A remote attacker could gain the ability to execute code by sending crafted messages to a Microsoft Server Message Block 1.0 (SMBv1) server.
    >
    > **SOLUTION:**
    > Customers are advised to refer to Microsoft Advisory MS17-010 for more details.
    > Patch:
    > Following are links for downloading patches to fix the vulnerabilities:

    What security control, if deployed, would likely have addressed this issue?

    A. Patch management

    B. File integrity monitoring

    C. Intrusion detection

    D. Threat hunting

9. Which one of the following tools is most likely to detect an XSS vulnerability?

    A. Static application test

    B. Web application vulnerability scanner

    C. Intrusion detection system

    D. Network vulnerability scanner

10. During a penetration test, Patrick deploys a toolkit on a compromised system and uses it to gain access to other systems on the same network. What term best describes this activity?

   A. Lateral movement

   B. Privilege escalation

   C. Footprinting

   D. OSINT

11. Kevin is participating in a security exercise for his organization. His role in the exercise is to use hacking techniques to attempt to gain access to the organization's systems. What role is Kevin playing in this exercise?

   A. Red team

   B. Blue team

   C. Purple team

   D. White team

12. Which one of the following assessment techniques is designed to solicit participation from external security experts and reward them for discovering vulnerabilities?

   A. Threat hunting

   B. Penetration testing

   C. Bug bounty

   D. Vulnerability scanning

13. Kyle is conducting a penetration test. After gaining access to an organization's database server, he installs a backdoor on the server to grant himself access in the future. What term best describes this action?

   A. Privilege escalation

   B. Lateral movement

   C. Maneuver

   D. Persistence

14. Which one of the following techniques would be considered passive reconnaissance?

   A. Port scans

   B. Vulnerability scans

   C. WHOIS lookups

   D. Footprinting

15. Brandon is conducting a penetration test to detect gaps in his organization's security controls. While conducting the test, Brandon should adopt which of the following mindsets?

   A. Defender's mindset

   B. Manager's mindset

   C. Executive's mindset

   D. Attacker's mindset

16. Bruce is conducting a penetration test for a client. The client provided him with details of their systems in advance. What type of test is Bruce conducting?

    A. Gray-box test

    B. Blue-box test

    C. White-box test

    D. Black-box test

17. Lila is working on a penetration testing team and she is unsure whether she is allowed to conduct social engineering as part of the test. What document should she consult to find this information?

    A. Contract

    B. Statement of work

    C. Rules of engagement

    D. Lessons learned report

18. Grace would like to determine the operating system running on a system that she is targeting in a penetration test. Which one of the following techniques will most directly provide her with this information?

    A. Port scanning

    B. Footprinting

    C. Vulnerability scanning

    D. Packet capture

19. Phil is conducting a penetration test and has gained access to a target system. The account he has on that system is a standard user account, and Phil is installing a tool that will allow him to gain root access. What term best describes this activity?

    A. Privilege escalation

    B. Lateral movement

    C. Pivoting

    D. Persistence

20. Jen is conducting a penetration test for a client. The client did not provide her with any details about their systems in advance of the test and Jen is determining this information using reconnaissance techniques. What type of test is Jen performing?

    A. Black box

    B. White box

    C. Gray box

    D. Blue box

Chapter

7

Cybersecurity Technology

THE CERTIFIED INFORMATION SECURITY MANAGER (CISM) DOMAINS AND SUBTOPICS COVERED IN THIS CHAPTER INCLUDE:

✓ Domain 3: Information Security Program

- B. Information Security Program Management

  - 3B1. Information Security Control Design and Selection

  - 3B2. Information Security Control Implementation and Integrations

THE CERTIFIED INFORMATION SECURITY MANAGER (CISM) SUPPORTING TASKS COVERED IN THIS CHAPTER INCLUDE:

✓ 25. Determine whether information security controls are appropriate and effectively manage risk to an acceptable level.

The cybersecurity field relies on a lot of technology to help achieve the goals of confidentiality, integrity, and availability. Although information security managers don't often find themselves in positions where they directly operate technology platforms, they do often lead the effort to select new security controls and also manage teams responsible for operating those controls. For this reason, it's crucial that information security managers understand the various cybersecurity technologies used by their teams.

Endpoint Security

Endpoint devices, such as laptop and desktop computers, mobile phones, and tablets, are the front lines in cybersecurity defensive strategies. They're at a high level of risk because they rest in the hands of end users who may intentionally or accidentally undermine the security mechanisms that protect these devices. For this reason, cybersecurity professionals pay careful attention to managing the secure configuration, monitoring, and management of endpoint systems.

Don't Get Hung Up on Technology

This chapter covers a lot of ground to make sure that you're exposed to all of the different cybersecurity technologies that you might find on the exam. It includes everything from cryptography and network security to cloud and code security. That's a tremendous amount of technical material.

You should certainly be familiar with these topics as you prepare for the CISM exam, but the most important thing to remember is that the CISM is *not* a technical exam. It is a management exam. You'll be asked questions about how to select and apply security controls, but you shouldn't expect to find detailed questions about the operations or design of those controls.

To help you put this in perspective, this chapter covers two of the CISM knowledge statements: K3.3 and K3.4. Those are two of the 26 objectives in Domain 3. That entire domain accounts for 27 percent of the material on the exam. So you'll likely find about 40 questions from this entire domain and there are 24 other exam objectives to cover. On average, this means that you'll only have a couple of questions drawn directly from the material in this chapter. So don't get overwhelmed or dive too deeply into the details here.

However, that doesn't mean that you should just skip over this material. Notice that I said you will only have a couple of questions drawn *directly* from this material. It's likely that you will find questions covering these topics that are more directly tied to other objectives, such as risk management and program design. The takeaway here is that you should have a *manager's* perspective on these topics, not a technician's perspective.

Malware Prevention

Malicious software, or *malware*, is one of the most common threats to endpoints. Malicious software may invade a network, spreading under its own power, or it may arrive on a system when a user clicks a malicious link or installs unsafe software. Once it has a foothold on a system, malware may be used to gain control of system resources and to steal sensitive information.

Antimalware software uses two different mechanisms to protect systems against malicious software:

- *Signature detection* uses databases of known malware patterns and scans the files and memory of a system for any data matching the pattern of known malicious software. If it finds suspect contents, it can then remove the content from the system or quarantine it for further analysis. When you're using signature detection, it is critical that you frequently update the virus definition file to ensure that you have current signatures for newly discovered malware.

- *Heuristic detection* takes a different approach. Instead of using patterns of known malicious activity, these systems attempt to model normal activity and then report when they discover anomalies—activity that deviates from that normal pattern.

Administrators typically install antimalware software on all the systems in their organization and then take advantage of centralized consoles to ensure the software remains updated and to receive incident reports from managed endpoints.

Endpoint Detection and Response

Today, virtually every system out there has basic malware protection installed. Organizations are now deploying more sophisticated tools, known as *endpoint detection and response (EDR)* platforms. EDR extends traditional malware protection to include four important capabilities:

- Detecting security incidents
- Containing incidents that are detected
- Investigating contained incidents
- Remediating endpoints back to their pre-compromised state

That's a tall order and these solutions aren't perfect, but they go a long way toward automating an organization's endpoint security capabilities and incident response workflow.

Data Loss Prevention

Data loss prevention (DLP) solutions provide technology that helps an organization enforce information handling policies and procedures to prevent data loss and theft. They search systems for stores of sensitive information that might be unsecured and monitor network traffic for potential attempts to remove sensitive information from the organization. They can act quickly to block the transmission before damage is done and alert administrators to the attempted breach.

DLP systems work in two different environments:

- *Host-based DLP* uses software agents installed on a single system that search the system for the presence of sensitive information. These searches often turn up Social Security numbers, credit card numbers, and other sensitive information in the most unlikely places! Detecting the presence of stored sensitive information allows security professionals to take prompt action to either remove it or secure it with encryption. Taking the time to secure or remove information now will be worth it in the long run if the device is lost, stolen, or compromised. Host-based DLP can also monitor system configuration and user actions, blocking undesirable actions. For example, some organizations use host-based DLP to block users from accessing USB-based removable media devices that they might use to carry information out of the organization's secure environment.

- *Network-based DLP* systems monitor outbound network traffic, watching for any transmissions that contain unencrypted sensitive information. They can then block those transmissions, preventing the unsecured loss of sensitive information. DLP systems may simply block traffic that violates the organization's policy, or, in some cases, they may automatically apply encryption to the content. This automatic encryption is commonly used with DLP systems that focus on email.

DLP systems also have two different types of detection mechanisms that they use to identify sensitive data:

- *Pattern matching* watches for the telltale signs of sensitive information. For example, if the DLP sees a number that is formatted like a credit card or Social Security number, it can automatically trigger an alert based on that pattern. Similarly, the DLP may contain a database of sensitive terms, such as "Top Secret" or "Business Confidential," and trigger when it sees those terms in a transmission.

- *Watermarking* allows systems or administrators to apply electronic tags to sensitive documents and then the DLP system can monitor systems and networks for unencrypted content containing those tags.

DLP systems may also operate as cloud-based managed security services. The service provider operates a DLP system that customers access in the cloud. This service delivery model relieves customers of the burden of operating and maintaining the DLP system themselves.

Change and Configuration Management

Configuration management tracks the way that specific endpoint devices are set up. Configuration management tracks both the operating systems settings and the inventory of software installed on a device. *Change management* programs provide organizations with a formal process for identifying, requesting, approving, and implementing changes to configurations.

Baselining is an important component of configuration management. A baseline is a snapshot of a system or application at a given point in time. It may be used to assess whether a system has changed outside of an approved change management process. System administrators may compare a running system to a baseline to identify all changes to the system and then compare those changes to a list of approved change requests.

Version control is also a critical component of change management programs, particularly in the areas of software and script development. Versioning assigns each release of a piece of software an incrementing version number that may be used to identify any given copy.

Configuration management should also create artifacts that may be used to help understand system configuration. For example, diagrams often play an important role in helping security professionals understand how a system was designed and configured. These can be crucial when performing time-sensitive troubleshooting or incident investigations.

Together, change and configuration management allow technology professionals to track the status of hardware, software, and firmware, ensuring that change occurs when desired but in a controlled fashion that minimizes risk to the organization.

Patch Management

Applying patches to operating systems is critical because it ensures that systems are not vulnerable to security exploits discovered by attackers. Each time an operating system vendor discovers a new vulnerability, they create a patch that corrects the issue. Promptly applying patches ensures a clean and tidy operating system.

In Windows, the Windows Update mechanism is the simplest way to apply security patches to systems as soon as they are released. On Linux systems, administrators may take advantage of a variety of update mechanisms depending on their specific Linux distributions and organizational practices.

As a security administrator, you should not only ensure that your systems are configured to receive updates, you should also analyze the output of patch management processes to ensure that those patches are applied. Configuration management tools can assist you with automating this work. They also help you keep track of patches to the applications that you run in your organization.

System Hardening

System hardening involves analyzing the default settings of your operating system and removing services and components that are not required to meet your business needs.

As you perform system hardening, you should accomplish a few important tasks:

- Remove unnecessary software and operating system components to configure the system for the least functionality required to perform its function. This is an activity known as reducing the attack surface. The fewer things you have installed on a system, the fewer opportunities for an attacker to exploit.

- Lock down the host firewall to only allow access to those open ports and services that are intended for use by other systems.

- Disable any default accounts and passwords that came with the operating system or applications you installed. These default accounts provide attackers with a starting point for brute-force attacks and, when configured with default passwords, will be quickly compromised if exposed to the Internet.

- Verify that system configuration settings match best practices. On Windows systems, this may mean modifying registry settings to configure your system to meet minimum security requirements. On Linux systems, you may need to modify configuration files to perform similar hardening tasks.

Network Security

Networks also play a crucial role in an organization's cybersecurity program. Endpoints, servers, and other devices all rely on the network to communicate with one another. Networks are often trusted to carry sensitive information within an organization. Cybersecurity professionals use a variety of controls to ensure the security of their networks.

Network Segmentation

Well-designed networks group systems into network segments based on their security level. This approach limits the risk that a compromised system on one network segment will be able to affect a system on a different network segment. It also makes it more difficult for a malicious insider to cause the organization damage.

Firewalls

Network *firewalls* serve as the security guards of a network, analyzing all attempts to connect to systems on a network and determining whether the request should be allowed or denied according to the organization's security policy. They also play an important role in network segmentation.

Firewalls often sit at the network perimeter, in between an organization's routers and the Internet. From this network location, they can easily see all inbound and outbound connections. Traffic on the internal network may flow between trusted systems unimpeded, but anything crossing the perimeter to or from the Internet must be evaluated by the firewall.

Typical border firewalls have three network interfaces because they connect three different security zones together, as shown in Figure 7.1.

FIGURE 7.1 Network firewalls divide networks into three zones.

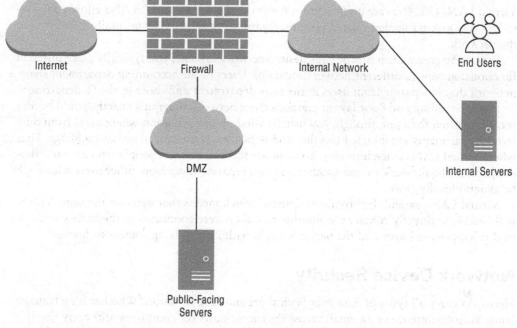

One interface connects to the Internet or another untrusted network. This is the interface between the protected networks and the outside world. Generally speaking, firewalls allow many different kinds of connections out to this network when initiated by a system on more trusted networks, but they block most inbound connection attempts, allowing only those that meet the organization's security policy.

A second interface connects to the organization's *intranet*. This is the internal network where most systems reside. This intranet zone may be further subdivided into segments for endpoint systems, wireless networks, guest networks, data center networks, and other business needs. The firewall may be configured to control access between those subnets, or the organization may use additional firewalls to segment those networks.

The third interface connects to the demilitarized zone (*DMZ*) network. The DMZ is a network where you can place systems that must accept connections from the outside world, such as a mail or web server. Those systems are placed in a separate security zone because they have a higher risk of compromise. If an attacker compromises a DMZ system, the firewall still blocks them from breaching the intranet. This approach is also known as a screened subnet.

Network designs using this philosophy often created an implicit trust in systems based on their network security zone. This approach is now going out of style in favor of a security philosophy known as *zero-trust*. Under the zero-trust approach, systems do not gain privileges based solely on their network location.

Virtual LANs

Virtual LANs (*VLANs*) are an important network security control. VLANs allow you to logically group together related systems, regardless of where they normally exist on the network.

When you create diagrams of your desired network layouts, you typically place different functional groups in different network locations. Users in the accounting department share a network that is separate from users in the sales department and those in the IT department.

If your building and floor layout matched those network diagrams exactly, you'd be all set. More often than not, though, you usually wind up in a situation where users from different departments are mingled together and departments are spread across buildings. That's where virtual LANs come into play. You can use them to connect people who are on different parts of the network to one another and also separate them from other users who might be geographically close.

Virtual LANs extend the broadcast domain, which means that users on the same VLAN will be able to directly contact one another as if they were connected to the same switch. All of this happens at Layer 2 of the network stack, without involving routers or firewalls.

Network Device Security

Networks carry all types of data over both short and long distances. Whether it's a transatlantic videoconference or an email across the room, many different networks carry the 1s and 0s that make communications work. Routers and switches are the core building blocks of these networks and require special security attention.

Switches do create networks, but they are limited to creating local networks. Switches generally operate at Layer 2 of the OSI model—the Data Link layer—where they work with MAC addresses only.

Some switches can perform limited functions at Layer 3 of the OSI model—the Network layer—where they can interpret IP addresses. In those cases, switches are beginning to take on the function of routers.

Routers play a higher-level role, connecting networks together by serving as a central aggregation point for network traffic heading to or from a large network. The router serves as the air traffic controller of the network, making decisions about the best paths for traffic to follow as it travels to its final destination. Routers also perform some security functions, using access control lists to limit the traffic that may enter or leave a network based on the organization's security policies. This type of filtering using access control lists does not pay attention to connection state and is known as *stateless inspection*.

Switches

Network engineers use *switches* to connect devices to networks. They are simple-looking devices that contain a large number of network ports. Switches may be very small, with 8 or fewer ports, or they can be quite large, with 500 or more ports.

Switches are normally hidden away inside wiring closets and other secure locations. Each switch port is connected to one end of a network cable. Those cables then disappear into special pipes known as conduits for distribution around a building.

When the cable reaches the final destination, it usually terminates in a neat-looking wall faceplate. This provides a way for users and technicians to connect and disconnect computers from the network easily without damaging the cables inside the wall or having unsightly unused wires lying about the room.

Some devices directly connect to switch ports through the use of wired networks. Many other devices don't use wires but instead depend on radio-based wireless networks. These networks are created by wireless access points (APs). These APs contain radios that send and receive network signals to mobile devices. The AP itself has a wired connection back to the switch, allowing the wireless devices to connect to the rest of the network.

Switch Physical Security

One of the most important security tasks for switches is maintaining the physical security of the device. Unlike routers, which are normally centrally located in secure data centers or network rooms, switches are generally spread all over the place, providing connectivity at the edge of the network in every building and floor throughout an organization. From a security perspective, this can be a nightmare because it is critical to keep those switches locked away where nobody can physically access them without authorization. The reason for this is simple: if someone gains access to your switch, they can take control of that portion of the network.

VLAN Security

Switch administrators should implement some common practices to ensure the secure implementation of VLANs:

Implement VLAN pruning.   Switches use a technology known as *VLAN trunking* to carry VLANs across the many switches that make up a network. This allows any switch port on the network to join any VLAN trunked to that switch. VLAN pruning implements the least privilege principle and only trunks VLANs to switches if the VLAN is needed on that switch. This requires a little more work on the part of network administrators, but it also reduces the risk of a compromised switch. For example, if you have a VLAN for the sales department and the sales department is contained within a single building, you should trunk that VLAN within the building but not into other buildings.

Block VLAN hopping.   Malicious users may attempt an attack known as *VLAN hopping* to change from their authorized VLAN to one containing resources that they would like to attack. They might do this through a variety of means, but most rely on pretending to be a switch and asking the switch to trunk VLANs to the malicious user's device. The countermeasures for this attack vary from device to device, but generally speaking, you should configure your switches to deny automatic VLAN trunking negotiation and only trunk VLANs when explicitly authorized by a network administrator.

Port Security

Port security protects against attackers disconnecting an authorized device from the wired network and replacing it with a rogue device that may eavesdrop on other users or attempt to access secure network resources. Port security works by limiting the MAC addresses that may be used on a particular switch port and requiring administrator intervention to change out a device. Port security works in two modes:

- In *static* mode, the administrator manually configures each switch port with the allowable MAC addresses. This is very time-consuming, but this MAC filtering approach is the most secure way to implement port security.

- In *dynamic*, or "sticky" mode, the administrator enables port security and then tells the switch to memorize the first MAC address that it sees on any given port and then restrict access to that MAC address. This makes configuration much faster but can be risky if you have unused but active switch ports.

Routers

Routers play a higher-level role, connecting networks together by serving as a central aggregation point for network traffic heading to or from a large network. The router makes decisions about the best paths for traffic to follow as it travels to its final destination. The router plays a role on the network that is similar to the way an air traffic controller organizes planes in the sky, sending them to their correct destination.

Routers also play an important role in network security. They are often located both physically and logically between the firewall and another network. Because they see traffic before network firewalls, they can perform filtering that reduces the load on the network firewall. Routers aren't great at performing complex filtering, but network administrators can configure them to perform basic screening of network traffic. Routers share some common functionality with firewalls, but they are definitely not a substitute for firewall technology. Firewalls differ from routers in several ways:

- Firewalls are purpose-specific devices and are much more efficient at performing complex filtering than routers.

- Firewalls have advanced rule capabilities. They allow you to create rules that are conditional upon the time of day, users involved, and other criteria.

- Firewalls offer more advanced security functionality. They can incorporate threat intelligence, perform application inspection, and integrate with intrusion prevention systems to provide enhanced protection to a network.

Firewalls do offer advanced security protection, but administrators may still choose to place some access control lists at the router level to filter traffic before it reaches the firewall to reduce the burden on downstream devices.

Routers also allow you to configure *quality of service (QoS)* controls that provide guaranteed bandwidth to high-priority applications. For example, you might prioritize videoconferencing traffic over routine file transfers.

Network Security Tools

In addition to using routers, switches, and firewalls to carry out security functions, network engineers also take advantage of several dedicated security tools, including virtual private networks, content filters, intrusion detection and prevention systems, and distributed denial-of-service (DDoS) protection systems.

Virtual Private Networks

Virtual private networks (VPNs) provide two important network security functions to IT administrators. First, *site-to-site VPNs* allow the secure interconnection of remote networks, such as connecting branch offices to each other or to a corporate headquarters. Second, *remote access VPNs* provide mobile workers with a mechanism to securely connect from remote locations back to the organization's network.

VPNs work by using encryption to create a virtual tunnel between two systems over the Internet. Everything that enters one end of the tunnel is encrypted, and then it is decrypted when it exits the other end of the tunnel. From the user's perspective, the network appears to function normally, but if an attacker gains access to traffic between the two secure networks, all they see is encrypted information that they can't read.

VPNs require an endpoint on the remote network that accepts VPN connections. Many different devices may serve as VPN endpoints, such as a firewall, router, server, or a dedicated *VPN concentrator*. All of these approaches provide secure VPN connections, but organizations that have high volumes of VPN often choose to use a dedicated VPN concentrator because these devices are efficient at handling VPN connections and can manage high-bandwidth traffic with ease.

If you don't have a high volume of VPN traffic, you might choose to use the firewall, router, or server approach. If you go that way, be warned that VPN traffic requires resource-intensive encryption, and that unlike VPN concentrators, firewalls, routers, and servers usually don't contain specialized hardware that accelerates encryption. Using them as VPN endpoints can cause performance issues.

For many years, most VPNs used a protocol called *Internet Protocol Security (IPsec)* to create these encrypted tunnels. Administrators looking to run VPN connections that support traffic at the Data Link layer could also run the *Layer 2 Tunneling Protocol (LT2P)* over an IPsec connection.

IPsec and L2TP provide robust, secure transport, but they are often difficult to configure and may be blocked by firewalls. For that reason, IPsec is often used for static, site-to-site VPN tunnels but is becoming less common for remote user VPNs.

Remote user VPNs now often rely on *Transport Layer Security (TLS)* technology, which works at the application layer. These VPNs work on any system with a web browser and use port 443 for communications—a port that is typically allowed through almost every firewall. *HTML5 VPNs* provide a web-based interface that allows users to work with internal network resources without actually establishing a presence on the internal network and instead using the web server in a proxying role.

When implementing a remote access VPN, administrators must choose from two different tunneling approaches:

- In a *full-tunnel VPN,* any traffic leaving the remote device is sent through the VPN back to the home network and protected by encryption. This includes not only traffic headed back to the corporate network, but all web browsing and other activity as well.

- In a *split-tunnel VPN,* some traffic is sent through the VPN while other traffic is sent out through the user's local network. The routing policy is set by the VPN administrator. In most cases, they configure the split tunnel to send traffic headed for corporate systems through the VPN while allowing regular Internet traffic to go directly to the destination over the local network. This approach was set up to reduce the burden on VPNs and to conserve bandwidth.

WARNING   Today, most security experts recommend against the use of split-tunnel VPNs. End users generally don't understand the difference and assume that, if they connect to a VPN, all of their network traffic is secure. This provides them with a false sense of security because some of their traffic is actually being sent directly over the Internet and may be subject to eavesdropping.

Another emerging trend is the *Always-On VPN.* In this strategy, all corporate mobile devices are configured to automatically connect to the VPN whenever they are powered on. This takes control away from the end user and ensures that traffic leaving the device is always protected by strong encryption.

Intrusion Detection and Prevention

Intrusion detection systems (IDS) and *intrusion prevention systems (IPS)* play an extremely important role in the defense of networks against hackers and other security threats. Intrusion detection systems sit on the network and monitor traffic, searching for signs of potentially malicious traffic.

For example, an intrusion detection system might notice that a request bound for a web server contains a SQL injection attack, a malformed packet is attempting to create a denial of service, a user's login attempt seems unusual based on the time of day and prior patterns, or that a system on the internal network is attempting to contact a botnet command-and-control server.

All of these situations are examples of security issues that administrators would obviously want to know about. Intrusion detection systems identify this type of situation and then alert administrators to the issue for further investigation.

In many cases, administrators are not available to immediately review alerts and take action or are simply overwhelmed by the sheer volume of alerts generated by an intrusion detection system.

That's where intrusion prevention comes into play. Intrusion prevention systems are just like intrusion detection systems but with a twist: they can take immediate corrective action in response to a detected threat. In most cases, this means taking action to remove the potentially malicious traffic from the network before it reaches endpoint systems. IPSs can achieve this goal through many different mechanisms of action. They might isolate network traffic, close network ports, automatically suspend compromised user accounts, or perform other remediation actions.

 Although many references treat intrusion detection systems (IDS) and intrusion prevention systems (IPS) as different technologies, the reality today is that the same products fill both functions. Any IPS can be set in an "alert only" mode that tells it to act as an IDS.

IDS Errors

Intrusion detection systems can make mistakes. Two different types of errors are caused by these systems, and monitoring those errors is an important part of security analytics:

- *False positive errors* occur when the system alerts administrators to an attack but the attack does not actually exist. This is an annoyance to the administrator, who wastes time investigating the alert, and may lead to administrators ignoring future alerts.

- *False negative errors* occur when an attack actually takes place but the intrusion detection system does not notice it.

IDS Detection Techniques

Intrusion detection and prevention systems use two different technologies to identify suspicious traffic. The most common and effective method is called *signature detection*. This approach works similarly to antivirus software.

Signature-based systems contain very large databases containing patterns of data (or signatures) known to be associated with malicious activity. When the system spots network traffic matching one of those signatures, it triggers an intrusion alert. This approach is also known as rule-based detection.

The downside is that a signature-based system cannot detect a previously unknown attack. If you're one of the first victims of a new attack, it will sneak right past a signature-detection system. The upside is that if the signatures are well designed, these systems work very well, with a low false positive rate. Signature detection is a reliable, time-tested technology.

The second method is known as *anomaly detection*. This model takes a completely different approach to the intrusion detection problem. Instead of trying to develop signatures for all possible malicious activity, the anomaly detection system tries to develop a model of normal activity and then report deviations from that model as suspicious.

For example, an anomaly detection system might notice that a user who normally connects to the VPN from home during the early evening hours is suddenly connecting from Asia in the middle of the night. The system can then either alert administrators or block the connection, depending on the policy. The models developed by these IDS and IPS systems are often application-aware and understand how to dissect the applications protocols in use during a network session.

Anomaly detection has the potential to notice new attack types, but it also has a high false positive error rate and is not widely used by security administrators.

Many modern intrusion detection and prevention systems combine signature detection and anomaly detection capabilities in the same product.

IDS Configurations

There are also differences in the way that intrusion prevention systems are set up and configured on the network. The two major approaches are in-band and out-of-band deployments.

In an *in-band deployment*, the intrusion prevention system sits directly on the network path and all communications must pass through it on their way to their final destination. In this approach, the IPS can block suspicious traffic from reaching its final destination. In-band deployments are also known as inline deployments. Although this approach allows an active response, it also adds the risk that an issue with the IPS can disrupt all network communications because the in-band IPS is a single point of failure.

In an *out-of-band deployment*, the IPS is not in the network path but sits outside the flow of network traffic. It is connected to a SPAN port on a switch, which allows it to receive copies of all traffic sent through the network to scan, but it cannot disrupt the flow of traffic. This approach is also known as *passive mode* because the IPS can still react by sending commands to block future traffic from offending systems, but it cannot stop the initial attack from entering the network because it only learns about that traffic after it has been sent.

DDoS Prevention

Most of the attack techniques used by hackers focus on undermining the confidentiality or integrity of data. One of the common goals of attackers is to steal sensitive information, such as credit card numbers or Social Security numbers, or alter information in an unauthorized fashion, such as increasing bank account balances or defacing a website.

Some attacks, however, focus on disrupting the legitimate use of a system. Unlike other attacks, these target the availability leg of the CIA triad. We call these attacks *denial-of-service (DoS)* attacks. These attacks make a system or resource unavailable to legitimate users by sending thousands or millions of requests to a network, server, or application, overwhelming it and making it unable to answer any requests. It is difficult to distinguish well-executed DoS attack requests from legitimate traffic.

There are two significant issues with this basic DoS approach from the attacker's perspective:

- *DoS attacks require large amounts of bandwidth.* Sending lots of requests that tie up the server requires a large network connection. It becomes a case of who has the bigger network connection.

- *DoS attacks are easy to block.* Once the victim recognizes they are under attack, they can simply block the IP addresses of the attackers.

Distributed denial-of-service (DDoS) attacks overcome these limitations by using botnets to overwhelm their target. The attack requests come from many different network locations, so it is difficult to distinguish them from legitimate requests.

DDoS attacks are a serious threat to system administrators because these attacks can quickly overwhelm a network with illegitimate traffic. Defending against them requires security professionals to understand them well and implement blocking technology on the network that identifies and weeds out suspected attack traffic before it reaches servers. This is often done with the cooperation of Internet service providers (ISPs) and third-party DDoS protection services.

Cloud Computing Security

Cloud computing can be an intimidating term, but the fundamental idea is straightforward: cloud service providers deliver computing services to their customers over the Internet. This could be as simple as Google providing their Gmail service to customers in a web browser or Amazon Web Services (AWS) providing virtualized servers to corporate clients who use them to build their own technology environment. In each of these cases, the provider builds an IT service and uses the Internet to deliver that service to its customers.

Here's a more formal definition of cloud computing from the National Institute of Standards and Technology (NIST):

> Cloud computing is a model for enabling ubiquitous, convenient, on-demand network access to a shared pool of configurable computing resources (e.g., networks, servers, storage, applications, and services) that can be rapidly provisioned and released with minimal management effort or service provider interaction.

Let's walk through some of the components of that definition. Cloud computing is ubiquitous and convenient. The resources provided by the cloud are available to customers wherever they may be. If you have access to the Internet, you can access the cloud. It doesn't matter whether you're sitting in your office or on the beach.

Cloud computing is also on demand. In most cases, you can provision and deprovision cloud resources in a few minutes with a few clicks. You can acquire new cloud resources almost immediately when you need them, and you can turn them off quickly (and stop paying for them!) when they are no longer required.

Many of the key benefits of the cloud derive from the fact that it uses a shared pool of resources that may be configured for different purposes by different users. This sharing allows *oversubscription* because not everyone will use all their resources at the same time, and it achieves economies of scale. The fact that many different users share resources in the same cloud infrastructure is known as *multitenancy*. In a multitenant environment, the same physical hardware might support the workloads and storage needs of many different customers, all of whom operate without any knowledge of or interaction with their fellow customers.

The cloud offers a variety of configurable computing resources. We'll talk about the different cloud service models later in this chapter, but you can acquire infrastructure components, platforms, or entire applications through cloud service providers and then configure them to meet your needs.

The rapid provisioning and releasing of cloud services also takes place with minimal management effort and service provider interaction. Unlike with on-premises hardware acquisition, you can provision cloud services yourself without dealing with account representatives and order processing times. If you need a new cloud server, you don't need to call up Microsoft, Amazon, or Google. You just click a few buttons on their website and you're good to go. From the perspective of most users, the cloud presents seemingly infinite capacity.

Benefits of the Cloud

As organizations consider the appropriate role of the cloud in their technology infrastructure, the essential question that they seek to answer is the appropriate balance of on-premises versus cloud/off-premises resources. The correct balance will vary from organization to organization. Understanding some of the major benefits provided by the cloud is helpful in finding that correct balance:

- *On-demand self-service computing*. Cloud resources are available when and where you need them. This provides developers and technologists with incredible agility, reducing cycle times and increasing the speed of deployment.

- *Scalability*. As the demand for a cloud-based service increases, customers can manually or automatically increase the capacity of their operations. In some cloud environments, the cloud service provider may do this in a manner that is completely transparent to the customer, scaling resources behind the scenes. Cloud providers achieve scalability in two ways:

  - *Vertical scaling* increases the capacity of existing servers, as shown in Figure 7.2(a). For example, you might change the number of CPU cores or the amount of memory assigned to a server. In the physical world, this means opening up a server and adding physical hardware. In the cloud, you can just click a few buttons and add memory or compute capacity.

  - *Horizontal scaling* adds more servers to a pool of clustered servers, as shown in Figure 7.2(b). If you run a website that supports 2,000 concurrent users with two servers, you might add a new server every time your typical usage increases by another 1,000 users. Cloud computing makes this quite easy since you can just replicate your existing server with a few clicks.

FIGURE 7.2   (a) Vertical scaling vs. (b) Horizontal scaling

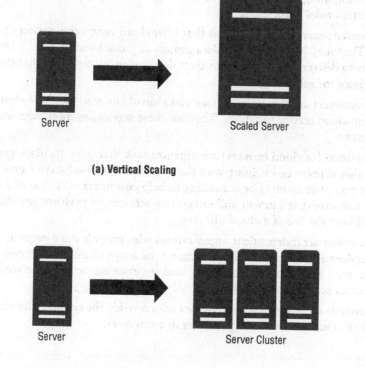

(a) Vertical Scaling

(b) Horizontal Scaling

- *Elasticity*. Elasticity and scalability are closely related. Scalability is focused on rapidly increasing capacity. Elasticity says that capacity should expand *and contract* as needs change to optimize costs. If your website starts to experience a burst in activity, elasticity allows you to automatically add servers until that capacity is met and then remove those servers when the capacity is no longer needed.

- *Measured service*. Everything you do in the cloud is measured by the provider. Providers track the number of seconds of processing time you consume, the amount of storage you occupy, the number of log entries that you generate, and many other measures. They use this information to be able to assess charges based on your usage. You pay for exactly what you request—no more and no less.

- *Agility* and *flexibility*. The speed to provision cloud resources and the ability to use them for short periods of time lends tremendous agility and flexibility to technology organizations. Developers and engineers who wish to try a new idea can rapidly spin up a test environment, evaluate the approach, and decide whether to move it into production with minimal effort and cost.

Cloud Roles

In any cloud computing environment, different organizations take on different roles. There are five important roles in the cloud:

- *Cloud service providers* are the firms that offer cloud computing services to their customers. They may build their own data centers or work hand-in-hand with other cloud providers to deliver their service, but their defining characteristic is that they offer a cloud service for sale.

- *Cloud consumers* are the organizations and individuals who purchase cloud services from cloud service providers. They use these services to meet their own business requirements.

- *Cloud partners* (or cloud brokers) are organizations that offer ancillary products or services that support or integrate with the offerings of a cloud service provider. Cloud partners may offer training or consulting to help customers make use of a cloud service, provide software development and integration services, or perform any other service that facilitates the use of a cloud offering.

- *Cloud auditors* are independent organizations who provide third-party assessments of cloud services and operations. Depending on the scope of the audit engagement, they may provide a general assessment of a cloud environment or focus on security controls for a narrow scope of operations.

- *Cloud carriers* serve as the intermediaries who provide the connectivity that allows the delivery of cloud services from providers to consumers.

The same organization may take on multiple roles. For example, if an organization purchases cloud infrastructure components from a cloud service provider, they are a cloud consumer. If they use those infrastructure components to build a cloud software application that they offer to their own customers, then they are also a cloud service provider themselves.

Cloud Service Models

We categorize the types of services offered by cloud service providers into several buckets based on the nature of the offering. The wide variety of services available in the cloud are often described as *anything as a service (XaaS)*, where X indicates the nature of the specific service. Although there are many different types of cloud services, we often describe them using three major service models: infrastructure as a service (IaaS), software as a service (SaaS), and platform as a service (PaaS).

Infrastructure as a Service (IaaS)

Infrastructure as a service (IaaS) offerings allow customers to purchase and interact with the basic building blocks of a technology infrastructure. These include computing, storage, and networks. Customers then have the flexibility to configure and manage those services in any way they like to meet their own business needs. The customer doesn't need to worry about the management of the underlying hardware, but they do have the ability to customize components to meet their needs. In the IaaS model, the cloud service provider is responsible for managing the physical facilities and the underlying hardware. The provider must also implement security controls that prevent customers from eavesdropping on each other or interfering with each other's use of the infrastructure environment.

Although there are dozens of IaaS providers in the marketplace today, the market is currently dominated by three major players: Amazon Web Services (AWS), Microsoft Azure, and Google Cloud Platform (GCP). These three providers serve the vast majority of IaaS customers and offer a wide breadth of computing, storage, and networking products, as well as supplementary services that reside higher in the stack, such as security monitoring, content delivery networks, and application streaming.

Software as a Service (SaaS)

Software as a service (SaaS) offerings provide customers with access to a fully managed application running in the cloud. The provider is responsible for everything from the operation of the physical data centers to the performance management of the application itself, although some of these tasks may be outsourced to other cloud service providers. In the SaaS model, the customer is only responsible for a limited configuration of the application itself, the selection of what data they wish to use with the cloud solution, and the use of application-provided access controls to limit access to that data.

The SaaS model is widely used to deliver applications ranging from web-based email to enterprise resource planning (ERP) and customer relationship management (CRM) suites. Customers enjoy continued access to cutting-edge software and typically pay for SaaS services using a subscription model. Users of the product normally access the application through a standard web browser and may even use a thin client device, such as the Google Chromebook, shown in Figure 7.3.

Platform as a Service (PaaS)

Platform as a service (PaaS) offerings fit into a middle ground between SaaS and IaaS solutions. In a PaaS offering, the service provider offers a platform where customers may run applications that they have developed themselves. The cloud service provider builds and manages the infrastructure and offers customers an execution environment, which may include code libraries, services, and tools that facilitate code execution.

FIGURE 7.3   Thin clients, such as this Samsung Google Chromebook, are sufficient to access SaaS applications.

Function as a service (FaaS) platforms are an example of PaaS computing. This approach allows customers to upload their own code functions to the provider and the provider will then execute those functions on a scheduled basis, in response to events, and/or on demand. The AWS Lambda service, shown in Figure 7.4, is an example of a FaaS/PaaS offering. Lambda allows customers to write code in Python, Java, C+, PowerShell, Node.js, Ruby, Go, and other programming languages. The Lambda function shown in Figure 7.4 is a Python function designed to read the current temperature from an Internet of Things (IoT) temperature sensor.

Because FaaS environments do not expose customers to the actual server instances executing their code, they are often referred to as *serverless computing* environments. However, this is somewhat of a misnomer, since FaaS environments most certainly do have servers running the code, but they do so in a manner that is transparent to the FaaS customer.

FIGURE 7.4   AWS Lambda function as a service environment

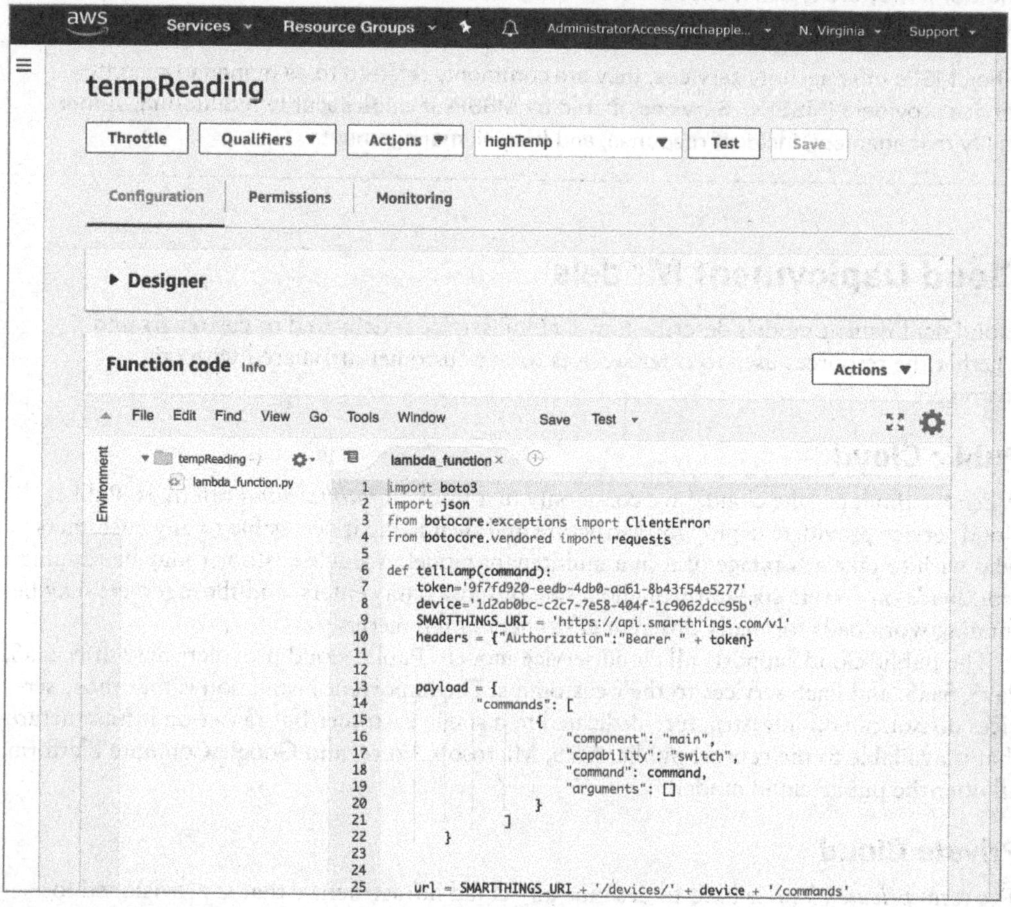

```
aws    Services ▾   Resource Groups ▾   ★   △   AdministratorAccess/mchapple... ▾      N. Virginia ▾   Support ▾

tempReading

[ Throttle ]  [ Qualifiers ▾ ]  [ Actions ▾ ]  [ highTemp            ▾ ]  [ Test ]  [ Save ]

Configuration     Permissions     Monitoring

▶ Designer

Function code  Info                                                          [ Actions ▾ ]

  ▲  File  Edit  Find  View  Go  Tools  Window      Save  Test ▾           ⌄⌄  ⚙

    ▼ 📁 tempReading    ⚙▾         lambda_function ×  ⊕
       lambda_function.py         1   import boto3
                                  2   import json
                                  3   from botocore.exceptions import ClientError
                                  4   from botocore.vendored import requests
                                  5
                                  6   def tellLamp(command):
                                  7       token='9f7fd920-eedb-4db0-aa61-8b43f54e5277'
                                  8       device='1d2ab0bc-c2c7-7e58-404f-1c9062dcc95b'
                                  9       SMARTTHINGS_URI = 'https://api.smartthings.com/v1'
                                  10      headers = {"Authorization":"Bearer " + token}
                                  11
                                  12
                                  13      payload = {
                                  14          "commands": [
                                  15              {
                                  16                  "component": "main",
                                  17                  "capability": "switch",
                                  18                  "command": command,
                                  19                  "arguments": []
                                  20              }
                                  21          ]
                                  22      }
                                  23
                                  24
                                  25      url = SMARTTHINGS_URI + '/devices/' + device + '/commands'
```

Managed Services

Organizations may also choose to outsource some or all of the management of their tech-nology infrastructure. *Managed service providers (MSPs)* are service organizations who provide information technology as a service to their customers. MSPs may handle an orga-nization's IT needs completely, or they may offer focused services such as network design and implementation, application monitoring, or cloud cost management. MSPs are not necessarily cloud service providers (CSPs) themselves (although they may be both MSP

(continues)

(continued)

and CSP). They are typically capable of working across a customer's total environment, including both cloud and on-premises deployments.

When MSPs offer security services, they are commonly referred to as managed security service providers (MSSPs). Services offered by MSSPs include security monitoring, vulnerability management, incident response, and firewall management.

Cloud Deployment Models

Cloud deployment models describe how a cloud service is delivered to customers and whether the resources used to offer services to one customer are shared with other customers.

Public Cloud

When we think of "the cloud," we commonly first think of *public cloud* offerings. Public cloud service providers deploy infrastructure and then make it accessible to any customers who wish to take advantage of it in a multitenant model. A single customer may be running workloads on servers spread throughout one or more data centers, and those servers may be running workloads for many different customers simultaneously.

The public cloud supports all cloud service models. Public cloud providers may offer IaaS, PaaS, SaaS, and FaaS services to their customers. The important distinction is that those services do not run on infrastructure dedicated to a single customer but rather on infrastructure that is available to the general public. AWS, Microsoft Azure, and Google Compute Platform all offer the public cloud model.

Private Cloud

The term *private cloud* is used to describe any cloud infrastructure that is provisioned for use by a single customer. This infrastructure may be built and managed by the organization that will be using the infrastructure, or it may be built and managed by a third party. The distinction here is that only one customer uses the environment. For this reason, private cloud services tend to have excess unused capacity to support peak demand and, as a result, are not as cost efficient as public cloud services.

The Intelligence Community Leverages a "Private Public" Cloud

The U.S. Intelligence Community (IC) has long been one of the largest, if not *the* largest, users of computing power in the world. In fact, many advances in computing began as projects in support of IC customers. As the private sector began a rapid migration to the public cloud, IC technologists took note but lamented that strict security requirements prevented them from using any multitenant environment for classified national security activities.

IC technologists worked with AWS to address this problem and, in 2014, launched the AWS Commercial Cloud Services (C2S) region that provides dedicated AWS services to IC customers. The region is operated by AWS but physically resides at a Central Intelligence Agency (CIA) facility and is completely air-gapped from the Internet, providing an incredibly high level of security.

The interesting thing about this approach is that it fits the definition of private cloud because AWS is operating the C2S region specifically for the IC, but it runs with the same tools and services available in the AWS public cloud, presumably at a much greater cost.

In 2017, AWS announced the launch of the AWS Secret Region, an even broader effort designed to support any classified work across the U.S. government. Microsoft also announced the availability of Azure Government Secret for the same purpose. The broad availability of those regions across government agencies makes the secret regions fit the definition of community cloud rather than private cloud.

Community Cloud

A *community cloud* service shares characteristics of both the public and private models. Community cloud services do run in a multitenant environment, but the tenants are limited to members of a specifically designed community. Community membership is normally defined based on a shared mission, similar security and compliance requirements, or other commonalities.

The HathiTrust digital library, shown in Figure 7.5, is an example of community cloud in action. Academic research libraries joined together to form a consortium that provides access to their collections of books. Students and faculty at HathiTrust member institutions may log into the community cloud service to access resources.

Hybrid Cloud

Hybrid cloud is a catch-all term used to describe cloud deployments that blend public, private, and/or community cloud services together. It is not simply purchasing both public and private cloud services and using them together. Hybrid cloud requires the use of technology that unifies the different cloud offerings into a single coherent platform.

For example, a firm might operate their own private cloud for the majority of their workloads and then leverage public cloud capacity when demand exceeds the capacity of their private cloud infrastructure. This approach is known as public cloud *bursting*.

AWS Outposts, shown in Figure 7.6, are examples of hybrid cloud computing. Customers of this service receive a rack of computing equipment that they install in their own data centers. The equipment in the rack is maintained by AWS but provisioned by the customer in the same manner as their AWS public cloud resources. This approach qualifies as hybrid cloud because customers can manage both their on-premises AWS Outposts private cloud deployment and their public cloud AWS services through the same management platform.

FIGURE 7.5   HathiTrust is an example of community cloud computing.

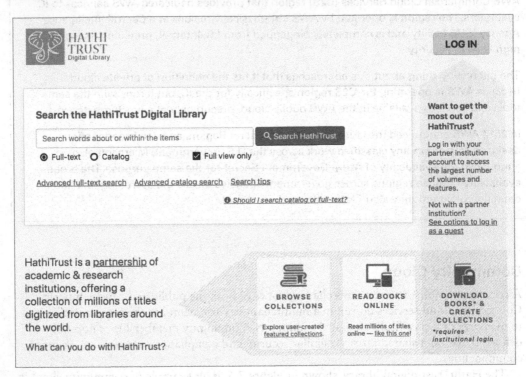

Shared Responsibility Model

In some ways, cybersecurity work in a cloud-centric environment is quite similar to on-premises cybersecurity. No matter where our systems are hosted, we still need to think about the confidentiality, integrity, and availability of our data and implement strong access controls and other mechanisms that protect those primary objectives.

However, cloud security operations also differ significantly from on-premises environments because cloud customers must divide responsibilities between one or more service providers and the customers' own cybersecurity teams. This type of operating environment is known as the *shared responsibility model*. Figure 7.7 shows the common division of responsibilities in IaaS, PaaS, and SaaS environments.

In some cases, this division of responsibility is straightforward. Cloud providers, by their nature, are always responsible for the security of both hardware and the physical data center environment. If the customer were handling either of these items, the solution would not fit the definition of cloud computing.

FIGURE 7.6   AWS Outposts offer hybrid cloud capability.

Source: Image property of Amazon Web Services; used with permission

FIGURE 7.7   Shared responsibility model for cloud computing

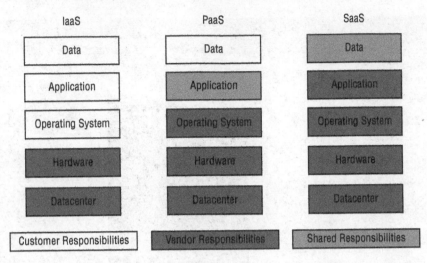

The differences in responsibility come higher up in the stack and vary depending on the nature of the cloud service being used. In an IaaS environment, the customer takes over security responsibility for everything that isn't infrastructure—the operating system, applications, and data that they run in the IaaS environment.

In a PaaS solution, the vendor also takes on responsibility for the operating system, whereas the customer retains responsibility for the data being placed into the environment and configuring its security. Responsibility for the application layer is shared between the service provider and the customer, and the exact division of responsibilities shifts based on the nature of the service. For example, if the PaaS platform provides runtime interpreters for customer code, the cloud provider is responsible for the security of those interpreters.

In an SaaS environment, the provider takes on almost all security responsibility. The customer retains some shared control over the data that they place in the SaaS environment and the configuration of access controls around that data, but the SaaS provider is being paid to take on the burden of most operational tasks, including cybersecurity.

> Be sure to clearly document the division of responsibilities for cybersecurity tasks. This is particularly important in situations requiring compliance with external regulations. For example, organizations subject to the Payment Card Industry Data Security Standard (PCI DSS) should work with cloud providers to document the specific controls and responsibilities for meeting each one of the many PCI DSS requirements. Cloud providers are familiar with this process, and many host websites provide detailed mappings of their controls to common compliance regimes.

Cloud Standards and Guidelines

The cybersecurity community offers a variety of reference documents to help organizations come to a common understanding of the cloud and cloud security issues.

The Cloud Reference Architecture, published by the National Institute for Standards and Technology (NIST) in their SP 500-292, offers a high-level taxonomy for cloud services. The cloud roles discussed earlier in this chapter are adapted from the NIST Cloud Reference Architecture. Figure 7.8 shows a high-level view of NIST's vision for how the elements of the architecture fit together.

FIGURE 7.8   Cloud Reference Architecture

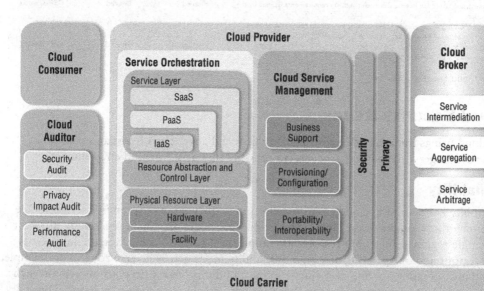

Source: NIST SP 500-292

The Cloud Security Alliance (CSA) is an industry organization focused on developing and promoting best practices in cloud security. They developed the Cloud Controls Matrix (CCM) as a reference document designed to help organizations understand the appropriate use of cloud security controls and map those controls to various regulatory standards. The CCM is a lengthy Excel spreadsheet, available for download from https://cloudsecurityalliance.org/artifacts/cloud-controls-matrix-v4. An excerpt appears in Figure 7.9.

FIGURE 7.9   Cloud Controls Matrix excerpt

Control Specification	IaaS	PaaS	SaaS
Establish, document, approve, communicate, apply, evaluate and maintain policies and procedures for application security to provide guidance to the appropriate planning, delivery and support of the organization's application security capabilities. Review and update the policies and procedures at least annually.	Shared	CSC-Owned	Shared
Establish, document and maintain baseline requirements for securing different applications.	Shared	Shared	CSP-Owned
Define and implement technical and operational metrics in alignment with business objectives, security requirements, and compliance obligations.	Shared	Shared	CSP-Owned
Define and implement a SDLC process for application design, development, deployment, and operation in accordance with security requirements defined by the organization.	Shared	Shared	CSP-Owned
Implement a testing strategy, including criteria for acceptance of new information systems, upgrades and new versions, which provides application security assurance and maintains compliance while enabling organizational speed of delivery goals. Automate when applicable and possible.	Shared	Shared	CSP-Owned

Source: Cloud Security Alliance

Cloud Security Issues

The cloud brings tremendous operational and financial advantages to organizations, but those advantages also come with new security issues that arise in cloud environments.

Availability

Availability issues exist in cloud environments, just as they do in on-premises settings. One of the major advantages of the cloud is that cloud providers may operate in many different geographic regions, and they often provide simple mechanisms for backing up data across those regions and/or operating in a high-availability mode across diverse zones. For example, a company operating a web server cluster in the cloud may choose to place servers on each major continent to serve customers in those regions and also to provide geographic diversity in the event of a large-scale issue in a particular geographic region.

Data Sovereignty

The distributed nature of cloud computing involves the use of geographically distant facilities to achieve high availability and to place content in close proximity to users. This may mean that a customer's data is stored and processed in data centers across many different countries, either with or without explicit notification. Unless customers understand how their data is stored, this could introduce legal concerns.

Data sovereignty is a principle that states that data is subject to the legal restrictions of any jurisdiction where it is collected, stored, or processed. Under this principle, a customer might wind up subject to the legal requirements of a jurisdiction where they have no involvement other than the fact that one of their cloud providers operates a data center within that jurisdiction.

Security professionals responsible for managing cloud services should be certain that they understand how their data is stored, processed, and transmitted across jurisdictions. They may also choose to encrypt data using keys that remain outside the providers' control to ensure that they maintain sole control over their data.

Some cloud providers offer explicit control over the use of resources in specific regions. For example, Figure 7.10 shows the controls used by Zoom users to block the use of data centers located in China or Hong Kong.

FIGURE 7.10   Limiting the data center regions used for a Zoom meeting

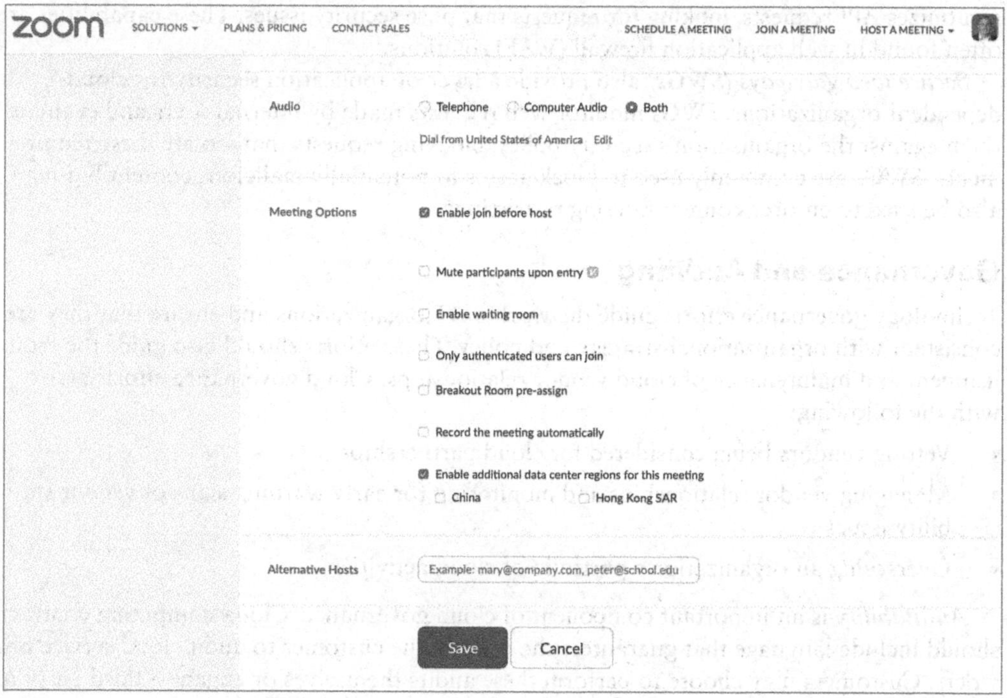

Virtualization Security

Virtual machine escape vulnerabilities are the most serious issue that may exist in a virtualized environment, particularly when a device is running several virtual systems of differing security levels. In an escape attack, the attacker has access to a single virtual guest system and then manages to leverage that access to intrude upon the resources assigned to a different virtual machine. The hypervisor is supposed to prevent this type of access by restricting a virtual machine's access to only those resources assigned to that machine. Escape attacks allow a process running on the virtual machine to "escape" those hypervisor restrictions.

Virtual machine sprawl occurs when IaaS users create virtual service instances and then forget about them or abandon them, leaving them to accrue costs and accumulate security issues over time. Organizations should maintain instance awareness to avoid VM sprawl issues.

Cloud Application Security

Cloud applications depend heavily on the use of application programming interfaces (APIs) to provide service integration and interoperability. In addition to implementing the secure coding practices discussed in Chapter 6, "Security Assessment and Testing," security analysts responsible for API-based applications should implement *API inspection* technology that scrutinizes API requests, looking for requests that pose security issues. These capabilities are often found in web application firewall (WAF) solutions.

Secure web gateways (SWGs) also provide a layer of application security for cloud-dependent organizations. SWGs monitor web requests made by internal users and evaluate them against the organization's security policy, blocking requests that violate these requirements. SWGs are commonly used to block access to potentially malicious content but may also be used to enforce content filtering restrictions.

Governance and Auditing

Technology governance efforts guide the work of IT organizations and ensure that they are consistent with organizational strategy and policy. These efforts should also guide the establishment and maintenance of cloud vendor relationships. Cloud governance efforts assist with the following:

- Vetting vendors being considered for cloud partnerships
- Managing vendor relationships and monitoring for early warning signs of vendor stability issues
- Overseeing an organization's portfolio of cloud activities

Auditability is an important component of cloud governance. Cloud computing contracts should include language that guarantees the right of the customer to audit cloud service providers. Customers may choose to perform these audits themselves or engage a third party to perform an independent audit. The use of auditing is essential to providing customers with the assurance that the provider is operating in a secure manner and meeting its contractual data protection obligations.

Cloud Security Controls

Cloud providers and third-party organizations offer a variety of solutions that help organizations achieve their security objectives in the cloud. Organizations may choose to adopt cloud-native controls offered by their cloud service provider, third-party solutions, or a combination of the two.

Controls offered by cloud service providers have the advantage of direct integration with the provider's offerings, often making them cost-effective and user-friendly. Third-party solutions are often more costly, but they bring the advantage of integrating with a variety of cloud providers, facilitating the management of multicloud environments.

Cloud Access Security Brokers

Most organizations use a variety of cloud service providers for different purposes. It's not unusual to find that a large organization purchases cloud services from dozens, or even hundreds, of different providers. This is especially true when organizations use highly specialized SaaS products. Managing security policies consistently across these services poses a major challenge for cybersecurity analysts.

Cloud access security brokers (CASBs) are software tools that serve as intermediaries between cloud service users and cloud service providers. This positioning allows them to monitor user activity and enforce policy requirements. CASBs operate using two different approaches:

- Inline CASB solutions physically or logically reside in the connection path between the user and the service. They may do this through a hardware appliance or an endpoint agent that routes requests through the CASB. This approach requires configuration of the network and/or endpoint devices. It provides the advantage of seeing requests before they are sent to the cloud service, allowing the CASB to block requests that violate policy.

- API-based CASB solutions interact not directly with the user but rather with the cloud provider through the provider's API. This approach provides direct access to the cloud service and does not require any user device configuration. However, it also does not allow the CASB to block requests that violate policy. API-based CASBs are limited to monitoring user activity and reporting on or correcting policy violations after the fact.

Resource Policies

Cloud providers offer *resource policies* that customers may use to limit the actions that users of their accounts may take. Implementing resource policies is a good security practice to limit the damage caused by an accidental command, a compromised account, or a malicious insider.

For example, a resource policy might prohibit affected users from using any resources outside specific geographic regions and restrict the services that they may use. Policies may also limit users to only launching smaller server instances in an effort to control costs.

Hardware Security Modules

Hardware security modules (HSMs) are special-purpose computing devices that manage encryption keys and also perform cryptographic operations in a highly efficient manner. HSMs are expensive to purchase and operate, but they provide an extremely high level of security when configured properly. One of their core benefits is that they can create and manage encryption keys without exposing the keys to a single human being, dramatically reducing the likelihood that the keys will be compromised.

Cloud service providers often use HSMs internally for the management of their own encryption keys and also offer HSM services to their customers as a secure method for managing customer keys without exposing them to the provider.

Cryptography

Cryptography is the practice of encoding information in such a manner that it cannot be decoded without access to the required decryption key. Cryptography consists of two main operations: *encryption*, which transforms plaintext information into ciphertext using an encryption key, and *decryption*, which transforms ciphertext back into plaintext using a decryption key.

Goals of Cryptography

Security practitioners use cryptographic systems to meet four fundamental goals: confidentiality, integrity, authentication, and nonrepudiation. Achieving each of these goals requires the satisfaction of a number of design requirements, and not all cryptosystems are intended to achieve all four goals. In the following sections, we'll examine each goal in detail and give a brief description of the technical requirements necessary to achieve it.

Confidentiality

Confidentiality ensures that data remains private in three different situations: when it is at rest, in transit, and in use.

Confidentiality is perhaps the most widely cited goal of cryptosystems—the preservation of secrecy for stored information or for communications between individuals and groups. Two main types of cryptosystems enforce confidentiality:

- *Symmetric cryptosystems* use a shared secret key available to all users of the cryptosystem.
- *Asymmetric cryptosystems* use individual combinations of public and private keys for each user of the system.

Both of these concepts are explored later in this chapter.

When developing a cryptographic system for the purpose of providing confidentiality, you must think about three types of data:

- *Data at rest*, or stored data, resides in a particular location awaiting access. Examples of data at rest include data stored on hard drives, backup tapes, cloud storage services, USB devices, and other storage media.

- *Data in motion*, or data on the wire, is transmitted between two systems. Data in motion might be traveling on a corporate network, a wireless network, or the public Internet.

- *Data in use* is active in a computer system where it may be accessed by a process running on that system.

Each of these situations poses different types of confidentiality risks. For example, data in motion may be susceptible to eavesdropping attacks, whereas data at rest is more susceptible to theft of physical devices. Data in use may be accessed by unauthorized processes if the operating system does not properly implement process isolation.

Obfuscation is a concept closely related to confidentiality. It is the practice of making it intentionally difficult for humans to understand how code works. This technique is often used to hide the inner workings of software, particularly when it contains sensitive intellectual property.

Integrity

Integrity ensures that data is not altered without authorization. If integrity mechanisms are in place, the recipient of a message can be certain that the message received is identical to the message that was sent. Similarly, integrity checks can ensure that stored data was not altered between the time it was created and the time it was accessed. Integrity controls protect against all forms of alteration, including intentional alteration by a third party attempting to insert false information, intentional deletion of portions of the data, and unintentional alteration by faults in the transmission process.

Message integrity is enforced through the use of encrypted message digests, known as *digital signatures*, created upon transmission of a message. The recipient of the message simply verifies that the message's digital signature is valid, ensuring that the message was not altered in transit. Integrity can be enforced by both public and secret key cryptosystems.

Authentication

Authentication verifies the claimed identity of system users and is a major function of cryptosystems. For example, suppose that Bob wants to establish a communications session with Alice and they are both participants in a shared secret communications system. Alice might use a challenge-response authentication technique to ensure that Bob is who he claims to be.

Figure 7.11 shows how this challenge-response protocol would work in action. In this example, the shared-secret code used by Alice and Bob is quite simple—the letters of each word are simply reversed. Bob first contacts Alice and identifies himself. Alice then sends a challenge message to Bob, asking him to encrypt a short message using the secret code known only to Alice and Bob. Bob replies with the encrypted message. After Alice verifies that the encrypted message is correct, she trusts that Bob himself is truly on the other end of the connection.

FIGURE 7.11   Challenge-response authentication protocol

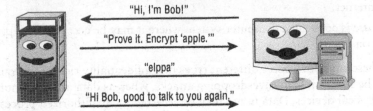

"Hi, I'm Bob!"

"Prove it. Encrypt 'apple.'"

"elppa"

"Hi Bob, good to talk to you again."

Nonrepudiation

Nonrepudiation provides assurance to the recipient that the message originated from the sender and not someone masquerading as the sender. It also prevents the sender from claiming that they never sent the message in the first place (also known as *repudiating* the message). Secret key, or symmetric key, cryptosystems (such as simple substitution ciphers) do not provide this guarantee of nonrepudiation. If Jim and Bob participate in a secret key communication system, they can both produce the same encrypted message using their shared secret key. Nonrepudiation is offered only by public key, or asymmetric, cryptosystems, a topic discussed later in this chapter.

Symmetric Key Algorithms

Symmetric key algorithms rely on a "shared secret" encryption key that is distributed to all members who participate in the communications. This key is used by all parties to both encrypt and decrypt messages, so the sender and the receiver both possess a copy of the shared key. The sender encrypts with the shared secret key and the receiver decrypts with it. When large-sized keys are used, symmetric encryption is very difficult to break. It is primarily employed to perform bulk encryption and provides only for the security service of confidentiality. Symmetric key cryptography can also be called *secret key cryptography* and *private key cryptography*. Figure 7.12 illustrates the symmetric key encryption and decryption processes.

FIGURE 7.12   Symmetric key cryptography

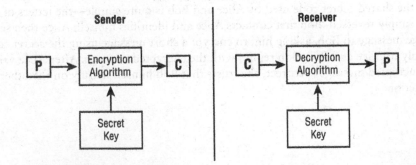

Sender	Receiver

P → Encryption Algorithm → C   C → Decryption Algorithm → P

Secret Key   Secret Key

The use of the term *private key* can be tricky because it is part of three different terms that are from two different types of cryptography: symmetric and asymmetric. The term *private key* by itself always means the private key from the key pair of public key cryptography (aka asymmetric). However, both *private key cryptography* and *shared private key* refer to symmetric cryptography. The meaning of the word *private* is stretched to refer to two people sharing a secret that they keep confidential. (The true meaning of *private is that only a single person* has a secret that's kept confidential.) Be sure to keep these confusing terms straight in your studies.

Symmetric key cryptography has several weaknesses:

Key distribution is a major problem.   Parties must have a secure method of exchanging the secret key before establishing communications with a symmetric key protocol. If a secure electronic channel is not available, an offline key distribution method must often be used (that is, out-of-band exchange).

Symmetric key cryptography does not implement nonrepudiation.   Because any communicating party can encrypt and decrypt messages with the shared secret key, there is no way to prove where a given message originated.

The algorithm is not scalable.   It is extremely difficult for large groups to communicate using symmetric key cryptography. Secure private communication between individuals in the group could be achieved only if each possible combination of users shared a private key.

Keys must be regenerated often.   Each time a participant leaves the group, all keys known by that participant must be discarded.

The major strength of symmetric key cryptography is the great speed at which it can operate. Symmetric key encryption is very fast, often 1,000 to 10,000 times faster than asymmetric algorithms. By nature of the mathematics involved, symmetric key cryptography also naturally lends itself to hardware implementations, creating the opportunity for even higher-speed operations.

The *Advanced Encryption Standard (AES)* is the most commonly used example of a symmetric encryption algorithm.

Asymmetric Cryptography

Asymmetric key algorithms, also known as *public key algorithms*, provide a solution to the weaknesses of symmetric key encryption. In these systems, each user has two keys: a public key, which is shared with all users, and a private key, which is kept secret and known only to the owner of the key pair. But here's a twist: opposite and related keys must be used in tandem to encrypt and decrypt. In other words, if the public key encrypts a message, then only the corresponding private key can decrypt it, and vice versa.

Figure 7.13 shows the algorithm used to encrypt and decrypt messages in a public key cryptosystem. Consider this example. If Alice wants to send a message to Bob using public key cryptography, she creates the message and then encrypts it using Bob's public key. The only possible way to decrypt this ciphertext is to use Bob's private key, and the only user with access to that key is Bob. Therefore, Alice can't even decrypt the message herself after she encrypts it. If Bob wants to send a reply to Alice, he simply encrypts the message using Alice's public key, and then Alice reads the message by decrypting it with her private key.

FIGURE 7.13 Asymmetric key cryptography

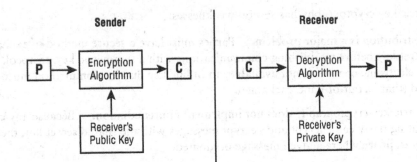

Asymmetric key algorithms also provide support for digital signature technology. Basically, if Bob wants to assure other users that a message with his name on it was actually sent by him, he first creates a message digest by using a hashing algorithm (you'll find more on hashing algorithms in the next section). Bob then encrypts that digest using his private key. Any user who wants to verify the signature simply decrypts the message digest using Bob's public key and then verifies that the decrypted message digest is accurate.

The following is a list of the major strengths of asymmetric key cryptography:

The addition of new users requires the generation of only one public-private key pair.   This same key pair is used to communicate with all users of the asymmetric cryptosystem. This makes the algorithm extremely scalable.

Users can be removed far more easily from asymmetric systems.   Asymmetric cryptosystems provide a key revocation mechanism that allows a key to be canceled, effectively removing a user from the system.

Key regeneration is required only when a user's private key is compromised.   If a user leaves the community, the system administrator simply needs to invalidate that user's keys. No other keys are compromised and therefore key regeneration is not required for any other user.

Asymmetric key encryption can provide integrity, authentication, and nonrepudiation.   If a user does not share their private key with other individuals, a message signed by that user can be shown to be accurate and from a specific source and cannot be later repudiated.

Key distribution is a simple process.   Users who want to participate in the system simply make their public key available to anyone with whom they want to communicate. There is no method by which the private key can be derived from the public key.

No preexisting communication link needs to exist.   Two individuals can begin communicating securely from the moment they start communicating. Asymmetric cryptography does not require a preexisting relationship to provide a secure mechanism for data exchange.

The major weakness of public key cryptography is its slow speed of operation. For this reason, many applications that require the secure transmission of large amounts of data use public key cryptography to establish a connection and then exchange a symmetric secret key. The remainder of the session then uses symmetric cryptography.

Common examples of asymmetric encryption algorithms include the Rivest Shamir Adelman (RSA) algorithm and Elliptic Curve Cryptography (ECC).

Hash Functions

Later in this chapter, you'll learn how cryptosystems implement digital signatures to provide proof that a message originated from a particular user of the cryptosystem and to ensure that the message was not modified while in transit between the two parties. Before you can completely understand that concept, we must first explain the concept of *hash functions*. We will explore the basics of hash functions and look at several common hash functions used in modern digital signature algorithms.

Hash functions have a very simple purpose—they take a potentially long message and generate a unique output value derived from the content of the message. This value is commonly referred to as the *message digest*. Message digests can be generated by the sender of a message and transmitted to the recipient along with the full message for two reasons.

First, the recipient can use the same hash function to recompute the message digest from the full message. They can then compare the computed message digest to the transmitted one to ensure that the message sent by the originator is the same one received by the recipient. If the message digests do not match, that means the message was somehow modified while in transit. It is important to note that the messages must be *exactly* identical for the digests to match. If the messages have even a slight difference in spacing, punctuation, or content, the message digest values will be completely different. It is not possible to tell the degree of difference between two messages by comparing the digests. Even a slight difference will generate totally different digest values.

Second, the message digest can be used to implement a digital signature algorithm. This concept is covered in "Digital Signatures" later in this chapter.

There are five basic requirements for a cryptographic hash function:

- They accept an input of any length.

- They produce an output of a fixed length, regardless of the length of the input.

- The hash value is relatively easy to compute.

- The hash function is one-way (meaning that it is extremely hard to determine the input when provided with the output).

- The hash function is *collision*-free (meaning that it is extremely hard to find two messages that produce the same hash value).

The Secure Hash Algorithm (SHA) versions 2 and 3 (SHA-2 and SHA-3) are government standard hash functions promoted by the National Institute of Standards and Technology (NIST).

Digital Signatures

Once you have chosen a cryptographically sound hashing algorithm, you can use it to implement a *digital signature* system. Digital signature infrastructures have two distinct goals:

- Digitally signed messages assure the recipient that the message truly came from the claimed sender. They enforce nonrepudiation (that is, they preclude the sender from later claiming that the message is a forgery).

- Digitally signed messages assure the recipient that the message was not altered while in transit between the sender and recipient. This protects against both malicious modification (a third party altering the meaning of the message) and unintentional modification (because of faults in the communications process, such as electrical interference).

Digital signature algorithms rely on a combination of the two major concepts already covered in this chapter—public key cryptography and hashing functions.

If Alice wants to digitally sign a message she's sending to Bob, she performs the following actions:

1. Alice generates a message digest of the original plaintext message using one of the cryptographically sound hashing algorithms, such as SHA-3.

2. Alice then encrypts only the message digest using her private key. This encrypted message digest is the digital signature.

3. Alice appends the signed message digest to the plaintext message.

4. Alice transmits the appended signature and message to Bob.

When Bob receives the digitally signed message, he reverses the procedure, as follows:

1. Bob decrypts the digital signature using Alice's public key.

2. Bob uses the same hashing function to create a message digest of the full plaintext message received from Alice.

3. Bob then compares the decrypted message digest he received from Alice with the message digest he computed himself. If the two digests match, he can be assured that the message he received was sent by Alice. If they do not match, either the message was not sent by Alice or the message was modified while in transit.

Digital signatures are used for more than just messages. Software vendors often use digital signature technology to authenticate code distributions that you download from the Internet, such as applets and software patches.

Note that the digital signature process does not provide any privacy in and of itself. It only ensures that the cryptographic goals of integrity, authentication, and nonrepudiation are met. However, if Alice wanted to ensure the privacy of her message to Bob, she could add a step to the message creation process. After appending the signed message digest to the plaintext message, Alice could encrypt the entire message with Bob's public key. When Bob receives the message, he would decrypt it with his own private key before following the steps just outlined.

Digital Certificates

Digital certificates provide communicating parties with the assurance that the people they are communicating with truly are who they claim to be. Digital certificates are essentially endorsed copies of an individual's public key. When users verify that a certificate was signed by a trusted certificate authority (CA), they know that the public key is legitimate.

Digital certificates contain specific identifying information, and their construction is governed by an international standard—X.509. Certificates that conform to X.509 contain the following certificate attributes:

- Version of X.509 to which the certificate conforms

- Serial number (from the certificate creator)

- Signature algorithm identifier (specifies the technique used by the certificate authority to digitally sign the contents of the certificate)

- Issuer name (identification of the certificate authority that issued the certificate)

- Validity period (specifies the dates and times—a starting date and time and an expiration date and time—during which the certificate is valid)

- Subject's *Common Name (CN)* that clearly describes the certificate owner (e.g., "certmike.com")

- Certificates may optionally contain *Subject Alternative Names (SAN)* that allow you to specify additional items (IP addresses, domain names, and so on) to be protected by the single certificate.

- Subject's public key (the most important data in the certificate—the actual public key the certificate owner used to set up secure communications)

Certificates may be issued for a variety of purposes. These include providing assurance for the public keys of:

- Computers/machines

- Individual users

- Email addresses
- Developers (code-signing certificates)

Certificate Authorities

Certificate authorities (CAs) are the glue that binds the public key infrastructure together. These neutral organizations offer notarization services for digital certificates. To obtain a digital certificate from a reputable CA, you must prove your identity to the satisfaction of the CA. The following list includes some of the major CAs who provide widely accepted digital certificates:

- Symantec
- IdenTrust
- Amazon Web Services
- GlobalSign
- Comodo
- Certum
- GoDaddy
- DigiCert
- Secom
- Entrust
- Actalis
- Trustwave

Nothing is preventing any organization from simply setting up shop as a CA. However, the certificates issued by a CA are only as good as the trust placed in the CA that issued them. This is an important item to consider when receiving a digital certificate from a third party. If you don't recognize and trust the name of the CA that issued the certificate, you shouldn't place any trust in the certificate at all. PKI relies on a hierarchy of trust relationships. If you configure your browser to trust a CA, it will automatically trust all of the digital certificates issued by that CA. Browser developers preconfigure browsers to trust the major CAs to avoid placing this burden on users.

Certificate authorities do not need to be third-party service providers. Many organizations operate internal CAs that provide *self-signed certificates* for use inside an organization. These certificates won't be trusted by the browsers of external users, but internal systems may be configured to trust the internal CA, saving the expense of obtaining certificates from a third-party CA.

Certificate Generation and Destruction

The technical concepts behind the public key infrastructure are relatively simple. In the following sections, we'll cover the processes used by certificate authorities to create, validate, and revoke client certificates.

Enrollment

When you want to obtain a digital certificate, you must first prove your identity to the CA in some manner; this process is called *enrollment*. As mentioned in the previous section, this sometimes involves physically appearing before an agent of the certification authority with the appropriate identification documents. Some certificate authorities provide other means of verification, including the use of credit report data and identity verification by trusted community leaders.

Once you've satisfied the certificate authority regarding your identity, you provide them with your public key in the form of a *certificate signing request (CSR)*. The CA next creates an X.509 digital certificate containing your identifying information and a copy of your public key. The CA then digitally signs the certificate using the CA's private key and provides you with a copy of your signed digital certificate. You may then safely distribute this certificate to anyone with whom you want to communicate securely.

Certificate authorities issue different types of certificates depending on the level of identity verification that they perform. The simplest, and most common, certificates are *domain validation (DV) certificates*, where the CA simply verifies that the certificate subject has control of the domain name. *Extended validation (EV) certificates* provide a higher level of assurance and the CA takes steps to verify that the certificate owner is a legitimate business before issuing the certificate.

Verification

When you receive a digital certificate from someone with whom you want to communicate, you *verify* the certificate by checking the CA's digital signature using the CA's public key. Next, you must check and ensure that the certificate was not revoked using a *certificate revocation list* (CRL) or the *Online Certificate Status Protocol (OCSP)*. At this point, you may assume that the public key listed in the certificate is authentic, provided that it satisfies the following requirements:

- The digital signature of the CA is authentic.
- You trust the CA.
- The certificate is not listed on a CRL.
- The certificate actually contains the data you are trusting.

The last point is a subtle but extremely important item. Before you trust an identifying piece of information about someone, be sure that it is actually contained within the certificate. If a certificate contains the email address (billjones@foo.com) but not the individual's name, you can be certain only that the public key contained therein is associated with that email address. The CA is not making any assertions about the actual identity of the billjones@foo.com email account. However, if the certificate contains the name Bill Jones along with an address and telephone number, the CA is vouching for that information as well.

Digital certificate verification algorithms are built into many popular web browsing and email clients, so you won't often need to get involved in the particulars of the process. However, it's important to have a solid understanding of the technical details taking place behind the scenes to make appropriate security judgments for your organization. It's also the reason that, when purchasing a certificate, you choose a CA that is widely trusted. If a CA either is not included in or is later pulled from the list of CAs trusted by a major browser, it will greatly limit the usefulness of your certificate.

Revocation

Occasionally, a certificate authority needs to *revoke* a certificate. This might occur for one of the following reasons:

- The certificate was compromised (for example, the certificate owner accidentally gave away the private key).
- The certificate was erroneously issued (for example, the CA mistakenly issued a certificate without proper verification).
- The details of the certificate changed (for example, the subject's name changed).
- The security association changed (for example, the subject is no longer employed by the organization sponsoring the certificate).

You can use three techniques to verify the authenticity of certificates and identify revoked certificates:

Certificate Revocation Lists (CRLs)   They are maintained by the various certificate authorities and contain the serial numbers of certificates that have been issued by a CA and that have been revoked along with the date and time the revocation went into effect. The major disadvantage of certificate revocation lists is that they must be downloaded and cross-referenced periodically, introducing a period of latency between the time a certificate is revoked and the time end users are notified of the revocation.

Online Certificate Status Protocol (OCSP)   This protocol eliminates the latency inherent in the use of certificate revocation lists by providing a means for real-time certificate verification. When a client receives a certificate, it sends an OCSP request to the CA's OCSP server. The server then responds with a status of valid, invalid, or unknown. The browser uses this information to determine whether the certificate is valid.

Certificate Stapling   The primary issue with OCSP is that it places a significant burden on the OCSP servers operated by certificate authorities. These servers must process requests from every single visitor to a website or other user of a digital certificate, verifying that the certificate is valid and not revoked.

Certificate stapling is an extension to the Online Certificate Status Protocol that relieves some of the burden placed on certificate authorities by the original protocol. When a user visits a website and initiates a secure connection, the website sends its certificate to the end user, who would normally then be responsible for contacting an OCSP server to verify the certificate's validity. In certificate stapling, the web server contacts the OCSP server itself and receives a signed and timestamped response from the OCSP server, which it then attaches, or staples, to the digital certificate. Then, when a user requests a secure web connection, the web server sends the certificate with the stapled OCSP response to the user. The user's browser then verifies that the certificate is authentic and also validates that the stapled OCSP response is genuine and recent. Because the CA signed the OCSP response, the user knows that it is from the certificate authority and the timestamp provides the user with assurance that the CA recently validated the certificate. From there, communication may continue as normal.

The time savings come when the next user visits the website. The web server can simply reuse the stapled certificate, without recontacting the OCSP server. As long as the timestamp is recent enough, the user will accept the stapled certificate without needing to contact the CA's OCSP server again. It's common to have stapled certificates with a validity period of 24 hours. That reduces the burden on an OCSP server from handling one request per user over the course of a day, which could be millions of requests, to handling one request per certificate per day. That's a tremendous reduction.

Code Security

Software is everywhere in our organizations. It ranges from customer-facing applications and services to smaller custom scripts written to support business needs. The process of designing, creating, supporting, and maintaining that software is known as the software development lifecycle (SDLC). As a security practitioner, you need to understand the SDLC and its security implications to ensure that the software your organization uses is well written and secure throughout its life span.

Software Development Life Cycle

The software development lifecycle (SDLC) describes the steps in a model for software development throughout its life. As shown in Figure 7.14, it maps software creation from an idea to requirements gathering and analysis to design, coding, testing, and rollout. Once software is in production, it also includes user training, maintenance, and decommissioning at the end of the software package's useful life.

Software development does not always follow a formal model, but most enterprise development for major applications does follow most, if not all, of these phases. In some cases, developers may even use elements of an SDLC model without realizing it!

The SDLC is useful for organizations and developers because it provides a consistent framework to structure workflow and planning for the development process. Despite these advantages, simply picking an SDLC model to implement may not always be the best choice. Certain types of work and projects fit better than others for each model, which makes choosing an effective SDLC model an important part of the process.

FIGURE 7.14   High-level SDLC view

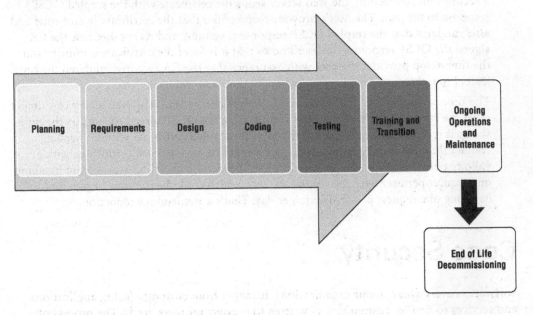

Software Development Phases

Regardless of which SDLC or process is chosen by your organization, a few phases appear in most SDLC models:

1. The *feasibility* phase involves conducting initial investigations into whether the effort should occur. Feasibility also looks at alternative solutions and high-level costs for each solution proposed. It results in a recommendation with a plan to move forward.

2. Once an effort has been deemed feasible, it will typically go through an *analysis and requirements definition* phase. In this phase, customer input is sought to determine what the desired functionality is, what the current system or application currently does and what it doesn't do, and what improvements are desired. Requirements may be ranked to determine which are most critical to the success of the project.

Security requirements definition is an important part of the analysis and requirements definition phase. It ensures that the application is designed to be secure and that secure coding practices are used.

3. The *design* phase includes design for functionality, architecture, integration points and techniques, dataflows, business processes, and any other elements that require design consideration.

4. The actual coding of the application occurs during the *development* phase. This phase may involve testing parts of the software, including *unit testing*, the testing of small components individually to ensure they function properly.

5. Although some testing is likely to occur in the development phase, formal testing with customers or others outside of the development team occurs in the *testing and integration* phase. Individual units or software components are integrated and then tested to ensure proper functionality. In addition, connections to outside services, data sources, and other integration may occur during this phase. During this phase, *user acceptance testing* (UAT) occurs to ensure that the users of the software are satisfied with its functionality.

6. The important task of ensuring that the end users are trained to use the software and that the software has entered general use occurs in the *training and transition* phase. This phase is sometimes called the acceptance, installation, and deployment phase.

7. Once a project reaches completion, the application or service will enter what is usually the longest phase: *ongoing operations and maintenance*. This phase includes patching, updating, minor modifications, and other work that goes into daily support.

8. The *disposition* phase occurs when a product or system reaches the end of its life. Although disposition is often ignored in the excitement of developing new products, it is an important phase for many reasons: shutting down old products can produce cost savings, replacing existing tools may require specific knowledge or additional effort, and data and systems may need to be preserved or properly disposed of.

The order of the phases may vary, with some progressing in a simple linear fashion and others taking an iterative or parallel approach. You will still see some form of each of these phases in successful software lifecycles.

Code Deployment Environments

Many organizations use multiple environments for their software and systems development and testing. The names and specific purposes for these systems vary depending on organizational needs, but the most common environments are as follows:

- The *development environment* is typically used for developers or other "builders" to do their work. Some workflows provide each developer with their own development environment; others use a shared development environment.

- The *test environment* is where the software or systems can be tested without impacting the production environment. In some schemes, this is preproduction, whereas in others a separate preproduction staging environment is used. *Quality assurance (QA)* activities take place in the test environment.

- The *staging environment* is a transition environment for code that has successfully cleared testing and is waiting to be deployed into production.

- The *production environment* is the live system. Software, patches, and other changes that have been tested and approved move to production.

Change management processes are typically followed for these environments. This provides accountability and oversight and may be required for audit or compliance purposes as well.

Software Development Models

The SDLC can be approached in many ways, and over time several formal models have been created to help provide a common framework for development. Although formal SDLC models can be very detailed, with specific practices, procedures, and documentation, many organizations choose the elements of one or more models that best fit their organizational style, workflow, and requirements.

Waterfall

The *Waterfall* methodology is a sequential model in which each phase is followed by the next one. Phases do not overlap, and each logically leads to the next. A typical six-phase Waterfall process is shown in Figure 7.15. In Phase 1, requirements are gathered and documented. Phase 2 involves analysis intended to build business rules and models. In Phase 3, a software architecture is designed, and coding and integration of the software occur in Phase 4. Once the software is complete, Phase 5 occurs, with testing and debugging being completed in this phase. Finally, the software enters an operational phase, with support, maintenance, and other operational activities happening on an ongoing basis.

FIGURE 7.15   The Waterfall SDLC model

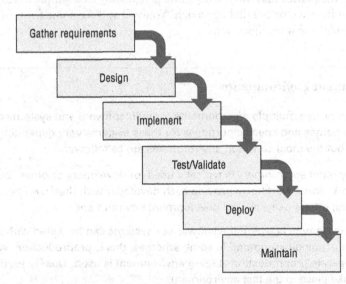

Waterfall has been replaced in many organizations because it is seen as relatively inflexible, but it remains in use for complex systems. Since Waterfall is not highly responsive to changes and does not account for internal iterative work, it is typically recommended for development efforts that involve a fixed scope and a known timeframe for delivery and that are using a stable, well-understood technology platform.

Spiral

The *Spiral* model uses the linear development concepts from the Waterfall model and adds an iterative process that revisits four phases multiple times during the development lifecycle to gather more detailed requirements, design functionality guided by the requirements, and build based on the design. In addition, the Spiral model puts significant emphasis on risk assessment as part of the SDLC, reviewing risks multiple times during the development process.

The Spiral model shown in Figure 7.16 uses four phases, which it repeatedly visits throughout the development lifecycle:

1. Identification, or requirements gathering, which initially gathers business requirements, system requirements, and more detailed requirements for subsystems or modules as the process continues.

2. Design, which involves conceptual, architectural, logical, and sometimes physical or final design.

3. Build, which produces an initial proof of concept and then further development releases until the final production build is produced.

4. Evaluation, which involves risk analysis for the development project intended to monitor the feasibility of delivering the software from a technical and managerial viewpoint. As the development cycle continues, this phase also involves customer testing and feedback to ensure customer acceptance.

FIGURE 7.16   The Spiral SDLC model

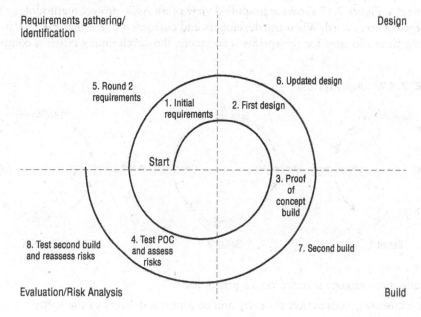

The Spiral model provides greater flexibility to handle changes in requirements as well as external influences such as the availability of customer feedback and development staff. It also allows the software development lifecycle to start earlier in the process than Waterfall does. Because Spiral revisits its process, it is possible for this model to result in rework or to identify design requirements later in the process that necessitate a significant design change due to more detailed requirements coming to light.

Agile

Agile software development is an iterative and incremental process, rather than the linear processes that Waterfall and Spiral use. Agile is rooted in the Manifesto for Agile Software Development, a document that has four basic premises:

- Individuals and interactions are more important than processes and tools.

- Working software is preferable to comprehensive documentation.

- Customer collaboration replaces contract negotiation.

- Responding to change is key, rather than following a plan.

If you are used to a Waterfall or Spiral development process, Agile is a significant departure from the planning, design, and documentation-centric approaches that Agile's predecessors use. Agile methods tend to break work up into smaller units, allowing work to be done more quickly and with less up-front planning. It focuses on adapting to needs, rather than predicting them, with major milestones identified early in the process but subject to change as the project continues to develop.

Work is typically broken up into short working sessions, called *sprints*, that can last days to a few weeks. Figure 7.17 shows a simplified view of an Agile project methodology with multiple sprints conducted. When the developers and customers agree that the task is done or when the time allocated for the sprints is complete, the development effort is completed.

FIGURE 7.17   Agile sprints

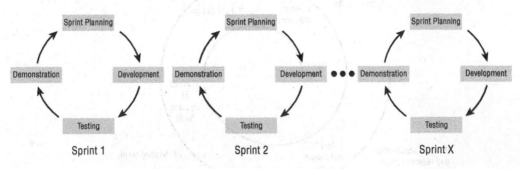

The Agile methodology is based on 12 principles:

- Ensure customer satisfaction via early and continuous delivery of the software.

- Welcome changing requirements, even late in the development process.

- Deliver working software frequently (in weeks rather than months).

- Ensure daily cooperation between developers and businesspeople.

- Projects should be built around motivated individuals who get the support, trust, and environment they need to succeed.

- Face-to-face conversations are the most efficient way to convey information inside the development team.

- Progress is measured by having working software.

- Development should be done at a sustainable pace that can be maintained on an ongoing basis.

- Pay continuous attention to technical excellence and good design.

- Simplicity—the art of maximizing the amount of work not done—is essential.

- The best architectures, requirements, and designs emerge from self-organizing teams.

- Teams should reflect on how to become more effective and then implement that behavior at regular intervals.

These principles drive an SDLC process that is less formally structured than Spiral or Waterfall but that has many opportunities for customer feedback and revision. It can react more nimbly to problems and will typically allow faster customer feedback—an advantage when security issues are discovered.

DevSecOps and DevOps

DevOps combines software development and IT operations to optimize the SDLC. This is done by using collections of tools called *toolchains* to improve the coding, building and testing, packaging, release, configuration and configuration management, and monitoring elements of a software development lifecycle.

Of course, DevOps should have security baked into it as well. The term *DevSecOps* describes security as part of the DevOps model. In this model, security is a shared responsibility that is part of the entire development and operations cycle. That means integrating security into the design, development, testing, and operational work done to produce applications and services.

The role of security practitioners in a DevSecOps model includes threat analysis and communications, planning, testing, providing feedback, and of course ongoing improvement and awareness responsibilities. Doing this requires a strong understanding of the organization's risk tolerance, as well as awareness of what the others involved in the DevSecOps environment are doing and when they are doing it. DevOps and DevSecOps are often combined with continuous integration and continuous deployment methodologies, where they can rely on automated security testing and integrated security tooling, including scanning, updates, and configuration management tools, to help ensure security.

Continuous Integration and Continuous Deployment

Continuous integration (CI) is a development practice that checks code into a shared repository on a consistent ongoing basis. In continuous integration environments, this can range from a few times a day to a very frequent process of check-ins and automated builds. The main goal of this approach is to enable the use of automation and scripting to improve efficiency.

Since continuous integration relies on an automated build process, it also requires automated testing. It is also often paired with *continuous deployment (CD)* (sometimes called continuous delivery), which rolls out tested changes into production automatically as soon as they have been tested.

Figure 7.18 shows a view of the continuous integration/continuous deployment pipeline.

FIGURE 7.18   The CI/CD pipeline

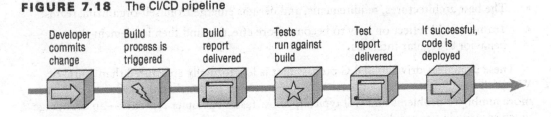

| Developer commits change | Build process is triggered | Build report delivered | Tests run against build | Test report delivered | If successful, code is deployed |

Using continuous integration and continuous deployment methods requires building *continuous validation* and automated security testing into the pipeline testing process. It can result in new vulnerabilities being deployed into production and could allow an untrusted or rogue developer to insert flaws into code that is deployed and then remove the code as part of a deployment in the next cycle. This means that logging, reporting, and *continuous monitoring* must all be designed to fit the CI/CD process.

Code Review

Reviewing the code that is written for an application provides several advantages. It helps to share knowledge of the code, and the experience gained in writing is better than simple documentation alone would be since it provides a personal understanding of the code and its functions. It also helps detect problems while enforcing coding best practices and standards by exposing the code to review during its development cycle. Finally, it ensures that multiple members of a team are aware of what the code is supposed to do and how it accomplishes its task.

There are a number of common *code review* processes, including both formal and Agile processes like pair programming, over-the-shoulder, and Fagan code reviews.

Pair Programming

Pair programming is an Agile software development technique that places two developers at one workstation. One developer writes code, while the other developer reviews their code as they write it. This is intended to provide real-time code review, and it ensures that multiple developers are familiar with the code that is written. In most pair programming environments, the developers are expected to change roles frequently, allowing both of them to spend time thinking about the code while at the keyboard and to think about the design and any issues in the code while reviewing it.

Pair programming adds additional cost to development since it requires two full-time developers. At the same time, it provides additional opportunities for review and analysis of the code and directly applies more experience to coding problems, potentially increasing the quality of the code.

Over-the-Shoulder

Over-the-shoulder code review also relies on a pair of developers, but rather than requiring constant interaction and hand-offs, over-the-shoulder requires the developer who wrote the code to explain the code to the other developer. This allows peer review of code and can also assist developers in understanding how the code works.

Pass-Around Code Reviews

Pass-around code review, sometimes known as email pass-around code review, is a form of manual peer review done by sending completed code to reviewers who check the code for issues. Pass-around reviews may involve more than one reviewer, allowing reviewers with different expertise and experience to contribute with their expertise. Although pass-around reviews allow more flexibility in *when* they occur than an over-the-shoulder review, they don't provide the same easy opportunity to learn about the code from the developer who wrote it that over-the-shoulder and pair programming offer, making documentation more important.

Tool-Assisted Reviews

Tool-assisted code reviews rely on formal or informal software-based tools to conduct code reviews. Tools like Atlassian's Crucible collaborative code review tool, Codacy's static code review tool, and Phabricator's Differential code review tool are all designed to improve the code review process. The wide variety of tools used for code review reflects not only the multitude of software development lifecycle options but also how organizations set up their design and review processes.

Fagan Inspection

Fagan inspection is a form of structured, formal code review intended to find a variety of problems during the development process. Fagan inspection specifies entry and exit criteria for processes, ensuring that a process is not started before appropriate diligence has been performed and also making sure that there are known criteria for moving to the next phase.

The Fagan inspection process shown in Figure 7.19 shows the six phases of a typical process:

1. Planning, including preparation of materials, attendees, and location

2. Overview, which prepares the team by reviewing the materials and assigning roles such as coder, reader, reviewer, and moderator

3. Preparation, which involves reviewing the code or other item being inspected and documents any issues or questions they may have

4. Meeting to identify defects based on the notes from the preparation phase

5. Rework to resolve issues

6. Follow-up by the moderator to ensure that all issues identified have been found and that no new defects were created during the resolution process

FIGURE 7.19   Fagan code review

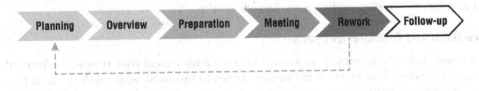

Formal methods for verification of software like the Fagan inspection and similar formal review processes can sound very expensive, but catching problems early can result in significant savings in time and cost. Fagan code reviews remain relatively rare since many of the "lightweight" review options are easier to implement, offer many of the same benefits, and are far less costly.

Software Security Testing

No matter how talented the development team for an application is, there will be some form of flaws in the code. Veracode's 2020 metrics for applications based on their testing showed that 76 percent of the applications they scanned exhibited at least one security issue during the testing process. That number points to a massive need for software security testing to continue to be better integrated into the software development lifecycle.

Veracode provides a useful yearly review of the state of software security. You can read more of the report at www.veracode.com/state-of-software-security-report.

A broad variety of manual and automatic testing tools and methods are available to security professionals and developers. Fortunately, automated tools have continued to improve, providing an easier way to verify that code is more secure.

The source code that is the basis of every application and program can contain a variety of bugs and flaws from programming and syntax errors to problems with business logic, error handling, and integration with other services and systems. It is important to be able to analyze the code to understand what the code does, how it performs that task, and where flaws may occur in the program itself. This is often done via static or dynamic code analysis along with testing methods like fuzzing. Once changes are made to code and it is deployed, it must be regression-tested to ensure that the fixes put in place didn't create new security issues!

Static Code Analysis

Static code analysis (sometimes called source code analysis) is conducted by reviewing the code for an application. Since static analysis uses the source code for an application, it can be seen as a type of white-box testing with full visibility to the testers. This can allow testers to find problems that other tests might miss, either because the logic is not exposed to other testing methods, or because of internal business logic problems.

Unlike many other methods, static analysis does not run the program; instead, it focuses on understanding how the program is written and what the code is intended to do. Static code analysis can be conducted using automated tools or manually by reviewing the code—a process sometimes called "code understanding." Automated static code analysis can be very effective at finding known issues, and manual static code analysis helps to identify programmer-induced errors.

Dynamic Code Analysis

Dynamic code analysis relies on the execution of the code while providing it with input to test the software. Much like static code analysis, dynamic code analysis may be done via automated tools or manually, but there is a strong preference for automated testing due to the volume of tests that need to be conducted in most dynamic code testing processes.

Fuzzing

Fuzz testing, or *fuzzing*, involves sending invalid or random data to an application to test its ability to handle unexpected data. The application is monitored to determine if it crashes, fails, or responds incorrectly. Fuzzing is typically automated due to the large amount of data that a fuzz test involves and is particularly useful for detecting input validation and logic issues as well as memory leaks and error handling. Unfortunately, fuzzing tends to only identify simple problems; it does not account for complex logic or business process issues and may not provide complete code coverage if its progress is not monitored.

Identity and Access Management

As security professionals, one of the most important things that we do is ensure that only authorized individuals gain access to information, systems, and networks under our protection. That's the role of *identity and access management (IAM)* programs.

Identification, Authentication, and Authorization

The access control process consists of three steps that you must understand. These steps are identification, authentication, and authorization.

During the first step of the process, *identification*, an individual makes a claim about their identity. The person trying to gain access doesn't present any proof at this point—they simply make an assertion. It's important to remember that the identification step is only a claim and the user could certainly be making a false claim!

Imagine a physical world scenario where you want to enter a secure office building where you have an appointment. During the identification step of the process, you might walk up to the security desk and say: "Hi, I'm Mike Chapple."

Proof comes into play during the second step of the process: *authentication*. During the authentication step, the individual proves their identity to the satisfaction of the access control system. In our office building example, the guard would likely wish to see my driver's license to confirm my identity.

Simply proving your identity isn't enough to gain access to a system, however. The access control system also needs to be satisfied that you are allowed to access the system. That's the third step of the access control process: *authorization*. In our office building example, the security guard might check a list of that day's appointments to see if it includes my name.

Exam Tip

When you get ready for the exam, you must remember the distinction between the identification and authentication phases. Be ready to identify the phase associated with an example of a mechanism.

So far, we've talked about identification, authentication, and authorization in the context of gaining access to a building. Let's talk about how they work in the electronic world. When we go to log in to a system, we often identify ourselves with a username, most likely composed of some combination of the letters from our names.

When we reach the authentication phase, we're commonly asked to enter a password. There are many other ways to authenticate, and we'll talk about those later in this chapter.

Finally, in the electronic world, authorization often takes the form of access control lists that itemize the specific filesystem permissions granted to an individual user or group of users. Users proceed through the identification, authentication, and authorization processes when they request access to a resource.

Authentication Techniques

Computer systems offer many different authentication techniques that allow users to prove their identity. Let's take a look at three different authentication factors: something you know, something you are, and something you have.

Something You Know

Passwords are the most common example of a "something you know" authentication factor. The user remembers their password and enters it in a system during the authentication process.

Users should choose strong passwords consisting of as many characters as possible and combine characters from multiple classes, such as uppercase and lowercase letters, digits, and symbols.

Something You Are

The second authentication factor is something you are, otherwise known as *biometric* authentication. Biometrics measures one of your physical characteristics, such as a fingerprint, eye pattern, face, or voice. Using biometric authentication requires specialized readers, such as the retinal scanner shown in Figure 7.20(a) or the fingerprint reader shown in Figure 7.20(b).

FIGURE 7.20 Biometric authentication with a (a) retinal scanner (b) fingerprint scanner

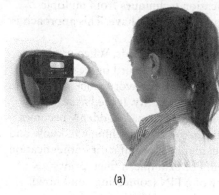

(a) (b)

Something You Have

The third authentication factor, something you have, requires the user to have physical possession of a device, such as a smartphone or authentication token keyfob like the one shown in Figure 7.21.

FIGURE 7.21   Authentication token

Multifactor Authentication

When used alone, any authentication factor provides some security for systems. However, they each have their own drawbacks. For example, an attacker might steal a user's password through a phishing attack. Once they have the password, they can then use that password to assume the user's identity. Other authentication factors aren't foolproof, either. If you use smartcard authentication to implement something you have, the user may lose the smartcard. Someone coming across it may then impersonate the user.

The solution to this problem is to combine authentication techniques from multiple factors, such as combining something you know with something you have. This approach is known as *multifactor authentication*.

Take the two techniques we just discussed: passwords and smartcards. When used alone, either one is subject to hackers either gaining knowledge of the password or stealing a smartcard. However, if an authentication system requires both a password (something you know) and a smartcard (something you have) it brings added security. If the hacker steals the password, they don't have the required smartcard, and vice versa. It suddenly becomes much more difficult for the attacker to gain access to the account. Something you know and something you have are different factors, so this is an example of multifactor authentication.

We can combine other authentication factors as well. For example, a fingerprint reader (something you are) might also require the entry of a PIN (something you know).

When evaluating multifactor authentication, remember that the techniques must be *different* factors. An approach that combines a password with the answer to a security question is *not* multifactor authentication because both factors are something you know.

Exam Tip

When you take the exam, you'll likely find a question about multifactor authentication. Be careful to ensure that the authentication techniques come from two different factors. Mistaking two "something you know" techniques for multifactor authentication is a common exam mistake!

Authentication Errors

The strength of an authentication mechanism may be measured by the number of errors that it generates. There are two basic types of errors in authentication systems.

False acceptance errors occur when the system misidentifies an individual as an authorized user and grants access that should be denied. This is a very serious error because it allows unauthorized access to the system, device, information, or facility. The frequency of these errors is measured by the *false acceptance rate (FAR)*.

False rejection errors occur when an authorized individual attempts to gain access to a system but is incorrectly denied access by the system. This is not as serious as a false acceptance because it does not jeopardize confidentiality or integrity, but it is still a serious error because it jeopardizes the availability of resources. The frequency of these errors is measured by the *false rejection rate (FRR)*.

The false acceptance rate and false rejection rates are not, by themselves, good measures of the strength of an authentication factor because they can be easily manipulated. At one extreme, administrators may configure the system to admit nobody at all, giving it a perfect false acceptance rate but also a very high false rejection rate. Similarly, if the system allows anyone access, it has a perfect false rejection rate but an unacceptably high false acceptance rate.

The solution to this is to use a balanced measure of strength called the *crossover error rate (CER)*. This is the efficacy rate that occurs when administrators tune the system to have equal false acceptance and false rejection rates. Figure 7.22 shows the relationship between the FAR, FRR, and CER. As you increase the sensitivity of a system, it increases the FRR but decreases the FAR. As you decrease the sensitivity of a system, it decreases the FRR but increases the FAR. In either case, the CER remains constant.

FIGURE 7.22   False acceptance rate (FAR), false rejection rate (FRR), and crossover error rate (CER)

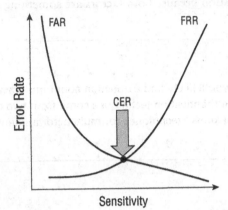

Single-Sign On and Federation

Federated identity management leverages the fact that a single individual may have accounts across a wide variety of systems. When organizations agree to federate their identity management systems, they share some of this information across the systems. This approach reduces the number of individual identities that a user must have and eases the burden on both the user and the organization.

You're probably already familiar with some federated identity management systems. When you log on to websites using your Google account, Facebook Connect, or Twitter account, you're using federated identity management.

Single-sign on (SSO) goes a step further and shares authenticated sessions across systems. Many organizations create SSO solutions within their organizations to help users avoid the burden of repeatedly authenticating.

In an SSO approach, users log on to the first SSO-enabled system they encounter and then that login session persists across other systems until it reaches its expiration. If the organization sets the expiration period to be the length of a business day, it means that users need to log in only once per day and then their single sign-on session will last the entire day.

Provisioning and Deprovisioning

Account administrators are responsible for managing the *provisioning* and *deprovisioning* of user accounts. When a new user joins the organization, administrators ensure that they go through the appropriate onboarding process and then provision a user account for that user. This involves creating authentication credentials and granting the user appropriate authorizations based on their job function.

When that user leaves the organization, administrators ensure that they go through an offboarding process that includes deprovisioning the account to remove their credentials and authorizations at the appropriate time. Administrators must act quickly to remove the user's access from computer systems. This prevents the user from accessing sensitive information or resources after their departure and is especially important when a user leaves the organization under unfavorable circumstances.

Security professionals should ensure that the organization has a strong process designed to remove access, preferably in an automated or semiautomated fashion. This process may have several workflows.

The normal workflow, for a planned departure, should automatically begin when a supervisor informs the Human Resources department that an employee is resigning or retiring. The account administration team should configure the user's account to automatically expire on the date they are leaving the organization.

An emergency workflow may be used when a user is suddenly terminated. This may occur under adverse circumstances when a user is fired. In those cases, the IT department should carefully coordinate with Human Resources to time the account termination precisely.

If account administrators fail to precisely time the access revocation, two undesirable situations may occur. First, if the account is terminated before the employee is informed of their termination, the employee may gain advance notice of the impending termination and take retaliatory action against the employer. Second, if the account is not terminated immediately upon the user being informed of their termination, the user may gain access to the system after being fired and take retaliatory action.

Suspending and terminating accounts in a timely manner boosts enterprise security by reducing the risk of unauthorized access.

Account Monitoring

Security administrators must pay careful attention to the permissions and use of end-user accounts to protect against security incidents. Let's take a look at some account monitoring practices that organizations should put in place.

The first is inaccurate permissions assigned to accounts that either prevent a user from doing their work or violate the principle of least privilege. These permissions are often the result of *privilege creep*, a condition that occurs when users switch jobs and gain new permissions but never have their old permissions revoked.

To protect against inaccurate permissions, administrators should perform regular user account reviews in cooperation with managers from around the organization. During each of these manual reviews, the administrators should pull a listing of all the permissions assigned to each account and then review that listing with managers to ensure that it is appropriate for the user's role, making any necessary adjustments. Administrators should pay careful attention to users who switched jobs since the last account review.

Another issue is the unauthorized use of permissions either by someone other than the legitimate user accessing the account or by the user performing some illegitimate action. Protecting against unauthorized use of permissions is tricky because it can be hard to detect. This requires the use of continuous account monitoring systems that watch for suspicious activity and alert administrators to strange actions.

For example, a continuous account monitoring system may flag violations of access policies, such as the following:

- Logons from strange geographic locations such as a user connecting from both the home office and a remote location in Eastern Europe at the same time; cases like this are known as impossible travel time logins and should be treated as risky logins.
- Logins from unusual network locations, such as a user who always logs in from the HR network suddenly appearing on a guest network.
- Logons at unusual times of day, such as a mail clerk logging into the system in the middle of the night.
- Deviations from normal behavior, such as users accessing files that they do not normally access.
- High volumes of activity that may represent bulk downloading of sensitive information. The specific circumstances that merit attention will vary from organization to organization, but performing this type of behavior-based continuous account monitoring is an important security control.

Summary

Security professionals use a wide variety of cybersecurity technologies to meet their organization's security requirements. These technologies begin at the endpoint where antimalware, data loss prevention, and endpoint detection and response platforms protect against the many risks encountered by end users as they use laptops, desktop computers, smartphones, tablets, and other devices.

Network security controls protect networks from intrusions and data sent over networks from eavesdropping. These controls include firewalls, virtual LANs, routers, switches, and virtual private networks. As organizations move to the cloud, this raises the need for cloud-focused security controls that protect information stored, processed, and transmitted in cloud environments.

Organizations that develop their own software must adopt strong software development security controls that ensure software meets the organization's security requirements. Encryption technology protects data both at rest and while in transit over a network, avoiding breaches of confidentiality. Identity and access management systems provide identification, authentication, and authorization services to restrict access to systems, information, and resources.

Exam Essentials

Know the role of endpoint security technologies in an enterprise cybersecurity program.   Antimalware software protects endpoint devices from many different threats. Antimalware software uses signature detection and heuristic detection to prevent malware infections. Endpoint detection and response (EDR) platforms manage the detection, containment, investigation, and remediation of endpoint security incidents. Data loss prevention (DLP) systems prevent the unauthorized exfiltration of sensitive data. Change and configuration management systems maintain secure system configurations, whereas patch management ensures that security updates are consistently applied. System hardening techniques close holes that might be exploited by an attacker.

Explain the role of network segmentation.   Network segmentation techniques place systems and users of different security levels on different network segments, containing the damage caused by a potential security incident. Firewalls provide segmentation of networks into security zones, whereas VLANs group users and devices by function.

Understand the security requirements for routers, switches, and other network devices.   Routers and switches must be protected against unauthorized physical access to avoid compromise. Switch security techniques include VLAN pruning, the prevention of VLAN hopping, and port security. Router security techniques include the use of access control lists to filter traffic and quality of service controls to prioritize important network use.

Explain the three major cloud service models.   In the anything-as-a-service (XaaS) approach to computing, there are three major cloud service models. Infrastructure-as-a-service (IaaS) offerings allow customers to purchase and interact with the basic building blocks of a technology infrastructure. Software-as-a-service (SaaS) offerings provide customers with access to a fully managed application running in the cloud. Platform-as-a-service (PaaS) offerings provide a platform where customers may run applications that they have developed themselves.

Describe the four major cloud deployment models.   *Public cloud* service providers deploy infrastructure and then make it accessible to any customers who wish to take advantage of it in a multitenant model. The term *private cloud* is used to describe any cloud infrastructure that is provisioned for use by a single customer. A *community cloud* service shares characteristics of both the public and private models. Community cloud services do run in a multitenant environment, but the tenants are limited to members of a specifically designed community. *Hybrid cloud* is a catch-all term used to describe cloud deployments that blend public, private, and/or community cloud services together.

Understand the shared responsibility model of cloud security.   Under the shared responsibility model of cloud security, cloud customers must divide responsibilities between one or more service providers and the customers' own cybersecurity teams. In an IaaS environment, the cloud provider takes on the most responsibility, providing security for everything below the operating system layer. In PaaS, the cloud provider takes over added responsibility for the security of the operating system itself. In SaaS, the cloud provider is responsible for the security of the entire environment, except for the configuration of access controls within the application and the choice of data to store in the service.

Understand secure software development concepts.   Software should be created using a standardized software development lifecycle that moves software through development, test, staging, and production environments. Developers should understand the issues associated with code reuse and software diversity. Web applications should be developed in alignment with industry-standard principles such as those developed by the Open Web Application Security Project (OWASP).

Explain secure code deployment and automation concepts.   Code repositories serve as a version control mechanism and centralized authority for the secure provisioning and deprovisioning of code. Developers and operations teams should work together on developing automated courses of action as they implement a DevOps approach to creating and deploying software. Software applications should be designed to support both scalability and elasticity.

Understand the goals of cryptography.   The four goals of cryptography are confidentiality, integrity, authentication, and nonrepudiation. Confidentiality is the use of encryption to protect sensitive information from prying eyes. Integrity is the use of cryptography to ensure that data is not maliciously or unintentionally altered. Authentication refers to the uses of encryption to validate the identity of individuals. Nonrepudiation ensures that individuals can prove to a third party that a message came from its purported sender.

Explain the differences between symmetric and asymmetric encryption.   Symmetric encryption uses the same shared secret key to encrypt and decrypt information. Users must have some mechanism to exchange these shared secret keys. Asymmetric encryption provides each user with a pair of keys: a public key, which is freely shared, and a private key, which is kept secret. Anything encrypted with one key from the pair may be decrypted with the other key from the same pair.

Explain how digital signatures provide nonrepudiation.   Digital signatures provide nonrepudiation by allowing a third party to verify the authenticity of a message. Senders create digital signatures by using a hash function to generate a message digest and then encrypting that digest with their own private key. Others may verify the digital signature by decrypting it with the sender's public key and comparing this decrypted message digest to one that they compute themselves using the hash function on the message.

Understand the purpose and use of digital certificates.   Digital certificates provide a trusted mechanism for sharing public keys with other individuals. Users and organizations obtain digital certificates from certificate authorities (CAs), who demonstrate their trust in the certificate by applying their digital signature. Recipients of the digital certificate can rely on the public key it contains if they trust the issuing CA and verify the CA's digital signature.

Explain the major components of an identity and access management program.   Identity and access management systems perform three major functions: identification, authentication, and authorization. Identification is the process of a user making a claim of identity, such as by providing a username. Authentication allows the user to prove their identity. Authentication may be done using something you know, something you have, or something you are. Multifactor authentication combines different authentication techniques to provide stronger security. Authorization ensures that authenticated users may only perform actions necessary to carry out their assigned responsibilities.

Review Questions

1. In which cloud security model does the cloud service provider bear the most responsibility for implementing security controls?

   A. IaaS

   B. FaaS

   C. PaaS

   D. SaaS

2. Adam is conducting software testing by reviewing the source code of the application. What type of code testing is Adam conducting?

   A. Mutation testing

   B. Static code analysis

   C. Dynamic code analysis

   D. Fuzzing

3. Helen would like to configure her organization's switches so that they do not allow systems connected to a switch to spoof MAC addresses. Which one of the following features would be helpful in this configuration?

   A. Loop protection

   B. Port security

   C. Flood guard

   D. Traffic encryption

4. Tim is working on a change to a web application used by his organization to fix a known bug. What environment should he be working in?

   A. Test

   B. Development

   C. Staging

   D. Production

5. Which one of the following statements about cloud computing is incorrect?

   A. Cloud computing offers ubiquitous, convenient access.

   B. Cloud computing customers store data on hardware that is shared with other customers.

   C. Cloud computing customers provision resources through the service provider's sales team.

   D. Cloud computing resources are accessed over a network.

6. Patricia is using a computer at a hotel business center, and she is concerned that the operating system on the device may be compromised. What is the best way for her to use this computer in a secure fashion?

   A. Use live boot media

   B. Connect to a VPN

   C. Run a malware scan

   D. Only access secure websites

7. Karim is investigating an alert generated by his organization's NIDS. The system alerted to a distributed denial-of-service attack, and Karim's investigation revealed that this type of attack did take place. What type of report has the system generated?

   A. False positive

   B. True negative

   C. True positive

   D. False negative

8. What type of security solution provides a hardware platform for the storage and management of encryption keys?

   A. HSM

   B. IPS

   C. SIEM

   D. SOAR

9. Ryan is investigating a security incident. He believes that the incident is originating from a single system on the Internet and targeting multiple systems on his network. What control could he put in place to stop the incident as quickly as possible?

   A. DDoS mitigation

   B. Host firewall rule

   C. Operating system update

   D. Network firewall rule

10. Kevin discovered that his web server was being overwhelmed by traffic, causing a CPU bottleneck. Using the interface offered by his cloud service provider, he added another CPU to the server. What term best describes Kevin's action?

   A. Elasticity

   B. Horizontal scaling

   C. Vertical scaling

   D. High availability

11. Every time Susan checks code into her organization's code repository, it is tested, validated, and then if accepted is immediately put into production. What is the term for this?

    A. Continuous integration

    B. Continuous delivery

    C. A security nightmare

    D. Agile development

12. Tom is building a multifactor authentication system that requires users to enter a passcode and then verifies that their face matches a photo stored in the system. What two factors is this system using?

    A. Something you know and something you have

    B. Something you have and something you know

    C. Something you have and something you are

    D. Something you know and something you are

13. Frank is evaluating the effectiveness of a biometric system. Which one of the following metrics would provide him with the best measure of the system's effectiveness?

    A. IRR

    B. CER

    C. FAR

    D. FRR

14. Gary is logging into a system and providing his fingerprint to gain access. What step of the IAM process is he performing?

    A. Identification

    B. Authorization

    C. Authentication

    D. Accounting

15. John is designing a system that will allow users from Acme Corporation, one of his organization's vendors, to access John's accounts payable system using the accounts provided by Acme Corporation. What type of authentication system is John attempting to design?

    A. Single sign-on

    B. Federated authentication

    C. Transitive trust

    D. Multifactor authentication

16. Howard is assessing the legal risks to his organization based on its handling of PII. The organization is based in the United States, handles the data of customers located in Europe, and stores information in Japanese data centers. What law would be most important to Howard during his assessment?

A. Japanese law

B. European Union law

C. U.S. law

D. All should have equal weight.

17. David would like to send Mike a message using an asymmetric encryption algorithm to provide confidentiality. What key should he use to encrypt the message?

A. David's public key

B. David's private key

C. Mike's public key

D. Mike's private key

18. When Mike receives the message that David encrypted for him in Question 17, what key should he use to decrypt the message?

A. David's public key

B. David's private key

C. Mike's public key

D. Mike's private key

19. If David wishes to digitally sign the message that he is sending Mike, what key would he use to create the digital signature?

A. David's public key

B. David's private key

C. Mike's public key

D. Mike's private key

20. When Mike receives the digitally signed message from David, what key should he use to verify the digital signature?

A. David's public key

B. David's private key

C. Mike's public key

D. Mike's private key

Chapter

8

Incident Response

THE CERTIFIED INFORMATION SECURITY MANAGER (CISM) DOMAINS AND SUBTOPICS COVERED IN THIS CHAPTER INCLUDE:

✓ **Domain 4: Incident Management**

- **A. Incident Management Readiness**

    - **4A1. Incident Response Plan**

    - **4A5. Incident Classification/Categorization**

    - **4A6. Incident Management Training, Testing, and Evaluation**

THE CERTIFIED INFORMATION SECURITY MANAGER (CISM) SUPPORTING TASKS COVERED IN THIS CHAPTER INCLUDE:

✓ **29. Establish and maintain an incident response plan, in alignment with the business continuity plan and disaster recovery plan.**

✓ **30. Establish and maintain an information security incident classification and categorization process.**

✓ **31. Develop and implement processes to ensure the timely identification of information security incidents.**

✓ **32. Establish and maintain processes to investigate and document information security incidents in accordance with legal and regulatory requirements.**

✓ **33. Establish and maintain incident handling process, including containment, notification, escalation, eradication, and recovery.**

✓ **34. Organize, train, equip, and assign responsibilities to incident response teams.**

✓ 35. Establish and maintain incident communication plans and processes for internal and external parties.

✓ 36. Evaluate incident management plans through testing and review, including table-top exercises, checklist review, and simulation testing at planned intervals.

✓ 37. Conduct post-incident reviews to facilitate continuous improvement, including root-cause analysis, lessons learned, corrective actions, and reassessment of risk.

No matter how well an organization prepares its cybersecurity defenses, sooner or later it will suffer a computer security incident that compromises the confidentiality, integrity, and availability of information or systems under its control. This incident may be a minor virus infection that is quickly remediated or a serious breach of personal information that comes into the national media spotlight. In either event, the organization must be prepared to conduct a coordinated, methodical response effort. Business leaders, technology leaders, cybersecurity experts, and technologists can plan for how they will handle these situations and prepare a well-thought-out response.

Security Incidents

Many IT professionals use the terms *security event* and *security incident* casually and interchangeably, but this is not correct. Members of a cybersecurity incident response team should use these terms carefully and according to their precise definitions within the organization. The National Institute for Standards and Technology (NIST) offers the following standard definitions for use throughout the U.S. government, and many private organizations choose to adopt them as well:

- An event is any observable occurrence in a system or network. A security event includes any observable occurrence that relates to a security function. For example, a user accessing a file stored on a server, an administrator changing permissions on a shared folder, and an attacker conducting a port scan are all examples of security events.

- An adverse event is any event that has negative consequences. Examples of adverse events include a malware infection on a system, a server crash, and a user accessing a file that they are not authorized to view.

- A security incident is a violation or imminent threat of violation of computer security policies, acceptable use policies, or standard security practices. Examples of security incidents include the accidental loss of sensitive information, an intrusion into a computer system by an attacker, the use of a keylogger on an executive's system to steal passwords, and the launch of a denial-of-service attack against a website.

Every security incident includes one or more security events, but not every security event is a security incident.

Computer security incident response teams (CSIRTs) are responsible for responding to computer security incidents that occur within an organization by following standardized response procedures and incorporating their subject matter expertise and professional judgment.

For brevity's sake, we will use the term "incident" as shorthand for "computer security incident" in the remainder of this book.

Phases of Incident Response

Organizations depend on the CSIRT members to respond calmly and consistently in the event of a security incident. The crisis-like atmosphere that surrounds many security incidents may lead to poor decision-making unless the organization has a clearly thought-out and refined process that describes how it will handle cybersecurity incident response. Figure 8.1 shows the simple incident response process advocated by NIST.

FIGURE 8.1   Incident response process

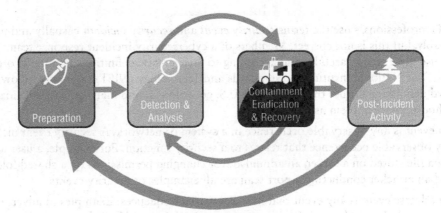

Source: NIST SP 800-61: *Computer Security Incident Handling Guide*

Notice that this process is not a simple progression of steps from start to finish. Instead, it includes loops that allow responders to return to prior phases as needed during the response. These loops reflect the reality of responses to actual cybersecurity incidents. Only in the simplest of incidents would an organization detect an incident, analyze data, conduct a recovery, and close out the incident in a straightforward sequence of steps. Instead, the containment process often includes several loops back through the detection and analysis phase to identify whether the incident has been successfully resolved. These loops are a normal part of the cybersecurity incident response process and should be expected.

Preparation

CSIRTs do not spring up out of thin air. As much as managers may wish it were so, they cannot simply will a CSIRT into existence by creating a policy document and assigning staff members to the CSIRT. Instead, the CSIRT requires careful preparation to ensure that the CSIRT has the proper policy foundation, has operating procedures that will be effective in the organization's computing environment, receives appropriate training, and is prepared to respond to an incident.

The preparation phase also includes building strong cybersecurity defenses to reduce the likelihood and impact of future incidents. This process of building a defense-in-depth approach to cybersecurity often includes personnel who might not be part of the CSIRT.

During the preparation phase, the organization should also assemble the hardware, software, and information required to conduct an incident investigation. NIST recommends that every organization's incident response toolkit should include, at a minimum, the following:

- Digital forensic workstations
- Backup devices
- Laptops for data collection, analysis, and reporting
- Spare server and networking equipment
- Blank removable media
- Portable printer
- Forensic and packet capture software
- Bootable USB media containing trusted copies of forensic tools
- Office supplies and evidence collection materials

 The preparation phase of the incident response plan is not a "one and done" planning process. Notice in Figure 8.1 that there is a loop from the post-incident activity phase back to the preparation phase. Whenever the organization is not actively involved in an incident response effort, it should be planning for the next incident.

During the preparation process, incident response teams should also define their standard notification and escalation procedures. Remember that anyone in the organization may be the first to identify a potential security incident. Procedures should clearly define how first responders report a potential incident to the CSIRT, the process for notifying the team members of an activation, and the criteria for escalating incident reports to management, as warranted.

Detection and Analysis

The detection and analysis phase of incident response is one of the trickiest to commit to a routine process. Although cybersecurity analysts have many tools at their disposal that may assist in identifying that a security incident is taking place, many incidents are only detected because of the trained eye of an experienced analyst.

NIST 800-61 describes four major categories of security event indicators:

- *Alerts* that originate from intrusion detection and prevention systems, security information and event management systems, antivirus software, file integrity–checking software, and/or third-party monitoring services
- *Logs* generated by operating systems, services, applications, network devices, and network flows
- *Publicly available information* about new vulnerabilities and exploits detected "in the wild" or in a controlled laboratory environment
- *People* from inside the organization or external sources who report suspicious activity that may indicate a security incident is in progress

When any of these information sources indicate that a security incident may be occurring, cybersecurity analysts should shift into the initial validation mode, where they attempt to determine whether an incident is taking place that merits further activation of the incident response process. This analysis is often more art than science and is very difficult work. NIST recommends the following actions to improve the timeliness and effectiveness of incident analysis:

Profile networks and systems to measure the characteristics of expected activity.   This will improve the organization's ability to identify abnormal activity during the detection and analysis process.

Understand normal behavior of users, systems, networks, and applications.   This behavior will vary between organizations, at different times of the day, week, and year and with changes in the business cycle. A solid understanding of normal behavior is critical to recognizing deviations from those patterns.

Create a logging policy that specifies the information that must be logged by systems, applications, and network devices.   The policy should also specify where those log records should be stored (preferably in a centralized log management system) and the retention period for logs.

Perform event correlation to combine information from multiple sources.   This function is typically performed by a *security information and event management (SIEM) system.*

Synchronize clocks across servers, workstations, and network devices.   This is done to facilitate the correlation of log entries from different systems. Organizations may easily achieve this objective by operating a *Network Time Protocol (NTP)* server.

Maintain an organization-wide knowledge base that contains critical information about systems and applications.   This knowledge base should include information about system profiles, usage patterns, and other information that may be useful to responders who are not familiar with the inner workings of a system.

Capture network traffic as soon as an incident is suspected.   If the organization does not routinely capture network traffic, responders should immediately begin packet captures during the detection and analysis phase. This information may provide critical details about an attacker's intentions and activity.

Filter information to reduce clutter.   Incident investigations generate massive amounts of information, and it is basically impossible to interpret it all without both inclusion and exclusion filters. Incident response teams may wish to create some predefined filters during the preparation phase to assist with future analysis efforts.

Seek assistance from external resources.   Responders should know the parameters for involving outside sources in their response efforts. This may be as simple as conducting a Google search for a strange error message, or it may involve full-fledged coordination with other response teams.

Containment, Eradication, and Recovery

During the incident detection and analysis phase, the CSIRT engages in primarily passive activities designed to uncover and analyze information about the incident. After completing this assessment, the team moves on to take active measures designed to contain the effects of the incident, eradicate the incident from the network, and recover normal operations.

At a high level, the containment, eradication, and recovery phase of the process is designed to achieve these objectives:

1. Select a containment strategy appropriate to the incident circumstances.
2. Implement the selected containment strategy to limit the damage caused by the incident.
3. Gather additional evidence as needed to support the response effort and potential legal action.
4. Identify the attacker(s) and attacking system(s).
5. Eradicate the effects of the incident and recover normal business operations.

Containing the Damage

Containment is the first activity that takes place during this phase, and it should begin as quickly as possible after analysts determine that an incident is underway. Containment activities are designed to isolate the incident and prevent it from spreading further. If that phrase sounds somewhat vague, that's because containment means very different things in the context of different types of security incidents. For example, if the organization is experiencing active exfiltration of data from a credit card processing system, incident responders might contain the damage by disconnecting that system from the network, preventing the attackers from continuing to exfiltrate information. On the other hand, if the organization is experiencing a denial-of-service attack against its website, disconnecting the network connection would simply help the attacker achieve its objective. In that case, containment might include placing filters on an upstream Internet connection that blocks all inbound traffic from networks involved in the attack or blocking web requests that bear a certain signature.

Exam Tip

When you take the exam, remember that containment is a critical priority. You want to stop the spread of any potential security threats before you worry about eradicating the damage or recovering operations.

Containment activities typically aren't perfect and often cause some collateral damage that disrupts normal business activity. Consider the two examples described in the previous paragraph. Disconnecting a credit card processing system from the network may bring transactions to a halt, potentially causing significant business losses. Similarly, blocking large swaths of inbound web traffic may render the site inaccessible to some legitimate users. Incident responders undertaking containment strategies must understand the potential side effects of their actions while weighing them against the greater benefit to the organization. Decisions such as these are one of the reasons that senior management may want to have input into the organization's incident response strategies and tactics.

Containment Strategy Criteria

Selecting appropriate containment strategies is one of the most difficult tasks facing incident responders. Containment approaches that are too drastic may have an unacceptable impact on business operations. On the other hand, responders who select weak containment approaches may find that the incident escalates to cause even more damage.

In the *Computer Security Incident Handling Guide*, NIST recommends using the following criteria to develop an appropriate containment strategy and weigh it against business interests:

- Potential damage to and theft of resources
- Need for evidence preservation

- Service availability (for example, network connectivity and services provided to external parties)

- Time and resources needed to implement the strategy

- Effectiveness of the strategy (for example, partial containment and full containment)

- Duration of the solution (for example, emergency workaround to be removed in four hours, temporary workaround to be removed in two weeks, or permanent solution)

Unfortunately, there's no formula or decision tree that guarantees responders will make the "right" decision while responding to an incident. Incident responders should understand these criteria, the intent of management, and their technical and business operating environment. Armed with this information, responders will be well-positioned to follow their best judgment and select an appropriate containment strategy.

WARNING   In any incident response, human health and safety should always be the highest priority. This may be a factor in situations where compromised systems or networks support safety-critical functions.

Segmentation

Cybersecurity analysts often use *network segmentation* as a proactive strategy to prevent the spread of future security incidents. For example, the network shown in Figure 8.2 is designed to segment different types of users from each other and from critical systems. An attacker who can gain access to the guest network would not be able to interact with systems belonging to employees or in the data center without traversing the network firewall.

FIGURE 8.2   Proactive network segmentation

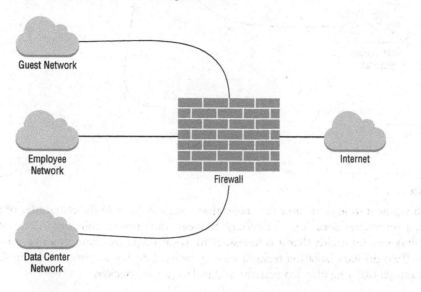

In addition to being used as a proactive control, network segmentation may play a crucial role in incident response. During the early stages of an incident, responders may realize that a portion of systems are compromised but wish to continue to observe the activity on those systems while they determine other appropriate responses. However, they certainly want to protect other systems on the network from those potentially compromised systems.

Figure 8.3 shows an example of how an organization might apply network segmentation during an incident response effort. Cybersecurity analysts suspect that several systems in the data center were compromised and build a separate virtual LAN (VLAN) to contain those systems. That VLAN, called the quarantine network, is segmented from the rest of the data center network and controlled by very strict firewall rules. Putting the systems on this network segment provides some degree of isolation, preventing them from damaging systems on other segments but allowing continued live analysis efforts.

FIGURE 8.3   Network segmentation for incident response

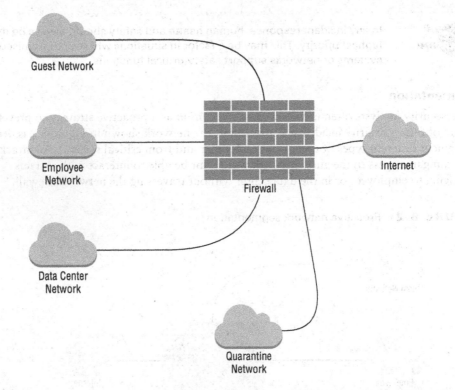

Isolation

Although segmentation does limit the access that attackers have to the remainder of the network, it sometimes doesn't go far enough to meet containment objectives. Cybersecurity analysts may instead decide that it is necessary to use stronger *isolation* practices to cut off an attack. Two primary isolation techniques may be used during a cybersecurity incident response effort: isolating affected systems and isolating the attacker.

Segmentation and isolation strategies carry with them significant risks to the organization. First, the attacker retains access to the compromised system, creating the potential for further expansion of the security incident. Second, the compromised system may be used to attack other systems on the Internet. In the best case scenario, an attack launched from the organization's network against a third party may lead to some difficult conversations with cybersecurity colleagues at other firms. In the worst case scenario, the courts may hold the organization liable for knowingly allowing the use of their network in an attack. Cybersecurity analysts considering a segmentation or isolation approach to containment should consult with both management and legal counsel.

ISOLATING AFFECTED SYSTEMS

Isolating affected systems is, quite simply, taking segmentation to the next level. Affected systems are completely disconnected from the remainder of the network, although they may still be able to communicate with each other and the attacker over the Internet. Figure 8.4 shows an example of taking the quarantine VLAN from the segmentation strategy and converting it to an isolation approach.

FIGURE 8.4   Network isolation for incident response

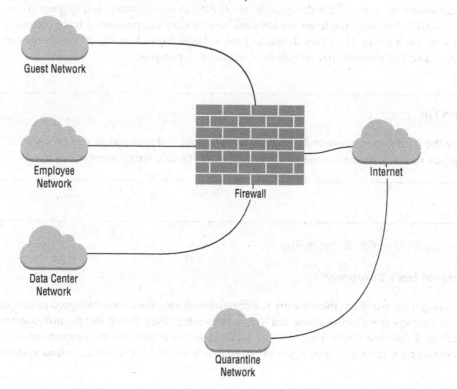

Guest Network

Employee Network

Firewall

Internet

Data Center Network

Quarantine Network

Notice that the only difference between Figures 8.3 and 8.4 is where the quarantine network is connected. In the segmentation approach, the network is connected to the firewall and may have some limited access to other networked systems. In the isolation approach, the quarantine network connects directly to the Internet and has no access to other systems. In reality, this approach may be implemented by simply altering firewall rules rather than bypassing the firewall entirely. The objective is to allow the attacker to continue accessing the isolated systems but restrict their ability to access other systems and cause further damage.

ISOLATING THE ATTACKER

Isolating the attacker is an interesting variation on the isolation strategy and depends on the use of *sandbox* systems that are set up purely to monitor attacker activity and that do not contain any information or resources of value to the attacker. Placing attackers in a sandboxed environment allows continued observation in a fairly safe, contained environment. Some organizations use honeypot systems for this purpose.

Removal

Removal of compromised systems from the network is the strongest containment technique in the cybersecurity analyst's incident response toolkit. As shown in Figure 8.5, removal differs from segmentation and isolation in that the affected systems are completely disconnected from other networks, although they may still be allowed to communicate with other compromised systems within the quarantine VLAN. In some cases, each suspect system may be physically disconnected from the network so that they are prevented from communicating even with each other. The exact details of removal will depend on the circumstances of the incident and the professional judgment of incident responders.

Exam Tip

Study the differences between segmentation, isolation, and removal as you prepare for the exam. Be ready to answer questions that ask you to identify which approach is in use.

🌐 Real World Scenario

Removal Isn't Foolproof

Removing a system from the network is a common containment step designed to prevent further damage from taking place, but NIST points out in their *Computer Security Incident Handling Guide* that it isn't foolproof. The guide presents a hypothetical example of an attacker using a simple ping as a sort of "dead man's switch" for a compromised system, designed to identify when the adversary detects the response and removes the system from the network.

In this scenario, the attacker simply sets up a periodic ping request to a known external host, such as the Google public DNS server located at 8.8.8.8. This server is almost always accessible from any network and the attacker can verify this connectivity after initially compromising a system.

The attacker can then write a simple script that monitors the results of those ping requests and, after detecting several consecutive failures, assumes that the attack was detected and the system was removed from the network. The script can then wipe out evidence of the attack or encrypt important information stored on the server.

The moral of the story is that although removal is a strong weapon in the containment toolkit, it isn't foolproof!

FIGURE 8.5   Network removal for incident response

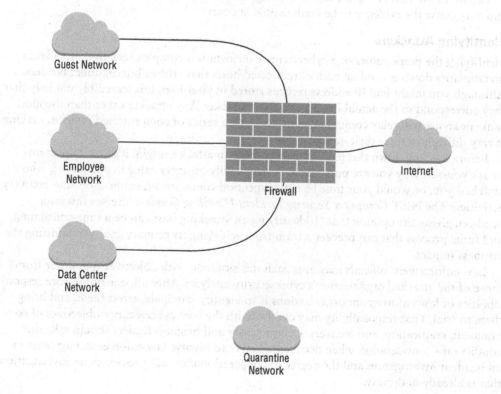

Evidence Gathering and Handling

The primary objective during the containment phase of incident response is to limit the damage to the organization and its resources. That objective may take precedence over other goals, but responders may still be interested in gathering evidence during the containment process. This evidence may be crucial in the continuing analysis of the incident for internal purposes, or it may be used during legal proceedings against the attacker.

If incident handlers suspect that evidence gathered during an investigation may be used in court, they should take special care to preserve and document evidence during their investigation. NIST recommends that investigators maintain a detailed evidence log that includes the following:

- Identifying information (for example, the location, serial number, model number, hostname, MAC addresses, and IP addresses of a computer)
- Name, title, and phone number of each individual who collected or handled the evidence during the investigation
- Time and date (including time zone) of each occurrence of evidence handling
- Locations where the evidence was stored

Failure to maintain accurate logs will bring the evidence chain of custody into question and may cause the evidence to be inadmissible in court.

Identifying Attackers

Identifying the perpetrators of a cybersecurity incident is a complex task that often leads investigators down a winding path of redirected hosts that crosses international borders. Although you might find IP address records stored in your logs, it is incredibly unlikely that they correspond to the actual IP address of the attacker. Any attacker other than the most rank amateurs will relay communications through a series of compromised systems, making it very difficult to trace their actual origin.

Before heading down this path of investigating an attack's origin, it's very important to ask yourself why you are pursuing it. Is there really business value in uncovering who attacked you, or would your time be better spent on containment, eradication, and recovery activities? The NIST *Computer Security Incident Handling Guide* addresses this issue head-on, giving the opinion that "[i]dentifying an attacking host can be a time-consuming and futile process that can prevent a team from achieving its primary goal—minimizing the business impact."

Law enforcement officials may approach this situation with objectives that differ from those of the attacked organization's cybersecurity analysts. After all, one of the core responsibilities of law enforcement organizations is to identify criminals, arrest them, and bring them to trial. That responsibility may conflict with the core cybersecurity objectives of containment, eradication, and recovery. Cybersecurity and business leaders should take this conflict into consideration when deciding whether to involve law enforcement agencies in an incident investigation and the degree of cooperation they will provide to an investigation that is already underway.

Law enforcement officers have tools at their disposal that aren't available to private cybersecurity analysts. If you do have a pressing need to identify an attacker, it may be wise to involve law enforcement. They can obtain search warrants that may prove invaluable during an investigation. Officers can serve search warrants on Internet service providers and other companies that may have log records that assist in untangling the winding trail of an attack. Additionally, law enforcement agencies may have access to sensitive government databases that contain information on known attackers and their methodologies.

Incident Eradication and Recovery

Once the cybersecurity team successfully contains an incident, it is time to move on to the *eradication* phase of the response. The primary purpose of eradication is to remove any of the artifacts of the incident that may remain on the organization's network. This could include the removal of any malicious code from the network, the sanitization of compromised media, and the securing of compromised user accounts.

The *recovery* phase of incident response focuses on restoring normal capabilities and services. It includes reconstituting resources and correcting security control deficiencies that may have led to the attack. This could include rebuilding and patching systems, reconfiguring firewalls, updating malware signatures, and similar activities. The goal of recovery is not just to rebuild the organization's network but to do so in a manner that reduces the likelihood of a successful future attack.

During the eradication and recovery effort, cybersecurity analysts should develop a clear understanding of the incident's root cause. This is critical to implementing a secure recovery that corrects control deficiencies that led to the original attack. After all, if you don't understand how an attacker breached your security controls in the first place, it will be hard to correct those controls so the attack doesn't reoccur. Understanding the root cause of an attack is a completely different activity than identifying the attacker. Root cause assessment is a critical component of incident recovery while, as mentioned earlier, identifying the attacker can be a costly distraction.

Root cause analysis also helps an organization identify other systems they operate that might share the same vulnerability. For example, if an attacker compromises a Cisco router and root cause analysis reveals an error in that device's configuration, administrators may correct the error on other routers they control to prevent a similar attack from compromising those devices.

Reconstruction and Reimaging

During an incident, attackers may compromise one or more systems through the use of malware, web application attacks, or other exploits. Once an attacker gains control of a system, security professionals should consider it completely compromised and untrustworthy. It is not safe to simply correct the security issue and move on because the attacker may still have an undetected foothold on the compromised system. Instead, the system should be rebuilt, either from scratch or by using an image or backup of the system from a known secure state.

Rebuilding and/or restoring systems should always be done with the incident root cause analysis in mind. If the system was compromised because it contained a security vulnerability, as opposed to through the use of a compromised user account, backups and images of that system likely have that same vulnerability. Even rebuilding the system from scratch may reintroduce the earlier vulnerability, rendering the system susceptible to the same attack. During the recovery phase, administrators should ensure that rebuilt or restored systems are remediated to address known security issues.

Patching Systems and Applications

During the incident recovery effort, cybersecurity analysts will patch operating systems and applications involved in the attack. This is also a good time to review the security patch status of all systems in the enterprise, addressing other security issues that may lurk behind the scenes.

Cybersecurity analysts should first focus their efforts on systems that were directly involved in the compromise and then work their way outward, addressing systems that were indirectly related to the compromise before touching systems that were not involved at all. Figure 8.6 shows the phased approach that cybersecurity analysts should take to patching systems and applications during the recovery phase.

FIGURE 8.6   Patching priorities

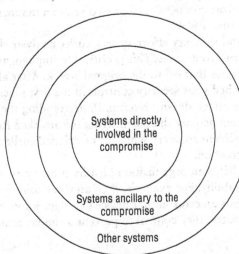

Systems directly involved in the compromise

Systems ancillary to the compromise

Other systems

Sanitization and Secure Disposal

During the recovery effort, cybersecurity analysts may need to dispose of or repurpose media from systems that were compromised during the incident. In those cases, special care should be taken to ensure that sensitive information that was stored on that media is not compromised. Responders don't want the recovery effort from one incident to lead to a second incident!

Generally speaking, there are three options available for the secure disposition of media containing sensitive information: clear, purge, and destroy. NIST defines these three activities in NIST SP 800-88: *Guidelines for Media Sanitization*:

- *Clear* applies logical techniques to sanitize data in all user-addressable storage locations for protection against simple non-invasive data recovery techniques; this is typically applied through the standard Read and Write commands to the storage device, such as by rewriting with a new value or using a menu option to reset the device to the factory state (where rewriting is not supported).

- *Purge* applies physical or logical techniques that render target data recovery infeasible using state-of-the-art laboratory techniques. Examples of purging activities include overwriting, block erase, and cryptographic erase activities when performed through the use of dedicated, standardized device commands. *Degaussing* is another form of purging that uses extremely strong magnetic fields to disrupt the data stored on a device.

- *Destroy* renders target data recovery infeasible using state-of-the-art laboratory techniques and results in the subsequent inability to use the media for storage of data. Destruction techniques include disintegration, pulverization, melting, and incinerating.

These three levels of data disposal are listed in increasing order of effectiveness as well as difficulty and cost. Physically incinerating a hard drive, for example, removes any possibility that data will be recovered but requires the use of an incinerator and renders the drive unusable for future purposes.

Figure 8.7 shows a flowchart designed to help security decision-makers choose appropriate techniques for destroying information and can be used to guide incident recovery efforts. Notice that the flowchart includes a validation phase after efforts to clear, purge, or destroy data. Validation ensures that the media sanitization was successful and that remnant data does not exist on the sanitized media.

Validating the Recovery Effort

Before concluding the recovery effort, incident responders should take time to verify that the recovery measures put in place were successful. The exact nature of this verification will depend on the technical circumstances of the incident and the organization's infrastructure. Four activities that should always be included in these validation efforts follow:

Validate that only authorized user accounts exist on every system and application in the organization.   In many cases, organizations already undertake periodic account reviews that verify the authorization for every account. This process should be used during the recovery validation effort.

Verify the proper restoration of permissions assigned to each account.   During the account review, responders should also verify that accounts do not have extraneous permissions that violate the principle of least privilege. This is true for normal user accounts, administrator accounts, and service accounts.

Verify that all systems are logging properly.   Every system and application should be configured to log security-related information to a level that is consistent with the organization's logging policy. Those log records should be sent to a centralized log repository that preserves them for archival use. The validation phase should include verification that these logs are properly configured and received by the repository.

Conduct vulnerability scans on all systems.   Vulnerability scans play an important role in verifying that systems are safeguarded against future attacks. Analysts should run thorough scans against systems and initiate remediation workflows where necessary.

FIGURE 8.7   Sanitization and disposition decision flow

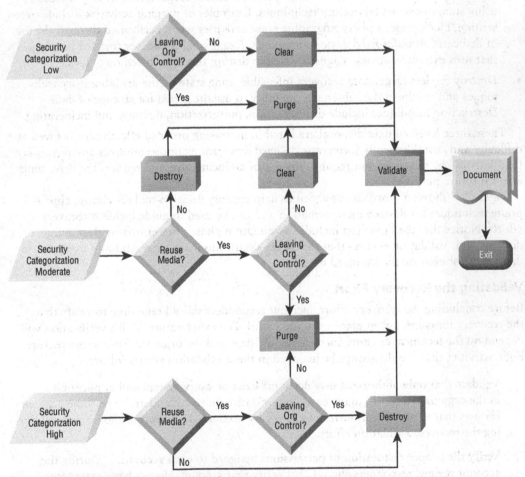

Source: NIST SP 800-88: *Guidelines for Media Sanitization*

These actions form the core of an incident recovery validation effort and should be complemented with other activities that validate the specific controls put in place during the containment, eradication, and recovery phase of incident response.

Post-Incident Activity

Security incidents don't end after security professionals remove attackers from the network or complete the recovery effort to restore normal business operations. Once the immediate danger passes and normal operations resume, the CSIRT enters the post-incident activity phase of incident response. During this phase, team members conduct a lessons-learned review and ensure that they meet internal and external evidence retention requirements.

Lessons-Learned Review

During the lessons-learned review, responders conduct a thorough review of the incident and their response, with a focus on improving procedures and tools for the next incident. This review is most effective if conducted during a meeting where everyone is present for the discussion (physically or virtually). Although some organizations try to conduct lessons-learned reviews in an offline manner, this approach does not lead to the back-and-forth discussion that often yields the greatest insight.

The lessons-learned review should be facilitated by an independent facilitator who was not involved in the incident response and who is perceived by everyone involved as an objective outsider. This allows the facilitator to productively guide the discussion without participants feeling that they are advancing a hidden agenda. NIST recommends that lessons-learned processes answer the following questions:

- Exactly what happened and at what times?
- What was the root cause of the incident?
- How well did staff and management perform in responding to the incident?
- Were the documented procedures followed? Were they adequate?
- What information was needed sooner?
- Were any steps or actions taken that might have inhibited the recovery?
- What would the staff and management do differently the next time a similar incident occurs?
- How could information sharing with other organizations have been improved?
- What corrective actions can prevent similar incidents in the future?
- What precursors or indicators should be watched for in the future to detect similar incidents?
- What additional tools or resources are needed to detect, analyze, and mitigate future incidents?

Once the group answers these questions, management must ensure that the organization takes follow-up actions, as appropriate. Lessons-learned reviews are only effective if they surface needed changes and those changes then occur to improve future incident response efforts.

The lessons-learned effort may result in the organization making changes to its cybersecurity program to reduce the risk of future incidents. When these remediations occur, the organization should reassess their level of risk at the conclusion of those remedial actions.

Evidence Retention

At the conclusion of an incident, the CSIRT has often gathered a large amount of evidence. The team leader should work with staff to identify both internal and external evidence retention requirements. If the incident may result in civil litigation or criminal prosecution, the team should consult attorneys prior to discarding any evidence. If there is no likelihood that the evidence will be used in court, the team should follow any retention policies that the organization has in place.

If the organization does not have an existing evidence retention policy for cybersecurity incidents, now would be a good time to create one. Many organizations choose to implement a two-year retention period for evidence not covered by other requirements. This allows incident handlers time to review the evidence at a later date during incident handling program reviews or while handling future similar incidents.

At the conclusion of the post-incident activity phase, the CSIRT deactivates, and the incident-handling cycle returns to the preparation and detection & analysis phases.

U.S. federal government agencies must retain all incident handling records for at least three years. This requirement appears in the National Archives General Records Schedule 3.2, Item 20. See www.archives .gov/files/records-mgmt/grs/grs03-2.pdf for more information.

Developing a Final Report

Every incident that activates the CSIRT should conclude with a formal written report that documents the incident for posterity. This serves several important purposes. First, it creates an institutional memory of the incident that is useful when developing new security controls and training new security team members. Second, it may serve as an important record of the incident if there is ever legal action that results from the incident. Finally, the act of creating the written report can help identify previously undetected deficiencies in the incident response process that may feed back through the lessons-learned process.

Important elements that the CSIRT should cover in a post-incident report include the following:

- Chronology of events for the incident and response efforts
- Root cause of the incident
- Location and description of evidence collected during the incident response process
- Specific actions taken by responders to contain, eradicate, and recover from the incident, including the rationale for those decisions
- Estimates of the impact of the incident on the organization and its stakeholders
- Results of post-recovery validation efforts
- Documentation of issues identified during the lessons-learned review

Incident summary reports should be classified in accordance with the organization's classification policy and stored in an appropriately secured manner. The organization should also have a defined retention period for incident reports and destroy old reports when they exceed that period.

Building the Incident Response Plan

One of the major responsibilities that organizations have during the preparation phase of incident response is building a solid incident response plan that will guide the program. This creates the policies, procedures, and other documentation required to support the program's ongoing efforts and ensure that response efforts are effective and timely.

Policy

The incident response policy serves as the cornerstone of an organization's incident response program. This policy should be written to guide efforts at a high level and provide the authority for incident response. The policy should be approved at the highest level possible within the organization, preferably by the chief executive officer. For this reason, policy authors should attempt to write the policy in a manner that makes it relatively timeless. This means that the policy should contain statements that provide authority for incident response, assign responsibility to the CSIRT, and describe the role of individual users and state organizational priorities. The policy is *not* the place to describe specific technologies, response procedures, or evidence-gathering techniques. Those details may change frequently and should be covered in more easily changeable procedure documents.

NIST recommends that incident response policies contain these key elements:

- Statement of management commitment
- Purpose and objectives of the policy
- Scope of the policy (to whom it applies and under what circumstances)
- Definition of cybersecurity incidents and related terms
- Organizational structure and definition of roles, responsibilities, and level of authority
- Prioritization or severity rating scheme for incidents
- Performance measures for the CSIRT
- Reporting and contact forms

Including these elements in the policy provides a solid foundation for the CSIRT's routine and crisis activities.

Procedures and Playbooks

Procedures provide the detailed, tactical information that CSIRT members need when responding to an incident. They represent the collective wisdom of team members and subject matter experts collected during periods of calm and ready to be applied in the event of an actual incident. CSIRTs often develop *playbooks* that describe the specific procedures that they will follow in the event of a specific type of cybersecurity incident. For example, a financial institution CSIRT might develop playbooks that cover:

- Breach of personal financial information
- Web server defacement
- Phishing attack targeted at customers
- Loss of a laptop
- General security incident not covered by another playbook

This is clearly not an exhaustive list, and each organization will develop playbooks that describe their response to both high severity and frequently occurring incident categories. The idea behind the playbook is that the team should be able to pick it up and find an operational plan for responding to the security incident that they may follow. Playbooks are especially important in the early hours of incident response to ensure that the team has a planned, measured response to the first reports of a potential incident.

For good examples of real-world cybersecurity incident playbooks, see the Ransomware Playbook, published by the Cyber Readiness Institute (https://cyberreadinessinstitute.org/wp-content/uploads/20-CRI-Ransomware-Playbook.pdf) or the Windows incident response playbook from the University of Central Florida (https://infosec.ucf.edu/wp-content/uploads/sites/2/2019/07/Procedure_for_Windows_Incident_Response.pdf).

Playbooks are designed to be step-by-step recipe-style responses to cybersecurity incidents. They should guide the team's response, but they are not a substitute for professional judgment. The responders handling an incident should have appropriate professional expertise and the authority to deviate from the playbook when circumstances require a different approach.

Documenting the Incident Response Plan

When developing the incident response plan documentation, organizations should pay particular attention to creating tools that may be useful during an incident response. These tools should provide clear guidance to response teams that may be quickly read and interpreted during a crisis situation. For example, the incident response checklist shown in Figure 8.8 provides a high-level overview of the incident response process in checklist form. The CSIRT leader may use this checklist to ensure that the team doesn't miss an important step in the heat of the crisis environment.

FIGURE 8.8   Incident response checklist

	Action	Completed
	Detection and Analysis	
1.	Determine whether an incident has occurred	
1.1	Analyze the precursors and indicators	
1.2	Look for correlating information	
1.3	Perform research (e.g., search engines, knowledge base)	
1.4	As soon as the handler believes an incident has occurred, begin documenting the investigation and gathering evidence	
2.	Prioritize handling the incident based on the relevant factors (functional impact, information impact, recoverability effort, etc.)	
3.	Report the incident to the appropriate internal personnel and external organizations	
	Containment, Eradication, and Recovery	
4.	Acquire, preserve, secure, and document evidence	
5.	Contain the incident	
6.	Eradicate the incident	
6.1	Identify and mitigate all vulnerabilities that were exploited	
6.2	Remove malware, inappropriate materials, and other components	
6.3	If more affected hosts are discovered (e.g., new malware infections), repeat the Detection and Analysis steps (1.1, 1.2) to identify all other affected hosts, then contain (5) and eradicate (6) the incident for them	
7.	Recover from the incident	
7.1	Return affected systems to an operationally ready state	
7.2	Confirm that the affected systems are functioning normally	
7.3	If necessary, implement additional monitoring to look for future related activity	
	Post-Incident Activity	
8.	Create a follow-up report	
9.	Hold a lessons-learned meeting (mandatory for major incidents, optional otherwise)	

Source: NIST SP 800-61: *Computer Security Incident Handling Guide*

The National Institute of Standards and Technology publishes a *Computer Security Incident Handling Guide* (SP 800-61) that contains a wealth of information that is useful to both government agencies and private organizations developing incident response plans. The current version of the guide, NIST SP 800-61 revision 2, is available online at http://nvlpubs.nist.gov/nistpubs/SpecialPublications/NIST.SP.800-61r2.pdf.

Creating an Incident Response Team

There are many different roles that should be represented in a CSIRT. Depending on the organization and its technical needs, some of these roles may be core team members who are always activated, whereas others may be called in as needed on an incident-by-incident basis. For example, a database administrator might be crucial when investigating the aftermath of a SQL injection attack but would probably not be very helpful when responding to a stolen laptop.

The core incident response team normally consists of cybersecurity professionals with specific expertise in incident response. In larger organizations, these may be full-time employees dedicated to incident response, whereas smaller organizations may call on cybersecurity experts who fill other roles for their "day jobs" to step into CSIRT roles in the aftermath of an incident.

The Role of Management

Management should have an active role in incident response efforts. The primary responsibility of IT managers and senior leadership is to provide the authority, resources, and time required to respond appropriately to a security incident. This includes ensuring that the CSIRT has the budget and staff required to plan for security incidents and access to subject matter experts during a response.

Management may also be called on during an incident response to make crucial business decisions about the need to shut down critical servers, communicate with law enforcement or the general public, and assess the impact of an incident on essential stakeholders.

In addition to the core team members, the CSIRT may include representation from the following:

- Technical subject matter experts whose knowledge may be required during a response. This includes system engineers, network administrators, database administrators, desktop experts, and application experts.
- IT support staff, who may be needed to carry out actions directed by the CSIRT.
- Legal counsel responsible for ensuring that the team's actions comply with legal, policy, and regulatory requirements and who can advise team leaders on compliance issues and communication with regulatory bodies.
- Human resources staff responsible for investigating potential employee malfeasance.
- Public relations and marketing staff, who can coordinate communications with the media and general public.

The CSIRT should be run by a designated leader with the clear authority to direct incident response efforts and serve as a liaison to management. This leader should be a skilled incident responder who is either assigned to lead the CSIRT as a full-time responsibility or who serves in a cybersecurity leadership position.

Incident Response Providers

In addition to including internal team members on the CSIRT, the organization may decide to outsource some or all of their actions to an incident response provider. Retaining an incident response provider gives the organization access to expertise that might not otherwise exist inside the firm. This may come at a significant expense, so the organizations should decide what types of incidents may be handled internally and which justify the use of an outside provider. Additionally, the organization should understand the provider's guaranteed response time and ensure that it has a plan in place to respond to the early stages of an incident before the provider assumes control.

CSIRT Scope of Control

The organization's incident response policy should clearly outline the scope of the CSIRT. This includes answers to the following questions:

- What triggers the activation of the CSIRT? Who is authorized to activate the CSIRT?
- Does the CSIRT cover the entire organization or is it responsible only for certain business units, information categories, or other divisions of responsibility?
- Is the CSIRT authorized to communicate with law enforcement, regulatory bodies, or other external parties and, if so, which ones?
- Does the CSIRT have internal communication and/or escalation responsibilities? If so, what triggers those requirements?

Coordination and Information Sharing

During an incident response effort, the CSIRT members often need to communicate and share information with both internal and external partners. Smooth information sharing is essential to an effective and efficient incident response, but it must be done within the clearly established parameters of an incident communication plan. The organization's incident response policies should limit communication to trusted parties and put controls in place to prevent the inadvertent release of sensitive information outside of those trusted partners.

Internal Communications

Internal communications among the CSIRT and with other employees within the organization should take place over secure communications channels that are designated in advance and tested for security. This may include email, instant messaging, message boards, and other collaboration tools that pass security muster. The key is to evaluate and standardize those communications tools in advance so that responders are not left to their own devices to identify tools in the heat of an incident.

External Communications

CSIRT members, business leaders, public relations teams, and legal counsel may all bring to the table requirements that may justify sharing limited or detailed information with external entities. The incident response plan should guide these efforts. Types of external communications may include the following:

- Law enforcement may wish to be involved when a cybersecurity incident appears to be criminal in nature. The organization may choose to cooperate or decline participation in an investigation but should always make this decision with the advice of legal counsel.

- Information sharing partners, such as the Information Sharing and Analysis Center (ISAC), provide community-based warnings of cybersecurity risks. The organization may choose to participate in one of these consortiums and, in some cases, share information about ongoing and past security incidents with partners in that consortium.

- Vendors may be able to provide information crucial to the response. The manufacturers of hardware and software used within the organization may be able to provide patches, troubleshooting advice, or other guidance crucial to the response effort.

- Other organizations may be actual or potential victims of the same attack. CSIRT members may wish to coordinate their incident response with other organizations.

- Communications with the media and the general public may be mandatory under regulatory or legislative reporting requirements, voluntary, or forced by media coverage of a security incident.

It is incumbent upon the CSIRT leader to control and coordinate external communications in a manner that meets regulatory requirements and best serves the response effort.

Classifying Incidents

Each time an incident occurs, the CSIRT should classify the incident by both the type of threat and the severity of the incident according to a standardized incident severity rating system. This classification aids other personnel in understanding the nature and severity of the incident and allows the comparison of the current incident to past and future incidents.

Threat Classification

In many cases, the incident will come from a known threat source that facilitates the rapid identification of the threat. NIST provides the following attack vectors that are useful for classifying threats:

External/Removable Media   An attack executed from removable media or a peripheral device—for example, malicious code spreading onto a system from an infected USB flash drive.

Attrition   An attack that employs brute-force methods to compromise, degrade, or destroy systems, networks, or services—for example, a DDoS attack intended to impair or deny access to a service or application or a brute-force attack against an authentication mechanism.

Web   An attack executed from a website or web-based application—for example, a cross-site scripting attack used to steal credentials or redirect to a site that exploits a browser vulnerability and installs malware.

Email   An attack executed via an email message or attachment—for example, exploit code disguised as an attached document or a link to a malicious website in the body of an email message.

Impersonation   An attack involving the replacement of something benign with something malicious—for example, spoofing, on-path attacks, rogue wireless access points, and SQL injection attacks all involve impersonation.

Improper Usage   Any incident resulting from the violation of an organization's acceptable usage policies by an authorized user, excluding the previous categories; for example, a user installs file-sharing software, leading to the loss of sensitive data, or a user performs illegal activities on a system.

Loss or Theft of Equipment   The loss or theft of a computing device or media used by the organization, such as a laptop, smartphone, or authentication token.

Unknown   An attack of unknown origin.

Other   An attack of known origin that does not fit into any of the previous categories.

In addition to understanding these attack vectors, cybersecurity analysts should be familiar with the concept of an *advanced persistent threat (APT)*. APT attackers are highly skilled and talented attackers focused on a specific objective. These attackers are often funded by nation-states, organized crime, and other sources with tremendous resources. APT attackers are known for taking advantage of *zero-day vulnerabilities*: vulnerabilities that are unknown to the security community and, as a result, are not included in security tests performed by vulnerability scanners and other tools and have no patches available to correct them.

Severity Classification

CSIRT members may investigate dozens, hundreds, or even thousands of security incidents each year, depending on the scope of their responsibilities and the size of the organization. Therefore, it is important to use a standardized process to communicate the severity of each incident to management and other stakeholders. Incident severity information assists in the prioritization and scope of incident response efforts.

Two important measures used to determine the incident severity are the scope of the impact and the types of data involved in the incident.

Scope of Impact

The scope of an incident's impact depends on the degree of impairment that it causes the organization as well as the effort required to recover from the incident.

Functional Impact

The functional impact of an incident is the degree of impairment that it causes to the organization. This may vary based on the criticality of the data, the system(s) or process(es) affected by the incident, and the organization's ability to continue providing services to users as an incident unfolds and in its aftermath. NIST recommends using four categories to describe the functional impact of an incident, as shown in Table 8.1.

TABLE 8.1   NIST functional impact categories

Category	Definition
None	No effect on the organization's ability to provide all services to all users.
Low	Minimal effect; the organization can still provide all critical services to all users but has lost efficiency.
Medium	Organization has lost the ability to provide a critical service to a subset of system users.
High	Organization is no longer able to provide some critical services to any users.

Source: NIST SP 800-61

There is one major gap in the functional impact assessment criteria provided by NIST: it does not include any assessment of the economic impact of a security incident on the organization. This may be because the NIST guidelines are primarily intended to serve a government audience. Organizations may wish to modify the categories in Table 8.1 to incorporate economic impact or measure financial impact using a separate scale, such as the one shown in Table 8.2.

TABLE 8.2   Economic impact categories

Category	Definition
None	The organization does not expect to experience any financial impact or the financial impact is negligible.
Low	The organization expects to experience a financial impact of $10,000 or less.
Medium	The organization expects to experience a financial impact of more than $10,000 but less than $500,000.
High	The organization expects to experience a financial impact of $500,000 or more.

The financial thresholds included in Table 8.2 are intended as examples only and should be adjusted according to the size of the organization. For example, a security incident causing a $500,000 loss may be crippling for a small business, whereas a Fortune 500 company may easily absorb this loss.

Recoverability Effort

In addition to measuring the functional and economic impact of a security incident, organizations should measure the time that services will be unavailable. This may be expressed as a function of the amount of downtime experienced by the service or the time required to recover from the incident. Table 8.3 shows the NIST-suggested recommendations for assessing the recoverability impact of a security incident.

TABLE 8.3   NIST recoverability effort categories

Category	Definition
Regular	Time to recovery is predictable with existing resources.
Supplemented	Time to recovery is predictable with additional resources.
Extended	Time to recovery is unpredictable; additional resources and outside help are needed.
Not Recoverable	Recovery from the incident is not possible (e.g., sensitive data exfiltrated and posted publicly); launch investigation.

Source: NIST SP 800-61

Data Types

The nature of the data involved in a security incident also contributes to the incident's severity. When a security incident affects the confidentiality or integrity of sensitive information, cybersecurity analysts should assign a data impact rating. The data impact rating scale recommended by NIST appears in Table 8.4.

TABLE 8.4   NIST information impact categories

Category	Definition
None	No information was exfiltrated, changed, deleted, or otherwise compromised.
Privacy breach	Sensitive personally identifiable information (PII) of taxpayers, employees, beneficiaries, and so on was accessed or exfiltrated.
Proprietary breach	Unclassified proprietary information, such as protected critical infrastructure information (PCII), was accessed or exfiltrated.
Integrity loss	Sensitive or proprietary information was changed or deleted.

Source: NIST SP 800-61

Although the impact scale presented in Table 8.4 is NIST's recommendation, it does have some significant shortcomings. Most notably, the definitions included in the table are skewed toward the types of information that might be possessed by a government agency and might not map well to information in the possession of a private organization. Some analysts might also object to the inclusion of "integrity loss" as a single category separate from the three classification-dependent breach categories.

Table 8.5 presents an alternative classification scheme that private organizations might use as the basis for their own information impact categorization schemes.

TABLE 8.5   Private organization information impact categories

Category	Definition
None	No information was exfiltrated, changed, deleted, or otherwise compromised.
Regulated information breach	Information regulated by an external compliance obligation was accessed or exfiltrated. This may include personally identifiable information (PII) that triggers a data breach notification law, protected health information (PHI) under HIPAA, and/or payment card information protected under PCI DSS. For organizations subject to the European Union's General Data Protection Regulation (GDPR), it should also include sensitive personal information (SPI) as defined under GDPR. SPI includes information from special categories, such as genetic data, trade union membership, and data concerning a person's sex life or sexual orientation.
Intellectual property breach	Sensitive intellectual property was accessed or exfiltrated. This may include product development plans, formulas, or other sensitive trade secrets.

(continues)

TABLE 8.5 Private organization information impact categories *(continued)*

Category	Definition
Confidential information breach	Corporate confidential information was accessed or exfiltrated. This includes information that is sensitive or classified as a high-value asset but does not fit under the categories of regulated information or intellectual property. Examples might include corporate financial information or information about mergers and acquisitions.
Integrity loss	Sensitive or proprietary information was changed or deleted.

As with the financial impact scale, organizations will need to customize the information impact categories in Table 8.5 to meet the unique requirements of their business processes.

Conducting Investigations

Every information security professional will, at one time or another, encounter a security incident that requires an investigation. In many cases, this investigation will be a brief, informal determination that the matter is not serious enough to warrant further action or the involvement of law enforcement authorities. However, in some cases, the threat posed or damage done will be severe enough to require a more formal inquiry. When this occurs, investigators must be careful to ensure that proper procedures are followed. Failure to abide by the correct procedures may violate the civil rights of the individual(s) being investigated and could result in a failed prosecution or even legal action against the investigator.

Investigation Types

Security practitioners may find themselves conducting investigations for a wide variety of reasons. Some of these investigations involve law enforcement and must follow rigorous standards designed to produce evidence that will be admissible in court. Other investigations support internal business processes and require much less rigor.

Administrative Investigations

Administrative investigations are internal investigations that examine either operational issues or a violation of the organization's policies. They may be conducted as part of a technical troubleshooting effort or in support of other administrative processes, such as HR disciplinary procedures.

Operational investigations examine issues related to the organization's computing infrastructure and have the primary goal of resolving operational issues. For example, an information technology (IT) team noticing performance issues on their web servers may conduct an operational investigation designed to determine the cause of the performance problems.

 Administrative investigations may quickly transition to another type of investigation. For example, an investigation into a performance issue may uncover evidence of a system intrusion that may then become a criminal investigation.

Operational investigations have the loosest standards for the collection of information. They are not intended to produce evidence because they are for internal operational purposes only. Therefore, administrators conducting an operational investigation will only conduct the analysis necessary to reach their operational conclusions. The collection need not be thorough or well documented, because resolving the issue is the primary goal.

In addition to resolving the operational issue, operational investigations often conduct a *root cause analysis* that seeks to identify the reason that an operational issue occurred. The root cause analysis often highlights issues that require remediation to prevent similar incidents in the future.

Administrative investigations that are not operational in nature may require a stronger standard of evidence, especially if they may result in sanctions against an individual. There is no set guideline for the appropriate standard of evidence in these investigations. Security professionals should consult with the sponsor of the investigation as well as their legal team to determine appropriate evidence collection, handling, and retention guidelines for administrative investigations.

Criminal Investigations

Criminal investigations, typically conducted by law enforcement personnel, investigate the alleged violation of criminal law. Criminal investigations may result in charging suspects with a crime and the prosecution of those charges in criminal court.

Most criminal cases must meet the *beyond a reasonable doubt* standard of evidence. Following this standard, the prosecution must demonstrate that the defendant committed the crime by presenting facts from which there are no other logical conclusions. For this reason, criminal investigations must follow very strict evidence collection and preservation processes.

Civil Investigations

Civil investigations typically do not involve law enforcement but rather involve internal employees and outside consultants working on behalf of a legal team. They prepare the evidence necessary to present a case in civil court, resolving a dispute between two parties.

Most civil cases do not follow the beyond-a-reasonable-doubt standard of proof. Instead, they use the weaker *preponderance of the evidence* standard. Meeting this standard simply requires that the evidence demonstrate that the outcome of the case is more likely than not. For this reason, evidence collection standards for civil investigations are not as rigorous as those used in criminal investigations.

Regulatory Investigations

Government agencies may conduct regulatory investigations when they believe that an individual or corporation has violated administrative law. Regulators typically conduct these investigations with a standard of proof commensurate with the venue where they expect to try their case. Regulatory investigations vary widely in scope and procedure and are often conducted by government agents.

Industry Standards

Some regulatory investigations may not involve government agencies. These are based on industry standards, such as the Payment Card Industry Data Security Standard (PCI DSS). These industry standards are not laws but are contractual obligations entered into by the participating organizations. In some cases, including PCI DSS, the organization may be required to submit to audits, assessments, and investigations conducted by an independent third party. Failure to participate in these investigations or negative investigation results may lead to fines or other sanctions. Therefore, investigations into violations of industry standards should be treated similarly to regulatory investigations.

Electronic Discovery

In legal proceedings, each side has a duty to preserve evidence related to the case and, through the discovery process, share information with their adversary in the proceedings. This discovery process applies to both paper records and electronic records and the electronic discovery (or eDiscovery) process facilitates the processing of electronic information for disclosure.

The Electronic Discovery Reference Model (EDRM) describes a standard process for conducting eDiscovery with nine aspects:

Information Governance ensures that information is well organized for future eDiscovery efforts.

Identification locates the information that may be responsive to a discovery request when the organization believes that litigation is likely.

Preservation ensures that potentially discoverable information is protected against alteration or deletion.

Collection gathers the relevant information centrally for use in the eDiscovery process.

Processing screens the collected information to perform a "rough cut" of irrelevant information, reducing the amount of information requiring detailed screening.

Review examines the remaining information to determine what information is relevant to the request and removing any information protected by attorney-client privilege.

Analysis performs a deeper inspection of the content and context of the remaining information.

Production places the information into a format that may be shared with others and delivers it to other parties, such as opposing counsel.

Presentation displays the information to witnesses, the court, and other parties.

> For more information on the EDRM, see `https://edrm.net/resources/frameworks-and-standards/edrm-model`.

Conducting eDiscovery is a complex process and requires careful coordination between information technology professionals and legal counsel.

Evidence

To successfully prosecute a crime, the prosecuting attorneys must provide sufficient evidence to prove an individual's guilt beyond a reasonable doubt. In the following sections, we'll explain the requirements that evidence must meet before it is allowed in court, the various types of evidence that may be introduced, and the requirements for handling and documenting evidence. The items of evidence that you maintain and may use in court are also known as *artifacts* and may include physical devices, such as computers, mobile devices, and network devices, the logs and data generated by those devices, and many other forms of evidence.

> The National Institute of Standards and Technology's Guide to Integrating Forensic Techniques into Incident Response (SP 800-86) is a great reference and is available at www.nist.gov/publications/guide-integrating-forensic-techniques-incident-response.

Admissible Evidence

There are three basic requirements for evidence to be introduced into a court of law. To be considered *admissible evidence*, it must meet all three of these requirements, as determined by the judge, prior to being discussed in open court:

- The evidence must be *relevant* to determining a fact.
- The fact that the evidence seeks to determine must be *material* (that is, related) to the case.
- The evidence must be *competent*, meaning it must have been obtained legally. Evidence that results from an illegal search would be inadmissible because it is not competent.

Types of Evidence

Many different types of evidence can be used in a court of law. Depending on the reference you consult, these may be grouped in many different ways. However, there are four major categories with which you should be familiar: real evidence, documentary evidence, testimonial evidence, and demonstrative evidence. Each has slightly different additional requirements for admissibility.

Real Evidence   *Real evidence* (also known as *object evidence*) consists of things that may actually be brought into a court of law. In common criminal proceedings, this may include items such as a murder weapon, clothing, or other physical objects. In a computer crime case, real evidence might include seized computer equipment, such as a keyboard with fingerprints on it or a hard drive from a hacker's computer system. Depending on the circumstances, real evidence may also be *conclusive evidence*, such as deoxyribonucleic acid (DNA), that is incontrovertible.

Documentary Evidence   *Documentary evidence* includes any written items brought into court to prove a fact at hand. This type of evidence must also be authenticated. For example, if an attorney wants to introduce a computer log as evidence, they have testimony from a witness (for example, the system administrator) confirming that the log was collected as a routine business practice and is indeed the actual log that the system collected.

Two additional evidence rules apply specifically to documentary evidence:

- The *best evidence rule* states that when a document is used as evidence in a court proceeding, the original document must be introduced. Copies or descriptions of original evidence (known as *secondary evidence*) will not be accepted as evidence unless certain exceptions to the rule apply.

- The *parol evidence rule* states that when an agreement between parties is put into written form, the written document is assumed to contain all the terms of the agreement and no verbal agreements may modify the written agreement.

    If documentary evidence meets the materiality, competency, and relevancy requirements and also complies with the best evidence and parol evidence rules, it can be admitted into court.

Chain of Evidence

Real evidence, like any type of evidence, must meet the relevancy, materiality, and competency requirements before being admitted into court. Additionally, real evidence must be authenticated. This can be done by a witness who can actually identify an object as unique (for example, "that knife with my name on the handle is the one that the intruder took off the table in my house and used to stab me") and unaltered, meaning that it has not been tampered with from the time of collection until the time of use in court.

(continues)

(continued)

In many cases, it is not possible for a witness to uniquely identify an object in court. In those cases, a *chain of evidence* (also known as a *chain of custody*) must be established. This documents everyone who handles evidence—including the police who originally collect it, the technicians who process it, and the lawyers who use it in court. The location of the evidence must be fully documented from the moment it was collected to the moment it appears in court to ensure that it is indeed the same item. This requires thorough labeling of evidence and comprehensive logs noting who had access to the evidence at specific times and the reasons they required such access.

When evidence is labeled to preserve the chain of custody, the label should include the following types of information regarding the collection:

- General description of the evidence

- Time and date the evidence was collected

- Exact location the evidence was collected from

- Name of the person collecting the evidence

- Relevant circumstances surrounding the collection

Each person who handles the evidence must sign the chain-of-custody log indicating the time they took direct responsibility for the evidence and the time they handed it off to the next person in the chain of custody. The chain must provide an unbroken sequence of events accounting for the evidence from the time it was collected until the time of the trial.

Testimonial Evidence *Testimonial evidence* is, quite simply, evidence consisting of the testimony of a witness, either verbal testimony in court or written testimony in a recorded deposition. Witnesses must take an oath agreeing to tell the truth, and they must have personal knowledge on which their testimony is based. Furthermore, witnesses must remember the basis for their testimony (they may consult written notes or records to aid their memory). Witnesses can offer *direct evidence*: oral testimony that proves or disproves a claim based on their own direct observation. The testimonial evidence of most witnesses must be strictly limited to direct evidence based on the witness's factual observations. However, this does not apply if a witness has been accepted by the court as an expert in a certain field. In that case, the witness may offer an *expert opinion* based on the other facts presented and their personal knowledge of the field.

Hearsay Rule

When a witness testifies in court, they must normally avoid the act of hearsay, meaning that they cannot testify about what someone else told them outside of court because the court has no way to substantiate that evidence and find it admissible.

That said, the hearsay rule is one that has many exceptions. These include past testimony given by a witness under oath that is no longer available, a statement made against the interest of the person making the statement, a dying utterance, public records, and many other situations.

An extremely important exception to this rule for forensic analysts is the business records exception to the hearsay rule. This says that business records, such as the logs generated by a computer system, may be admitted as evidence if they were made at the time of the event by someone or something with direct knowledge, they were kept in the course of regular business activity, and that keeping those records is a regular practice of the organization.

Records admitted under the business records exception must be accompanied by the testimony of an individual qualified to show that these criteria were met. This exception is commonly used to introduce system logs and other records generated by computer systems.

Demonstrative Evidence *Demonstrative evidence* is evidence used to support testimonial evidence. It consists of items that may or may not be admitted into evidence themselves but are used to help a witness explain a concept or clarify an issue. For example, demonstrative evidence might include a diagram explaining the contents of a network packet or showing the process used to conduct a distributed denial-of-service attack. The admissibility of demonstrative evidence is a matter left to the trial court, with the general principle that demonstrative evidence must assist the jury in understanding a case.

Artifacts, Evidence Collection, and Forensic Procedures

Collecting digital evidence is a tricky process and should be attempted only by professional forensic technicians. The International Organization on Computer Evidence (IOCE) outlines six principles to guide digital evidence technicians as they perform media, network, and software analyses in the pursuit of forensically recovered evidence:

- When dealing with digital evidence, all of the general forensic and procedural principles must be applied.

- Upon seizing digital evidence, actions taken should not change that evidence.

- When it is necessary for a person to access original digital evidence, that person should be trained for the purpose.

- All activity relating to the seizure, access, storage, or transfer of digital evidence must be fully documented, preserved, and available for review.

- An individual is responsible for all actions taken with respect to digital evidence while it is in their possession.

- Any agency that is responsible for seizing, accessing, storing, or transferring digital evidence is responsible for compliance with these principles.

As you conduct forensic evidence collection, it is important to preserve the original evidence. Remember that the very conduct of your investigation may alter the evidence you are evaluating. Therefore, when analyzing digital evidence, it's best to work with a copy of the actual evidence whenever possible. For example, when conducting an investigation into the contents of a hard drive, make an image of that drive, seal the original drive in an evidence bag, and then use the disk image for your investigation.

Media Analysis   Media analysis, a branch of computer forensic analysis, involves the identification and extraction of information from storage media. This may include magnetic media (e.g., hard disks and tapes) or optical media (e.g., CDs, DVDs, and Blu-ray discs).

Techniques used for media analysis may include the recovery of deleted files from unallocated sectors of the physical disk, the live analysis of storage media connected to a computer system (especially useful when examining encrypted media), and the static analysis of forensic images of storage media.

When gathering information from storage devices, analysts should never access hard drives or other media from a live system. Instead, they should power off the system (after collecting other evidence), remove the storage device, and then attach the storage device to a dedicated forensic workstation, using a *write blocker*. Write blockers are hardware adapters that physically sever the portion of the cable used to connect the storage device that would write data to the device, reducing the likelihood of accidental tampering with the device.

After connecting the device to a live workstation, the analyst should immediately calculate a cryptographic hash of the device contents and then use forensic tools to create a forensic image of the device: a bitwise copy of the data stored on the device. The analyst should then compute the cryptographic hash of that image to ensure that it is identical to the original media contents.

After creating and verifying a forensic image, the original image file should be preserved as evidence. Analysts should create copies of that image (verifying the integrity of the hash) and then use those images for any analysis. This careful process reduces the likelihood of error and ensures the preservation of the chain of custody.

In-Memory Analysis   Investigators often wish to collect information from the memory of live systems. This is a tricky undertaking, since it can be difficult to work with memory without actually altering its contents. When gathering the contents of memory, analysts should use trusted tools to generate a *memory dump* file and place it on a forensically prepared device, such as a USB drive. This memory dump file contains all the contents collected from memory and may then be used for analysis. As with other types of digital evidence, the analyst collecting the memory dump should compute a cryptographic hash of the dump file to later prove its authenticity. Any analysis performed on the file should not touch the original collected dump but work from copies of that dump file.

Network Analysis   Forensic investigators are also often interested in the activity that took place over the network during a security incident. This is often difficult to reconstruct due to the volatility of network data—if it isn't deliberately recorded at the time it occurs, it generally is not preserved.

Network forensic analysis, therefore, often depends on either prior knowledge that an incident is underway or the use of preexisting security controls that log network activity. These include:

- Intrusion detection and prevention system logs
- Network flow data captured by a flow monitoring system
- Packet captures deliberately collected during an incident
- Logs from firewalls and other network security devices

When collecting data directly from a network during a live analysis, forensic technicians should use a SPAN port on a switch (which mirrors data sent to one or more other ports for analysis) or a network tap, which is a hardware device that performs the same function as a SPAN port. Both of these approaches generate packet dumps without actually altering the network traffic being exchanged between two systems. When this is not possible, the analyst may run a software protocol analyzer on one of the communicating systems, but this approach is not as reliable as using a dedicated hardware device.

After collecting network packets, they should be treated in the same manner as any other digital evidence. The tools creating the packet capture should write them to forensically prepared media. Analysts should compute cryptographic hashes of the original evidence files and work only with copies of those original files.

The task of the network forensic analyst is to collect and correlate information from these disparate sources and produce as comprehensive a picture of network activity as possible.

Software Analysis   Forensic analysts may also be called on to conduct forensic reviews of applications or the activity that takes place within a running application. In some cases, when malicious insiders are suspected, the forensic analyst may be asked to conduct a review of software code, looking for backdoors, logic bombs, or other security vulnerabilities.

In other cases, forensic analysts may be asked to review and interpret the log files from application or database servers, seeking other signs of malicious activity, such as SQL injection attacks, privilege escalations, or other application attacks.

Software analysis may also include the validation of file hash values against known file types. The National Software Reference Library (NSRL), maintained by the National Institute of Standards and Technology, includes the cryptographic hash values for over

130,000,000 known applications, making it easier for forensic analysts to detect authentic and manipulated files. For more information on the NSRL, see www.nist.gov/itl/ssd/software-quality-group/national-software-reference-library-nsrl.

Hardware/Embedded Device Analysis   Forensic analysts often must review the contents of hardware and embedded devices. This may include a review of

- Personal computers
- Smartphones
- Tablet computers
- Embedded computers in cars, security systems, and other devices

Analysts conducting these reviews must have specialized knowledge of the systems under review. This often requires calling in expert consultants who are familiar with the memory, storage systems, and operating systems of such devices. Because of the complex interactions between software, hardware, and storage, the discipline of hardware analysis requires skills in both media analysis and software analysis.

The Scientific Working Group for Digital Evidence (www.swgde.org/home) is a consortium of forensic analysts led by the U.S. Federal Bureau of Investigation (FBI). They produce detailed guidance on gathering digital evidence from many different sources and are invaluable references for working digital forensic analysts.

Plan Training, Testing, and Evaluation

As organizations build out their incident response programs, they must ensure that everyone understands their role in incident response. Training programs should touch every team member and be tailored to each individual's role in incident response efforts. For example, a receptionist might simply need to understand that they must report security incidents to the security operations center (SOC). Incident response team members, on the other hand, will need detailed technical training on their responsibilities. Other employees may fit somewhere in between those two extremes and should receive role-specific training.

Organizations should regularly test their incident response plans to ensure that they continue to meet the organization's security objectives. The results of these tests may identify potential revisions to the plan that will improve future incident response efforts. Common incident response test types include the following:

- **Checklist reviews** provide each team member with a copy of their incident response checklists and ask them to walk through their expected actions to ensure that they understand their role and that the steps on the checklist remain relevant.

- **Tabletop exercises** gather the team in a central location and lead them through a discussion of how they would respond to a given incident scenario.

- **Incident simulations** move beyond tabletop exercises and actually ask the team to carry out some or all portions of the incident response effort in response to a provided scenario.

Testing cybersecurity incident response plans is a critical component of any organization's incident response strategy. Testing reassures the organization that the plan will function properly in the event of an actual incident and provides a critical training exercise for the team members who would respond to a real-world cybersecurity crisis.

In addition to conducting tests, organizations should collect key indicators and metrics to measure the health of their incident response program. NIST suggests monitoring the following key metrics for each incident:

- Number of incidents handled
- Total amount of labor spent working on each incident
- Elapsed time from the beginning of the incident to discovery
- Elapsed time from discovery to an initial impact assessment
- Elapsed time for each stage of the containment, eradication, and recovery process
- How long it took the CSIRT to respond to the initial report of the incident
- How long it took to escalate the incident to management and/or external authorities
- Compliance with established policies and procedures
- Determining whether the cause of the incident was identified successfully
- Determining whether the incident is a recurrence of a previous incident
- Calculating the estimated monetary damage
- Measuring the difference between the initial impact assessment and the final impact assessment

Organizations should use these metrics as a starting point and design a set of customized indicators that best meet the management goals of their cybersecurity program.

Summary

Incident response programs provide organizations with the ability to respond to security issues in a calm, repeatable manner. Security incidents occur when there is a known, suspected, or imminent violation of an organization's security policies. When a security incident occurs, the organization should activate its computer security incident response team (CSIRT).

The CSIRT guides the organization through the four stages of incident response: preparation; detection and analysis; containment, eradication, and recovery; and post-incident activities. During the preparation phase, the organization ensures that the CSIRT has the proper policy foundation, has operating procedures that will be effective in the organization's computing environment, receives appropriate training, and is prepared to respond to an incident.

During the detection and analysis phase, the organization watches for signs of security incidents. This includes monitoring alerts, logs, publicly available information, and reports from internal and external staff about security anomalies. When the organization suspects a security incident, it moves into the containment, eradication, and recovery phase, which is designed to limit the damage and restore normal operations as quickly as possible.

Restoration of normal activity doesn't signal the end of incident response efforts. At the conclusion of an incident, the post-incident activities phase provides the organization with the opportunity to reflect upon the incident by conducting a lessons-learned review. During this phase, the organization should also ensure that evidence is retained for future use according to policy.

Exam Essentials

Security events are occurrences that may escalate into a security incident.   An event is any observable occurrence in a system or network. A security event includes any observable occurrence that relates to a security function. A security incident is a violation or imminent threat of violation of computer security policies, acceptable use policies, or standard security practices. Every incident consists of one or more events, but every event is not an incident.

The cybersecurity incident response process has four phases.   The four phases of incident response are preparation; detection and analysis; containment, eradication, and recovery; and post-incident activities. The process is not a simple progression of steps from start to finish. Instead, it includes loops that allow responders to return to prior phases as needed during the response.

Security event indicators include alerts, logs, publicly available information, and people.   Alerts originate from intrusion detection and prevention systems, security information and event management systems, antivirus software, file integrity checking software, and third-party monitoring services. Logs are generated by operating systems, services, applications, network devices, and network flows. Publicly available information exists about new vulnerabilities and exploits detected "in the wild" or in a controlled laboratory environment. People from inside the organization or external sources report suspicious activity that may indicate that a security incident is in progress.

Policies, procedures, and playbooks guide incident response efforts.   The incident response policy serves as the cornerstone of an organization's incident response program. This policy should be written to guide efforts at a high level and provide the authority for incident response. Procedures provide the detailed, tactical information that CSIRT members need when responding to an incident. CSIRTs often develop playbooks that describe the specific procedures that they will follow in the event of a specific type of cybersecurity incident.

Incident response teams should represent diverse stakeholders. The core incident response team normally consists of cybersecurity professionals with specific expertise in incident response. In addition to the core team members, the CSIRT may include representation from technical subject matter experts, IT support staff, legal counsel, human resources staff, and public relations and marketing teams.

Incidents may be classified according to the attack vector where they originate. Common attack vectors for security incidents include external/removable media, attrition, the web, email, impersonation, improper usage, loss or theft of equipment, and other/ unknown sources.

Response teams classify the severity of an incident. The functional impact of an incident is the degree of impairment that it causes to the organization. The economic impact is the amount of financial loss that the organization incurs. In addition to measuring the functional and economic impact of a security incident, organizations should measure the time that services will be unavailable and the recoverability effort. Finally, the nature of the data involved in an incident also contributes to the severity of the information impact.

Review Questions

1. Which one of the following is an example of a computer security incident?

    A. User accesses a secure file

    B. Administrator changes a file's permission settings

    C. Intruder breaks into a building

    D. Former employee crashes a server

2. During which phase of the incident response process would an organization implement defenses designed to reduce the likelihood of a security incident?

    A. Preparation

    B. Detection and analysis

    C. Containment, eradication, and recovery

    D. Post-incident activity

3. Alan is responsible for developing his organization's detection and analysis capabilities. He would like to purchase a system that can combine log records from multiple sources to detect potential security incidents. What type of system is best suited to meet Alan's security objective?

    A. IPS

    B. IDS

    C. SIEM

    D. Firewall

4. Ben is working to classify the functional impact of an incident. The incident has disabled email service for approximately 30 percent of his organization's staff. How should Ben classify the functional impact of this incident according to the NIST scale?

    A. None

    B. Low

    C. Medium

    D. High

5. Which phase of the incident response process would include measures designed to limit the damage caused by an ongoing breach?

    A. Preparation

    B. Detection and analysis

    C. Containment, eradication, and recovery

    D. Post-incident activity

6. Grace is the CSIRT leader for a business unit within NASA, a federal agency. What is the minimum amount of time that Grace must retain incident handling records?

   A. Six months

   B. One year

   C. Two years

   D. Three years

7. Karen is responding to a security incident that resulted from an intruder stealing files from a U.S. federal government agency. Those files contained unencrypted information about protected critical infrastructure. How should Karen rate the information impact of this loss?

   A. None

   B. Privacy breach

   C. Proprietary breach

   D. Integrity loss

8. Matt is concerned about the fact that log records from his organization contain conflicting timestamps due to unsynchronized clocks. What protocol can he use to synchronize clocks throughout the enterprise?

   A. NTP

   B. FTP

   C. ARP

   D. SSH

9. Which one of the following document types would outline the authority of a CSIRT responding to a security incident?

   A. Policy

   B. Procedure

   C. Playbook

   D. Baseline

10. A cross-site scripting attack is an example of what type of threat vector?

    A. Impersonation

    B. Email

    C. Attrition

    D. Web

11. Which one of the following parties is not commonly the target of periodic external communications during an incident involving the theft of sensitive product development plans?

    A. The perpetrator

    B. Law enforcement

    C. Vendors

    D. Information sharing partners

12. Robert is finishing a draft of a proposed incident response policy for his organization. Who would be the most appropriate person to sign the policy?

    A. CEO

    B. Director of security

    C. CIO

    D. CSIRT leader

13. Which one of the following is not an objective of the containment, eradication, and recovery phase of incident response?

    A. Detect an incident in progress

    B. Implement a containment strategy

    C. Identify the attackers

    D. Eradicate the effects of the incident

14. Renee is responding to a security incident that resulted in the unavailability of a website critical to her company's operations. She is unsure of the amount of time and effort that it will take to recover the website. How should Renee classify the recoverability effort?

    A. Regular

    B. Supplemented

    C. Extended

    D. Not recoverable

15. Which one of the following is an example of an attrition attack?

    A. SQL injection

    B. Theft of a laptop

    C. User installs file-sharing software

    D. Brute-force password attack

16. Who is the best facilitator for a post-incident lessons-learned session?

    A. CEO

    B. CSIRT leader

    C. Independent facilitator

    D. First responder

17. Which one of the following elements is not normally found in an incident response policy?

    A. Performance measures for the CSIRT

    B. Definition of cybersecurity incidents

    C. Definition of roles, responsibilities, and levels of authority

    D. Procedures for rebuilding systems

18. An on-path attack is an example of what type of threat vector?

   A. Attrition

   B. Impersonation

   C. Web

   D. Email

19. Tommy is the CSIRT leader for his organization and is responding to a newly discovered security incident. What document is most likely to contain step-by-step instructions that he might follow in the early hours of the response effort?

   A. Policy

   B. Baseline

   C. Playbook

   D. Textbook

20. Hank is responding to a security event where the CEO of his company had her laptop stolen. The laptop was encrypted but contained sensitive information about the company's employees. How should Hank classify the information impact of this security event?

   A. None

   B. Privacy breach

   C. Proprietary breach

   D. Integrity loss

Chapter 9

Business Continuity and Disaster Recovery

THE CERTIFIED INFORMATION SECURITY MANAGER (CISM) DOMAINS AND SUBTOPICS COVERED IN THIS CHAPTER INCLUDE:

✓ **Domain 4: Incident Management**

  ▪ **A. Incident Management Readiness**

    ▪ **4A2. Business Impact Analysis (BIA)**

    ▪ **4A3. Business Continuity Plan (BCP)**

    ▪ **4A4. Disaster Recovery Plan (DRP)**

Despite our best intentions, disasters of one form or another eventually strike every organization. Whether it's a natural disaster, such as a hurricane, earthquake, or pandemic, or a human-made calamity, such as a building fire, burst water pipe, or cybersecurity incident, every organization will encounter events that threaten their operations or even their very existence.

Resilient organizations have plans and procedures in place to help mitigate the effects a disaster has on their continuing operations and to speed the return to normal operations. Business continuity planning (BCP) helps your organization assess priorities and design resilient processes that will allow continued operations in the event of a disaster. Disaster recovery planning (DRP) is the technical complement to the business-focused BCP exercise. It includes the technical controls that prevent disruptions and facilitate the restoration of service as quickly as possible after a disruption occurs.

Together, the disaster recovery and business continuity plans kick in and guide the actions of emergency-response personnel until the end goal is reached—which is to see the business restored to full operating capacity in its primary operations facilities.

Planning for Business Continuity

Business continuity planning (BCP) involves assessing the risks to organizational processes and creating policies, plans, and procedures to minimize the impact those risks might have on the organization if they were to occur. BCP is used to maintain the continuous operation of a business in the event of an emergency. The goal of BCP planners is to implement a combination of policies, procedures, and processes so that a potentially disruptive event has as little impact on the business as possible.

BCP focuses on maintaining business operations with reduced or restricted infrastructure capabilities or resources. As long as the continuity of the organization's ability to perform its mission-critical work tasks is maintained, BCP can be used to manage and restore the environment.

Business Continuity Planning vs. Disaster Recovery Planning

CISM candidates often become confused about the difference between business continuity planning (BCP) and disaster recovery planning (DRP). They might try to sequence them in a particular order or draw firm lines between the two activities. The reality of the situation is that these lines are blurry in real life and don't lend themselves to neat and clean categorization.

The distinction between the two is one of perspective. Both activities help prepare an organization for a disaster. They intend to keep operations running continuously, when possible, and recover functions as quickly as possible if a disruption occurs. The perspective difference is that business continuity activities are typically strategically focused and center themselves on business processes and operations. Disaster recovery plans tend to be more tactical and describe technical activities such as recovery sites, backups, and fault tolerance.

In any event, don't get hung up on the difference between the two. We've yet to see an exam question force anyone to draw a solid line between the two activities. It's much more important that you understand the processes and technologies involved in these two related disciplines.

The overall goal of BCP is to provide a quick, calm, and efficient response in the event of an emergency and to enhance a company's ability to recover from a disruptive event promptly. The BCP process has four main steps:

- Project scope and planning
- Business impact analysis
- Continuity planning
- Plan approval and implementation

The next four sections of this chapter cover each of these phases in detail. The last portion of this chapter will introduce some of the critical elements you should consider when compiling documentation of your organization's business continuity plan.

 The top priority of BCP and DRP is always *people*. The primary concern is to get people out of harm's way; then you can address IT recovery and restoration issues.

Project Scope and Planning

As with any formalized business process, the development of a resilient business continuity plan requires the use of a proven methodology. Organizations should approach the planning process with several goals in mind:

- Perform a structured review of the business's organization from a crisis planning point of view.
- Create a BCP team with the approval of senior management.
- Assess the resources available to participate in business continuity activities.
- Analyze the legal and regulatory landscape that governs an organization's response to a catastrophic event.

The exact process you use will depend on the size and nature of your organization and its business. There isn't a "one-size-fits-all" guide to business continuity project planning. You should consult with project planning professionals in your organization and determine the approach that will work best within your organizational culture.

The purpose of this phase is to ensure that the organization dedicates sufficient time and attention to both developing the project scope and plan and then documenting those activities for future reference.

Organizational Review

One of the first tasks of the team responsible for business continuity planning is to perform an analysis of the business organization to identify all departments and individuals who have a stake in the BCP process. Here are some areas to consider:

- Operational departments that are responsible for the core services the business provides to its clients

- Critical support services, such as the IT department, facilities and maintenance personnel, and other groups responsible for the upkeep of systems that support the operational departments

- Security teams responsible for physical security, since they are many times the first responders to an incident and are also responsible for the physical safeguarding of the primary facility and alternate processing facility

- Senior executives and other key individuals essential for the ongoing viability of the organization

This identification process is critical for two reasons. First, it provides the groundwork necessary to help identify potential members of the BCP team (see the next section). Second, it builds the foundation for the remainder of the BCP process.

Typically, the team spearheading the BCP effort performs the business organization analysis. Some organizations employ a dedicated business continuity manager to lead these efforts, whereas others treat it as a part-time responsibility for another IT leader. Either approach is acceptable because the output of the analysis commonly guides the selection of the remaining BCP team members. However, a thorough review of this analysis should be one of the first tasks assigned to the full BCP team when it convenes. This step is critical because the individuals performing the initial analysis may have overlooked critical business functions known to BCP team members that represent other parts of the organization. If the team were to continue without revising the organizational analysis, the entire BCP process might be negatively affected, resulting in the development of a plan that does not fully address the emergency-response needs of the organization as a whole.

When developing a business continuity plan, be sure to consider the locations of your headquarters and branch offices. The plan should account for a disaster that occurs at any location where your organization conducts its business, including your own physical locations and those of your cloud service providers.

BCP Team Selection

In some organizations, the IT and/or security departments bear the sole responsibility for business continuity planning, and no other operational or support departments provide input. Those departments may not even know of the plan's existence until a disaster looms on the horizon or actually strikes the organization. This is a critical flaw! The isolated development of a business continuity plan can spell disaster in two ways. First, the plan itself may not take into account knowledge possessed only by the individuals responsible for the day-to-day operation of the business. Second, it keeps operational elements "in the dark" about plan specifics until implementation becomes necessary. These two factors may lead to disengaged units disagreeing with provisions of the plan and failing to implement it properly. They also deny organizations the benefits achieved by a structured training and testing program for the plan.

To prevent these situations from adversely impacting the BCP process, the individuals responsible for the effort should take special care when selecting the BCP team. The team should include, at a minimum, the following individuals:

- Representatives from each of the organization's departments responsible for the core services performed by the business

- Business unit team members from the functional areas identified by the organizational analysis

- IT subject-matter experts with technical expertise in areas covered by the BCP

- Cybersecurity team members with knowledge of the BCP process

- Physical security and facility management teams responsible for the physical plant

- Attorneys familiar with corporate legal, regulatory, and contractual responsibilities

- Human resources team members who can address staffing issues and the impact on individual employees

- Public relations team members who need to conduct similar planning for how they will communicate with stakeholders and the public in the event of a disruption

- Senior management representatives with the ability to set the vision, define priorities, and allocate resources

---

Tips for Selecting an Effective BCP Team

Select your team carefully! You need to strike a balance between representing different points of view and creating a team with explosive personality differences. Your goal should be to create a group that is as diverse as possible and still operates in harmony.

Take some time to think about the BCP team membership and who would be appropriate for your organization's technical, financial, and political environment. Who would you include?

Each team member brings a unique perspective to the BCP process and will have individual biases. For example, representatives from operational departments will often consider their department the most critical to the organization's continued viability. Although these biases may at first seem divisive, the leader of the BCP effort should embrace them and harness them productively. If used effectively, the biases will help achieve a healthy balance in the final plan as each representative advocates the needs of their department. On the other hand, without effective leadership, these biases may devolve into destructive turf battles that derail the BCP effort and harm the organization as a whole.

Resource Requirements

After the team validates the organizational review, it should turn to an assessment of the resources required by the BCP effort. This assessment involves the resources needed by three distinct BCP phases:

BCP Development   The BCP team will require some resources to perform the four elements of the BCP process (project scope and planning, business impact analysis, continuity planning, and approval and implementation). It's more than likely that the major resource consumed by this BCP phase will be the effort expended by members of the BCP team and the support staff they call on to assist in the development of the plan.

BCP Testing, Training, and Maintenance   The testing, training, and maintenance phases of BCP will require some hardware and software commitments. Still, once again, the major commitment in this phase will be the effort of the employees involved in those activities.

BCP Implementation   When a disaster strikes and the BCP team deems it necessary to conduct a full-scale implementation of the business continuity plan, the implementation will require significant resources. Those resources include a large amount of effort (BCP will likely become the focus of a large part, if not all, of the organization) as well as direct financial expenses. For this reason, the team must use its BCP implementation powers judiciously yet decisively.

An effective business continuity plan requires the expenditure of significant resources, ranging from the purchase and deployment of redundant computing facilities to the pencils and paper used by team members scratching out the first drafts of the plan. However, as you saw earlier, personnel is one of the most significant resources consumed by the BCP process. Many security professionals overlook the importance of accounting for labor, but you can rest assured that senior management will not. Business leaders are keenly aware of the effect that time-consuming side activities have on the operational productivity of their organizations and the real cost of personnel in terms of salary, benefits, and lost opportunities. These concerns become especially paramount when you are requesting the time of senior executives.

You should expect that leaders responsible for resource utilization management will put your BCP proposal under a microscope, and you should prepare to defend the necessity of your plan with coherent, logical arguments that address the business case for BCP.

Legal and Regulatory Requirements

Many industries may find themselves bound by federal, state, and local laws or regulations that require them to implement various degrees of BCP. We've already discussed one example in this chapter—the officers and directors of publicly traded firms have a fiduciary responsibility to exercise due diligence in the execution of their business continuity duties. In other circumstances, the requirements (and consequences of failure) might be even more severe. Emergency services, such as police, fire, and emergency medical operations, have a responsibility to the community to continue operations in the event of a disaster. Indeed, their services become even more critical in an emergency that threatens public safety. Failure to implement an effective BCP could result in the loss of life or property and decrease public confidence in the government.

In many countries, financial institutions, such as banks, brokerages, and the firms that process their data, are subject to strict government and international banking and securities regulations. These regulations are necessarily strict because their purpose is to ensure the continued operation of the institution as a crucial part of the economy. When pharmaceutical manufacturers must produce products in less-than-optimal circumstances following a disaster or in response to a rapidly emerging pandemic, they are required to certify the purity of their products to government regulators. There are countless other examples of industries that are necessary to continue operating in the event of an emergency by various laws and regulations.

Even if you're not bound by any of these considerations, you might have contractual obligations to your clients that require you to implement sound BCP practices. If your contracts include commitments to customers expressed as *service-level agreements* (SLAs), you might find yourself in breach of those contracts if a disaster interrupts your ability to service your clients. Many clients may feel sorry for you and want to continue using your products/services, but their own business requirements might force them to sever the relationship and find new suppliers.

On the flip side of the coin, developing a strong, documented business continuity plan can help your organization win new clients and additional business from existing clients. If you can show your customers the sound procedures you have in place to continue serving them in the event of a disaster, they'll place greater confidence in your firm and be more likely to choose you as their preferred vendor. That's not a bad position to be in!

All of these concerns point to one conclusion—it's essential to include your organization's legal counsel in the BCP process. They are intimately familiar with the legal, regulatory, and contractual obligations that apply to your organization. They can help your team implement a plan that meets those requirements while ensuring the continued viability of the organization to the benefit of all—employees, shareholders, suppliers, and customers alike.

Laws regarding computing systems, business practices, and disaster management change frequently. They also vary from jurisdiction to jurisdiction. Be sure to keep your attorneys involved throughout the lifetime of your BCP, including the testing and maintenance phases. If you restrict their involvement to a preimplementation review of the plan, you may not become aware of the impact that changing laws and regulations have on your corporate responsibilities.

Business Impact Analysis

Once your BCP team completes the four stages of preparing to create a business continuity plan, it's time to dive into the heart of the work—the *business impact analysis* (BIA). The BIA identifies the business processes and tasks that are critical to an organization's ongoing viability and the threats posed to those resources. It also assesses the likelihood that each threat will occur and the impact those occurrences will have on the business. The results of the BIA provide you with quantitative measures that can help you prioritize the commitment of business continuity resources to the various local, regional, and global risk exposures facing your organization.

It's important to realize that there are two different types of analyses that business planners use when facing a decision:

Quantitative Impact Assessment   Involves the use of numbers and formulas to reach a decision. This type of data often expresses options in terms of the dollar value to the business.

Qualitative Impact Assessment   Takes non-numerical factors, such as reputation, investor/customer confidence, workforce stability, and other concerns, into account. This type of data often results in categories of prioritization (such as high, medium, and low).

Quantitative analysis and qualitative assessment both play an essential role in the BCP process. However, most people tend to favor one type of analysis over the other. When selecting the individual members of the BCP team, try to achieve a balance between people who prefer each strategy. This approach helps develop a well-rounded BCP and will benefit the organization in the long run.

The BIA process described in this chapter approaches the problem from both quantitative and qualitative points of view. However, it's tempting for a BCP team to "go with the numbers" and perform a quantitative assessment while neglecting the somewhat more subjective qualitative assessment. The BCP team should perform a qualitative analysis of the factors affecting your BCP process. For example, if your business is highly dependent on a few important clients, your management team is probably willing to suffer a significant short-term financial loss to retain those clients in the long term. The BCP team must sit down and discuss (preferably with the involvement of senior management) qualitative concerns to develop a comprehensive approach that satisfies all stakeholders.

 As you work your way through the BIA process, you will find that it is quite similar to the risk assessment process covered in Chapter 3, "Information Risk Management." The techniques used are very similar because both use standard risk evaluation techniques. The major difference is that the risk assessment process is focused on individual assets, whereas the BCP focuses on business processes and tasks.

Identifying Priorities

The first BIA task facing the BCP team is identifying business priorities. Depending on your line of business, certain activities are essential to your day-to-day operations when disaster strikes. You should create a comprehensive list of critical business functions and rank them in order of importance. Although this task may seem somewhat daunting, it's not as hard as it looks.

These critical business functions will vary from organization to organization, based on each organization's mission. They are the activities that, if disrupted, would jeopardize the organization's ability to achieve its goals. For example, an online retailer would treat the ability to sell products from their website and fulfill those orders promptly as critical business functions.

A great way to divide the workload of this process among the team members is to assign each participant the responsibility of drawing up a prioritized list that covers the business functions for which their department is responsible. When the entire BCP team convenes, team members can use those prioritized lists to create a master prioritized list for the organization as a whole. One caution with this approach—if your team is not truly representative of the organization, you may miss critical priorities. Be sure to gather input from all parts of the organization, especially from any areas not represented on the BCP team.

This process helps identify business priorities from a qualitative point of view. Recall that we're describing an attempt to develop both qualitative and quantitative BIAs simultaneously. To begin the quantitative assessment, the BCP team should develop a list of organization assets and then assign an *asset value* (AV) in monetary terms to each asset. Teams creating this list may draw on other existing documentation within the organization, such as accounting information, insurance policies, and configuration management systems. These values form the basis of risk calculations performed later in the BIA.

The second quantitative measure that the team must develop is the *maximum tolerable downtime* (MTD), sometimes also known as *maximum tolerable outage* (MTO). The MTD is the maximum length of time a business function can tolerate a disruption before suffering irreparable harm. The MTD provides valuable information when you're performing both BCP and DRP planning. The organization's list of critical business functions plays a crucial role in this process. The MTD for critical business functions should be lower than the

MTD for activities not identified as critical. Returning to the example of an online retailer, the MTD for the website selling products may be only a few minutes, whereas the MTD for their internal email system might be measured in hours.

The *recovery time objective* (RTO) for each business function is the amount of time in which you think you can feasibly recover the function in the event of a disruption. This value is closely related to the MTD. Once you have defined your recovery objectives, you can design and plan the procedures necessary to accomplish the recovery tasks.

As you conduct your BCP work, ensure that your RTOs are less than your MTDs, resulting in a situation in which a function should never be unavailable beyond the maximum tolerable downtime.

While the RTO and MTD measure the time to recover operations and the impact of that recovery time on operations, organizations must also pay attention to the potential data loss that might occur during an availability incident. Depending on the way that information is collected, stored, and processed, some data loss may take place.

The *recovery point objective (RPO)* is the data loss equivalent to the time-focused RTO. The RPO defines the point in time before the incident when the organization should be able to recover data from a critical business process. For example, an organization might perform database transaction log backups every 15 minutes. In that case, the RPO would be 15 minutes, meaning that the organization may lose up to 15 minutes' worth of data after an incident. If an incident takes place at 8:30 a.m., the last transaction log backup must have occurred sometime between 8:15 a.m. and 8:30 a.m. Depending on the precise timing of the incident and the backup, the organization may have irretrievably lost between 0 and 15 minutes of data.

Risk Identification

The next phase of the BIA is the identification of risks posed to your organization. During this phase, you'll have an easy time identifying some common threats, but you might need to exercise some creativity to come up with more obscure (but very real!) risks.

Risks come in two forms: natural risks and person-made risks. The following list includes some events that pose natural threats:

- Violent storms/hurricanes/tornadoes/blizzards
- Lightning strikes
- Earthquakes
- Mudslides/avalanches
- Volcanic eruptions
- Pandemics

   Person-made threats include the following events:

- Terrorist acts/wars/civil unrest
- Theft/vandalism

- Fires/explosions
- Prolonged power outages
- Building collapses
- Transportation failures
- Internet disruptions
- Service provider outages
- Economic crises

Remember, these are by no means all-inclusive lists. They merely identify some common risks that many organizations face. You may want to use them as a starting point, but a full listing of risks facing your organization will require input from all members of the BCP team.

The risk identification portion of the process is purely qualitative. At this point in the process, the BCP team should not be concerned about the likelihood that each type of risk will materialize or the amount of damage such an occurrence would inflict upon the continued operation of the business. The results of this analysis will drive both the qualitative and quantitative portions of the remaining BIA tasks.

Business Impact Analysis and the Cloud

As you conduct your business impact analysis, don't forget to take into account any cloud vendors on which your organization relies. Depending on the nature of the cloud service, the vendor's own business continuity arrangements may have a critical impact on your organization's business operations as well.

Consider, for example, a firm that outsourced email and calendaring to a third-party software-as-a-service (SaaS) provider. Does the contract with that provider include details about the provider's SLA and commitments for restoring operations in the event of a disaster?

Also, remember that having a contract is not normally considered to be performing sufficient due diligence when choosing a cloud provider. You should also verify that they have the controls in place to deliver on their contractual commitments. Although it may not be possible for you to physically visit the vendor's facilities to verify their control implementation, you can always do the next best thing—send someone else!

Now, before you go off identifying an emissary and booking flights, realize that many of your vendor's customers are probably asking the same question. For this reason, the vendor may have already hired an independent auditing firm to conduct an assessment of its controls. They can make the results of this assessment available to you in the form of a Service Organization Control (SOC) report.

(continues)

(continued)

Keep in mind that there are three different versions of the SOC report. The simplest of these, a SOC 1 report, covers only internal controls over financial reporting. If you want to verify the security, privacy, and availability controls, you'll want to review either an SOC 2 or SOC 3 report. The American Institute of Certified Public Accountants (AICPA) sets and maintains the standards surrounding these reports to maintain consistency between auditors from different accounting firms.

For more information on this topic, see the AICPA's document comparing the SOC report types at www.aicpa.org/interestareas/frc/assuranceadvisoryservices/ serviceorganization-management.html.

Likelihood Assessment

The preceding step consisted of the BCP team's drawing up a comprehensive list of the events that can be a threat to an organization. You probably recognized that some events are much more likely to happen than others. For example, an earthquake is a much more plausible risk than a tropical storm for a business located in Southern California. A company based in Florida might have the exact opposite likelihood that each risk would occur.

To account for these differences, the next phase of the business impact analysis identifies the likelihood that each risk will occur. We describe this likelihood using the same process used for the risk assessment in Chapter 3. First, we determine the *annualized rate of occurrence* (ARO) that reflects the number of times a business expects to experience a given disaster each year. This annualization process simplifies comparing the magnitude of very different risks.

The BCP team should determine an ARO for each risk identified in the previous section. Base these numbers on corporate history, professional experience of team members, and advice from experts, such as meteorologists, seismologists, fire prevention professionals, and other consultants, as needed.

> **TIP** In addition to the government resources identified in this chapter, insurance companies develop large repositories of risk information as part of their actuarial processes. You may be able to obtain this information from them to assist in your BCP efforts. After all, you have a mutual interest in preventing damage to your business!

In many cases, you may be able to find likelihood assessments for some risks prepared by experts at no cost to you. For example, the U.S. Geological Survey (USGS) developed an earthquake hazard map that illustrates the ARO for earthquakes in various regions of the United States. Similarly, the Federal Emergency Management Agency (FEMA) coordinates the development of detailed flood maps of local communities throughout the United States. These resources are available online and offer a wealth of information to organizations performing a business impact analysis.

Impact Analysis

As you may have surmised based on its name, the impact analysis is one of the most critical portions of the business impact analysis. In this phase, you analyze the data gathered during risk identification and likelihood assessment and attempt to determine what impact each one of the identified risks would have on the business if it were to occur.

From a quantitative point of view, we will cover three specific metrics: the exposure factor, the single loss expectancy, and the annualized loss expectancy. Each one of these values describes a particular risk/asset combination evaluated during the previous phases.

The *exposure factor* (EF) is the amount of damage that the risk poses to the asset, expressed as a percentage of the asset's value (AV). For example, if the BCP team consults with fire experts and determines that a building fire would destroy 70 percent of the building, the exposure factor of the building to fire is 70 percent.

The *single loss expectancy* (SLE) is the monetary loss expected each time the risk materializes. You can compute the SLE using the following formula:

$$SLE = AV \times EF$$

Continuing with the preceding example, if the building is worth $500,000, the single loss expectancy would be 70 percent of $500,000, or $350,000. You can interpret this figure to mean that you could expect a single fire in the building would cause $350,000 worth of damage.

The *annualized loss expectancy* (ALE) is the monetary loss that the business expects to occur as a result of the risk harming the asset during a typical year. The SLE is the amount of damage you expect each time a disaster strikes, and the ARO (from the likelihood analysis) is the number of times you expect a disaster to occur each year. You compute the ALE by simply multiplying those two numbers:

$$ALE = ARO \times SLE$$

Returning once again to our building example, fire experts might predict that a fire will occur in the building approximately once every 30 years, specifically determining that there is a 0.03 chance of a fire in any given year. The ALE is then 3 percent of the $350,000 SLE, or $10,500. You can interpret this figure to mean that the business should expect to lose $10,500 each year due to a fire in the building.

Obviously, a fire will not occur each year—this figure represents the average cost over the approximately 30 years between fires. It's not especially useful for budgeting considerations but proves invaluable when attempting to prioritize the assignment of BCP resources to a given risk. Of course, a business leader may decide that the risk of fire remains unacceptable and take actions that contradict the quantitative analysis. That's where qualitative assessment comes into play.

Be sure you're familiar with the quantitative formulas contained in this chapter, and the concepts of asset value, exposure factor, the annualized rate of occurrence, single loss expectancy, and annualized loss expectancy. Know the formulas and be able to work through a scenario.

From a qualitative point of view, you must consider the nonmonetary impact that interruptions might have on your business. For example, you might want to consider the following:

- Loss of goodwill among your clients
- Loss of employees to other jobs after prolonged downtime
- Social/ethical responsibilities to the community
- Negative publicity

It's difficult to put dollar values on items like these to include them in the quantitative portion of the impact analysis, but they are equally important. After all, if you decimate your client base, you won't have a business to return to when you're ready to resume operations!

Resource Prioritization

The final step of the BIA is to prioritize the allocation of business continuity resources to the various risks that you identified and assessed in earlier phases of the BIA.

From a quantitative point of view, this process is fairly straightforward. You simply create a list of all the risks you analyzed during the BIA process and sort them in descending order according to the ALE computed during the impact analysis phase. This step provides you with a prioritized list of the risks that you should address. Select as many items as you're willing and able to handle simultaneously from the top of the list and work your way down. Eventually, you'll reach a point at which you've exhausted either the list of risks (unlikely!) or all your available resources (much more likely!).

Recall from the previous section that we also stressed the importance of addressing qualitatively important concerns. In earlier sections about the BIA, we treated quantitative and qualitative analysis as mainly separate functions with some overlap in the analysis. Now it's time to merge the two prioritized lists, which is more of an art than a science. You must work with the BCP team and representatives from the senior management team and combine the two lists into a single prioritized list.

Qualitative concerns may justify elevating or lowering the priority of risks that already exist on the ALE-sorted quantitative list. For example, if you run a fire suppression company, your number-one priority might be the prevention of a fire in your principal place of business even though an earthquake might cause more physical damage. The potential loss of reputation within the business community resulting from the destruction of a fire suppression company by fire might be too challenging to overcome and result in the eventual collapse of the business, justifying the increased priority.

Continuity Planning

The first two phases of the BCP process (project scope and planning and the business impact analysis) focus on determining how the BCP process will work and prioritizing the business assets that you must protect against interruption. The next phase of BCP development, continuity planning, focuses on developing and implementing a continuity strategy to minimize the impact that the realized risks might have on protected assets.

In this section, you'll learn about the subtasks involved in continuity planning:

- Strategy development
- Provisions and processes
- Plan approval
- Plan implementation
- Training and education

Strategy Development

The strategy development phase bridges the gap between the business impact analysis and the continuity planning phases of BCP development. The BCP team must now take the prioritized list of concerns raised by the quantitative and qualitative resource prioritization exercises and determine which risks will be addressed by the business continuity plan. Fully addressing all the contingencies would require the implementation of provisions and processes that maintain a zero-downtime posture in the face of every possible risk. For obvious reasons, implementing a policy this comprehensive is impossible.

The BCP team should look back to the MTD estimates created during the early stages of the BIA and determine which risks are deemed acceptable and which must be mitigated by the BCP continuity provisions. Some of these decisions are obvious—the risk of a blizzard striking an operations facility in Egypt is negligible and constitutes an acceptable risk. The risk of a monsoon in New Delhi is severe enough that BCP provisions must mitigate it.

Once the BCP team determines which risks require mitigation and the level of resources that will be committed to each mitigation task, they are ready to move on to the provisions and processes phase of continuity planning.

Provisions and Processes

The provisions and processes phase of continuity planning is the meat of the entire business continuity plan. In this task, the BCP team designs the specific procedures and mechanisms that will mitigate the risks deemed unacceptable during the strategy development stage. Three categories of assets must be protected through BCP provisions and processes: people, buildings/facilities, and infrastructure. In the next three sections, we'll explore some of the techniques you can use to safeguard these categories.

People

First, you must ensure that the people within your organization are safe before, during, and after an emergency. Once you've achieved that goal, you must make provisions to allow your employees to conduct both their BCP and operational tasks in as normal a manner as possible, given the circumstances.

WARNING   Don't lose sight of the fact that people are your most valuable asset. The safety of people must always come before the organization's business goals. Be sure that your business continuity plan makes adequate provisions for the security of your employees, customers, suppliers, and any other individuals who may be affected.

Management should provide team members with all the resources they need to complete their assigned tasks. At the same time, if circumstances dictate that people be present in the workplace for extended periods, arrangements must be made for shelter and food. Any continuity plan that requires these provisions should include detailed instructions for the BCP team in the event of a disaster. The organization should maintain stockpiles of provisions sufficient to feed the operational and support groups for an extended time in an accessible location. Plans should specify the periodic rotation of those stockpiles to prevent spoilage.

Buildings and Facilities

Many businesses require specialized facilities to carry out their critical operations. These might include standard office facilities, manufacturing plants, operations centers, warehouses, distribution/logistics centers, and repair/maintenance depots, among others. When you perform your BIA, you will identify those facilities that play a critical role in your organization's continued viability. Your continuity plan should address two areas for each critical facility:

Hardening Provisions   Your BCP should outline mechanisms and procedures that can be put in place to protect your existing facilities against the risks defined in the strategy development phase. Hardening provisions might include steps as simple as patching a leaky roof or as complex as installing reinforced hurricane shutters and fireproof walls.

Alternate Sites   If it's not feasible to harden a facility against a risk, your BCP should identify alternate sites where business activities can resume immediately (or at least in a time that's shorter than the maximum tolerable downtime for all affected critical business functions). We'll discuss a few of the facility types that might be useful in this stage later in this chapter. Typically, an alternate site is associated with disaster recovery planning (DRP) rather than BCP. The organization might identify the need for an alternate site during BCP development, but it takes an actual interruption to trigger the use of the site, making it fall under the DRP.

Infrastructure

Every business depends on some sort of infrastructure for its critical processes. For many companies, a vital part of this infrastructure is an IT backbone of communications and computer systems that process orders, manage the supply chain, handle customer interaction, and perform other business functions. This backbone consists of servers, workstations, and critical communications links between sites. The BCP must address how the organization will protect these systems against risks identified during the strategy development phase. As with buildings and facilities, there are two main methods of providing this protection:

Physically Hardening Systems You can protect systems against the risks by introducing protective measures such as computer-safe fire suppression systems and uninterruptible power supplies.

Alternative Systems You can also protect business functions by introducing redundancy (either redundant components or completely redundant systems/communications links that rely on different facilities).

These same principles apply to whatever infrastructure components serve your critical business processes—transportation systems, electrical power grids, banking and financial systems, water supplies, and so on.

As organizations move many of their technology operations to the cloud, this doesn't reduce their reliance on physical infrastructure. Although the company may no longer operate the infrastructure itself, it still relies on the physical infrastructure of its cloud service provider and should take measures to ensure it is comfortable with the level of continuity planning conducted by that provider. A disruption at a key cloud provider that affects one of the organization's own critical business functions can be just as damaging as a failure of the organization's own infrastructure.

Plan Approval and Implementation

Once the BCP team completes the design phase of the BCP document, it's time to gain top-level management endorsement of the plan. If you were fortunate enough to have senior management involvement throughout the development phases of the plan, this should be a relatively straightforward process. On the other hand, if this is your first time approaching management with the BCP document, you should be prepared to provide a lengthy explanation of the plan's purpose and specific provisions.

Senior management buy-in is essential to the success of the overall BCP effort.

Plan Approval

If possible, you should attempt to have the plan endorsed by the top executive in your business—the chief executive officer, chairperson, president, or similar business leader. This move demonstrates the importance of the plan to the entire organization and showcases the business leader's commitment to business continuity. The signature of such an individual on the plan also gives it much greater weight and credibility in the eyes of other senior managers, who might otherwise brush it off as a necessary but trivial IT initiative.

Plan Implementation

Once you've received approval from senior management, it's time to dive in and start implementing your plan. The BCP team should get together and develop an implementation schedule that utilizes the resources dedicated to the program to achieve the stated process and provision goals in as prompt a manner as possible, given the scope of the modifications and the organization's attitude toward continuity planning.

After fully deploying resources, the BCP team should supervise the design and implementation of a BCP maintenance program. This program ensures that the plan remains responsive to evolving business needs.

Training and Education

Training and education are essential elements of the BCP implementation. All personnel who will be involved in the plan (either directly or indirectly) should receive some sort of training on the overall plan as well as their individual responsibilities.

Everyone in the organization should receive at least a plan overview briefing. These briefings provide employees with the confidence that business leaders have considered the possible risks posed to the continued operation of the business and have put a plan in place to mitigate the impact on the organization should a disruption occur.

People with direct BCP responsibilities should be trained and evaluated on their specific BCP tasks to ensure that they can complete them efficiently when disaster strikes. Furthermore, at least one backup person should be trained for every BCP task to provide redundancy in the event personnel are injured or cannot reach the workplace during an emergency.

BCP Documentation

Documentation is a critical step in the business continuity planning process. Committing your BCP methodology to paper provides several significant benefits:

- It ensures that BCP personnel have a written continuity document to reference in the event of an emergency, even if senior BCP team members are not present to guide the effort.

- It provides a historical record of the BCP process that will be useful to future personnel seeking to both understand the reasoning behind various procedures and implement necessary changes in the plan.

- It forces the team members to commit their thoughts to paper—a process that often facilitates the identification of flaws in the plan. Having the plan on paper also allows draft documents to be distributed to individuals not on the BCP team for a "sanity check."

In the following sections, we'll explore some of the essential components of the written business continuity plan.

Continuity Planning Goals

First, the plan should describe the goals of continuity planning as set forth by the BCP team and senior management. These goals should be decided at or before the first BCP team meeting and will most likely remain unchanged throughout the life of the BCP.

The most common goal of the BCP is quite simple: to ensure the continuous operation of the business in the face of an emergency. Other goals may also be inserted in this section of the document to meet organizational needs. For example, you might have an objective that your customer call center experience no more than 15 consecutive minutes of downtime or that your backup servers be able to handle 75 percent of your processing load within one hour of plan activation.

Statement of Importance

The *statement of importance* reflects the criticality of the BCP to the organization's continued viability. This document commonly takes the form of a letter to the organization's employees, stating the reason that the organization devoted significant resources to the BCP development process and requesting the cooperation of all personnel in the BCP implementation phase.

Here's where the importance of senior executive buy-in comes into play. If you can put out this letter under the signature of the chief executive officer (CEO) or an officer at a similar level, the plan will carry tremendous weight as you attempt to implement changes throughout the organization. If you have the signature of a lower-level manager, you may encounter resistance as you try to work with portions of the organization outside of that individual's direct control.

Statement of Priorities

The *statement of priorities* flows directly from the "identify priorities" phase of the business impact analysis. It simply involves listing the functions considered critical to continued business operations in a prioritized order. When listing these priorities, you should also include a statement that they were developed as part of the BCP process and reflect the importance of the functions to continued business operations in the event of an emergency and nothing more. Otherwise, the list of priorities could be used for unintended purposes and result in a political turf battle between competing organizations to the detriment of the business continuity plan.

Statement of Organizational Responsibility

The *statement of organizational responsibility* also comes from a senior-level executive and can be incorporated into the same letter as the statement of importance. It echoes the sentiment that "business continuity is everyone's responsibility!" The statement of organizational responsibility restates the organization's commitment to business continuity planning. It informs employees, vendors, and affiliates that the organization expects them to do everything they can to assist with the BCP process.

Statement of Urgency and Timing

The *statement of urgency and timing* expresses the criticality of implementing the BCP and outlines the implementation timetable decided on by the BCP team and agreed to by upper management. The wording of this statement will depend on the actual urgency assigned to the BCP process by your organization's leadership. Consider including a detailed implementation timeline to foster a sense of urgency.

Risk Assessment

The *risk assessment* portion of the BCP documentation essentially recaps the decision-making process undertaken during the business impact analysis. It should include a discussion of all the critical business functions considered during the BIA as well as the quantitative and qualitative analyses performed to assess the risks to those functions. Include the actual AV, EF, ARO, SLE, and ALE figures in the quantitative analysis. Also, describe the thought process behind the analysis to the reader. Finally, keep in mind that the assessment reflects a point-in-time evaluation, and the team must update it regularly to reflect changing conditions.

Risk Acceptance/Mitigation

The *risk acceptance/mitigation* section of the BCP documentation contains the outcome of the strategy development portion of the BCP process. It should cover each risk identified in the risk analysis portion of the document and outline one of two thought processes:

- For risks that were deemed acceptable, it should outline the reasons the risk was considered acceptable as well as potential future events that might warrant a reconsideration of this determination.

- For risks that were deemed unacceptable, it should outline the risk management provisions and processes put into place to reduce the risk to the organization's continued viability.

 It's far too easy to look at a difficult risk mitigation challenge and say, "We accept this risk" before moving on to less difficult things. Business continuity planners should resist these statements and ask business leaders to document their risk acceptance decisions formally. If auditors later scrutinize your business continuity plan, they will most certainly look for formal artifacts of any risk acceptance decisions made in the BCP process.

Vital Records Program

The BCP documentation should also outline a vital records program for the organization. This document states where critical business records will be stored and the procedures for making and storing backup copies of those records.

One of the biggest challenges in implementing a vital records program is often identifying the essential records in the first place. As many organizations transitioned from paper-based to digital workflows, they often lost the rigor that existed around creating and maintaining formal file structures. Vital records may now be distributed among a wide variety of IT systems and cloud services. Some may be stored on central servers accessible to groups, whereas others may be located in digital repositories assigned to an individual employee.

If that messy state of affairs sounds like your current reality, you may want to begin your vital records program by identifying the records that are truly critical to your business. Sit down with functional leaders and ask, "If we needed to rebuild our organization today in a completely new location without access to any of our computers or files, what records would you need?" Asking the question in this way forces the team to visualize the actual process of recreating operations and, as they walk through the steps in their minds, will produce an inventory of the organization's vital records. This inventory may evolve as people remember other important information sources, so you should consider using multiple conversations to finalize it.

Once you've identified the records that your organization considers vital, the next task is a formidable one: find them! You should be able to identify the storage locations for each document identified in your vital records inventory. Once you've completed this task, you can then use this vital records inventory to inform the rest of your business continuity planning efforts.

Emergency-Response Guidelines

The emergency-response guidelines outline the organizational and individual responsibilities for an immediate response to an emergency. This document provides the first employees to detect an emergency with the steps they should take to activate the provisions of the BCP that do not start automatically. These guidelines should include the following:

- Immediate response procedures (security and safety procedures, fire suppression procedures, notification of appropriate emergency-response agencies, and so on)
- A list of the individuals to notify of the incident (executives, BCP team members, and so on)
- Secondary response procedures that first responders should take while waiting for the BCP team to assemble

Your guidelines should be easily accessible to everyone in the organization who may be among the first responders to a crisis incident. Any time a disruption strikes, time is of the essence. Slowdowns in activating your business continuity procedures may result in undesirable downtime for your business operations.

Maintenance

The BCP documentation and the plan itself must be living documents. Every organization encounters nearly constant change, and this dynamic nature ensures that the business's continuity requirements will also evolve. The BCP team should not disband after the plan is developed but should still meet periodically to discuss the plan and review the results of plan tests to ensure that it continues to meet organizational needs.

Minor changes to the plan do not require conducting the full BCP development process from scratch; the BCP team may make them at an informal meeting by unanimous consent. However, keep in mind that drastic changes in an organization's mission or resources may require going back to the BCP drawing board and beginning again.

Any time you make a change to the BCP, you must practice reasonable version control. All older versions of the BCP should be physically destroyed and replaced by the most current version so that no confusion exists as to the correct implementation of the BCP.

It is also a good practice to include BCP components in job descriptions to ensure that the BCP remains fresh and to increase the likelihood that team members carry out their BCP responsibilities correctly. Including BCP responsibilities in an employee's job description also makes them fair game for the performance review process.

Testing and Exercises

The BCP documentation should also outline a formalized exercise program to ensure that the plan remains current. Exercises also verify that team members receive adequate training to perform their duties in the event of a disaster. The testing process is quite similar to that used for the disaster recovery plan, so we'll reserve the discussion of the specific test types for later in this chapter.

The Nature of Disaster

Disaster recovery planning brings order to the chaos that surrounds the interruption of an organization's normal activities. By its very nature, a *disaster recovery plan* is designed to cover situations where tensions are already high and cooler heads may not naturally prevail. Picture the circumstances in which you might find it necessary to implement DRP measures—a hurricane destroys your main operations facility; a fire devastates your main processing center; terrorist activity closes off access to a major metropolitan area. Any event that stops, prevents, or interrupts an organization's ability to perform its work tasks (or threatens to do so) is considered a disaster. The moment that information technology (IT) becomes unable to support mission-critical processes is the moment DRP kicks in to manage the restoration and recovery procedures.

A disaster recovery plan should be set up so that it can almost run on autopilot. The DRP should also be designed to reduce decision-making activities during a disaster as much as possible. Essential personnel should be well trained in their duties and responsibilities in the wake of a disaster and also know the steps they need to take to get the organization up and running as soon as possible. We'll begin by analyzing some of the possible disasters that might strike your organization and the particular threats that they pose.

To plan for natural and unnatural disasters in the workplace, you must first understand their various forms, as explained in the following sections.

Natural Disasters

Natural disasters reflect the occasional fury of our habitat—violent occurrences that result from changes in the earth's surface or atmosphere that are beyond human control. In some cases, such as hurricanes, scientists have developed sophisticated predictive models that provide ample warning before a disaster strikes. Others, such as earthquakes, can cause devastation at a moment's notice. A disaster recovery plan should provide mechanisms for responding to both types of disasters, either with a gradual buildup of response forces or as an immediate reaction to a rapidly emerging crisis.

Earthquakes

Earthquakes are caused by the shifting of seismic plates and can occur almost anywhere in the world without warning. However, they are far more likely to occur along known fault lines that exist in many areas of the world. A well-known example is the San Andreas Fault, which poses a significant risk to portions of the western United States. If you live in a region along a fault line where earthquakes are likely, your DRP should address the procedures your business will implement should a seismic event interrupt your normal activities.

The United States Geological Survey (USGS) publishes earthquake hazard information for locations in the United States. A summary map of the risk appears in Figure 9.1. You can consult the USGS to determine more specific earthquake risk information for areas where your organization has physical facilities.

Floods

Flooding can occur almost anywhere in the world at any time of the year. Some flooding results from the gradual accumulation of rainwater in rivers, lakes, and other bodies of water that then overflow their banks and flood the community. Other floods, known as *flash floods*, strike when a sudden severe storm dumps more rainwater on an area than the ground can absorb in a short period of time. Floods can also occur when dams are breached. Large waves caused by seismic activity, or *tsunamis*, combine the awesome power and weight of water with flooding, as we saw during the 2011 tsunami in Japan. This tsunami amply demonstrated the enormous destructive capabilities of water and the havoc it can wreak on various businesses and economies when it triggered an unprecedented nuclear disaster at Fukushima.

According to government statistics, flooding is responsible for approximately $8 billion (that's billion with a *b*!) in damage to businesses and homes each year in the United States. It's important that your DRP make appropriate response plans for the eventuality that a flood may strike your facilities.

FIGURE 9.1   U.S. earthquake risk map

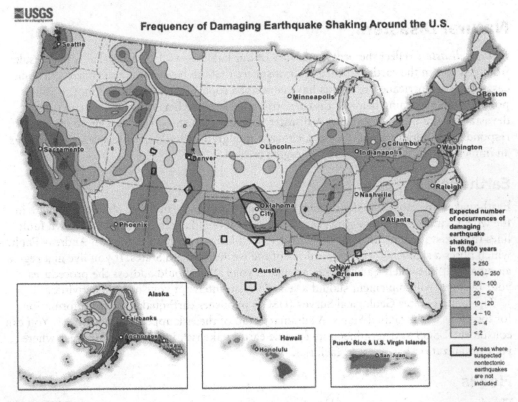

Source: USGS

 WARNING When you evaluate a firm's risk of damage from flooding to develop business continuity and disaster recovery plans, it's also a good idea to check with responsible individuals and ensure that your organization has sufficient insurance in place to protect it from the financial impact of a flood. In the United States, most general business policies do not cover flood damage, and you should investigate obtaining specialized government-backed flood insurance under FEMA's National Flood Insurance Program. Outside the U.S., commercial insurance providers may offer these policies.

Although flooding is theoretically possible in almost any region of the world, it is much more likely to occur in certain areas. FEMA's National Flood Insurance Program is responsible for completing a flood risk assessment for the entire United States and providing this data to citizens in graphical form. You can view flood maps online at http://msc.fema.gov/portal.

This site also provides valuable information on recorded earthquakes, hurricanes, windstorms, hailstorms, and other natural disasters to help you prepare your organization's risk assessment.

Figure 9.2 shows a flood map for a portion of the downtown region of Miami, Florida. When viewing flood maps, like the example shown in Figure 9.2, you'll find that they often combine several different types of confusing terminology. First, the shading indicates the likelihood of a flood occurring in an area. Areas shaded with the darkest color are described as falling within the "100-year flood plain." This means that the government estimates the chance of flooding in that area are 1 in 100, or 1.0 percent. Those shaded more lightly lie within the "500-year flood plain," meaning that there is a 1 in 500, or 0.2 percent, annual risk of flood.

These maps also contain information about the impact of a flood, measured in terms of the depth of flooding expected during a flooding event. Those are described as zones having many different letter codes, which you will not need to memorize for the CISM exam.

For a more detailed tutorial on reading flood maps and current map information, visit `www.fema.gov/sites/default/files/2020-07/how-to-read-flood-insurance-rate-map-tutorial.txt`.

FIGURE 9.2   Flood hazard map for Miami–Dade County, Florida

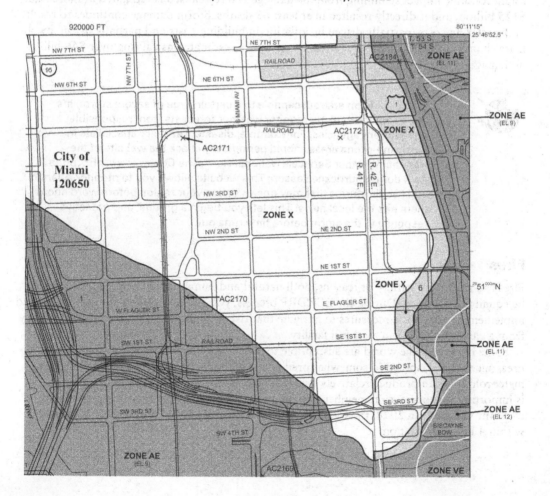

Storms

Storms come in many forms and pose diverse risks to a business. Prolonged periods of intense rainfall bring the risk of flash flooding described in the previous section. Hurricanes and tornadoes come with the threat of winds exceeding 100 miles per hour that undermine the structural integrity of buildings and turn everyday objects such as trees, lawn furniture, and even vehicles into deadly missiles. Hailstorms bring a rapid onslaught of destructive ice chunks falling from the sky. Many storms also bring the risk of lightning, which can cause severe damage to sensitive electronic components. For this reason, your business continuity plan should detail appropriate mechanisms to protect against lightning-induced damage, and your disaster recovery plan should include adequate provisions for power outages and equipment damage that might result from a lightning strike. Never underestimate the damage that a single storm can do.

In 2017, the Category 4 Atlantic hurricane Harvey marked one of the costliest, deadliest, and strongest hurricanes ever to make landfall in the continental United States. It bored a path of destruction through Texas, destroying both natural and human-made features. The total economic impact stemming from the damage Harvey caused is estimated at more than $125 billion, and it directly resulted in at least 63 deaths. Storm damage continues to result in devastating costs, partially driven by inflation in building costs and partially driven by climate change. In 2020, an active hurricane season was estimated as causing over $46 billion in damage.

If you live in an area susceptible to a certain type of severe storm, it's important to regularly monitor weather forecasts from responsible government agencies. For example, disaster recovery specialists in hurricane-prone areas should periodically check the website of the National Weather Service's National Hurricane Center (www.nhc.noaa.gov) during hurricane season. This website allows you to monitor Atlantic and Pacific storms that may pose a risk to your region before word about them hits the local news. This lets you begin a gradual and proactive response to the storm before time runs out.

Fires

Fires can start for a variety of reasons, both natural and human-made, but both forms can be equally devastating. During the BCP/DRP process, you should evaluate the risk of fire and implement at least basic measures to mitigate that risk and prepare the business for recovery from a catastrophic fire in a critical facility.

Some regions of the world are susceptible to wildfires during the warm season. These fires, once started, spread in somewhat predictable patterns, and fire experts working with meteorologists can produce relatively accurate forecasts of a wildfire's potential path. It is important, of course, to remember that wildfires can behave unpredictably and require constant vigilance. In 2018, the Camp Fire in California destroyed the town of Paradise within 4 hours of ignition.

The damage caused by forest fires continues to increase, driven by climate change and other factors. In 2020, the state of California experienced over 9,600 fires burning over 4.3 million acres of the state. To put that in context, 4 percent of the land area of the state of California burned in a single year.

As with many other types of large-scale natural disasters, you can obtain valuable information about impending threats on the web. In the United States, the National Interagency Fire Center posts daily fire updates and forecasts on its website: www.nifc.gov/fireInfo/nfn.htm. Other countries have similar warning systems in place.

Pandemics

Pandemics pose a significant health and safety risk to society and have the potential to disrupt business operations in a manner unlike many other disasters. Rather than causing physical damage, pandemics threaten the safety of individuals and prevent them from gathering in large numbers, shutting down offices and other facilities.

The COVID-19 coronavirus pandemic that began in 2020 was the most severe example to occur in the past century, but numerous other smaller outbreaks have occurred, including the SARS outbreak, avian flu, and swine flu. Although major outbreaks like COVID-19 may be infrequent, the severity of this risk requires careful planning, including building contingency plans for how businesses will operate in a pandemic response mode and what types of insurance may or may not provide coverage in response to a pandemic.

Other Natural Events

Some regions of the world are prone to localized types of natural disasters. During the BCP/DRP process, your assessment team should analyze all of your organization's operating locations and gauge the impact that such events might have on your business. For example, many parts of the world are subject to volcanic eruptions. If you conduct operations in an area in close proximity to an active or dormant volcano, your DRP should probably address this eventuality. Other localized natural occurrences include monsoons in Asia, tsunamis in the South Pacific, avalanches in mountainous regions, and mudslides in the western United States.

If your business is geographically diverse, it is prudent to include local emergency-response experts on your planning team. At the very least, make use of local resources such as government emergency preparedness teams, civil defense organizations, and insurance claim offices to help guide your efforts. These organizations possess a wealth of knowledge and are usually more than happy to help you prepare your organization for the unexpected—after all, every organization that successfully weathers a natural disaster is one less organization that requires a portion of their valuable recovery resources after disaster strikes.

Human-Made Disasters

Our advanced civilization has become increasingly dependent on complex interactions between technological, logistical, and natural systems. The same complex interactions that make our sophisticated society possible also present a number of potential vulnerabilities from both intentional and unintentional human-made *disasters*. In the following sections, we'll examine a few of the more common disasters to help you analyze your organization's vulnerabilities when preparing a business continuity plan and disaster recovery plan.

Fires

Earlier in the chapter, we explained how some regions of the world are susceptible to wildfires during the warm season, and these types of fires can be described as natural disasters. Many smaller-scale fires result from human action—be it carelessness, faulty electrical wiring, improper fire protection practices, arson, or other reasons. Studies from the Insurance Information Institute indicate that there are at least 1,000 building fires in the United States *every day*. If such a fire strikes your organization, do you have the proper preventive measures in place to quickly contain it? If the fire destroys your facilities, how quickly does your disaster recovery plan allow you to resume operations elsewhere?

Acts of Terrorism

Since the terrorist attacks on September 11, 2001, businesses are increasingly concerned about risks posed by terrorist threats. These attacks caused many small businesses to fail because they did not have business continuity/disaster recovery plans in place that were adequate to ensure their continued viability. Many larger businesses experienced significant losses that caused severe long-term damage. The Insurance Information Institute issued a study one year after the attacks that estimated the total damage from the attacks in New York City at $40 billion (yes, that's with a *b* again!).

WARNING

General business insurance may not properly cover an organization against acts of terrorism. In years past, most policies either covered acts of terrorism or didn't mention them explicitly. After suffering catastrophic terrorism-related losses, many insurance companies responded by amending policies to exclude losses from terrorist activity. Policy riders and endorsements are sometimes available but often at extremely high cost. If your business continuity or disaster recovery plan includes insurance as a means of financial recovery (as it probably should!), you'd be well advised to check your policies and contact your insurance professionals to ensure that you're still covered.

Power Outages

Even the most basic disaster recovery plan contains provisions to deal with the threat of a short power outage. Critical business systems are often protected by uninterruptible power supply (UPS) devices to keep them running at least long enough to complete a proper shutdown or to get emergency generators up and working. Even so, could your organization keep operating during a sustained power outage?

After Hurricane Harvey made landfall in 2017, millions of people in Texas lost power. Similar power outages occurred in 2020 in response to the California wildfires. Does your business continuity plan include provisions to keep your business viable during a prolonged period without power? If so, what is your planning horizon? Do you need enough fuel and other supplies to last for 48 hours? 7 days? Does your disaster recovery plan make ample preparations for the timely restoration of power even if the commercial power grid remains unavailable? All of these decisions should be made based on the requirements in your business continuity and disaster recovery plans.

Check your UPSs regularly! These critical devices are often overlooked until they become necessary. Many UPSs contain self-testing mechanisms that report problems automatically, but it's still a good idea to subject them to regular testing. Also, be sure to audit the number and type of devices plugged into each UPS. It's amazing how many people think it's okay to add "just one more system" to a UPS, and you don't want to be surprised when the device can't handle the load during a real power outage! UPS systems and backup generators are discussed more thoroughly later in this chapter.

Today's technology-driven organizations depend increasingly on electric power, so your BCP/DRP team should consider provisioning alternative power sources that can run business systems for an extended period of time. An adequate backup generator could make a huge difference when the survival of your business is at stake.

Network, Utility, and Infrastructure Failures

When planners consider the impact that utility outages may have on their organizations, they naturally think first about the impact of a power outage. However, keep other utilities in mind, too. Do any of your critical business systems rely on water, sewers, natural gas, or other utilities? Also consider regional infrastructure such as highways, airports, and railroads. Any of these systems can suffer failures that might not be related to weather or other conditions described in this chapter. Many businesses depend on one or more of these infrastructure elements to move people or materials. Their failure can paralyze your business's ability to continue functioning.

You must also think about your Internet connectivity as a utility service. Do you have sufficient redundancy in your connectivity options to survive or recover quickly from a disaster? If you have redundant providers, do they have any single points of failure? For example, do they both enter your building in a single fiber conduit that could be severed? If there are no alternative fiber ingress points, can you supplement a fiber connection with wireless connectivity? Do your alternate processing sites have sufficient network capacity to carry the full burden of operations in the event of a disaster?

If you quickly answered "no" to the question whether you have critical business systems that rely on water, sewers, natural gas, or other utilities, think again. Do you consider people a critical business system? If a major storm knocks out the water supply to your facilities and you need to keep those facilities up and running, can you supply your employees with enough drinking water to meet their needs?

What about your fire protection systems? If any of them are water-based, is there a holding tank system in place that contains ample water to extinguish a serious building fire if the public water system is unavailable? Fires often cause serious damage in areas ravaged by storms, earthquakes, and other disasters that might also interrupt the delivery of water.

Hardware/Software Failures

Like it or not, computer systems fail. Hardware components simply wear out and refuse to continue performing, or they suffer physical damage. Software systems contain bugs or fall prey to improper or unexpected inputs. For this reason, BCP/DRP teams must provide adequate redundancy in their systems. If zero downtime is a mandatory requirement, one solution is to use fully redundant failover servers in separate locations attached to separate communications links and infrastructures (also designed to operate in a failover mode). If one server is damaged or destroyed, the other will instantly take over the processing load. For more information on this concept, see the section "Remote Mirroring" later in this chapter.

Because of financial constraints, it isn't always feasible to maintain fully redundant systems. In those circumstances, the BCP/DRP team should address how replacement parts can be quickly obtained and installed. As many parts as possible should be kept in a local parts inventory for quick replacement; this is especially true for hard-to-find parts that must otherwise be shipped in. After all, how many organizations could do without telephones for three days while a critical private branch exchange (PBX) component is en route from an overseas location to be installed on site?

Strikes/Picketing

When designing your business continuity and disaster recovery plans, don't forget about the importance of the human factor in emergency planning. One form of human-made disaster that is often overlooked is the possibility of a strike or other labor crisis. If a large number of your employees walk out at the same time, what impact would that have on your business? How long would you be able to sustain operations without the regular full-time employees that staff a certain area? Your BCP and DRP teams should address these concerns and provide alternative plans should a labor crisis occur. Labor issues normally fall outside the purview of cybersecurity teams, offering a great example of an issue that should be included in a disaster recovery plan, but requires input and leadership from other business functions, such as human resources and operations.

Theft/Vandalism

Earlier, we talked about the threat that terrorist activities pose to an organization. Theft and vandalism represent the same kind of threat on a much smaller scale. In most cases, however, there's a far greater chance that your organization will be affected by theft or vandalism than by a terrorist attack. The theft or destruction of a critical infrastructure component, such as scrappers stealing copper wires or vandals destroying sensors, can negatively impact critical business functions.

Insurance provides some financial protection against these events (subject to deductibles and limitations of coverage), but acts of this kind can cause serious damage to your business, on both a short-term and long-term basis. Your business continuity and disaster recovery plans should include adequate preventive measures to control the frequency of these occurrences as well as contingency plans to mitigate the effects that theft and vandalism have on ongoing operations.

Cybersecurity Incidents

When we conduct business continuity planning and disaster recovery planning, we often first think of physical disasters that might damage our equipment, facilities, and data. It's also important to consider the risk posed by cybersecurity incidents. Chapter 8, "Incident Response," discussed these cybersecurity risks in detail and described the incident response mechanisms used by organizations reacting to cybersecurity incidents.

Cybersecurity incidents that disrupt business activity or threaten to do so may cause an organization to invoke business continuity and disaster recovery plans. For this reason, the teams conducting BCP/DRP efforts should carefully coordinate with cybersecurity incident response teams and ensure that the plans are tightly integrated.

System Resilience, High Availability, and Fault Tolerance

Technical controls that add to system resilience and fault tolerance directly affect availability, one of the core goals of the CIA security triad (confidentiality, integrity, and availability). A primary goal of system resilience and fault tolerance is to eliminate single points of failure in critical business systems.

A *single point of failure (SPOF)* is any component that can cause an entire system to fail. If a computer has data on a single disk, failure of the disk can cause the computer to fail, so the disk is a single point of failure. If a database-dependent website includes multiple web servers all served by a single database server, the database server is a single point of failure.

System resilience refers to the ability of a system to maintain an acceptable level of service during an adverse event. This could be a hardware fault managed by fault-tolerant components, or it could be an attack managed by other controls such as effective intrusion prevention systems. In some contexts, it refers to the ability of a system to return to a previous state after an adverse event. For example, if a primary server in a failover cluster fails, fault tolerance ensures that the system fails over to another server. System resilience implies that the cluster can fail back to the original server after the original server is repaired.

Fault tolerance is the ability of a system to suffer a fault but continue to operate. Fault tolerance is achieved by adding redundant components such as additional disks within a properly configured redundant array of inexpensive disks (RAID) array or additional servers within a failover clustered configuration.

High availability is the use of redundant technology components to allow a system to quickly recover from a failure after experiencing a brief disruption. High availability is often achieved through the use of load balancing and failover servers.

Technology professionals measure the objective and effectiveness of these controls by the percentage of the time that a system is available. For example, a fairly low availability threshold would be to specify that a system must be available 99.9 percent of the time (or "three nines" of availability). This means that the system may only experience 0.1 percent of downtime during whatever period is measured. If you apply this metric to a 30-day month of system operation, 99.9 percent availability would require less than 44 minutes of downtime. If you move to a 99.999 percent (or "five nines") requirement, the system would only be permitted 26 seconds of downtime per month.

Of course, the stronger your availability requirement, the more difficult it will be to meet. Achieving higher availability targets on a consistent basis requires the use of high availability, fault tolerance, and system resilience controls.

Protecting Hard Drives

A common way that fault tolerance and system resilience is added for computers is with a RAID array. A RAID array includes two or more disks, and most RAID configurations will continue to operate even after one of the disks fails. Some of the common RAID configurations are as follows:

RAID-0   This is also called striping. It uses two or more disks and improves the disk subsystem performance, but it does not provide fault tolerance.

RAID-1   This is also called mirroring. It uses two disks that each hold the same data. If one disk fails, the other disk includes the data so that a system can continue to operate after a single disk fails. Depending on the hardware used and which drive fails, the system may be able to continue to operate without intervention, or the system may need to be manually configured to use the drive that didn't fail.

RAID-5   This is also called striping with parity. It uses three or more disks with the equivalent of one disk holding parity information. This parity information allows the reconstruction of data through mathematical calculations if a single disk is lost. If any single disk fails, the RAID array will continue to operate, though it will be slower.

RAID-6   This offers an alternative approach to disk striping with parity. It functions in the same manner as RAID-5 but stores parity information on two disks, protecting against the failure of two separate disks, but requiring a minimum of four disks to implement.

RAID-10   This is also known as RAID 1 + 0 or a stripe of mirrors and is configured as two or more mirrors (RAID-1) with each mirror configured in a striped (RAID-0) configuration. It uses at least four disks but can support more as long as an even number of disks are added. It will continue to operate even if multiple disks fail, as long as at least one drive in each mirror continues to function. For example, if it had three mirrored sets (called M1, M2, and M3 for this example) it would have a total of six disks. If one drive in M1, one in M2, and one in M3 all failed, the array would continue to operate. However, if two drives in any of the mirrors failed, such as both drives in M1, the entire array would fail.

 Fault tolerance is not the same as a backup. Occasionally, management may balk at the cost of backup tapes and point to the RAID, saying that the data is already backed up. However, if a catastrophic hardware failure destroys a RAID array, all the data is lost unless a backup exists. Similarly, if an accidental deletion or corruption destroys data, it cannot be restored if a backup doesn't exist.

Both software- and hardware-based RAID solutions are available. Software-based systems require the operating system to manage the disks in the array and can reduce overall system performance. They are relatively inexpensive since they don't require any additional hardware other than the additional disk(s). Hardware RAID systems are generally more efficient and reliable. Although a hardware RAID is more expensive, the benefits typically outweigh the costs when used to increase availability of a critical component.

Hardware-based RAID arrays typically include spare drives that can be logically added to the array. For example, a hardware-based RAID-5 could include five disks, with three disks in a RAID-5 array and two spare disks. If one disk fails, the hardware senses the failure and logically swaps out the faulty drive with a good spare. Additionally, most hardware-based arrays support hot swapping, allowing technicians to replace failed disks without powering down the system. A cold-swappable RAID requires the system to be powered down to replace a faulty drive.

Protecting Servers

Fault tolerance can be added for critical servers with failover clusters. A failover cluster includes two or more servers, and if one of the servers fails, another server in the cluster can take over its load in an automatic process called *failover*. Failover clusters can include multiple servers (not just two), and they can also provide fault tolerance for multiple services or applications.

As an example of a failover cluster, consider Figure 9.3. It shows multiple components put together to provide reliable web access for a heavily accessed website that uses a database. DB1 and DB2 are two database servers configured in a failover cluster. At any given time, only one server will function as the active database server, and the second server will be inactive. For example, if DB1 is the active server it will perform all the database services for the website. DB2 monitors DB1 to ensure it is operational, and if DB2 senses a failure in DB1, it will cause the cluster to automatically fail over to DB2.

FIGURE 9.3   Failover cluster with network load balancing

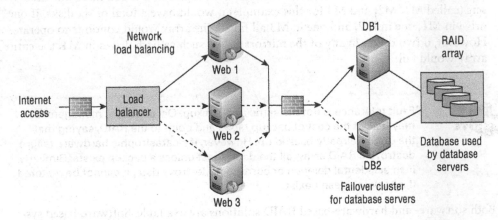

In Figure 9.3, you can see that both DB1 and DB2 have access to the data in the database. This data is stored on a RAID array providing fault tolerance for the disks.

Additionally, the three web servers are configured in a network load-balancing cluster. The load balancer can be hardware or software based, and it balances the client load across the three servers. It makes it easy to add additional web servers to handle an increased load while also balancing the load among all the servers. If any of the servers fail, the load balancer can sense the failure and stop sending traffic to that server. Although network load balancing is primarily used to increase the scalability of a system so that it can handle more traffic, it also provides a measure of fault tolerance.

If you're running your servers in the cloud, you may be able to take advantage of fault tolerance services offered by your cloud provider. For example, many IaaS providers offer load-balancing services that automatically scale resources on an as-needed basis. These services also incorporate health checking that can automatically restart servers that are not functioning properly.

Similarly, when designing cloud environments, be sure to consider the availability of data centers in different regions of the world. If you are already load balancing multiple servers, you may be able to place those servers in different geographic regions and availability zones within those regions to add resiliency in addition to scalability.

Failover clusters are not the only method of fault tolerance for servers. Some systems provide automatic fault tolerance for servers, allowing a server to fail without losing access to the provided service. For example, in a Microsoft domain with two or more domain controllers, each domain controller will regularly replicate Active Directory data with the others so that all the domain controllers have the same data. If one fails, computers within the domain can still find the other domain controller(s) and the network can continue to operate. Similarly, many database server products include methods to replicate database content with other servers so that all servers have the same content. Three of these methods—electronic vaulting, remote journaling, and remote mirroring—are discussed later in this chapter.

Protecting Power Sources

Fault tolerance can be added for power sources with an *uninterruptible power supply* (UPS), a generator, or both. In general, a UPS provides battery-supplied power for a short period of time between 5 and 30 minutes, and a generator provides long-term power. The goal of a UPS is to provide power long enough to complete a logical shutdown of a system or until a generator is powered on and provides stable power.

Generators provide power to systems during long-term power outages. The length of time that a generator will provide power is dependent on the fuel, and it's possible for a site to stay on generator power as long as it has fuel and the generator remains functional. Generators also require a steady fuel supply—they commonly use diesel fuel, natural gas, or propane. In addition to making sure that you have sufficient fuel on hand, you should also take steps to ensure that you can be delivered fuel on a regular basis in the event of an extended emergency. Remember, if the disaster is widespread, there will be significant demand for a limited fuel supply. If you have contracts in place with suppliers, you're much more likely to receive fuel in a timely manner. It's also important to understand that some fuel degrades over time and must be replaced on a regular basis if it is not used.

Recovery Strategy

When a disaster interrupts your business, your disaster recovery plan should kick in nearly automatically and begin providing support for recovery operations. The disaster recovery plan should be designed so that the first employees on the scene can immediately begin the recovery effort in an organized fashion, even if members of the official DRP team have not yet arrived on site. In the following sections, we'll cover critical subtasks involved in crafting an effective disaster recovery plan that can guide rapid restoration of regular business processes and resumption of activity at the primary business location.

In addition to improving your response capabilities, purchasing insurance can reduce the impact of financial losses. When selecting insurance, be sure to purchase sufficient coverage to enable you to recover from a disaster. Simple value coverage may be insufficient to encompass actual replacement costs. If your property insurance includes an actual cash value (ACV) clause, then your damaged property will be compensated based on the fair market value of the items on the date of loss less all accumulated depreciation since the time of their purchase. The important point here is that unless you have a replacement cost clause in your insurance coverage, your organization is likely to pay out of pocket for some of the losses it might sustain. Many insurance providers offer cybersecurity liability policies that specifically cover breaches of confidentiality, integrity, and availability.

Valuable paper insurance coverage provides protection for inscribed, printed, and written documents and manuscripts and other printed business records. However, it does not cover damage to paper money and printed security certificates.

Business Unit and Functional Priorities

To recover your business operations with the greatest possible efficiency, you must engineer your disaster recovery plan so that those business units with the highest priority are recovered first. You must identify and prioritize critical business functions as well so you can define which functions you want to restore after a disaster or failure and in what order. The business impact analysis (BIA) you developed during your business continuity work is an excellent resource when performing this task.

To achieve this goal, the DRP team must first identify the critical business units that are vital to achieving your organization's mission and agree on an order of prioritization, and they must do likewise with business functions. And take note: Not all critical business functions will necessarily be carried out in critical business units, so the final results of this analysis will very probably comprise a superset of critical business units plus other select units.

If this process sounds familiar, it should! This is very much like the prioritization task the BCP team performs during the business impact analysis. In fact, most organizations will complete a BIA as part of their business continuity planning process. This analysis identifies vulnerabilities, develops strategies to minimize risk, and ultimately produces a BIA report that describes the potential risks that an organization faces and identifies critical business units and functions. A BIA also identifies costs related to failures that include loss of cash flow, equipment replacement, salaries paid to clear work backlogs, profit losses, opportunity costs from the inability to attract new business, and so forth. Such failures are assessed in terms of potential impacts on finances, personnel, safety, legal compliance, contract fulfillment, and quality assurance, preferably in monetary terms to make impacts comparable and to set budgetary expectations. With all this BIA information in hand, you should use the resulting documentation as the basis for this prioritization task.

At a minimum, the output from this task should be a simple listing of business units in priority order. However, a more detailed list, broken down into specific business processes listed in order of priority, would be a much more useful deliverable. This business process–oriented list is more reflective of real-world conditions, but it requires considerable additional effort. It will, however, greatly assist in the recovery effort—after all, not every task performed by the highest-priority business unit will be of the highest priority. You might find that it would be best to restore the highest-priority unit to 50 percent capacity and then move on to lower-priority units to achieve some minimum operating capacity across the organization before attempting a full recovery effort.

By the same token, the same exercise must be completed for critical business processes and functions. Not only can these things involve multiple business units and cross the lines between them, but they also define the operational elements that must be restored in the wake of a disaster or other business interruption. Here also, the final result should be a checklist of items in priority order, each with its own risk and cost assessment, and a corresponding set of recovery objectives and milestones. As discussed earlier in this chapter, these include the maximum tolerable downtime (MTD), recovery time objective (RTO), and recovery point objective (RPO). Business continuity planners can analyze these metrics to identify situations that require intervention and additional controls.

Crisis Management

If a disaster strikes your organization, panic is likely to set in. The best way to combat this is with an organized disaster recovery plan. The individuals in your business who are most likely to first notice an emergency situation (that is, security guards, technical personnel, and so on) should be fully trained in disaster recovery procedures and know the proper notification procedures and immediate response mechanisms.

Many things that normally seem like common sense (such as calling emergency services in the event of a fire) may slip the minds of panicked employees seeking to flee an emergency. The best way to combat this is with continuous training on disaster recovery responsibilities. Returning to the fire example, all employees should be trained to activate the fire alarm or contact emergency officials when they spot a fire (after, of course, taking the appropriate measures to protect themselves). After all, it's better that the fire department receives 10 different phone calls reporting a fire at your organization than it is for everyone to assume that someone else already took care of it.

Crisis management steps in to cover crises of all forms. These may include more commonplace disasters, such as a facility fire, or more extraordinary events, such as a global pandemic. Organizations may also activate their crisis management programs for events with little impact on technology, such as a public relations disaster.

Crisis management is a science and an art form. If your training budget permits, investing in crisis training for your key employees is a good idea. This ensures that at least some of your employees know how to handle emergency situations properly and can provide all-important "on-the-scene" leadership to panic-stricken co-workers.

Emergency Communications

When a disaster strikes, it is important that the organization be able to communicate internally as well as with the outside world. A disaster of any significance is easily noticed, but if an organization is unable to keep the outside world informed of its recovery status, the public is apt to fear the worst and assume that the organization is unable to recover. It is also essential that the organization be able to communicate internally during a disaster so that employees know what is expected of them—whether they are to return to work or report to another location, for instance.

Employees participating in disaster recovery efforts should be instructed to refer media inquiries to the public relations team. You don't want employees naively providing unvarnished assessments of the situation based on partial information to the media and then having those assessments wind up in print.

In some cases, the circumstances that brought about the disaster to begin with may have also damaged some or all normal means of communications. A violent storm or an earthquake may have also knocked out telecommunications systems; at that point, it's too late to try to figure out other means of communicating both internally and externally.

Workgroup Recovery

When designing a disaster recovery plan, it's important to keep your goal in mind—the restoration of workgroups to the point that they can resume their activities in their usual work locations. It's easy to get sidetracked and think of disaster recovery as purely an IT effort focused on restoring systems and processes to working order.

To facilitate this effort, it's sometimes best to develop separate recovery facilities for different workgroups. For example, if you have several subsidiary organizations that are in different locations and that perform tasks similar to the tasks that workgroups at your office perform, you may want to consider temporarily relocating those workgroups to the other facility and having them communicate electronically and via telephone with other business units until they're ready to return to the main operations facility.

Larger organizations may have difficulty finding recovery facilities capable of handling the entire business operation. This is another example of a circumstance in which independent recovery of different workgroups is appropriate.

Alternate Processing Sites

One of the most important elements of the disaster recovery plan is the selection of alternate processing sites to be used when the primary sites are unavailable. Many options are available when considering recovery facilities, limited only by the creative minds of disaster recovery planners and available resources. In the following sections, we cover several types of sites commonly used in disaster recovery planning: cold sites, warm sites, hot sites, mobile sites, and cloud computing.

Cold Sites

Cold sites are standby facilities large enough to handle the processing load of an organization and equipped with appropriate electrical and environmental support systems. They may be large warehouses, empty office buildings, or other similar structures. However, a cold site has no computing facilities (hardware or software) preinstalled and also has no active broadband communications links. Many cold sites do have at least a few copper telephone lines, and some sites may have standby links that can be activated with minimal notification.

🌐 Real World Scenario

Cold Site Setup

A cold site setup is well depicted in the film *Boiler Room*, which involves a chop-shop investment firm telemarketing bogus pharmaceutical investment deals to prospective clients. In this fictional case, the "disaster" is human-made, but the concept is much the same, even if the timing is quite different.

Under threat of exposure and a pending law enforcement raid, the firm establishes a nearby building that is empty, save for a few banks of phones on dusty concrete floors in a mock-up of a cold recovery site. Granted, this work is both fictional and illegal, but it illustrates a very real and legitimate reason for maintaining a redundant failover recovery site for the purpose of business continuity.

Research the various forms of recovery sites, and then consider which among them is best suited for your particular business needs and budget. A cold site is the least expensive option and perhaps the most practical. A warm site contains the data links and preconfigured equipment necessary to begin restoring operations but no usable data or information. The most expensive option is a hot site, which fully replicates your existing business infrastructure and is ready to take over for the primary site on short notice.

The major advantage of a cold site is its relatively low cost—there's no computing base to maintain and no monthly telecommunications bill when the site is idle. However, the drawbacks of such a site are obvious—there is a tremendous lag between the time the decision is made to activate the site and the time when that site is ready to support business operations. Servers and workstations must be brought in and configured. Data must be restored from backup tapes. Communications links must be activated or established. The time to activate a cold site is often measured in weeks, making a quick recovery close to impossible and often yielding a false sense of security. It's also worth observing that the substantial time, effort, and expense required to activate and transfer operations to a cold site make this approach the most difficult to test.

Hot Sites

A *hot site* is the exact opposite of the cold site. In this configuration, a backup facility is maintained in constant working order, with a full complement of servers, workstations, and communications links ready to assume primary operations responsibilities. The servers and workstations are all preconfigured and loaded with appropriate operating system and application software.

The data on the primary site servers is periodically or continuously replicated to corresponding servers at the hot site, ensuring that the hot site has up-to-date data. Depending on the bandwidth available between the sites, hot site data may be replicated instantaneously. If that is the case, operators could move operations to the hot site at a moment's notice. If that's not the case, disaster recovery managers have three options to activate the hot site:

- If there is sufficient time before the primary site must be shut down, they can force replication between the two sites right before the transition of operational control.

- If replication is impossible, managers may carry backup tapes of the transaction logs from the primary site to the hot site and manually reapply any transactions that took place since the last replication.

- If there are no available backups and it isn't possible to force replication, the disaster recovery team may simply accept the loss of some portion of the data. This should only be done when the loss is within the organization's recovery point objective (RPO).

The advantages of a hot site are obvious—the level of disaster recovery protection provided by this type of site is unsurpassed. However, the cost is *extremely* high. Maintaining a hot site essentially doubles an organization's budget for hardware, software, and services and requires the use of additional employees to maintain the site.

WARNING   If you use a hot site, never forget that it has copies of your production data. Be sure to provide that site with the same level of technical and physical security controls you provide at your primary site.

If an organization wants to maintain a hot site but wants to reduce the expense of equipment and maintenance, it might opt to use a shared hot site facility managed by an outside contractor. However, the inherent danger in these facilities is that they may be overtaxed in the event of a widespread disaster and be unable to service all clients simultaneously. If your organization considers such an arrangement, be sure to investigate these issues thoroughly, both before signing the contract and periodically during the contract term.

Another method of reducing the expense of a hot site is to use the hot site as a development or test environment. Developers can replicate data to the hot site in real time both for test purposes and to provide a live replica of the production environment. This reduces cost by having the hot site provide a useful service to the organization even when it is not actively being used for disaster operations.

Warm Sites

Warm sites occupy the middle ground between hot and cold sites for disaster recovery specialists. They always contain the equipment and data circuits necessary to rapidly establish operations. As with hot sites, this equipment is usually preconfigured and ready to run appropriate applications to support an organization's operations. Unlike hot sites, however, warm sites do not typically contain copies of the client's data. The main requirement in bringing a warm site to full operational status is the transportation of appropriate backup media to the site and restoration of critical data on the standby servers.

Activation of a warm site typically takes at least 12 hours from the time a disaster is declared. This does not mean that any site that can be activated in less than 12 hours qualifies as a hot site, however; switchover times for most hot sites are often measured in seconds or minutes, and complete cutovers seldom take more than an hour or two.

Warm sites avoid significant telecommunications and personnel costs inherent in maintaining a near–real-time copy of the operational data environment. As with hot sites and cold sites, warm sites may also be obtained on a shared facility basis. If you choose this option, be sure that you have a "no lockout" policy written into your contract guaranteeing you the use of an appropriate facility even during a period of high demand. It's a good idea to take this concept one step further and physically inspect the facilities and the contractor's operational plan to reassure yourself that the facility will indeed be able to back up the "no lockout" guarantee should push ever come to shove.

Mobile Sites

Mobile sites are non-mainstream alternatives to traditional recovery sites. They typically consist of self-contained trailers or other easily relocated units. These sites include all the environmental control systems necessary to maintain a safe computing environment. Larger corporations sometimes maintain these sites on a "fly-away" basis, ready to deploy them to any operating location around the world via air, rail, sea, or surface transportation. Smaller firms might contract with a mobile site vendor in their local area to provide these services on an as-needed basis.

If your disaster recovery plan depends on a workgroup recovery strategy, mobile sites are an excellent way to implement that approach. They are often large enough to accommodate entire (small!) workgroups.

Mobile sites are usually configured as cold sites or warm sites, depending on the disaster recovery plan they are designed to support. It is also possible to configure a mobile site as a hot site, but this is unusual because you seldom know in advance where a mobile site will need to be deployed.

Cloud Computing

Many organizations now turn to cloud computing as their preferred disaster recovery option. Infrastructure as a Service (IaaS) providers, such as Amazon Web Services (AWS),

Microsoft Azure, and Google Compute Engine, offer on-demand service at low cost. Companies wishing to maintain their own data centers may choose to use these IaaS options as backup service providers. Storing ready-to-run images with cloud providers is often quite cost effective and allows the organization to avoid incurring most of the operating cost until the cloud site activates in a disaster.

Organizations that already operate their technology resources in the cloud don't get a free pass on disaster recovery. They must also think about how they will handle issues that arise within their cloud environment. They should then design and configure their use of cloud services to take advantage of redundancy options, geographic dispersion, and similar considerations.

Database Recovery

Many organizations rely on databases to process and track operations, sales, logistics, and other activities vital to their continued viability. For this reason, it's essential that you include database recovery techniques in your disaster recovery plans. It's a wise idea to have a database specialist on the DRP team who can provide input as to the technical feasibility of various ideas. After all, you shouldn't allocate several hours to restore a database backup when it's impossible to complete a restoration in less than half a day!

In the following sections, we'll cover the three main techniques used to create offsite copies of database content: electronic vaulting, remote journaling, and remote mirroring. Each one has specific benefits and drawbacks, so you'll need to analyze your organization's computing requirements and available resources to select the option best suited to your firm and within the boundaries of your RPO. Selecting solutions that lose data beyond your RPO pose unwarranted risk, while selecting those that are more aggressive than your RPO may incur unnecessary costs.

Electronic Vaulting

In an *electronic vaulting* scenario, database backups are moved to a remote site using bulk transfers. The remote location may be a dedicated alternative recovery site (such as a hot site) or simply an offsite location managed within the company or by a contractor for the purpose of maintaining backup data.

If you use electronic vaulting, remember that there may be a significant delay between the time you declare a disaster and the time your database is ready for operation with current data. If you decide to activate a recovery site, technicians will need to retrieve the appropriate backups from the electronic vault and apply them to the soon-to-be production servers at the recovery site.

As with any type of backup scenario, be certain to periodically test your electronic vaulting setup. A great method for testing backup solutions is to give disaster recovery personnel a "surprise test," asking them to restore data from a certain day.

It's important to know that electronic vaulting introduces the potential for significant data loss. In the event of a disaster, you will only be able to recover information as of the time of the last vaulting operation.

Remote Journaling

With *remote journaling*, data transfers are performed in a more expeditious manner. Data transfers still occur in a bulk transfer mode, but they occur on a more frequent basis, usually once every hour and sometimes more frequently. Unlike electronic vaulting scenarios, where entire database backup files are transferred, remote journaling setups transfer copies of the database transaction logs containing the transactions that occurred since the previous bulk transfer.

Remote journaling is similar to electronic vaulting in that transaction logs transferred to the remote site are not applied to a live database server but are maintained in a backup device. When a disaster is declared, technicians retrieve the appropriate transaction logs and apply them to the production database, bringing the database up to the current production state.

Remote Mirroring

Remote mirroring is the most advanced database backup solution. Not surprisingly, it's also the most expensive! Remote mirroring goes beyond the technology used by remote journaling and electronic vaulting; with remote mirroring, a live database server is maintained at the backup site. The remote server receives copies of the database modifications at the same time they are applied to the production server at the primary site. Therefore, the mirrored server is ready to take over an operational role at a moment's notice.

Remote mirroring is a popular database backup strategy for organizations seeking to implement a hot site. However, when weighing the feasibility of a remote mirroring solution, be sure to take into account the infrastructure and personnel costs required to support the mirrored server as well as the processing overhead that will be added to each database transaction on the mirrored server. Also, don't forget that the remote location and server will require the same level of security controls to protect any sensitive data they contain.

Cloud-based database platforms may include redundancy capabilities as a built-in feature. If you operate databases in the cloud, consider investigating these options to simplify your disaster recovery planning efforts, but be sure to understand the limitations of the specific service you consider!

Recovery Plan Development

Once you've established your business unit priorities and have a good idea of the appropriate alternative recovery sites for your organization, it's time to put pen to paper and begin drafting a true disaster recovery plan. Don't expect to sit down and write the full plan in one sitting. It's likely that the DRP team will go through many draft documents before reaching a final written document that satisfies the operational needs of critical business units and falls within the resource, time, and expense constraints of the disaster recovery budget and available personnel.

In the following sections, we explore some important items to include in your disaster recovery plan. Depending on the size of your organization and the number of people involved in the DRP effort, it may be a good idea to maintain multiple types of plan documents, intended for different audiences. The following list includes various types of documents worth considering:

- Executive summary providing a high-level overview of the plan

- Department-specific plans

- Technical guides for IT personnel responsible for implementing and maintaining critical backup systems

- Checklists for individuals on the disaster recovery team

- Full copies of the plan for critical disaster recovery team members

Using custom-tailored documents becomes especially important when a disaster occurs or is imminent. Personnel who need to refresh themselves on the disaster recovery procedures that affect various parts of the organization will be able to refer to their department-specific plans. Critical disaster recovery team members will have checklists to help guide their actions amid the chaotic atmosphere of a disaster. IT personnel will have technical guides helping them get the alternate sites up and running. Finally, managers and public relations personnel will have a simple document that provides them a high-level view of the coordinated symphony that is an active disaster recovery effort without requiring interpretation from team members busy with tasks directly related to that effort.

Visit the Professional Practices library at https://drii.org/ resources/professionalpractices/EN to examine a collection of documents that explain how to work through and document your planning processes for BCP and disaster recovery. Other good standard documents in this area include the BCI Good Practice Guideline (GPG) (www.thebci.org/training-qualifications/good-practice-guidelines.html), ISO 27001 (www.iso.org/isoiec-27001-information-security.html), and NIST SP 800-34, "Contingency Planning Guide for Federal Information Systems" (https://csrc.nist .gov/publications/detail/sp/800-34/rev-1/final).

Emergency Response

A disaster recovery plan should contain simple yet comprehensive instructions for essential personnel to follow immediately upon recognizing that a disaster is in progress or is imminent. These instructions will vary widely depending on the nature of the disaster, the type of personnel responding to the incident, and the time available before facilities need to be evacuated and/or equipment shut down. For example, instructions for a large-scale fire will be much more concise than the instructions for how to prepare for a hurricane that is still 48 hours away from a predicted landfall near an operational site. Emergency-response plans are often put together in the form of checklists provided to responders. When designing such checklists, keep one essential design principle in mind: arrange the checklist tasks in order of priority, with the most important task first!

It's essential to remember that these checklists will be executed in the midst of a crisis. It is extremely likely that responders will not be able to complete the entire checklist, especially in the event of a short-notice disaster. For this reason, you should put the most essential tasks (that is, "Activate the building alarm") first on the checklist. The lower an item on the list, the lower the likelihood that it will be completed before an evacuation/shutdown takes place.

Among these essential tasks is the formal declaration of a disaster. The response plan should include clear criteria for activation of the disaster recovery plan, define who has the authority to declare a disaster, and then review notification procedures, as discussed in the next section.

Personnel and Communications

A disaster recovery plan should also contain a list of personnel to contact in the event of a disaster. Usually, this includes key members of the DRP team as well as personnel who execute critical disaster recovery tasks throughout the organization. This response checklist should include alternate means of contact (that is, pager numbers, mobile phone numbers, and so on) as well as backup contacts for each role should the primary contact be incommunicado or unable to reach the recovery site for one reason or another.

The Power of Checklists

Checklists are invaluable tools in the face of disaster. They provide a sense of order amid the chaotic events surrounding a disaster. Do what you must to ensure that response checklists provide first responders with a clear plan to protect life and property and ensure the continuity of operations.

A checklist for response to a building fire might include the following steps:

1. Activate the building alarm system.

2. Ensure that an orderly evacuation is in progress.

(continues)

(continued)

3. If reasonable to do so, consider fighting the fire with available fire extinguishers or other fire suppression equipment.

4. After leaving the building, use a mobile telephone to call emergency services (911 in the U.S.) to ensure that emergency authorities received the alarm notification. Provide additional information on any required emergency response.

5. Ensure that any injured personnel receive appropriate medical treatment.

6. Activate the organization's disaster recovery plan to ensure continuity of operations.

Be sure to consult with the individuals in your organization responsible for privacy before assembling and disseminating a telephone notification checklist. You may need to comply with special policies regarding the use of home telephone numbers and other personal information in the checklist.

The notification checklist should be supplied to all personnel who might respond to a disaster. This enables prompt notification of key personnel. Many firms organize their notification checklists in a "telephone tree" style: each member of the tree contacts the person below them, spreading the notification burden among members of the team instead of relying on one person to make lots of telephone calls.

If you choose to implement a telephone tree notification scheme, be sure to add a safety net. Have the last person in each chain contact the originator to confirm that their entire chain has been notified. This lets you rest assured that the disaster recovery team activation is smoothly underway.

Assessment

When the disaster recovery team arrives on site, one of their first tasks is to assess the situation. This normally occurs in a rolling fashion, with the first responders performing a very simple assessment to triage activity and get the disaster response underway. As the incident progresses, more detailed assessments will take place to gauge the effectiveness of disaster recovery efforts and prioritize the assignment of resources.

Backups and Offsite Storage

Backups play an important role in the disaster recovery plan. They are copies of data stored on tape, disk, the cloud, or other media as a last-ditch recovery option. If a disaster causes data loss, administrators may turn to backups to recover lost data.

Your disaster recovery plan (especially the technical guide) should fully address the backup strategy pursued by your organization. Indeed, this is one of the most important elements of any business continuity plan and disaster recovery plan.

Many system administrators are already familiar with various types of backups, so you'll benefit by bringing one or more individuals with specific technical expertise in this area onto the BCP/DRP team to provide expert guidance. There are three main types of backups:

Full Backups   As the name implies, *full backups* store a complete copy of the data contained on the protected device. Full backups duplicate every file on the system regardless of the setting of the archive bit. Once a full backup is complete, the archive bit on every file is reset, turned off, or set to 0.

Incremental Backups   *Incremental backups* store only those files that have been modified since the time of the most recent full or incremental backup. Only files that have the archive bit turned on, enabled, or set to 1 are duplicated. Once an incremental backup is complete, the archive bit on all duplicated files is reset, turned off, or set to 0.

Differential Backups   *Differential backups* store all files that have been modified since the time of the most recent full backup. Only files that have the archive bit turned on, enabled, or set to 1 are duplicated. However, unlike full and incremental backups, the differential backup process does not change the archive bit.

Some operating systems do not actually use an archive bit to achieve this goal and instead analyze file system timestamps. This difference in implementation doesn't affect the types of data stored by each backup type.

The most important difference between incremental and differential backups is the time needed to restore data in the event of an emergency. If you use a combination of full and differential backups, you will need to restore only two backups—the most recent full backup and the most recent differential backup. On the other hand, if your strategy combines full backups with incremental backups, you will need to restore the most recent full backup as well as all incremental backups performed since that full backup. The trade-off is the time required to *create* the backups—differential backups don't take as long to restore, but they take longer to create than incremental ones.

The storage of the backup media is equally critical. It may be convenient to store backup media in or near the primary operations center to easily fulfill user requests for backup data, but you'll definitely need to keep copies of the media in at least one offsite location to provide redundancy should your primary operating location be suddenly destroyed. One common strategy used by many organizations is to store backups in a cloud service that is itself geographically redundant. This allows the organization to retrieve the backups from any location after a disaster. Note that using geographically diverse sites may introduce new regulatory requirements when the information resides in different jurisdictions.

Using Backups

In case of system failure, many companies use one of two common methods to restore data from backups. In the first situation, they run a full backup on Monday night and then run differential backups every other night of the week. If a failure occurs Saturday morning, they restore Monday's full backup and then restore only Friday's differential backup. In the second situation, they run a full backup on Monday night and run incremental backups every other night of the week. If a failure occurs Saturday morning, they restore Monday's full backup and then restore each incremental backup in original chronological order (that is, Wednesday's, then Friday's, and so on).

Most organizations adopt a backup strategy that utilizes more than one of the three backup types along with a media rotation scheme. Both allow backup administrators access to a sufficiently large range of backups to complete user requests and provide fault tolerance while minimizing the amount of money that must be spent on backup media. A common strategy is to perform full backups over the weekend and incremental or differential backups on a nightly basis. The specific method of backup and all the particulars of the backup procedure are dependent on your organization's fault-tolerance requirements, as defined by your RPO values. If you are unable to survive minor amounts of data loss, your ability to tolerate faults is low. However, if hours or days of data can be lost without serious consequence, your tolerance of faults is high. You should design your backup solution accordingly.

Disk-to-Disk Backup

Over the past decade, disk storage has become increasingly inexpensive. With drive capacities now measured in terabytes, tape and optical media can't cope with data volume requirements anymore. Many enterprises now use disk-to-disk (D2D) backup solutions for some portion of their disaster recovery strategy.

Many backup technologies are designed around the tape paradigm. *Virtual tape libraries (VTL)* support the use of disks with this model by using software to make disk storage appear as tapes to backup software.

One important note: Organizations seeking to adopt an entirely disk-to-disk approach must remember to maintain geographical diversity. Some of those disks have to be located offsite. Many organizations solve this problem by hiring managed service providers to manage remote backup locations.

As transfer and storage costs come down, cloud-based backup solutions are becoming very cost effective. You may wish to consider using such a service as an alternative to physically transporting backup tapes to a remote location.

Utilities

As discussed in previous sections of this chapter, your organization is reliant on several utilities to provide critical elements of your infrastructure—electric power, water, natural gas, sewer service, and so on. Your disaster recovery plan should contain contact information and procedures to troubleshoot these services if problems arise during a disaster.

Logistics and Supplies

The logistical problems surrounding a disaster recovery operation are immense. You will suddenly face the problem of moving large sets of people, equipment, and supplies to alternate recovery sites. It's also possible that the people will be living at those sites for an extended period of time and that the disaster recovery team will be responsible for providing them with food, water, shelter, and appropriate facilities. Your disaster recovery plan should contain provisions for this type of operation if it falls within the scope of your expected operational needs.

Training, Awareness, and Documentation

As with a business continuity plan, it is essential that you provide training to all personnel who will be involved in the disaster recovery effort. The level of training required will vary according to an individual's role in the effort and their position within the company. When designing a training plan, consider including the following elements:

- Orientation training for all new employees
- Initial training for employees taking on a new disaster recovery role for the first time
- Detailed refresher training for disaster recovery team members
- Brief awareness refreshers for all other employees (can be accomplished as part of other meetings and through a medium like email newsletters sent to all employees)

The disaster recovery plan should also be fully documented. Earlier in this chapter, we discussed several documentation options available to you. Be sure you implement the necessary documentation programs and modify the documentation as changes to the plan occur. Because of the rapidly changing nature of the disaster recovery and business continuity plans, you might consider publication on a secured portion of your organization's intranet.

Testing and Maintenance

Every disaster recovery plan must be tested on a periodic basis to ensure that the plan's provisions are viable and that it meets an organization's changing needs. The types of tests that you conduct will depend on the types of recovery facilities available to you, the culture of your organization, and the availability of disaster recovery team members. The five main test types—checklist tests, structured walk-throughs, simulation tests, parallel tests, and full-interruption tests—are discussed in the remaining sections of this chapter.

For more information on this topic, consult NIST Special Publication 800-84, "Guide to Test, Training, and Exercise Programs for IT Plans and Capabilities Recommendations", available at https://csrc.nist.gov/publications/detail/sp/800-84/final.

Read-Through Test

The *read-through test* is one of the simplest tests to conduct, but it's also one of the most critical ones. In this test, you distribute copies of disaster recovery plans to the members of the disaster recovery team for review. This lets you accomplish three goals simultaneously:

- It ensures that key personnel are aware of their responsibilities and have that knowledge refreshed periodically.

- It provides individuals with an opportunity to review the plans for obsolete information and update any items that require modification because of changes within the organization.

- In large organizations, it helps identify situations in which key personnel have left the company and nobody bothered to reassign their disaster recovery responsibilities. This is also a good reason why disaster recovery responsibilities should be included in job descriptions.

Structured Walk-Through

A *structured walk-through* takes testing one step further. In this type of test, often referred to as a *table-top exercise*, members of the disaster recovery team gather in a large conference room and role-play a disaster scenario. Usually, the exact scenario is known only to the test moderator, who presents the details to the team at the meeting. The team members then refer to their copies of the disaster recovery plan and discuss the appropriate responses to that particular type of disaster.

Walk-throughs may vary in their scope and intent. Some exercises may include taking physical actions or at least considering their impact on the exercise. For example, a walk-through might require that everyone leave the building and return home to participate in the exercise.

Simulation Test

Simulation tests are similar to the structured walk-throughs. In simulation tests, disaster recovery team members are presented with a scenario and asked to develop an appropriate response. Unlike with the tests previously discussed, some of these response measures are then tested. This may involve the interruption of noncritical business activities and the use of some operational personnel.

Parallel Test

Parallel tests represent the next level in testing and involve relocating personnel to the alternate recovery site and implementing site activation procedures. The employees relocated to the site perform their disaster recovery responsibilities just as they would for an actual disaster. The only difference is that operations at the main facility are not interrupted. That site retains full responsibility for conducting the day-to-day business of the organization.

Full-Interruption Test

Full-interruption tests operate like parallel tests, but they involve actually shutting down operations at the primary site and shifting them to the recovery site. These tests involve a significant risk, as they require the operational shutdown of the primary site and transfer to the recovery site, followed by the reverse process to restore operations at the primary site. For this reason, full-interruption tests are extremely difficult to arrange, and you often encounter resistance from management.

Lessons Learned

At the conclusion of any disaster recovery operation or other security incident, the organization should conduct a *lessons learned* session. The lessons learned process is designed to provide everyone involved with the incident response effort an opportunity to reflect on their individual role in the incident and the team's response overall. It is an opportunity to improve the processes and technologies used in incident response to better respond to future security crises.

The most common way to conduct lessons learned is to gather everyone in the same room, or connect them via videoconference or telephone, and ask a trained facilitator to lead a lessons learned session. Ideally, this facilitator should have played no role in the incident response, leaving them with no preconceived notions about the response. The facilitator should be a neutral party who simply helps guide the conversation.

Time is of the essence with the lessons learned session because, as time passes, details quickly become fuzzy and memories are lost. The more quickly you conduct a lessons learned session, the more likely it is that you will receive valuable feedback that can help guide future responses.

In SP 800-61, NIST offers a series of questions to use in the lessons learned process. They include the following:

- Exactly what happened and at what times?
- How well did staff and management perform in dealing with the incident?
- Were documented procedures followed?
- Were the procedures adequate?
- Were any steps or actions taken that might have inhibited the recovery?
- What would the staff and management do differently the next time a similar incident occurs?
- How could information sharing with other organizations have been improved?
- What corrective actions can prevent similar incidents in the future?
- What precursors or indicators should be watched for in the future to detect similar incidents?
- What additional tools or resources are needed to detect, analyze, and mitigate future incidents?

The responses to these questions, if given honestly, will provide valuable insight into the state of the organization's incident response program. They can help provide a roadmap of future improvements designed to bolster disaster recovery. The facilitator should work with the team leader to document the lessons learned in a report that includes suggested process improvement actions.

Maintenance

Remember that a disaster recovery plan is a living document. As your organization's needs change, you must adapt the disaster recovery plan to meet those changed needs to follow suit. You will discover many necessary modifications by using a well-organized and coordinated testing plan. Minor changes may often be made through a series of telephone conversations or emails, whereas major changes may require one or more meetings of the full disaster recovery team.

A disaster recovery planner should refer to the organization's business continuity plan as a template for its recovery efforts. This and all the supportive material may need to comply with applicable regulations and reflect current business needs. Business processes such as payroll and order generation should contain specified metrics mapped to related IT systems and infrastructure.

Most organizations apply formal change management processes so that whenever the IT infrastructure changes, all relevant documentation is updated and checked to reflect such changes. Regularly scheduled fire drills and dry runs to ensure that all elements of the DRP are used properly to keep staff trained present a perfect opportunity to integrate changes into regular maintenance and change management procedures. Design, implement, and document changes each time you go through these processes and exercises. Know where everything is, and keep each element of the DRP working properly. In case of emergency, use your recovery plan. Finally, make sure the staff stays trained to keep their skills sharp—for existing support personnel—and use simulated exercises to bring new people up to speed quickly.

Summary

Every organization dependent on technological resources for its survival should have a comprehensive business continuity plan in place to ensure the sustained viability of the organization when emergencies take place. Several important concepts underlie solid business continuity planning practices, including project scope and planning, business impact analysis, continuity planning, and approval and implementation.

Disaster recovery planning is critical to a comprehensive information security program. DRPs serve as a valuable complement to business continuity plans and ensure that the proper technical controls are in place to keep the business functioning and to restore service after a disruption.

An organization's disaster recovery plan is one of the most important documents under the purview of security professionals. It should provide guidance to the personnel responsible for ensuring the continuity of operations in the face of disaster. The DRP provides an orderly sequence of events designed to activate alternate processing sites while simultaneously restoring the primary site to operational status. Once you've successfully developed your DRP, you must train personnel on its use, ensure that you maintain accurate documentation, and conduct periodic tests to keep the plan fresh in the minds of responders.

Exam Essentials

Understand the four steps of the business continuity planning process. Business continuity planning involves four distinct phases: project scope and planning, business impact analysis, continuity planning, and approval and implementation. Each task contributes to the overall goal of ensuring that business operations continue uninterrupted in the face of an emergency.

Describe how to perform the business organization analysis. In the business organization analysis, the individuals responsible for leading the BCP process determine which departments and individuals have a stake in the business continuity plan. This analysis serves as the foundation for BCP team selection and, after validation by the BCP team, is used to guide the next stages of BCP development.

List the necessary members of the business continuity planning team. The BCP team should contain, at a minimum, representatives from each of the operational and support departments; technical experts from the IT department; physical and IT security personnel with BCP skills; legal representatives familiar with corporate legal, regulatory, and contractual responsibilities; and representatives from senior management. Additional team members depend on the structure and nature of the organization.

Know the legal and regulatory requirements that face business continuity planners. Business leaders must exercise due diligence to ensure that shareholders' interests are protected in the event disaster strikes. Some industries are also subject to federal, state, and local regulations that mandate specific BCP procedures. Many businesses also have contractual obligations to their clients that they must meet before, during, and after a disaster.

Explain the steps of the business impact analysis process. The five stages of the business impact analysis process are the identification of priorities, risk identification, likelihood assessment, impact analysis, and resource prioritization.

Describe the process used to develop a continuity strategy. During the strategy development phase, the BCP team determines which risks they will mitigate. In the provisions and processes phase, the team designs mechanisms and procedures that will mitigate identified risks. The plan must then be approved by senior management and implemented. Personnel must also receive training on their roles in the BCP process.

Explain the importance of comprehensively documenting an organization's business continuity and disaster recovery plans. Committing the plan to writing provides the organization with a written record of the procedures to follow when disaster strikes. It prevents the "it's in my head" syndrome and ensures the orderly progress of events in an emergency.

Be familiar with the common types of recovery facilities. The common types of recovery facilities are cold sites, warm sites, hot sites, mobile sites, and multiple sites. Be sure you understand the benefits and drawbacks for each such facility.

Understand the technologies that may assist with database backup. Databases benefit from three backup technologies. Electronic vaulting is used to transfer database backups to a remote site as part of a bulk transfer. In remote journaling, data transfers occur on a more frequent basis. With remote mirroring technology, database transactions are mirrored at the backup site in real time.

Explain the common processes used in disaster recovery programs. These programs should take a comprehensive approach to planning and include considerations related to the initial response effort, personnel involved, communication among the team and with internal and external entities, assessment of response efforts, and restoration of services. DR programs should also include training and awareness efforts to ensure personnel understand their responsibilities and lessons learned sessions to continuously improve the program.

Know the five types of disaster recovery plan tests and the impact each has on normal business operations. The five types of disaster recovery plan tests are: read-through tests, structured walk-throughs, simulation tests, parallel tests, and full-interruption tests. Checklist tests are purely paperwork exercises, whereas structured walk-throughs involve a project team meeting. Neither has an impact on business operations. Simulation tests may shut down noncritical business units. Parallel tests involve relocating personnel but do not affect day-to-day operations. Full-interruption tests involve shutting down primary systems and shifting responsibility to the recovery facility.

Review Questions

1. Tracy is preparing for her organization's annual business continuity exercise, but she encounters resistance from some managers who don't see the exercise as important and feel that it is a waste of resources. She has already told the managers that it will only take half a day for their employees to participate. What argument could Tracy make to best address these concerns?

   A. The exercise is required by policy.

   B. The exercise is already scheduled, and canceling it would be difficult.

   C. The exercise is crucial to ensuring that the organization is prepared for emergencies.

   D. The exercise will not be very time-consuming.

2. The board of directors of Clashmore Circuits is conducting an annual review of the business continuity planning process to ensure that adequate measures are in place to minimize the effect of a disaster on the organization's continued viability. What obligation are they satisfying with this review?

   A. Corporate responsibility

   B. Disaster requirement

   C. Due diligence

   D. Going concern responsibility

3. Renee is reporting the results of her organization's BIA to senior leaders. They express frustration at all of the details, and one of them says, "Look, we just need to know how much we should expect these risks to cost us each year." What measure could Renee provide to best answer this question?

   A. ARO

   B. SLE

   C. ALE

   D. EF

4. Jake is conducting a business impact analysis for his organization. As part of the process, he asks leaders from different units to provide input on how long the enterprise resource planning (ERP) system could be unavailable without causing irreparable harm to the organization. What measure is he seeking to determine?

   A. SLE

   B. EF

   C. MTD

   D. ARO

5. You are concerned about the risk that an avalanche poses to your $3 million shipping facility. Based on expert opinion, you determine that there is a 5 percent chance that an avalanche will occur each year. Experts advise you that an avalanche would completely destroy your building and require you to rebuild on the same land. Ninety percent of the $3 million value of the facility is attributed to the building, and 10 percent is attributed to the land itself. What is the single loss expectancy (SLE) of your shipping facility to avalanches?

   A. $3 million

   B. $2,700,000

   C. $270,000

   D. $135,000

6. You are concerned about the risk that a hurricane poses to your corporate headquarters in South Florida. The building itself is valued at $15 million. After consulting with the National Weather Service, you determine that there is a 10 percent likelihood that a hurricane will strike over the course of a year. You hire a team of architects and engineers who determine that the average hurricane would destroy approximately 50 percent of the building. What is the annualized loss expectancy (ALE)?

   A. $750,000

   B. $1.5 million

   C. $7.5 million

   D. $15 million

7. Brian is developing continuity plan provisions and processes for his organization. What resource should he protect as the highest priority in those plans?

   A. Physical plant

   B. Infrastructure

   C. Financial

   D. People

8. Ricky is conducting the quantitative portion of his organization's business impact analysis. Which one of the following concerns is *least* suitable for quantitative measurement during this assessment?

   A. Loss of a plant

   B. Damage to a vehicle

   C. Negative publicity

   D. Power outage

9. Darren is concerned about the risk of a serious power outage affecting his organization's data center. He consults the organization's business impact analysis and determines that the ARO of a power outage is 20 percent. He notes that the assessment took place three years ago and no power outage has occurred. What ARO should he use in this year's assessment, assuming that none of the circumstances underlying the analysis have changed?

   A. 20 percent

   B. 50 percent

   C. 75 percent

   D. 100 percent

10. Of the individuals listed, who would provide the best endorsement for a business continuity plan's statement of importance?

   A. Vice president of business operations

   B. Chief information officer

   C. Chief executive officer

   D. Business continuity manager

11. Kevin is attempting to determine an appropriate backup frequency for his organization's database server and wants to ensure that any data loss is within the organization's risk appetite. Which one of the following security process metrics would best assist him with this task?

   A. RTO

   B. MTD

   C. RPO

   D. MTBF

12. Brian's organization recently suffered a disaster and wants to improve their disaster recovery program based on their experience. Which one of the following activities will best assist with this task?

   A. Training programs

   B. Awareness efforts

   C. BIA review

   D. Lessons learned

13. Adam is reviewing the fault tolerance controls used by his organization and realizes that they currently have a single point of failure in the disks used to support a critical server. Which one of the following controls can provide fault tolerance for these disks?

   A. Load balancing

   B. RAID

   C. Clustering

   D. HA pairs

14. Brad is helping to design a disaster recovery strategy for his organization and is analyzing possible storage locations for backup data. He is not certain where the organization will recover operations in the event of a disaster and would like to choose an option that allows them the flexibility to easily retrieve data from any DR site. Which one of the following storage locations provides the best option for Brad?

A. Primary data center

B. Field office

C. Cloud computing

D. IT manager's home

15. Tonya is reviewing the flood risk to her organization and learns that their primary data center resides within a 100-year flood plain. What conclusion can she draw from this information?

A. The last flood of any kind to hit the area was more than 100 years ago.

B. The odds of a flood at this level are 1 in 100 in any given year.

C. The area is expected to be safe from flooding for at least 100 years.

D. The last significant flood to hit the area was more than 100 years ago.

16. Bryn runs a corporate website and currently uses a single server, which is capable of handling the site's entire load. She is concerned, however, that an outage on that server could cause the organization to exceed its RTO. What action could she take that would best protect against this risk?

A. Install dual power supplies in the server

B. Replace the server's hard drives with RAID arrays

C. Deploy multiple servers behind a load balancer

D. Perform regular backups of the server

17. Nolan is considering the use of several different types of alternate processing facilities for his organization's data center. Which one of the following alternative processing sites takes the longest time to activate but has the lowest cost to implement?

A. Hot site

B. Mobile site

C. Cold site

D. Warm site

18. Harry is conducting a disaster recovery test. He moved a group of personnel to the alternate recovery site where they are mimicking the operations of the primary site but do not have operational responsibility. What type of disaster recovery test is he performing?

A. Checklist test

B. Structured walkthrough

C. Simulation test

D. Parallel test

19. What type of backup involves always storing copies of all files modified since the most recent full backup?

    A. Differential backups

    B. Partial backup

    C. Incremental backups

    D. Database backup

20. You operate a grain processing business and are developing your restoration priorities. Which one of the following systems would likely be your highest priority?

    A. Order-processing system

    B. Fire suppression system

    C. Payroll system

    D. Website

Appendix

Answers to the Review Questions

Chapter 1: Today's Information Security Manager

1. **D.** Managerial controls are procedural mechanisms that focus on the mechanics of the risk management process. Threat assessment is an example of one of these activities.

2. **B.** The breach of credit card information may cause many different impacts on the organization, including compliance, operational, and financial risks. However, in this scenario, Jade's primary concern is violating PCI DSS, making the concern a compliance risk.

3. **C.** The defacement of a website alters content without authorization and is, therefore, a violation of the integrity objective. The attackers may also have breached the confidentiality or availability of the website, but the scenario does not provide us with enough information to draw those conclusions.

4. **C.** The most important consideration when gaining stakeholder support for security initiatives is demonstrating the alignment between a request and the objectives of the business. While managers should certainly use plain language and communicate in the format desired by leaders, these are secondary considerations. Adopting emerging technologies is not necessary to underscore the importance of security initiatives.

5. **D.** Deterrent controls are designed to prevent an attacker from attempting to violate security policies in the first place. Preventive controls would attempt to block an attack that was about to take place. Corrective controls would remediate the issues that arose during an attack.

6. **D.** All individuals within an organization have some responsibility for protecting data. However, the data owner is the senior-most leader who bears ultimate responsibility for this protection. The data owner may delegate some authority and/or responsibility to data stewards, data custodians, and end users, but they still bear ultimate responsibility.

7. **C.** The availability of this cybersecurity insurance offering is an external factor that the organization might exploit to better achieve its objectives and, therefore, should be classified as an opportunity. Strengths and weaknesses are internal characteristics of the organization. Threats are external factors that pose a risk to the organization.

8. **A.** Technical controls enforce confidentiality, integrity, and availability in the digital space. Examples of technical security controls include firewall rules, access control lists, intrusion prevention systems, and encryption.

9. **B.** As the ultimate stakeholder for the initiative, Dan is the accountable individual and should be labeled with an "A" in the RACI matrix. Others who are directly contributing to the effort would be labeled as responsible ("R"). Stakeholders who are not directly working on the SOC implementation would be labeled as either consulted ("C") or informed ("I"), as appropriate.

10. **A.** The risk that Tony is contemplating could fit any one of these categories. However, his primary concern is that the company may no longer be able to do business if the risk materializes. This is a strategic risk.

11. C. Although it is possible that a frequent flyer account number, or any other account number for that matter, could be used in identity theft, it is far more likely that identity thieves would use core identity documents. These include driver's licenses, passports, and Social Security numbers.

12. A. As an organization analyzes its risk environment, technical and business leaders determine the level of protection required to preserve the confidentiality, integrity, and availability of their information and systems. They express these requirements by writing the control objectives that the organization wishes to achieve. These control objectives are statements of a desired security state.

13. A. It may be true that these individuals fit into more than one, or even all, of these categories. However, the key element in the question is that the users have administrative access to systems. Therefore, they are best described as privileged users.

14. D. The CISO should report to a senior-level decision-maker in the organization and not to the leader of another technology function. Therefore, the senior D director for identity and access management is an inappropriate reporting structure. The CIO, CRO, and CEO would all be appropriate supervisors for a CISO.

15. D. The use of full-disk encryption is intended to prevent a security incident from occurring if a device is lost or stolen. Therefore, this is a preventive control gap.

16. E. This goal is specific in that it describes the implementation of an IPS. It is also measurable since it states a clear objective of reducing intrusions by 50 percent. We do not have enough information about the organization to determine whether it is achievable or relevant. It is definitely not time-bound because it contains no deadline. Toni could remedy this situation by adding a deliverable date to the goal.

17. C. The disclosure of sensitive information to unauthorized individuals is a violation of the principle of confidentiality.

18. B. The three primary objectives of cybersecurity professionals are confidentiality, integrity, and availability.

19. C. The span of control is the number of employees who directly report to a manager. Most organizations consider 5–10 employees to be an appropriate span of control.

20. E. This is an example of a Managed organization: one that begins to implement organized processes on a per-project basis but is still operating in reactive mode. At the Initial level, the organization has unpredictable processes that are poorly controlled. When an organization achieves Level 3: Defined, it has standard processes that are used organization-wide and are adapted for use within each project. Level 4: Quantitatively Managed organizations build measurement and controls on top of their processes to allow them to quickly identify and remediate deficiencies and address control gaps before issues arise. At the top tier of the CMMI, Level 5: Optimizing organizations use a continuous process improvement approach to adjust and fine-tune the way that they work to achieve peak efficiency and effectiveness.

Chapter 2: Information Security Governance and Compliance

1. B. The key term in this scenario is "one way." This indicates that compliance with the document is not mandatory, so Joe must be authoring a guideline. Policies, standards, and procedures are all mandatory.

2. B. Governance programs should be flexible and dynamic, rather than static. They should adapt to changes in the environment, as needed. They should be tailored to the enterprise's needs and cover the enterprise end-to-end. They should clearly distinguish between governance and management activities.

3. C. The General Data Protection Regulation (GDPR) implements privacy requirements for handling the personal information of EU residents. The Health Insurance Portability and Accountability Act (HIPAA) includes security and privacy rules that affect health-care providers, health insurers, and health information clearinghouses. The Family Educational Rights and Privacy Act (FERPA) applies to educational institutions. The Payment Card Industry Data Security Standard (PCI DSS) applies to credit and debit card information.

4. B. The five security functions described in the NIST Cybersecurity Framework are identify, protect, detect, respond, and recover.

5. C. The International Organization for Standardization (ISO) publishes ISO 27701, covering privacy controls. ISO 27001 and 27002 cover cybersecurity, and ISO 31000 covers risk management.

6. D. Policies require approval from the highest level of management, usually the CEO. Other documents may often be approved by other managers, such as the CISO.

7. C. Master service agreements (MSAs) provide an umbrella contract for the work that a vendor does with an organization over an extended period of time. The MSA typically includes detailed security and privacy requirements. Each time the organization enters into a new project with the vendor, they may then create a statement of work (SOW) that contains project-specific details and references the MSA.

8. B. All of these organizations produce security standards and benchmarks. However, only the Center for Internet Security (CIS) is known for producing independent benchmarks covering a wide variety of software and hardware.

9. C. In the corporate governance model for publicly traded organizations, the shareholders who own the corporation delegate control of the corporation to the elected members of the board of directors. The board is then responsible for selecting the CEO, reviewing the CEO's performance, and terminating the CEO when necessary.

10. B. Security policies do not normally contain prescriptive technical guidance, such as a requirement to use a specific encryption algorithm. This type of detail would normally be found in a security standard.

11. A. The fact that the auditor will not be assessing the effectiveness of the controls means that this is a Type 1 report, not a Type 2 report. The fact that it will be shared only under NDA means that it is an SOC 2 assessment.

12. C. The common elements of a business case include a scope statement, a strategic context, a cost analysis, an evaluation of alternatives, a project plan, and a management plan. Organizations may develop rollback plans for high-risk changes, but those rollback plans are not a standard component of the business case.

13. D. The Payment Card Industry Data Security Standard (PCI DSS) provides detailed rules about the storage, processing, and transmission of credit and debit card information. PCI DSS is not a law but rather a contractual obligation that applies to credit card merchants and service providers.

14. A. Policies should be developed in a manner that obtains input from all relevant stakeholders, but it is not necessary to obtain agreement or approval from all stakeholders. Policies should follow normal corporate policy approval processes and should be written in a manner that fits within the organizational culture and "tone at the top." Once an information security policy is approved, it commonly falls to the information security manager to communicate and implement the policy.

15. D. A complete business case should include all relevant financial and human resources costs for an initiative, including both one-time and recurring costs.

16. D. The chief executive officer (CEO) bears ultimate responsibility for the efficiency and effectiveness of the organization in all respects. The chief information officer (CIO), chief information security officer (CISO), and chief financial officer (CFO) are all accountable to the CEO or other senior leader for the areas under their span of control.

17. D. Any of these terms could reasonably be used to describe this engagement. However, the term *audit* best describes this effort because of the formal nature of the review and the fact that it was requested by the board.

18. A. The five COBIT domains are:

- Evaluate, Direct, and Monitor (EDM)
- Align, Plan, and Organize (APO)
- Build, Acquire, and Implement (BAI)
- Deliver, Service, and Support (DSS)
- Monitor, Evaluate, and Assess (MEA)

19. D. The NIST Cybersecurity Framework is designed to help organizations describe their current cybersecurity posture, describe their target state for cybersecurity, identify and prioritize opportunities for improvement, assess progress, and communicate with stakeholders about risk. It does not create specific technology requirements.

20. C. Requests for an exception to a security policy would not normally include a proposed revision to the policy. Exceptions are documented variances from the policy because of specific technical and/or business requirements. They do not alter the original policy, which remains in force for systems not covered by the exception.

Chapter 3: Information Risk Management

1. C. By applying the patch, Jen has removed the vulnerability from her server. This also has the effect of eliminating this particular risk. Jen cannot control the external threat of an attacker attempting to gain access to her server.

2. C. Installing a web application firewall reduces the probability that an attack will reach the web server. Vulnerabilities may still exist in the web application, and the threat of an external attack is unchanged. The impact of a successful SQL injection attack is also unchanged by a web application firewall.

3. C. The asset at risk in this case is the customer database. Losing control of the database would result in a $500,000 fine, so the asset value (AV) is $500,000.

4. D. The attack would result in the total loss of customer data stored in the database, making the exposure factor (EF) 100 percent.

5. C. We compute the single loss expectancy (SLE) by multiplying the asset value (AV) ($500,000) and the exposure factor (EF) (100%) to get an SLE of $500,000.

6. A. Aziz's threat intelligence research determined that the threat has a 5 percent likelihood of occurrence each year. This is an ARO of 0.05.

7. B. We compute the annualized loss expectancy (ALE) by multiplying the SLE ($500,000) and the ARO (0.05) to get an ALE of $25,000.

8. C. Installing new controls or upgrading existing controls is an effort to reduce the probability or magnitude of a risk. This is an example of a risk mitigation activity.

9. B. Changing business processes or activities to eliminate a risk is an example of risk avoidance.

10. D. Insurance policies use a risk transference strategy by shifting some or all of the financial risk from the organization to an insurance company.

11. A. When an organization decides to take no further action to address the remaining risk, they are choosing a strategy of risk acceptance.

12. A. Under the General Data Protection Regulation (GDPR), the data protection officer (DPO) is an individual who is assigned the direct responsibility for carrying out an organization's privacy program.

13. A. In this case, the physicians maintain the data ownership role. They have chosen to outsource data processing to Helen's organization, making that organization a data processor.

14. C. The recovery time objective (RTO) is the amount of time that the organization can tolerate a system being down before it is repaired. That is the metric that Gene has identified in this scenario.

15. B. This is a tricky question as it is possible to find all of these categories of information in patient records. However, they are most likely to contain protected health information (PHI). PHI could also be described as a subcategory of personally identifiable information (PII), but PHI is a better description. It is also possible that the records might contain payment card information (PCI) or personal financial information (PFI), but that is less likely than PHI.

16. C. Organizations should only use data for the purposes disclosed during the collection of that data. In this case, the organization collected data for technical support purposes and is now using it for marketing purposes. That violates the principle of purpose limitation.

17. C. Top Secret is the highest level of classification under the U.S. system and, therefore, requires the highest level of security control.

18. A. Tokenization techniques use a lookup table and are designed to be reversible. Masking and hashing techniques replace the data with values that can't be reversed back to the original data if performed properly. Shredding, when conducted properly, physically destroys data so that it may not be recovered.

19. B. Data controllers are the entities who determine the reasons for processing personal information and direct the methods of processing that data. This term is used primarily in European law, and it serves as a substitute for the term *data owner* to avoid a presumption that anyone who collects data has an ownership interest in that data.

20. D. The residual risk is the risk that remains after an organization implements controls designed to mitigate, avoid, and/or transfer the inherent risk.

Chapter 4: Cybersecurity Threats

1. B. Although higher levels of detail can be useful, they aren't a common measure used to assess threat intelligence. Instead, the timeliness, accuracy, and relevance of the information are considered critical to determining whether you should use the threat information.

2. C. STIX is an XML-based language, allowing it to be easily extended and modified while also using standard XML-based editors, readers, and other tools.

3. A. Attacks that are conducted as part of an authorized penetration test are white-hat hacking attacks, regardless of whether they are conducted by internal employees or an external firm. Kolin is, therefore, engaged in white-hat hacking. If he were acting on his own, without authorization, his status would depend on his intent. If he had malicious intent, his activity would be considered black-hat hacking. If he simply intended to report vulnerabilities to the hospital, his attack would be considered gray hat. Green hat is not a commonly used category of attacker.

4. A. Advanced persistent threats (APTs) are most commonly associated with nation-state actors. It is unlikely that an APT group would leverage the unsophisticated services of a script kiddie. It is also unlikely that a hacktivist would have access to APT resources. Although APTs may take advantage of insider access, they are most commonly associated with nation-state actors.

5. D. The U.S. government created the Information Sharing and Analysis Centers (ISACs). ISACs help infrastructure owners and operators share threat information, and they provide tools and assistance to their members.

6. A. Nation-state actors are government-sponsored, and they typically have the greatest access to resources, including tools, money, and talent.

7. A. Email is the most common threat vector exploited by attackers who use phishing and other social engineering tactics to gain access to an organization. The other vectors listed here—direct access, wireless, and removable media—all require physical proximity to an organization and are not easily executed from a remote location.

8. D. The Chinese military and U.S. government are examples of nation-state actors and advanced persistent threats (APTs). The Russian mafia is an example of a criminal syndicate. Anonymous is the world's most prominent hacktivist group.

9. A. Behavioral assessments are very useful when you are attempting to identify insider threats. Since insider threats are often hard to distinguish from normal behavior, the context of the actions performed—such as after-hours logins, misuse of credentials, logins from abnormal locations, or abnormal patterns—and other behavioral indicators are often used.

10. D. TAXII, the Trusted Automated Exchange of Intelligence Information protocol, is specifically designed to communicate cyberthreat information at the application layer. OpenIOC is a compromise indicator framework, and STIX is a threat description language.

11. A. Tampering with equipment before it reaches the intended user is an example of a supply chain threat. It is also possible to describe this attack as a direct access attack because it involved physical access to the device, but supply chain is a more relevant answer. You should be prepared to select the best possible choice from several possible correct answers when you take the exam. Exam questions often use this type of misdirection.

12. B. All of these resources might contain information about the technical details of TLS, but Internet Request for Comments (RFC) documents are the definitive technical standards for Internet protocols. Consulting the RFCs would be Ken's best option.

13. C. All of these items could be concerning, depending on the circumstances. However, API keys should *never* be found in public repositories because they may grant unauthorized individuals access to information and resources.

14. A. Threat maps are graphical tools that display information about the geographic locations of attackers and their targets. These tools are most often used as interesting marketing gimmicks, but they can also help identify possible threat sources.

15. B. Specific details of attacks that may be used to identify compromises are known as indicators of compromise (IoCs). This data may also be described as an adversary tactic, technique, or procedure (TTP), but the fact that it is a set of file signatures makes it more closely match the definition of an IoC.

16. A. The developers in question are using unapproved technology for business purposes. This is the classic definition of shadow IT. It is possible to describe this as data exfiltration, but there is no indication that the data security has been compromised, so shadow IT is a better description here. Remember, you will often be asked to choose the best answer from multiple correct answers on the exam.

17. A. Tom's greatest concern should be that running unsupported software exposes his organization to the risk of new, unpatchable vulnerabilities. It is certainly true that Tom will no longer receive technical support, but this is a less important issue from a security perspective. There is no indication in this scenario that discontinuing the product will result in the theft of customer information or increased costs.

18. C. Port scans are an active reconnaissance technique that probe target systems and would not be considered open source intelligence (OSINT). Search engine research, DNS lookups, and WHOIS queries are all open source resources.

19. A, C. As a government contractor, Snowden had authorized access to classified information and exploited this access to make an unauthorized disclosure of that information. This clearly makes him fit into the category of an insider. He did so with political motivations, making him fit the category of hacktivist as well.

20. C. Renee was not authorized to perform this security testing, so her work does not fit into the category of white-hat hacking. However, she also does not have malicious intent, so her work cannot be categorized as a black-hat attack. Instead, it fits somewhere in between the two extremes and would best be described as gray-hat hacking.

Chapter 5: Information Security Program Development and Management

1. B. Information security program charters commonly contain high-level organizational items, such as a scope statement, statement of roles and responsibilities, and description of the governance structure. A project schedule is a more tactical document that would not normally be included in a program-level charter due to its changing nature.

2. C. Privilege creep occurs when an employee transfers within the organization and does not have their old privileges revoked. Privilege creep may occur when transfers are not properly processed and, if left unchecked, violates the principle of least privilege.

3. C. The best-case scenario is that expenses are close to the budgeted amount but do not exceed the actual budget. Budget overages are difficult because funds may not be available to cover all expenses. When expenses are significantly under budget, the organization suffers an opportunity cost because those funds could have been used for other purposes or returned to shareholders as profit.

4. D. Steering committees help facilitate alignment between security and business objectives. The security manager can convene a group that represents business units and get their input in the development of security plans. The change advisory board (CAB) is designed to manage change requests, not to provide input on security activities. Senior leadership teams and the board operate at an executive level and would not likely have the time or expertise to participate in this effort.

5. D. The information security program charter should contain program documentation procedures that formalize how the organization will establish, communicate, and maintain information security standards and other documents. This would not be found in a short scope statement, a request for change (RFC), or a nondisclosure agreement (NDA).

6. D. Awareness efforts are not designed to impart new knowledge but simply to remind employees of security information they have already learned. Of the techniques listed here, only posters are an awareness mechanism. All of the other techniques are training tools designed to impart new knowledge.

7. A. Data ownership language should be legally binding and part of the master agreement with the vendor. As it is such an important topic, it should be included in the formal contract with the vendor. It is not appropriate subject matter for a nondisclosure agreement (NDA) that focuses on confidentiality or a less formal vehicle, such as a memorandum of understanding (MOU) or statement of work (SOW).

8. D. Key performance indicators (KPIs) are metrics that demonstrate the success of the security program in achieving its objectives. KPIs are mutually agreed-upon measures that evaluate whether a security program is meeting its defined goals. Generally speaking, KPIs are a look back at historical performance, providing a measuring stick to evaluate the past success of the program. Key goal indicators (KGIs) are similar to KPIs but measure progress toward defined goals. For example, if an organization has a goal to eliminate all stored Social Security numbers (SSNs), a KGI might track the percentage of SSNs removed. Key risk indicators (KRIs) are measures that seek to quantify the security risk facing an organization. KRIs, unlike KPIs and KGIs, are a look forward. They attempt to show how much risk exists that may jeopardize the future security of the organization. KMIs are not a standard metric for cybersecurity programs.

9. D. This is an operational expense, since it is a payroll expenditure, rather than a large purchase of capital equipment. The cost of hiring an employee is a recurring cost, rather than a one-time cost. The scenario does not identify whether the expense was budgeted or unbudgeted.

10. A. Gary's organization uses a fiscal year beginning on January 1. This means that the fiscal year and calendar year are aligned and they will always be the same. June 2024 is a month during the calendar year 2024 and, because the fiscal year is aligned with the calendar year, it is also the fiscal year 2024.

11. B. When following the separation of duties principle, organizations divide critical tasks into discrete components and ensure that no one individual has the ability to perform both actions. This prevents a single rogue individual from performing that task in an unauthorized manner.

12. D. Mandatory vacation programs require that employees take continuous periods of time off each year and revoke their system privileges during that time. The purpose of these required vacation periods is to disrupt any attempt to engage in the cover-up actions necessary to hide fraud and result in exposing the threat. Separation of duties, least privilege, and defense-in-depth controls all may help prevent the fraud in the first place but are unlikely to speed the detection of fraud that has already occurred.

13. A. Charles is tracking a key performance indicator (KPI). A KPI is used to measure performance (and success). Without a definition of success, this would simply be a metric, but Charles is working toward a known goal and can measure against it. There is not a return investment calculation in this problem, and the measure is not a control.

14. B. Certifications help employees validate their skills and are an important recruiting and retention tool. Training programs help employees keep their skills current and develop skills in new areas of cybersecurity. Awareness efforts are meant to reinforce security knowledge. Accreditation processes are used to formally certify systems in government and military applications.

15. C. In a formal change management program, all changes require an RFC, no matter how minor. However, some routine changes have preapproved status and may be made as soon as the RFC is submitted. RFCs for these changes are automatically approved. Once someone submits an RFC for review, it must be approved by a relevant authority. For minor changes, this may simply be the person's manager. In the case of major changes, the organization's CAB may review and approve the change. The primary purpose of change management is to minimize the probability and impact of disruptions to IT services due to changes. Change management does support audits, but this is not the primary purpose of the function.

16. A. Background screening often includes criminal background checks, sex offender registry lookups, reference checks, and employment/education verification. In some cases, organizations may perform credit checks to further investigate an employee's background, although obtaining and using this information requires written consent and is heavily regulated, so many organizations skip this part of checks.

17. A. The most appropriate standard to use as a baseline when evaluating vendors is to determine whether the vendor's security controls meet the organization's own standards. Compliance with laws and regulations should be included in that requirement and are a necessary, but not sufficient, condition for working with the vendor. Vendor compliance with their own policies also fits into the category of necessary, but not sufficient, controls, since the vendor's policy may be weaker than the organization's own requirements. The elimination of all identified security risks is an impossible requirement for a potential vendor to meet.

18. B. The current governance structure allows these subsidiaries to remain independent. Therefore, it is not appropriate to include them in the parent organization's program or replace their programs. Instead, Abe should limit the portion of the organization included in his program, which is a limitation of scope.

19. C. Key risk indicators (KRIs) are measures that seek to quantify the security risk facing an organization. KRIs, unlike KPIs and KGIs, are a look forward. They attempt to show how much risk exists that may jeopardize the future security of the organization. Key performance indicators (KPIs) are metrics that demonstrate the success of the security program in achieving its objectives. KPIs are mutually agreed-upon measures that evaluate whether a security program is meeting its defined goals. Generally speaking, KPIs are a look back at historical performance, providing a measuring stick to evaluate the past success of the program. Key goal indicators (KGIs) are similar to KPIs but measure progress toward defined goals. For example, if an organization has a goal to eliminate all stored Social Security numbers (SSNs), a KGI might track the percentage of SSNs removed. KMIs are not a standard metric for cybersecurity programs.

20. D. One common mistake made by information security managers is to develop a dashboard or web page with updated metrics and then simply inform stakeholders that they may view those metrics whenever they like. This approach has two major drawbacks. First, stakeholders who are not involved in security on a day-to-day basis are unlikely to revisit the site unless prompted to do so periodically. Second, providing metrics is only one piece of the picture. Security managers should also provide context for those metrics to explain changes and update stakeholders on the progress of the program.

Chapter 6: Security Assessment and Testing

1. C. Threat hunting is an assessment technique that makes an assumption of compromise and then searches the organization for indicators of compromise that confirm the assumption. Vulnerability scanning, penetration testing, and war driving are all assessment techniques that probe for vulnerabilities but do not assume that a compromise has already taken place.

2. D. Credentialed scans require only read-only access to target servers. Renee should follow the principle of least privilege and limit the access available to the scanner.

3. C. Ryan should first run his scan against a test environment to identify likely vulnerabilities and assess whether the scan itself might disrupt business activities.

4. C. The scenario does not provide us with enough information to determine whether this exercise involved red team, blue team, or purple team tactics, and in fact, those exercises typically involve live access to systems. Tabletop exercises, on the other hand, are designed to walk teams through a scenario, and that is what Tina is doing in this instance.

5. A. A false positive error occurs when the vulnerability scanner reports a vulnerability that does not actually exist.

6. B. By allowing students to change their own grades, this vulnerability provides a pathway to unauthorized alteration of information. Brian should recommend that the school deploy integrity controls that prevent unauthorized modifications.

7. D. There is no reason that an organization can't run vulnerability scans on weekends or holidays. On the other hand, vulnerability scan possibilities may be limited by technical constraints, regulatory requirements, and license limitations.

8. A. This vulnerability is corrected by a patch that was released by Microsoft in 2017. A strong patch management program would have identified and remediated the missing patch.

9. B. Intrusion detection systems do not detect vulnerabilities; they detect attacks. The remaining three tools could all possibly discover a cross-site scripting (XSS) vulnerability, but a web application vulnerability scanner is the most likely to detect it because it is specifically designed to test web applications.

10. A. Moving from one compromised system to other systems on the same network is known as lateral movement. Privilege escalation attacks increase the level of access that an attacker has to an already compromised system. Footprinting and OSINT are reconnaissance techniques.

11. A. Offensive hacking is used by red teams as they attempt to gain access to systems on the target network. Blue teams are responsible for managing the organization's defenses. White teams serve as the neutral moderators of the exercise. Purple teaming is conducted after an exercise to bring together the red and blue teams for knowledge sharing.

12. C. Bug bounty programs are designed to allow external security experts to test systems and uncover previously unknown vulnerabilities. Bug bounty programs offer successful testers financial rewards to incentivize their participation.

13. D. Backdoors are a persistence tool, designed to make sure that the attacker's access persists after the original vulnerability is remediated. Kyle can use this backdoor to gain access to the system in the future, even if the original exploit that he used to gain access is no longer effective.

14. C. WHOIS lookups use external registries and are an example of open source intelligence (OSINT), which is a passive reconnaissance technique. Port scans, vulnerability scans, and footprinting all require active engagement with the target and are, therefore, active reconnaissance.

15. D. Penetration testers must take a very different approach in their thinking. Instead of trying to defend against all possible threats, they only need to find a single vulnerability that they might exploit to achieve their goals. To find these flaws, they must think like the adversary who might attack the system in the real world. This approach is commonly known as adopting the *hacker mindset*.

16. C. White-box tests are performed with full knowledge of the underlying technology, configurations, and settings that make up the target. Black-box tests are intended to replicate what an attacker would encounter. Testers are not provided with access to or information about an environment, but instead, they must gather information, discover vulnerabilities, and make their way through an infrastructure or systems as an attacker would. Gray-box tests are a blend of black-box and white-box testing. Blue-box tests are not a type of penetration test.

17. C. The rules of engagement provide technical details on the parameters of the test. This level of detail would not normally be found in a contract or statement of work. The lessons learned report is not produced until after the test.

18. B. All of these techniques might provide Grace with information about the operating system running on a device. However, footprinting is a technique specifically designed to elicit this information.

19. A. Privilege escalation is the act of increasing the level of access that an attacker has to a system. It is a common exploit to launch after gaining initial access to a system in an attempt to gain administrative access (otherwise known as root or superuser access).

20. A. Black-box tests are intended to replicate what an attacker would encounter. Testers are not provided with access to or information about an environment, and instead, they must gather information, discover vulnerabilities, and make their way through an infrastructure or systems like an attacker would. White-box tests are performed with full knowledge of the underlying technology, configurations, and settings that make up the target. Gray-box tests are a blend of black-box and white-box testing. Blue-box tests are not a type of penetration test.

Chapter 7: Cybersecurity Technology

1. D. The cloud service provider bears the most responsibility for implementing security controls in an SaaS environment and the least responsibility in an IaaS environment. This is due to the division of responsibilities under the cloud computing shared responsibility model.

2. B. Adam is conducting static code analysis by reviewing the source code. Dynamic code analysis requires running the program, and both mutation testing and fuzzing are types of dynamic analysis.

3. B. Port security restricts the number of unique MAC addresses that may originate from a single switch port. It is commonly used to prevent someone from unplugging an authorized device from the network and connecting an unauthorized device but may also be used to prevent existing devices from spoofing MAC addresses of other devices.

4. B. Developers working on active changes to code should always work in the development environment. The test environment is where the software or systems can be tested without impacting the production environment. The staging environment is a transition environment for code that has successfully cleared testing and is waiting to be deployed into production. The production environment is the live system. Software, patches, and other changes that have been tested and approved move to production.

5. C. One of the important characteristics of cloud computing is that customers can access resources on-demand with minimal service provider interaction. Cloud customers do not need to contact a sales representative each time they wish to provision a resource but can normally do so on a self-service basis.

6. A. If Patricia's major concern is a compromised operating system, she can bypass the operating system on the device by booting it from live boot media and running her own operating system on the hardware. Running a malware scan may provide her with some information but may not detect all compromises, and Patricia likely does not have the necessary permissions to correct any issues. Using a VPN or accessing secure sites would not protect her against a compromised operating system, as the operating system would be able to view the contents of her communication prior to encryption.

7. C. In a true positive report, the system reports an attack when an attack actually exists. A false positive report occurs when the system reports an attack that did not take place. A true negative report occurs when the system reports no attack and no attack took place. A false negative report occurs when the system does not report an attack that did take place.

8. A. Hardware security modules (HSMs) provide an effective way to manage encryption keys. These hardware devices store and manage encryption keys in a secure manner that prevents humans from ever needing to work directly with the keys.

9. D. The attack in question could be most quickly stopped with a network firewall rule blocking all traffic from the origin system. Host firewall rules would also address the issue but would be more time-consuming to create on every system. An operating system update would not stop attack traffic. There is also no indication that a DDoS attack is underway, so a DDoS mitigation service would not be helpful.

10. C. This is an example of adding additional capacity to an existing server, which is also known as vertical scaling. Kevin could also have used horizontal scaling by adding additional web servers. Elasticity involves the ability to both add and remove capacity on demand, and though it does describe this scenario, it's not as good a description as vertical scaling. There is no mention of increasing the server's availability.

11. B. Although this example includes continuous integration, the important thing to notice is that the code is then deployed into production. This means that Susan is operating in a continuous deployment environment, where code is both continually integrated and deployed. Agile is a development methodology that often uses CI/CD, but we cannot determine if Susan is using an Agile methodology.

12. D. Facial recognition technology is an example of a biometric authentication technique, or "something you are." A passcode is an example of a knowledge-based authentication technique, or "something you know."

13. B. The false rejection rate (FRR) identifies the number of times that an individual who should be allowed access to a facility is rejected. The false acceptance rate (FAR) identifies the number of times that an individual who should not be allowed access to a facility is admitted. Both the FAR and FRR may be manipulated by changing system settings. The crossover error rate (CER) is the rate at which the FRR and FAR are equal and is less prone to manipulation. Therefore, the CER is the best measure for Fred to use. IRR is not a measure of biometric system effectiveness.

14. C. Gary is proving his identity with his fingerprint, a biometric mechanism. Steps that prove your identity are examples of authentication techniques.

15. B. This type of authentication, where one domain trusts users from another domain, is called federation. Federation may involve transitive trusts, where the trusts may be followed through a series of domains, but this scenario only describes the use of two domains. And it also only describes the use of credentials for a single system and not for a multiple-system scenario where single sign-on would be relevant. There is no requirement described for the use of multifactor authentication, which would require the use of two or more diverse authentication techniques.

16. D. The principle of data sovereignty states that data is subject to the legal restrictions of any jurisdiction where it is collected, stored, or processed. In this case, Howard needs to assess the laws of all three jurisdictions.

17. C. When encrypting a confidential message using an asymmetric encryption algorithm, the person performing the encryption does so using the recipient's public key.

18. D. In an asymmetric encryption algorithm, the recipient of a confidential message uses their own private key to decrypt messages that they receive.

19. B. The sender of a message may digitally sign the message by encrypting a message digest with the sender's own private key.

20. A. The recipient of a digitally signed message may verify the digital signature by decrypting it with the public key of the individual who signed the message.

Chapter 8: Incident Response

1. D. A former employee crashing a server is an example of a computer security incident because it is an actual violation of the availability of that system. An intruder breaking into a building may be a security event, but it is not necessarily a computer security event unless they perform some action affecting a computer system. A user accessing a secure file and an administrator changing a file permission settings are examples of security events but are not security incidents.

2. A. Organizations should build solid, defense-in-depth approaches to cybersecurity during the preparation phase of the incident response process. The controls built during this phase serve to reduce the likelihood and impact of future incidents.

3. C. A security information and event management (SIEM) system correlates log entries from multiple sources and attempts to identify potential security incidents.

4. C. The definition of a medium functional impact is that the organization has lost the ability to provide a critical service to a subset of system users. That accurately describes the situation that Ben finds himself in. Assigning a low functional impact is only done when the organization can provide all critical services to all users at diminished efficiency. Assigning a high functional impact is only done if a critical service is not available to all users.

5. C. The containment protocols included in the containment, eradication, and recovery phases are designed to limit the damage caused by an ongoing security incident.

6. D. National Archives General Records Schedule (GRS) 24 requires that all U.S. federal agencies retain incident handling records for at least three years.

7. C. In a proprietary breach, unclassified proprietary information is accessed or exfiltrated. Protected critical infrastructure information (PCII) is an example of unclassified proprietary information.

8. A. The Network Time Protocol (NTP) provides a common source of time information that allows the synchronizing of clocks throughout an enterprise.

9. A. An organization's incident response policy should contain a clear description of the authority assigned to the CSIRT while responding to an active security incident.

10. D. A web attack is an attack executed from a website or web-based application—for example, a cross-site scripting attack used to steal credentials or redirect to a site that exploits a browser vulnerability and installs malware.

11. A. CSIRT members do not normally communicate directly with the perpetrator of a cyber-security incident. Although team members may have contact with the perpetrator in the case of ransomware attacks, this would not normally be the case during an incident involving the theft of information. It is far more likely that the CSIRT would be in routine contact with vendors, law enforcement, and information sharing partners as the incident unfolds.

12. A. The incident response policy provides the CSIRT with the authority needed to do their job. Therefore, it should be approved by the highest possible level of authority within the organization, preferably the CEO.

13. A. Detection of a potential incident occurs during the detection and analysis phase of incident response. The other activities listed might all be objectives of the containment, eradication, and recovery phase.

14. C. Extended recoverability effort occurs when the time to recovery is unpredictable. In those cases, additional resources and outside help are typically needed.

15. D. An attrition attack employs brute-force methods to compromise, degrade, or destroy systems, networks, or services—for example, a DDoS attack intended to impair or deny access to a service or application or a brute-force attack against an authentication mechanism.

16. C. Lessons learned sessions are most effective when facilitated by an independent party who was not involved in the incident response effort.

17. D. Procedures for rebuilding systems are highly technical and would normally be included in a playbook or procedure document rather than an incident response policy.

18. B. An impersonation attack involves the replacement of something benign with something malicious—spoofing, on-path attacks, rogue wireless access points, and SQL injection attacks all involve impersonation.

19. C. Incident response playbooks contain detailed step-by-step instructions that guide the early response to a cybersecurity incident. Organizations typically have playbooks prepared for high-severity and frequently occurring incident types.

20. A. The event described in this scenario would not qualify as a security incident with measurable information impact. Although the laptop did contain information that might cause a privacy breach, that breach was avoided by the use of encryption to protect the contents of the laptop.

Chapter 9: Business Continuity and Disaster Recovery

1. C. This question requires that you exercise some judgment, as do many questions on the CISM exam. All of these answers are plausible things that Tracy could bring up, but we're looking for the best answer. In this case, that is ensuring that the organization is ready for an emergency—a mission-critical goal. Telling managers that the exercise is already scheduled or required by policy doesn't address their concerns that it is a waste of time. Telling them that it won't be time-consuming is not likely to be an effective argument because they are already raising concerns about the amount of time requested.

2. C. A firm's officers and directors are legally bound to exercise due diligence in conducting their activities. This concept creates a fiduciary responsibility on their part to ensure that adequate business continuity plans are in place. This is an element of corporate responsibility, but that term is vague and not commonly used to describe a board's responsibilities. Disaster requirement and going concern responsibilities are also not risk management terms.

3. C. The annualized loss expectancy (ALE) represents the amount of money a business expects to lose to a given risk each year. This figure is quite useful when performing a quantitative prioritization of business continuity resource allocation.

4. C. The maximum tolerable downtime (MTD) represents the longest period a business function can be unavailable before causing irreparable harm to the business. This figure is useful when determining the level of business continuity resources to assign to a particular function.

5. B. The single loss expectancy (SLE) is the product of the asset value (AV) and the exposure factor (EF). From the scenario, you know that the AV is $3 million and the EF is 90 percent, based on that the same land can be used to rebuild the facility. This yields an SLE of $2,700,000.

6. A. This problem requires you to compute the ALE, which is the product of the SLE and ARO. From the scenario, you know that the ARO is 0.10 (or 10 percent). From the scenario presented, you know that the SLE is $7.5 million. This yields an ALE of $750,000.

7. D. The safety of human life must always be the paramount concern in business continuity planning. Be sure that your plan reflects this priority, especially in the written documentation that is disseminated to your organization's employees!

8. C. It is difficult to put a dollar figure on the business lost because of negative publicity. Therefore, this type of concern is better evaluated through qualitative analysis. The other items listed here are all more easily quantifiable.

9. A. The annualized rate of occurrence (ARO) is the likelihood that the risk will materialize in any given year. The fact that a power outage did not occur in any of the past three years doesn't change the probability that one will occur in the upcoming year. Unless other circumstances have changed, the ARO should remain the same.

10. C. You should strive to have the highest-ranking person possible sign the BCP's statement of importance. Of the choices given, the chief executive officer (CEO) is the highest ranking.

11. C. The recovery point objective (RPO) specifies the maximum amount of data that may be lost during a disaster and should be used to guide backup strategies. The maximum tolerable downtime (MTD) and recovery time objective (RTO) are related to the duration of an outage, rather than the amount of data lost. The mean time between failures (MTBF) is related to the frequency of failure events.

12. D. The lessons learned session captures discoveries made during the disaster recovery process and facilitates continuous improvement. It may identify deficiencies in training and awareness or the BIA.

13. B. Redundant arrays of inexpensive disks (RAID) are a fault tolerance control that allows an organization's storage service to withstand the loss of one or more individual disks. Load balancing, clustering, and HA pairs are all fault-tolerance services designed for server compute capacity, not storage.

14. C. Cloud computing services provide an excellent location for backup storage because they are accessible from any location. The primary data center is a poor choice, as it may be damaged during a disaster. A field office is reasonable, but it is in a specific location and is not as flexible as a cloud-based approach. The IT manager's home is a poor choice, as the IT manager may leave the organization or may not have appropriate environmental and physical security controls in place.

15. B. The term *100-year flood plain* is used to describe an area where flooding is expected once every 100 years. It is, however, more mathematically correct to say that this label indicates a 1 percent probability of flooding in any given year.

16. C. All of these are good practices that could help improve the quality of service that Bryn provides from her website. Installing dual power supplies or deploying RAID arrays could reduce the likelihood of a server failure, but these measures only protect against a single risk each. Deploying multiple servers behind a load balancer is the best option because it protects against any type of risk that would cause a server failure. Backups are an important control for recovering operations after a disaster and different backup strategies could indeed alter the RTO, but it is even better if Bryn can design a web architecture that lowers the risk of the outage occurring in the first place.

17. C. The cold site contains none of the equipment necessary to restore operations. All of the equipment must be brought in and configured and data must be restored to it before operations can commence. This often takes weeks, but cold sites also have the lowest cost to implement. Hot sites, warm sites, and mobile sites all have quicker recovery times.

18. D. The parallel test involves relocating personnel to the alternate recovery site and implementing site activation procedures. Checklist tests, structured walkthroughs, and simulations are all test types that do not involve actually activating the alternate site.

19. A. Differential backups involve always storing copies of all files modified since the most recent full backup regardless of any incremental or differential backups created during the intervening time period.

20. B. People should always be your highest priority in business continuity planning. As a life safety system, fire suppression systems should always receive high prioritization.

Index

A

access, revoking, 135
access management, 136–138
access point (AP), 189
accidental alteration, 9
account maintenance, 137
account monitoring, 137–138, 239–240
accountable roles, within information security, 7–8
accounting, 133, 136
action plans, for information security strategy, 19–20
actor, threat, 12, 92, 94–99
actual cash value (ACV) clause, 332
Acunetix, 157
adaptive tier (NIST Cybersecurity Framework), 51
administrative investigation, regarding security incident, 279–280
admissible evidence, from security incident, 282
Advanced Encryption Standard (AES), 215
advanced persistent threat (APT), 92, 96–97, 275
agent-based scanning, 153
Agile, 228–229, 231
agreements, 37–38, 134
algorithm, for encryption, 166
Align, Plan, and Organize (APO) objective, 48
alteration (DAD Triad), 8–9
Always-On VPN, 192
Amazon Web Services (AWS), 199, 203
annualized loss expectancy (ALE), 69–70, 309
annualized rate of occurrence (ARO), 68, 308
anomaly detection, 193–194
Anonymous hacking group, 95
antimalware software, 183
anything as a service (XaaS), 198
application programming interfaces (API), 210
application scanning, 157
applications, cloud security of, 210
approval statement, of information security program, 120
Arachni, 157, 158
artifact, from security incident, 282
assessment

defined, 57
within disaster recovery planning (DRP), 343
likelihood, 308
qualitative/quantitative impact, 304
of risk, 68–72
of supply chains, 71
of threat intelligence, 105–106
asset classification, 81
asset criticality information, 147
asset inventory, 147
asset management, 50
asset return agreement, 134
asset value (AV), 68
asymmetric cryptosystem, 212
asymmetric key algorithm, 215–217
attacker, within security incident, 262–263
attestation process, 137
audit, 56, 138–139, 210
auditor, cloud service, 198
Australian Signals Directorate Cyber Security Centre, 103
authentication, 213–214, 234–238
authorization step, of access control process, 234
Automated Indicator Sharing (AIS) program, 103
availability, 2, 3, 25, 208
AWS Outposts, 203–204
Azure (Microsoft), 199

B

backup, 329, 342–344
baselining, 185
BCI Good Practice Guideline (GPG), 340
benchmarks, 54–56
best evidence rule, 283
biometric authentication, 235
black-box test, 171
black-hat hacker, 93
board of directors, 34
budget, security, 127–130
bug bounty program, 171

Build, Acquire, and Implement (BAI) objective, 48
business alignment, 120–121
business case, development of, 36–37
business continuity planning (BCP)
    business impact analysis (BIA) and, 304–310
    continuity planning phase of, 310–313
    documentation within, 314–318
    exam essentials for, 349–350
    legal and regulatory requirements
        within, 303–304
    organizational review within, 300
    overview of, 298–299
    plan approval and implementation phase
        of, 313–318
    project scope and planning within, 299–304
    provisions and processes phase of, 311–313
    resource requirements for, 302–303
    review questions and answers for,
        351–355, 374–376
    strategy development phase of, 311
    team selection within, 301–302
    training within, 314
business environment, 17
business impact analysis (BIA), 79, 304–310, 332
business leaders, information security
    manager as, 3–4
business partnership agreement (BPA), 37
business purpose, of information security
    program, 119
business strategy, alignment with, 16–17
business unit, functional properties and, 332–333

C

Camp Fire, 322
Capability Maturity Model Integration
    (CMMI), 15
capital expenses (CapEx), 128
capture the flag (CTF) exercises, 124, 175
carrier, cloud service, 198
Center for Internet Security (CIS), 55
Centers for Medicare and Medicaid Services
    (CMS), 39–40
certificate authorities (CA), 220
certificate revocation list (CRL), 221, 222
certificate signing request (CSR), 221
certificate stapling, 222–223
certification program, 53, 126
chain of command, within policy development, 46

chain of evidence, 283–284
change advisory board (CAB), 138
change management, 138, 185
charter, of information security program, 118–121
checklist, within disaster recovery planning
    (DRP), 341–342
chief audit executive, 5
chief executive officer (CEO), 5, 34–35
chief information officer (CIO), 4–6
chief information security officer (CISO), 4–7, 139
chief operating officer (COO), 5
chief risk officer (CRO), 5
chief security officer (CSO), 5
CIA Triad, 3, 9, 25, 168
Cisco, 103
civil investigation, regarding security
    incident, 280–281
closed source intelligence, 104–105
cloud access security broker (CASB), 211
cloud computing
    benefits of, 196–197
    business impact analysis (BIA) and, 307–308
    community, 203
    defined, 195
    deployment models of, 202–204
    as disaster recovery option, 337–338
    hybrid, 203
    private, 202–203
    public, 202
    redundancy capabilities within, 339
    roles within, 198
    service models within, 198–202
    standards and guidelines within, 207–208
    as threat vector, 100
cloud computing security, 195–196,
    204–206, 208–212
Cloud Controls Matrix (CCM), 207–208
Cloud Reference Architecture, 207
Cloud Security Alliance (CSA), 207
code deployment environment, 225
code security, 223–233
cold site, 335
communication, 19, 20, 274, 334, 341–342
community cloud, 203
compensating control, 22, 44–45
compliance risk, 11
Computer Emergency Readiness Team (CERT)
    (CISA), 103
Computer Security Incident Handling Guide,
    256–257, 260–262, 271

computer security incident response team (CSIRT), 252, 253, 272–274, 289
computer-based training (CBT), 123
confidentiality, 2, 3, 25, 81, 213
configuration management systems, 161, 185
configuration review, 150
conflict of interest, with information security, 5
consulted roles within information security, 7–8
consumer, cloud service, 198
containment, from security incident, 255–263
continuity planning, for BCP, 310–313
continuous account monitoring system, 137
continuous development (CD), 230
continuous integration (CI), 230
control objective, 13–14, 20–21
Control Objectives for Information Technology (COBIT), 14, 47–49
control risk, 76
controller, data, 82
corporate governance, 33–35
corrective control, 22
cost analysis, 36
COVID-19 pandemic, 323
credentialed scanning, 152
credit check, 134
criminal investigation, regarding security incident, 280
criminal syndicates, 96
crisis management, 333
cross-cutting crime factor, as cybercrime, 96
crossover error rate (CER), of authentication, 237–238
cryptography
    asymmetric, 215–217
    authentication within, 213–214
    certificate generation and destruction within, 220–223
    confidentiality within, 212–213
    defined, 212
    digital certificates within, 219–220
    digital signatures within, 218–219
    goals of, 212–214
    hash functions within, 217–218
    integrity within, 213
    nonrepudiation within, 214
    symmetric key algorithms within, 214–215
culture, within policy development, 46
custodian, data, 18, 82
customer, as data owners, 131
cyberattacks, 19

cyber-dependent crime, 96
cybersecurity, 2, 6–7, 18–19
Cybersecurity and Infrastructure Security Agency (CISA), 102
Cybersecurity Framework (CSF), 49–52
cybersecurity professionals, 3
cybersecurity technology
    configuration management, 185
    data loss prevention (DLP), 184
    DDoS prevention within, 194–195
    endpoint detection and response (EDR) platform, 183
    endpoint security, 182–186
    exam essentials for, 241–243
    intrusion detection and prevention, 192–194
    malware prevention, 183
    network security, 186–195
    network segmentation, 186–188
    patch management, 185
    review questions and answers for, 244–247, 370–372
    system hardening, 185–186
    virtual private networks (VPNs), 191–192
cybersecurity threat
    actors within, 12, 92, 94–99
    advanced persistent threat (APT) as, 96–97
    classifying, 92–93
    competitors as, 98–99
    criminal syndicates as, 96
    data and intelligence within, 101–109
    exam essentials for, 109–110
    hacktivist as, 94–96
    insider attack as, 97–98
    intent/motivation of, 93
    internal, 96
    internal *versus* external, 92
    overview of, 92–100
    resources/funding for, 93
    review questions and answers for, 111–114, 363–365
    script kiddie as, 94
    shadow IT as, 98
    sophistication/capability level of, 92
    threat vectors within, 99–100

D

DAD Triad, 8–9
dark web, 96, 98–99, 103–104
data

breach, 47, 84
controller, 82
custodian, 18, 82
data loss prevention (DLP), 23–24, 184
encryption, 23
exfiltration, 8
loss, 8
masking, 84
minimization, 24–25, 83
in motion, 23, 213
obfuscation, 24–25, 83
owners/ownership, 18, 82, 131
in processing, 23
processor, 18, 82
protection, 23–25
protection officer, 82–83
at rest, 23, 212
retention of, 83
roles and responsibilities within, 82–83
sensitive information within, 80
sovereignty, 208–209
steward, 18, 82
subject, 82
threat, 101–109
in use, 213
database recovery, 338–340
debug mode, 164–165
decryption, 212
defensive behaviors, of penetration testing, 172
Defined level of CMMI, 15
de-identification process, 24, 83–84
Deliver, Service, and Support (DSS) objective, 48
demilitarized zone (DMZ) network, 187
demonstrative evidence, from security incident, 285
denial (DAD Triad), 9
denial-of-service (DoS), 69, 194
Department of Homeland Security, 107
deprovisioning, 238–239
detection and analysis phase, of security incident
    response, 254–255
detective control, 22
deterrent control, 22
device security, network, 188–191
DevOps, 229–230
DevSecOps, 229–230
differential backups, 343
digital certificates, 219–223
digital signature, 213, 218–219
direct access, as threat vector, 100
direct evidence, from security incident, 284
Director of Incident Response, 6
Director of Policy and Compliance, 6

Director of Security Engineering, 6
Director of Security Operations, 6
disaster, types of, 78–79
disaster recovery planning (DRP)
    alternate processing sites within, 334–338
    assessment within, 342
    backups within, 342–344
    business units within, 332–333
    checklists within, 341–342
    crisis management within, 333
    database recovery within, 338–340
    emergency communications within, 334
    emergency response of, 341
    exam essentials for, 349–350
    logistics and supplies within, 345
    maintenance within, 348–349
    offsite storage within, 342–344
    overview of, 78–79, 298–299, 318–327
    personnel within, 341–342
    review questions and answers for,
        351–355, 374–376
    strategy for, 331–339
    testing within, 346–348
    training within, 345–349
    utility plan within, 345
    workgroup recovery within, 334
disclosure (DAD Triad), 8
disk-to-disk (D2D) backup, 344
distributed denial-of-service (DDoS), 9,
    72–75, 194–195
documentary evidence, from security incident, 283
domain validation (DV) certificate, 221
dynamic code analysis, 233
dynamic testing, 157

E

earthquake, 319, 320
Electronic Discovery Reference Model
    (EDRM), 281–282
Electronic Signature Guidelines (Washington
    state), 43–44
electronic vaulting, 338–339
email, as threat vector, 99
emergency response guidelines, 317, 341
employees, 133–135
encryption, 21, 23, 166–167, 212
end of life (EOL) agreement, 38
end of service life (EOSL) agreement, 38
endpoint detection and response (EDR)
    platform, 183

endpoint security, 182–186

enforcement mechanism, of information security program, 120

enrollment, within digital certificates, 221

enterprise risk management (ERM), 65, 78

eradication phase, of security incident, 263–266

Evaluate, Direct, and Monitor (EDM) objective, 48

evaluation of alternatives, within business cases, 36

evidence, from security incident, 268, 282–288

evidence production procedure, 43

exam essentials
  for business continuity, 349–350
  for cybersecurity technology, 241–243
  for cybersecurity threat, 109–110
  for disaster recovery planning (DRP), 349–350
  for incident response, 290–291
  for information risk management, 85
  for information security, 57–58
  information security manager, 25–26
  for information security program, 139–140
  for security assessment, 176

exception process, to security framework, 44–45

exit interview, 135

expenses, 128–129

exploitation frameworks, of penetration testing, 174

exposure factor (EF), 69, 309

extended validation (EV) certificate, 221

external risk, 66

F

Fagan inspection, 231–232

failover, 329–331

false acceptance rate (FAR), of authentication, 237–238

false positive error (vulnerability scanning), 161

false rejection rate (FRR), of authentication, 237–238

Family Educational Rights and Privacy Act (FERPA), 47

fault tolerance, 328, 331

federated identity management, 238

FEMA, 320, 321

File Transfer Protocol (FTP), 166

filtering, of routers, 188

financial information, 80

financial managers, 133

financial risk, 10

FireEye, 105

fires, 322–324

firewall, 21, 186–188, 190

fiscal year, 127–128

flooding, 319–321

footprinting, 173

FTP-Secure (FTPS), 166

full backups, 343

full-interruption test, 347

full-tunnel VPN, 192

function as a service (FaaS), 200

functional impact, of security incident, 276–277

fuzzing, 233

G

gamification, 124

gap analysis, 13–14

General Data Protection Regulation (GDPR), 47, 68, 83, 84

"get out of jail free" card, within penetration testing, 172

Google Cloud Platform (GCP), 199

governance, 33–38, 210

governance, risk, and compliance (GRC) program, 35

governance framework, 48

government information, 80–81

Gramm-Leach-Bliley Act (GLBA), 46

gray-box test, 171

gray-hat hacker, 93

Guidelines for Media Sanitization, 265

H

hackers, 93, 168–169

hacktivist, 94–96

hard drive, RAID array for, 328–329

hardware security module (HSM), 211–212

hardware/embedded device analysis, 288

Harvey, hurricane, 322, 325

hash functions, within cryptography, 217–218

hashing, 24, 83

HathiTrust, 203, 204

Health Insurance Portability and Accountability Act (HIPAA), 11, 46

hearsay rule, 284–285

heat map, 76–77

heuristic detection, 183

high availability, 328

high-risk user, training regarding, 19

hiring, 126, 133–134
host-based DLP, 23–24, 184
hot site, 336
HTML5 VPNs, 192
Human Resources (HR), 133–135
human-made disasters, 324–327
hybrid cloud, 203

I

identification step, of access control process, 234
identity and access management (IAM), 234–240
identity theft, 10
impact, magnitude of risk, 67
impossible travel time login, 137
in-band deployment, of intrusion detection system
    (IDS), 194
incident impact, 9–12
incremental backups, 343
incremental budgeting, 127
independent director, 34
indicator management of threat, 107–108
indicators of compromise (IoCs), 101
industry-specific standards, 42
information classification, 80–81
information risk management
    disaster recovery planning within, 78–79
    exam essentials for, 85
    overview of, 65
    privacy within, 79–84
    review questions and answers for,
        86–89, 362–363
    risk analyzing within, 65–78
    risk treatment and response within, 72–75
information security
    assessment of, 57
    audit of, 56
    benchmarks for, 54–56
    cybersecurity versus, 6–7
    defined, 7
    exam essentials for, 57–58
    laws and regulation compliance within, 46–47
    objectives of, 2–3
    quality control of, 56–57
    review questions and answers for,
        59–62, 360–361
    risks within, 8–12
    roles and responsibilities within, 7–8
    secure configuration guide of, 54–56
    standard frameworks within, 47–56
    verification of, 56–57

Information Security and Privacy Program Charter
    (University of Pennsylvania), 119
information security governance, 35–36
information security managers, 2–8,
    25–30, 358–359
information security policy framework, 38–46
information security program
    accounting and, 133
    approval statement of, 120
    audit and, 138–139
    with business functions, 130–139
    charter of, 118–121
    contracting and, 131–132
    defined, 117
    enforcement mechanisms of, 120
    establishing new, 117–121
    exam essentials for, 139–140
    existing program maintenance of, 121–123
    governance structure and processes of, 120
    Human Resources (HR) and, 133–135
    information technology and, 135–138
    metrics and monitoring of, 121–123
    overview of, 117
    procurement and, 130
    program documentation procedures of, 120
    reporting of, 123
    review process of, 120
    review questions and answers for,
        141–144, 365–368
    scope defining of, 118
    security awareness of, 123–125
    security patches within, 162
    security team within, 125–126
    stakeholders within, 119
    statement of authority within, 119
    vendor evaluation and, 130–131
information security strategy, 12–20
Information Sharing and Analysis Center
    (ISAC), 108
information technology, 135–138
Information Technology Infrastructure Library
    (ITIL), 122
informed roles within information security, 7–8
infrastructure as a service (IaaS), 199,
    206, 337–338
infrastructure vulnerability scanning, 156–157
inherent risk, 75
initial access, of penetration testing, 173
Initial level of CMMI, 15
in-memory analysis, 286
insider attack, 97–98
integrity, 2, 3, 25, 213

intellectual property (IP) theft, 67
intelligence, threat, 101–109
Intelligence Community (IC), 202–203
interactive testing, 157
interface, network, 187
internal risk, 67
International Organization for Standardization (ISO), 33, 53, 54
Internet Protocol Security (IPsec), 191
intranet, 187
intrusion detection system (IDS), 22, 192–194
intrusion prevention system (IPS), 192–194
intrusive plug-in, 151
investigations, regarding security incidents, 279–288
ISACA, COBIT and, 47–49
ISO 27001, 53
ISO 27002, 54
ISO 27004, 54
ISO 27701, 54
ISO 31000, 54
ISO Standard 27036, 133
isolation, within security incident, 258–260

J

job rotation, 136

K

key goal indicator (KGI), 122
key performance indicator (KPI), 122
key risk indicator (KRI), 72, 122–123
known environment test, 170

L

Lambda service, 200–201
lateral movement, of penetration testing, 174
law enforcement, security incident involvement of, 263
laws, compliance with, 46–47
Layer 2 Tunneling Protocol (LT2P), 191
leadership, support from, 17

least privilege principle, 136
legacy system, 67
lessons-learned review, following security incident, 267
lessons-learned review, for disaster recovery, 347–348
lifecycle, vendor, 136
likelihood of occurrence of risk, 67
lines of authority, for CISO, 4–5
Linux, 185
log reviews, 161, 254

M

malware prevention, 183
Managed level of CMMI, 15
managed security service provider (MSSP), 202
managed service provider (MSP), 201–202
management, within incident response, 272
management plan, within business cases, 37
management team, within corporate governance model, 34
managerial control, 21
managers, information security, 2–8, 25–30, 358–359
mandatory vacation policy, 137
Mandiant, 96–97
Manifesto for Agile Software Development, 228
masking, 25
master service agreement (MSA), 37
maturity models, 14–15, 49
maximum tolerable downtime (MTD), 305–306
mean time between failures (MTBF), 79
mean time to repair (MTTR), 79
media analysis, 286
memorandum of understanding (MOU), 37
memory dump file, 286
message digest, 217
Metasploit, 174
metrics, for information security program, 121–123
Microsoft, 103, 163–164, 199
Minimum Security Standards for Electronic Information (University of California (UC) at Berkeley), 40–41
MISP Threat Sharing, 102
mobile site, 337
Monitor, Evaluate, and Assess (MEA) objective, 48

monitoring procedure, within information security policy framework, 43
multifactor authentication, 236–237
multiparty risk, 67
multitenancy, 195

N

National Council of ISACs, 108
National Institute of Standards and Technology (NIST)
    Computer Security Incident Handling Guide, 256–257, 260–262, 271
    cybersecurity framework of, 49–52
    frameworks from, 33
    Guidelines for Media Sanitization, 265
    response plan policies from, 269
    Risk Management Framework (RMF) of, 52–53
National Software Reference Library (NSRL), 287–288
nation-state attack, 97
natural disaster, 319–323
Nessus, 148–150, 155, 156, 160
network analysis, 287
network security, 186–195
network segmentation, 186–188, 257–258
Network Time Protocol (NTP) server, 255
network-based DLP, 24, 184
Nikto, 157, 158
nondisclosure agreement (NDA), 37, 134
nonintrusive plug-in, 151
nonrepudiation, within cryptography, 214

O

OASIS GitHub, 107
obfuscation, 213
object evidence, from security incident, 283
offboarding, vendor, 132–133
officer, 4
onboarding, vendor, 132
on-demand self-service computing, 196
Online Certificate Status Protocol (OCSP), 221, 222
Open Indicators of Compromise (OpenIOC), 108
open source intelligence (OSINT), 101–104
Open Threat Exchange, 101

OpenVAS, 156
operating system, unsupported, 163–164
operational control, 21
operational expenses (OpEx), 129
operational risk, 11
opportunity (of SWOT analysis), 13, 14
Optimizing level of CMMI, 15
Organization for the Advancement of Structured Information Standards (OASIS), 107
organizational budgeting, 127
out-of-band deployment, of IPS, 194
Outposts, AWS, 203–204
oversubscription, 195
over-the-shoulder code review, 231
owners, data, 18

P

pair programming, 231
pandemics, 323
parallel test, 347
parol evidence rule, 283
partial implementation tier (NIST Cybersecurity Framework), 51
partially known environment test, 171
partner, cloud service, 198
pass-around code review, 231
passive mode approach, of IPS, 194
passwords, 235–237
patch management, 162, 185
patching procedure, 43, 264
pattern matching, 24, 184
Payment Card Industry Data Security Standard (PCI DSS), 22, 45, 46, 148, 206, 281
Payment Card Industry Forensic Investigators (PFI), 42–43
payment fraud, as cybercrime, 96
penetration testing, 167–174
people, as asset, 311–312
permissions, 137, 172
persistence, of penetration testing, 174
personal information, inventory of, 80
personally identifiable information (PII), 80
phishing, 124, 236
physical control, 22
pivoting, of penetration testing, 174
platform as a service (PaaS), 199–201, 206
playbook, for incident response plan, 270
plug-ins, 150, 151, 154–155

policy, 33, 38–40, 45–46, 269
port security, 190
power outages, 324–325
power source, protection for, 331
pre-employment screening, 133–134
preparation phase, of security incident
    response, 253
presumption of compromise philosophy, 170
preventive control, 21
privacy
    breach notifications of, 84
    data roles and responsibilities within, 82–83
    information classification in, 80–81
    information lifecycle within, 83
    overview of, 79–84
    sensitive information inventory within, 80
    technologies within, 83–84
private cloud, 202–203
private key cryptography, 214–215
privilege creep, 134, 239
privilege escalation, of penetration testing, 174
privileged user, training regarding, 19
processing sites, alternate, 334–338
processor, data, 18, 82
procurement, information security
    program and, 130
procurement process, risk management within,
    78
Professional Practices library, 340
proprietary threat intelligence, 104–105
protected health information (PHI), 11, 80
provider, cloud service, 198
provisioning, 238–239
public cloud, 202
public key algorithm, 215–217
purple teaming, 175
purpose limitation, 83

Q

qualitative impact assessment, 304
qualitative risk assessment, 68, 70–71
quality control, 56–57
Qualys, 153, 156
quantitative impact assessment, 304
quantitative risk assessment, 68–70
Quantitatively Managed level of CMMI, 15

R

RACI matrix, 7–8
RAID array, 328–329
rainbow table attack, 25, 84
Ransomware Playbook, 270
Rapid7 Nexpose, 156
read-through test, 346
real evidence, from security incident, 283
reconnaissance, within penetration testing, 173
recovery phase, of security incident, 263–266
recovery plan development, 340–345
recovery point objective (RPO), 79, 306
recovery time objective (RTO), 79, 306
regulations, compliance with, 46–47
regulatory environment, 17
regulatory investigation, regarding security
    incident, 281
regulatory requirement, 148
remote access VPNs, 191
remote journaling, 339
remote mirroring, 339
removable media, as threat vector, 100
removal, within security incident, 260–261
repeatable tier (NIST Cybersecurity
    Framework), 51
reputational risk, 10
request for change (RFC), 138
request for proposal (RFP), 131
residual risk, 76
resource policy, for cloud computing, 211
response plan, for security incident, 269–271
response team, for incident security, 272–273
responsible roles within information security, 7–8
review questions and answers
    for business continuity and disaster
        recovery, 374–376
    for cybersecurity technology,
        244–247, 370–372
    for cybersecurity threat, 111–114,
        363–365
    for incident response, 292–295,
        372–374
    information risk management, 86–89, 362–363
    for information security, 59–62, 360–361
    for information security managers,
        27–30, 358–359
    for information security program,
        141–144, 365–368

for security assessment, 177–180,
    368–370
risk
    acceptance, 75
    analyzing, 65–72, 75–78
    appetite, 76, 148
    assessment of, 68–72
    avoidance, 74
    calculation, 67–68
    compliance, 11
    control, 76
    cross categories of, 11–12
    defined, 65–66
    enterprise management of, 78
    external, 66
    financial, 10
    identification process of, 66–67, 306–308
    of information security, 8–12
    inherent, 75
    intellectual property (IP) theft, 67
    internal, 67
    legacy system, 67
    likelihood of ocurrence of, 67
    magnitude of impact of, 67
    matrix, 76–77
    mitigation, 73–74
    multiparty, 67
    operational, 11
    reassessing, 71–72
    reporting of, 76–77
    reputational, 10
    residual, 76
    response of, 72–75
    software compliance/licensing, 67
    strategic, 10–11
    tolerance of, 17
    transference, 74
    treatment of, 72–75
risk acceptance/mitigation, of BCP
    documentation, 316
risk assessment, of BCP documentation, 316
risk informed tier (NIST Cybersecurity
    Framework), 51
Risk Management Framework (RMF) (NIST
    framework), 52–53
role-based training, 123–124
root cause analysis, 280
router, 188, 190–191
rules of engagement (RoE), for penetration
    testing, 171–173

S

sandbox system, 260
sanitization phase, following security
    incident, 264–265
SANS Internet Storm Center, 103
Sarbanes-Oxley (SOX) Act, 47
scalability, of cloud computing, 196
scan perspective, 153–154
scan target, 146–147
scanning, vulnerability
    agent-based, 153
    application, 157
    configuration of, 149–154
    credentialed, 152
    false positives within, 161
    frequency determination of,
        148–149
    infrastructure vulnerability, 156–157
    maintenance of, 154–155
    plug-ins for, 150, 151, 154–155
    reviewing and interpreting reports of, 159–160
    sensitivity levels within, 150–151
    server-based, 153
    supplementing network, 152–153
    validating results of, 160–161
    web application, 157–158
Scientific Working Group for Digital Evidence, 288
scope, of information security program, 118
scope statement, 36, 119
screened subnet, 187
script kiddie, 94
secret information, 80
secret key cryptography, 214
secure configuration guide, 54–56
Secure File Transfer Protocol (SFTP), 166
Secure Shell (SSH), 166
secure web gateway (SWG), 210
security assessment, 168, 175, 177–180, 368–374.
    See also vulnerability management
security awareness, 124–125
security budget, 127–130
security control, 20–22, 56–57, 168
security expert, 3–4
security incident
    attacker identification within, 262–263
    classifying, 274–279
    containing the damage from, 255–263
    containment, eradication, and recovery phase of
        response to, 255–266

coordination and information sharing
within, 273–274
data types within, 277–279
defined, 8
detection and analysis phase of response
to, 254–255
eradication and recovery within, 263–266
evidence gathering and handling within, 262
evidence regarding, 282–290
evidence retention following, 268
exam essentials for, 290–291
final report development following, 268–269
investigations regarding, 279–288
isolation within, 258–260
law enforcement role within, 263
lessons-learned review following, 267
overview of, 251–252
phases of response to, 252
plan testing and evaluation for, 288–289
post-incident activity, 267–269
preparation phase of response to, 253
removal process within, 260–261
response plan building for, 269–271
response team for, 272–273
review questions and answers for,
292–295, 372–374
segmentation within, 257–258
security information and event management
(SIEM), 161, 254
security team, 5–7, 125–126
security training, for information security
program, 123–125
security vulnerabilities
encryption, weak, 166–167
error messages regarding, 164–165
legacy platforms, 163–164
overview of, 161–167
patch management, 162
protocols, insecure, 165–166
training and exercises for, 174–175
weak configurations within, 164
self-signed certificates, 220
Senki, 101
sensitive information, inventory of, 80
separation of duties principle, 136
server-based scanning, 153
serverless computing environments, 200
servers, protection for, 329–331
service organization control (SOC), 56, 307–308
service-level agreement (SLA), 37

severity classification, of security incident, 276–279
shadow IT, 98
shared responsibility model, 204–206
shareholders, within corporate
governance model, 34
signature detection, 183, 193
signature-based system, 193
simulation test, 347
single loss expectancy (SLE), 69, 309
single point of failure (SPOF),
327
single points of failure, 79
single-sign on (SSO), 238
site-to-site VPNs, 191
SMART goals, 16
social media, 18, 99
software
analysis of, 287–288
antimalware, 183
compliance/licensing risk, 67
development, risk management within, 78
development models of, 226–229
development phases of, 224–225
failures of, 326
scanner, vulnerabilities of, 154
security testing of, 232–233
software development life cycle
(SDLC), 223–224
software as a service (SaaS), 199, 206
software development life cycle (SDLC), 223–224,
226–229
Spamhaus, 103
span of control, 6
spiral model, of software development, 227–228
split-tunnel VPN, 192
SSL cipher vulnerability, 167
stakeholders, 7, 45, 119
stateless inspection, 188
statement of authority, of information security
program, 119
statement of importance, 315
statement of organizational responsibility, 315
statement of priorities, 315
statement of urgency and timing, 316
statement of work (SOW), 37
static code analysis, 233
static testing, 157
steering committee, 121
steward, data, 18, 82

STOP tag, 73–74
storms, 322
strategic context, 36
strategic risk, 10–11
strategy development phase, of BCP, 311
strength (of SWOT analysis), 13, 14
strikes/picketing, 326
Structured Threat Information Expression
    (STIX), 107
structured walk-through, 346
Stuxnet, 97
subject, data, 82
supply chain, assessment of, 71
switches, 188, 189
SWOT analysis, 13, 14
symmetric cryptosystem, 212
symmetric key algorithms, 214–215
system hardening, 185–186
system resilience, 327–328
systems development, risk management within, 78

T

table-top exercise, 346
tactics, techniques, and procedures (TTP), 109
technical control, 21
Telnet, 165–166
template, scanning, 150
terrorism, 96, 324
testimonial evidence, from security incident, 284
theft/vandalism, 327
third-party relationship, 18, 37–38, 100
threat
    actor, 12, 92, 94–99
    classification of, 275
    data, 101–109
    defined, 65–66
    feed failure within, 104
    hunting, 170
    indicator management and exchange
        of, 107–108
    intelligence, 101–109
    landscape, 17
    map, 105
    research of, 12
    of SWOT analysis, 13, 14
    vector, 12, 99–100

ThreatConnect, 106
Threatfeeds, 102
tokenization, 25, 84
tool-assisted code review, 231
top secret information, 80
training, 123–126, 174–175, 314
Transport Layer Security (TLS), 191–192
Trusted Automated Exchange of Intelligence
    Information (TAXII), 107

U

UK Centre for the Protection of National
    Infrastructure, 108
unclassified information, 81
uninterruptible power supply (UPS), 324–325
unit testing, of software development, 224
University of California (UC) at Berkeley, 41–42
University of Notre Dame, 39
University of Pennsylvania, 119
unknown environment test, 171
unsupported operating systems, 163–164
U.S. Department of Defense Cyber Crime
    Center, 103
U.S. Department of Energy, 124–125
U.S. Department of Health and Human Services, 11
USB drive, as threat vector, 100
user acceptance testing (UAT), 225
user training, 123–124

V

vacation, policies of, 137
vendor due diligence, 130–131
vendors, 131–136
Veracode, 232
verification, security control, 56–57
version control, 185
virtual LAN (VLAN), 188–190, 258, 259
virtual machine escape, 209
virtual machine sprawl, 210
virtual private network (VPN), 191–192
virtual tape library (VTL), 344
VirusShare, 103
Visa, 42–43

vital records program, of BCP
documentation, 316–317
VPN concentrator, 191
vulnerability, 65–66, 161–167
vulnerability database, 101
vulnerability feeds, 154
vulnerability management
    network scan supplementation, 152–153
    overview of, 146
    reviewing and interpreting scan reports
        within, 159–160
    scan configuration of, 149–154
    scan frequency within, 148–149
    scan perspective within, 153–154
    scan results validation within, 160–161
    scan sensitivity levels within, 150–151
    scan target identification within, 146–147
    scanner maintenance within, 154–155
    scanning tools for, 155–158

W

war driving, 173
war flying, 173
warm site, 337
Washington, state of, *Electronic Signature
    Guidelines*, 43–44
Waterfall methodology, of software
    development, 226
watermarking, 24, 184
Wayne State University, 119
weakness (of SWOT analysis), 13, 14
web application scanning, 157–158
websites
    AICPA, 308
    Anonymous hacking group, 95
    Australian Signals Directorate Cyber Security
        Centre, 103
    Automated Indicator Sharing (AIS)
        program, 103
    BCI Good Practice Guideline (GPG), 340
    Center for Internet Security (CIS), 55
    Cisco, 103
    Cloud Controls Matrix (CCM), 207
    Computer Emergency Readiness Team
        (CERT), 103

    *Computer Security Incident Handling
        Guide*, 271
    Cyber Readiness Institute, 270
    Department of Homeland Security, 107
    Electronic Discovery Reference Model
        (EDRM), 281
    Electronic Signature Guidelines (Washington
        state), 44
    FEMA, 320, 321
    FireEye, 105
    "Guide to Test, Training, and Exercise
        Programs for IT Plans and Capabilities
        Recommendations," 346
    Information Security and Privacy Program
        Charter (University of Pennsylvania),
        119
    ISO Standard 27036, 133
    Microsoft, 103
    *Minimum Security Standards for Electronic
        Information* (University of California (UC)
        at Berkeley), 40–41
    MISP Threat Sharing, 102
    National Archives General Records
        Schedule, 268
    National Council of ISACs, 108
    National Hurricane Center, 322
    National Software Reference Library
        (NSRL), 287
    NIST Cybersecurity Framework Core, 50
    OASIS GitHub, 107
    Open Threat Exchange, 101
    Professional Practices, 340
    Ransomware Playbook, 270
    Risk Management Framework (RMF) (NIST
        framework), 52
    SANS Internet Storm Center, 103
    Scientific Working Group for Digital
        Evidence, 288
    Senki, 101
    Spamhaus, 103
    ThreatConnect, 106
    Threatfeeds, 102
    UK Centre for the Protection of National
        Infrastructure, 108
    U.S. Department of Defense Cyber Crime
        Center, 103
    Veracode, 232
    VirusShare, 103

Wayne State University Information Security Program, 119

What to Do if Compromised (Visa), 42

What to Do if Compromised (Visa), 42

white-box test, 170

white-hat hacker, 93

Windows Server (Microsoft), 55–56, 163–164, 185

wireless network, as threat vector, 100

workgroup, recovery of, 334

write blocker, 286

X

XaaS (anything as a service), 198

Z

zero-based budgeting, 127

zero-day attack, 97

zero-day vulnerability, 275

zero-trust approach, 188

Zoom, 209

Get Certified!

 Security +

 CISSP

 CISM

 CySA +

 PenTest+

SSCP

 Data +

CCSP

 CIPP/US

90 Days To Your Next Certification

Mike Chapple offers **FREE ONLINE STUDY GROUPS** that complement this book and will help prepare you for your next technology certification.

Visit CertMike.com to learn more!

Comprehensive Online Learning Environment

Register to gain one year of FREE access to the Sybex online interactive learning environment and test bank to help you study for your Certified Information Security Manager (CISM) certification exam—included with your purchase of this book!

The online test bank includes the following:

- **Assessment Test** to help you focus your study on specific objectives
- **Chapter Tests** to reinforce what you've learned
- **Practice Exams** to test your knowledge of the material
- **Digital Flashcards** to reinforce your learning and provide last-minute test prep before the exam
- **Searchable Glossary** to define the key terms you'll need to know for the exam

Register and Access the Online Test Bank

To register your book and get access to the online test bank, follow these steps:

1. Go to www.wiley.com/go/sybextestprep.
2. Select your book from the list.
3. Complete the required registration information, including answering the security verification t prove book ownership. You will be emailed a PIN code.
4. Follow the directions in the email or go to www.wiley.com/go/sybextestprep. Find your book in the list there and click Register Or Login.
5. Enter the PIN code you received and click the Activate button.
6. On the Create an Account or Login page, enter your username and password, and click Login o create a new account. A success message will appear.
7. Once you are logged in, you will see the online test bank you have registered and should click the Go To Test Bank button to begin.

SYBEX

A Wiley Bra